SINGING TO THE JINAS

Singing to the Jinas

Jain Laywomen, Maṇḍaḷ Singing, and the Negotiations of Jain Devotion

M. WHITNEY KELTING

OXFORD
UNIVERSITY PRESS
2001

OXFORD
UNIVERSITY PRESS

Oxford New York
Athens Auckland Bangkok Bogotá Buenos Aires Calcutta
Cape Town Chennai Dar es Salaam Delhi Florence Hong Kong Istanbul
Karachi Kuala Lumpur Madrid Melbourne Mexico City Mumbai Nairobi
Paris São Paulo Shanghai Singapore Taipei Tokyo Toronto Warsaw

and associated companies in
Berlin Ibadan

Published by Oxford University Press, Inc
198 Madison Avenue, New York, New York 10016

Oxford is a registered trademark of Oxford University Press

Library of Congress Cataloging-in-Publication Data
Kelting, Mary Whitney.
Singing to the Jinas : Jain laywomen, Mandal singing, and the negotiations
of Jain devotion / by M. Whitney Kelting.
p. cm.
Includes bibliographical references and index.
ISBN 0-19-514011-7
1. Women in Jainism. 2. Jainism—Rituals. I. Title.
BL1375.W65 K45 2001
294.4'082—dc21 00-036728

1 3 5 7 9 8 6 4 2

Printed in the United States of America
on acid free paper

For Steven

મન વાંછિત ફળિયા રે તુજ આલંબને,
કર જોડીને મોહન કહે મનરંગ જો ॥

Preface

Maṇḍaḷ means "a circle; a ring; a circumference; a compass; an assemblage; a company; a district" (Belsare 1993). When I was invited into the Śrī Pārśva Mahilā Maṇḍaḷ (Pārśva Women's Singing Circle), it was an entrance into many such circles where women order their worlds—not a place where women go when excluded from male activities or a space to which women are resigned, but a chosen space at the center of various women's communities. I chose to work within these circles rather than to stand outside the circles looking in, thus relinquishing much of the authoritative directive of my research.

It was hot on my first day of research, and I stood in the scorching sun out in front of the corrugated steel walls of the Ajitnāth Temple (the Jain temple where I performed the bulk of my research) in Shivajinagar waiting to meet Mr. Pungaliya—my only real contact in Pune. When he arrived, we went inside the temple and he told me all the Jinas' names and introduced me to Arun, the *pujārī*. Arun asked me questions about what I was there to do. I said that I wanted to talk to Jain laywomen and singers. Arun told me to follow him, and off he sped through the alleys of Shivajinagar where the first tea of the afternoon was being boiled and men were preparing to go back to work. He took me up three flights of stairs to an apartment. There I was told to go to the back bedroom and wait. After a while, a woman came in, told me to turn on my tape recorder and started to sing. I had met Ranjana (see photograph). The sound of her singing and her forceful character guided much of my research time.

It was not long before the place I had in Ranjana's room expanded to the whole Alandikar household. I began to spend time going to events or talking with her mother-in-law, Dadiji; her co-sisters-in-law (the wives of Ranjana's husband's brothers who all live in a joint family), Lata, Nita, and Kavita; and the young daugh-

Ranjana and author, Indrayani Express Train, July 1997. (Photo by Steven C. Runge)

ters of these women, Soni, Moni, Kajal, and Rashmi. From this home, I was taken to meet other women related to the Alandikar family. A month after starting my research we celebrated Divali and I met most of the other relatives; perhaps most important, I met the one sister-in-law, Hema, and her daughter, Sveta, who lived in another town, and Dadiji's two daughters, Padma and Vimal, who would return to their mother's house for special events and for extended visits during the hot season. A family has inner and outer circles. I slowly made sense of some of the literally hundreds of outer-circle relatives I met during my research.

One Saturday soon after I met her, Ranjana took me to meet her maṇḍaḷ (a performance singing collective) and introduced me to the members who were there that week. I explained that I was studying Jain women and their singing. Though it was clear that they thought it was funny that I wanted to make recordings of their rehearsal, they allowed me to do so. Once I became aware of them, I went to every maṇḍaḷ event and practice. It was at a practice that I met Maluben, the president of the maṇḍaḷ, who insisted I come to her house for tea and to meet her daughter, Sheelu, who was visiting from her husband's house. Maluben immediately began asking questions about my notebook to make sure I was accurately recording each event; she asked me to translate my notes and then offered commentary on them. During one week Ranjana and I stopped by Savitaben's house, across the street from the temple, to discuss maṇḍaḷ matters, and soon I was visiting Savitaben, whose arrestingly lovely voice pronounced the beauty of Jain devotional music. In her house, I met the women involved in maṇḍaḷ activities: her co-sisters-in-law, especially Kamalben and Ushaben, and a young daughter-in-law, Prithi (who is also Kavita's sister). I began to talk more with other women from the maṇḍaḷ: Kamalben, Vina,

Sharmila, Asha and her daughter Doli, and particularly Pramilaben (the maṇḍaḷ treasurer) and her niece Manisha (who ran the young women's group). At their Dīvāḷī program, the Pārśva Maṇḍaḷ publicly declared me a member. The circles widened quickly and sometimes I went from centers directly to other centers, bypassing peripheries. I went home with Ranjana to her mother's house in Karad and made trips to other households connected to the Alandikars by marriage: Nita's aunt (her mother's sister) and her brother, Ranjana's sisters and nieces, Lata's mother and sister, Padma's mother-in-law's house, and so on. I learned that the connections extend not in one location but through the paths of marriages.

It is in the context of these interconnected groups of women that I study Jain religiosity and *stavan* (hymn) singing. The stavan themselves have concentric circles of understanding. When I first asked a woman, Why do you sing that stavan?, I got a response based on aesthetic judgments which, when I asked further, became a comment on her personal devotion. The maṇḍaḷ made decisions according to their understanding of the intersection between meaning and context. This book moves from Western academic theory to women's personal experiences which after time provides a base from which readers can reorient themselves within the center of one world from which they may see the rest.

My dissertation thesis, from which much of this book is drawn, ended with an epilogue, a translation of a letter I wrote to the maṇḍaḷ to explain what my thesis was about and what they had contributed to scholarship on Jains. During my research time, the women often asked why I was studying them. I had short answers to the question, but as I finished writing I arrived at a more complex answer. I decided to include this letter at the beginning of this book (though it reflects the structures and understandings of that thesis) because it characterizes some of the ways in which this book addresses those women as much as it does the scholarly community. A few of the women can read English, though slowly, and have read sections of that thesis and this book with me during my two subsequent research trips (in 1997 and 1999) to Pune. But before I submitted my thesis and returned to Pune, I wanted to explain how I had used their words and singing. The letter asks questions and makes statements that reflect the expectations and interests of the women to whom I wrote—expectations and interests that are very different from those of academic readers. I have retained this letter as a whole—it is only a few pages—rather than editing for academic interest. Perhaps it will leave readers with the memory that research is an exchange between people whose work and play (the "real work," as the poet Gary Snyder called it) are woven into the seamless fabric of living. My field notes contain recipes, directions to people's houses, the names of prospective brides for one woman's son, the names of the latest Hindi film music cassettes, and children's drawings and homework practice, as well as the pages and pages of notes on topics directly addressed in this book. These intrusions are in fact just the opposite: The world of stavan singing is just one of many in Jain women's lives and it is entwined with these other worlds in some predictable and some unexpected ways.

While writing this book, I incurred a vast karmic debt to the many people who gave me so much of their time, skills, and support; any mistakes within are in those places where I resisted their better judgments. I start by thanking my entire family (and I mean all of you)—and especially my parents, Howard Kelting and Whitney

Keen—whose support has been Herculean and their love endless. I thank those dear friends with whom I have debated details of much of this book and from whom I have gained so much inspiration: Brian Axel, Wendy Bellermann, Matthew and Melissa Burke, Ria Davidis and Michael Jones-Correa, Dena Davis, Julie and Mohsen Kurd, Jeff McKibben, Mekhala Natavar, Warren Senders and Vijaya Sundaram, the late Janis Shough, and Mary Jane Smith. Thanks to the religious studies department at St. Lawrence University for granting me the schedules that permitted my finishing this book, and my students (especially my Jainism class) for their cheerful enthusiasm for the project that kept their professor energized but at times distracted. Kudos to Carol Barkley for preparing my photographs under my concerned eye. At the University of Wisconsin, I thank first and foremost my graduate adviser David Knipe for his continuous support of my project. Thanks to Joe Elder, V. Narayana Rao, and, especially, Kirin Narayan. Thanks to my language teachers for the building blocks of my research: especially Mithilesh Misra, Manindra Verma, Usha Nilsson, Gautam Vajracarya, and the late Dhamiben Shah. Others who have cheered me on and helped me think through sections were Marcus Banks, John Carman, Kathleen Erndl, Mary McGee, and Leslie Orr. In Pune I spoke with several scholars about issues in my research, especially Phil Engblom, Jan Houben, Anne Feldhaus, and Tom Kerr. Thanks to Nanda Pandhare (and her family) whose utter competence and good cheer kept our home free from the hassles of the world. Thanks to Cynthia Read at Oxford University Press for her continued support of this project. Thanks to two anonymous readers at Oxford University Press who gave me extensive and productive comments. Alan Babb also shared with me his very helpful thoughts after reading the penultimate draft which helped me finish up. Paul Dundas deserves special thanks for cheers and for answering so many queries about Jain history and specific texts and doctrines. John Cort has asked me so many fruitful questions, guided me through several rough passages in this study, and encouraged me to focus on this book when my mind wandered toward other projects; I cannot thank him enough.

The research on which my doctoral thesis (and by extension much of this book) was based was conducted while on a doctoral dissertation fellowship (September 1993–September 1994) from the American Institute of Indian Studies. I was also generously supported during my thesis write-up period with a Charlotte Newcombe doctoral dissertation fellowship (September 1994–September 1995). At AIIS-Pune office, thanks to Madhav Bhandare and Shantaram Gavade. I was officially affiliated with the L. D. Institute of Indology in Ahmedabad, thanks to them for my affiliation and, especially Dalsukhbhai Malvania, for advice during my visit. An earlier draft of chapter 8 appears as an article in Olle Qvarnström and N. K. Wagle, eds., *Approaches to Jain Studies: Philosophy, Logic, Rituals and Symbols* (Toronto: University of Toronto Centre for South Asian Studies, 1999). Thanks to Olle Quarnström for inviting me to participate. I include shared material courtesy of the Centre for South Asian Studies, University of Toronto, Canada. At the head of each chapter and throughout the book, I quote stavan in full or in part. These versions of the stavan were transcribed in Gujarātī and Hindi from field recordings or directly from singers into my fieldnotes. Although some of these stavan are occasionally published in Jain pamphlets, I was unable to identify anyone to ask for permission for their publication in this book. All of the translations (and photographs) in this book are my own unless they are marked otherwise.

It is impossible to find the right words (harder still in English) to describe the gifts of time, knowledge, attention, patience, and love that I received from the many Jains who helped my project. The Ajitnāth Saṅgh of Shivajinagar welcomed me, gave me open access to their temple, books, time and programs, encouraged my research and questions when it surely would have been easier to avoid me and taught me much about not only being Jains and being Gujarātīs, but about being good people. The Śrī Pārśva Mahilā Maṇḍaḷ included me in their programs, considered me as an (admittedly peculiar) adjunct to the maṇḍaḷ and defended my position (as well as that of my tape recorder and camera) at several events as one of their own: I hope that their intelligence and complexity shine through the text of this book. Special thanks to Maluben Shah, Sheelu Shah, Savita Shah, Pramila Shah, and Manisha Shah for especially consistent support and for taking my project seriously from the beginning. I thank Arun Pandey who serves as Ajitnāth temple's pujārī for making sure I always knew the when and where of temple events and for, after only an hour of talk, realizing that I should talk to Ranjana.

If it is impossible to find the words to thank the congregation and the maṇḍaḷ, how do I thank the Alandikar family for all they gave me? I thank them all individually: Dadaji (the late Shantilal Deepchand Shah), Dadiji, Motakaka, Latakaki, Satishkaka, Ranjanakaki, Ashokkaka, Nitakaki, Kamleshkaka, Kavitakaki, Mukesh (and now Vaishali and Jyoti), Kalpesh, Rupesh, Manesh, Soni, Nilesh, Moni, Tushar, Kunal, Kajal and Rashmi. However even within this small group, I want to add extra appreciation for Dadi's love and support which made my research an important part of my living. Thanks to the others from Sirur (now living in Chinchwad): Sureshkaka, Hemakaki, Sandip, Reshma, Sreyas, Sangita, and Sveta; in Dombivli: Ashokphua, Padmaphoi, Arati, Aparna, and Dipa; in Junnar: Vinodphua, Vimalphoi, Dinesh, Bhabhi, and Girish. Thanks also in Pune to Monika, Utkarsh, Minaben, Chimankaka, Pramodkaka, Pushpaphoi, and the late, and dearly missed, Lilaphoi. I want to thank the Ambalāl Shah family in Karad who welcomed us into their home and made us feel at home in India. I must make further mention of all I have received from Ranjana; I am blessed to have met a woman of such intelligence, empathy, deep and abiding interest in the world, strength of will, wry humor, and a temperament which, though similar to mine, gave more when I sometimes could not. Had I not met her, I would have written a different and far inferior book. My last and most special thanks go to my husband, Steve Runge, for being there metaphorically and literally through everything.

Canton, New York M. W. K.
October 2000

Praise to Śrī Ajitnāth
Praise to Śrī Śankheśvar Pārśvanāth

Be blessed, worshipful ones in the auspicious village of Shivajinagar, the Pārśva Maṇḍaḷ and the women of the Ajitnāth congregation and to all those who are younger and older; accept from America, your sister Whitney's homage and likewise her blessing.

Jay Jinendra! How is everyone? Everyone's health is good, no? Is everyone in your houses well? Everyone's little ones are doing well, too, I hope? How did their exams go? Today I finished my thesis. How about that? I hope that Steve and I will return quickly to Shivajinagar and, of course, I will bring the book with me.

When I was still in India, you all asked me about this book; I did not know yet the whole meaning and purpose of the book because I was still doing research. While writing, things became clearer, so maybe I can answer your questions now. I cannot fit a whole book into one letter just as I could not fit all of your ideas into one book. My wish is that someday, sitting together, we will read the book.

Before going to India, I read a lot of books about Jains. In them, there was nothing much written about women. The lives of women and their love and intelligence were nowhere in those books. When we were staying with all of you, I was given so much from all of you. From your affection and your intelligence, I have learned so much. When I arrived at Ajitnāth Temple for the first time, I knew nothing about laywomen's religion. I wanted to study singing and women. Arun took me to Ranjana's house; it was there that I began. I did *pūjā* every day with Ranjana and then everyone else in the family, and I started going to *maṇḍaḷ*. Every day, I met another woman and each of you gave me a lot of your time and thoughts which I have put in this book. In my year with you, I spent much time performing pūjā, seeing the maṇḍaḷ programs, learning *stavan*, and I wrote about these times in the book.

In America, people know very little about Jainism and still less about Jain women. Yet I feel you have so much to offer. I think you all know so much about Jainism. All the time, just in living, you understand and explain Jain philosophy and theology: in worship, in making food, in raising your little ones, and in the way you run your homes. In this book I wrote about your Jainism. I put my hope with God that when you read this, you'll think the book is okay. Here, people will read this book and some of my words are for them, but every word is for you. You have given me so much, and because of this, this book is also your book.

In the first chapter, I give a history of Shivajinagar and Pune. This is, of course, a history of your fathers-in-law's families because women's history is not from one place, is it? Then I answer some questions about history, philosophy, and sociology with regard to the congregation. I also tell a little bit about how you use Gujarāti (and Mārvāḍī) in the stavan and the ways that you live as Gujarātīs (and Mārvāḍīs) and Jains in Maharashtra.

In Jainism, there are ideal women—*Mahāsatī*s, female mendicants, and *dīkṣārthī*s—but for laywomen, religion is a little different; you stay in a family. The second chapter describes fasts and fasting: the long eight- and thirty-day fasts, the Āyambil Oli and the Akṣaynidhi fast and the reasons you performed them; fasts and ordinations are times when women reach for those ideals in the books. But the way those ideals are understood is a bit different for women and men, laity and mendicants, no?

Each of you collected many stavan in your diaries, most of which you learned from other women. There were published stavan books and cassettes as well. In your coming and going from your mother's home to your mother-in-law's home, as well as in visiting others, you learned stavan. The third chapter explains the different places I found stavan, and the particular ways you learned and taught stavan while I was with you. I see the stavan learning and collecting as connected to the way women find ties with their friends and relatives wherever they go.

In the fourth chapter, I write a history of stavan and pūjā texts—that they arose out of *raso* and *pada* literature in the medieval times. I write about what stavan lyrics sound like and the ways similes are used; I talk about the different poetic devices and the melodies. Many of the stavan used *rās-garbā* melodies and were chosen for the way that they fit with the performances of pūjās. I think it has a lot to do with the whole performance with the *dānḍiya-rās* and *garbā*, as well as the instruments and the way you sing. But as important as Gujarātī music and language is, there is a Jain aesthetic deriving from Śānt Ras, especially the precision of performance—like how everything was practiced until the melody, the words, the *dānḍiya* action and the pūjā itself had a good fit.

The fifth chapter gives the meaning of the stavan lyrics and the way that certain stavan are performed in certain pūjās and at certain times. You said to me that the stavan could be described as "beautiful," "having good meaning," and "being good for performance with a manḍaḷ." I included the ways stavan have categories and how the "beautiful" ones were often the ones you sang in the temple in the morning. I also wrote about which stavan went where in the pūjās—how "Kesarīyā, O Kesarīyā" was sung with each offering and how "Bring, O Bring" was sung to give appreciation to each person at the pūjā and how when Arun was putting the decorations on Mahāvīr you often sang "My Golden Throne." Each of these makes sense being sung when it was, and this sense comes from how you understand the song and the pūjā, no? In the end, I write about the songs Ranjana, Savita, Nita, and Maluben especially liked, and how these special stavan spoke beautifully about the Jina's grace and the types of devotion each of you have.

In the sixth chapter, I talk about morning pūjā, and I explain the importance of having the right sentiment. I tell how each laywoman chooses exactly what to do during pūjā, but that those choices come from a bigger group of things all called pūjā. When you taught me (and the little ones) pūjā, you were careful to show how many things can be called pūjā; but in life, few of you can spend that much time in the temple each day, so you must choose. As you wanted, I told them all about pūjā clothes and when you shouldn't do pūjā. I hope people will better understand Jain temple practice and devotion.

The seventh chapter is all about formal pūjās: Snātra, Pañcakalyāṇak, Vāstuk Pūjās and the way the maṇḍaḷ performed them. Here, you were less free to choose the songs and the way the pūjā goes because it has to fit with the text and the pūjā, no? I talked about how the pūjā contest at Goḍījī was a place where you made sure you were not making mistakes—I did tell them that the maṇḍaḷ had gotten third place out of all of Pune. From the pūjā contest and how women went to other maṇḍaḷs' pūjās, there was a shared sense of what should be done. The women were the ones who went to these pūjās. The Mahāvīr Nirvāṇ program's dances and drama did the same thing for the girls, too, but here the women are watching. Finally, I use the Navānu Prakārī Pūjā as an example of the ways that the maṇḍaḷ figured out what was most important to the pūjā when trying to do a big program and how the maṇḍaḷ used the auction to raise money for the temple, but the pūjā itself was performed in a way that the merit was still shared.

In the last chapter, I talk about that Vāstuk Pūjā we went to when the family did not seem to want to do more than watch the pūjā. No one was ready to do the pūjā, do you remember? After this pūjā everyone was talking—there was a conflict over whether or not the pūjā was very meritorious. Each of you had an answer to this question based on understanding the relationship between knowledge, gifting, and devotion. The general answer said that if the person giving the money (or sponsoring the pūjā) was not devoted enough to know how to perform pūjā or say the prayers, it would be hard to perform a pūjā with the correct sentiment. Actually, this is similar to some of the medieval *ācārya*s' ideas about intention and merit.

In your years, you have learned so much about laywomen's religion and Jainism in general as well. Along with the pūjā and the stavan, you understand Jain theology—that's the work between laywomen and god, isn't it?—and then you teach this religion to your children and to me, too. In this way, it is so important to understand Jain laywomen's religion, so one can see the way Jainism continues through the centuries.

I want to include this letter in the book. It gives another way of seeing the whole book and reminds the reader of your central place in this book and of the great gift each of you has given me. In your lives, you teach truth and nonviolence, and so your homes have so much peace. You always have a lot of work to do at home, but in between you gave so much. This book is my first one, but I hope to write others. A book is like a baby, no? Everyone eat *barfi*, because I have, in finishing this book, begotten a daughter. I wrote this book with hard labor and with that, your words have made it possible. But a book—like a daughter—one day leaves your house. My hope is that she finds acceptance and brings happiness wherever she goes. You are all *māsī* now, aren't you?

It is late now in my home, but in yours, everyone is having their morning tea. My letter is finished. Give my love to everyone and have Ajitnāth *darśan* for me. Please know that our time together has just begun. I send my love with this letter.

Your sister,
Whitney

Contents

Note on Translation and Transliteration

My research was conducted in a mixture of Hindī (Mārvāḍī and sometimes that elusive tongue, Bombay Hindī) and Gujarātī. All the translations in this book were done by me unless otherwise indicated. If no source is given for the text itself (usually in the case of the *stavan*), that text was transcribed from my tape recordings or collected orally into my field notes. Translation in itself is an imperfect art. I have given the meanings as accurately as possible while maintaining some of the original feel of the texts. The stavan (hymns) were almost all in Gujarātī or at least used Gujarātī grammar, though they were commonly written in a mixture of Devanagari and Gujarātī script. The printed texts to which I refer were almost all in Gujarātī script, regardless of whether they were in Gujarātī, Hindī, Prakrit, or Sanskrit. The endless weaving of languages through the texts and our conversations makes transliteration quite difficult: Do I spell a word as spoken, as written, or as deemed correctly spelled (by whom)? I transliterated those words for which I felt there were no adequate translations in English. Thus *pūjā* is not translated as "worship," though *sādhus* and *sādhvīs* combined I felt comfortable calling "mendicants." To do so, I have used a standardized transliteration format recommended by the ALA-LC. I retain the spellings used in the printed quotes from texts, even if words have been spelled "incorrectly." When transcribing stavan from recordings or transcribing conversations, I have retained the phonetics of the speech—unless the women corrected my spellings of the words when they looked at my transcriptions. Thus readers should be aware that the transliteration system occasionally reflects the spelling of the written word and not the pronunciation. For example, the word written as *kesar* was pronounced *keśar*. As a rule, I did not include the final *a* (pronounced in Prakrit and Sanskrit) as it was not pronounced in Gujarātī and Hindī. The exceptions (aren't there always exceptions) are in words that would end with a consonant that is difficult to pronounce without the final a or other words in which I (with my imperfect ear) heard the final a voiced by the speakers. For example, the word *mantr* was pronounced *mantra* and *mokṣ* seemed to retain the edge of the a in the pronounciation *mokṣa*, but I use *karma* rather than further confusing the reader with the women's actual pronunciation *karam*. I do not use diacriticals with people's names, but I do use diacriticals for names of cities to reflect the pronunciation of the women with whom I spoke. Throughout the book I have used an *s* to make these transliterated words plural after the English pluralization except for the word *stavan* which is given as stavan for both singular and plural. Finally, I have put these words in italics on their first usage unless they are proper names. I am sure there are mistaken judgments and inconsistencies, and for this I ask the readers' forgiveness.

SINGING TO THE JINAS

1

We came, we came, we came right here.
We are so happy to celebrate the housewarming *pūjā*.

We went to the houses of our brothers in Shivajinagar,
We devoutly celebrated the pūjā in our sisters' homes,
  O—We came to see God.

The Pārśva Maṇḍaḷ came right here
From devotion, we celebrated wildly.
  O—We devoutly celebrated with all our senses.

I say, we came to your door, God, because we have devotion.
The whole women's *maṇḍaḷ* is very happy.
  O—We came to Shivajinagar's God.

We decorated his image with all our gems.
O God, you are in the hearts of all my sisters.
  O—Because we are devoted, we performed your worship.

Transcription and translation of recording of ritual performance in Pune, Maharashtra, on 21 February 1994. Courtesy Śrī Pārśva Mahilā Maṇḍaḷ.

Hearing and Listening to the Voices of the Śrāvikā

Knowledge came to the first listeners—the first Jain laity—in undifferentiated perfect sounds emanating from the Jina at the assembly hall of his first sermon. Jain theology, like many other theologies in South Asia, travels in the form of sound: pure speech, incantation, sermon, prayer, narrative, and song. *Śrāvikā* means "a woman who listens," and the term now refers to Jain laywomen. Anyone who studies religion knows that words matter and contexts speak. Jain faith begins as an act of listening. This listening is accompanied by song, the songs performed in celebration of the presence of the Jina (in the *stavan* above, God[1]) who teaches the faith to the faithful. The laywomen who are enjoined to do this listening are the same women whose voices later carry the melody of Jain theology. The genre these women control—a type of devotional song called stavan—is the most widely known and internalized source of Jain theology, or, more accurately, theologies. These theologies are constructed and reconstructed by the careful and repeated use of stavan in particular religious contexts. I do not want readers to approach these questions abstractly but rather to see them as the human questions that they are. Religious practice and theology are experienced by individuals and constructed within the context of negotiations about practice and theology in one's community. It is this tension between individual and shared theologies that drives this book. To understand how this singing forms and reformulates theologies and what these theologies say about Jainism, readers first need to arrive at where they might listen and hear.

Locating the Location

Pune is three and a half hours east from Bombay (hereafter, Mumbaī)[2] on the Deccan Queen Express Train. To get to Ajitnāth Temple, get off the train at the Shivajinagar Train Station. Shivajinagar is across the Mula River from the oldest part of Pune. The neighborhood is loosely defined as the area between the Shivaji bridge and the Shivajinagar rail and bus stations. Ajitnāth Temple and the homes of many Jains who worship there are within the triangle formed by Shivaji and Jangli Maharaj Roads and the river. In the triangle, there are many Ganapatī temples, a popular but tiny Hanuman temple, a Śitalā Mā temple, a small but active mosque, and a standing image of Ambedkar in his blue suit. Most of the children—if they go to school—wear the ultra-turquoise uniforms of the nearby Marāṭhī-medium Modern School. Shivajinagar, crossed by some large roads (the Mumbaī-Pune Road, Shivaji Road, Jangli Maharaj Road), is a mix of shop-lined streets, alleys, and narrow lanes. The architecture is a haphazard mix of a few old wada-style homes, some bungalows, row houses, cement apartment buildings, tin-roofed single rooms where the men sleep out front on charpoys, and a few new one-story *pakka* houses, which were built while I was doing this research (see figure 1-1). In short, it is a remarkably diverse neighborhood, religiously and economically.

Tell the ricksha driver that you want to go to the Shivaji Statue at the Military Academy Chauk (near Modern Chauk). Ask the flower seller (to the right on the in-

FIGURE 1-1. View of Shivajinagar, Pune, from Ranjana's room, 1994.

tersection, near the ricksha stand) for the Jain temple. He'll point you down the correct street. The temple is on the right side behind newly carved high stone walls, which recently replaced the previous walls of corrugated steel (see figure 1-2). It is made of white marble, carved after the style of the central temple at the most famous and most visited Śvetāmbar Jain pilgrimage site, Śatruñjay.[3] Leave your shoes at the base of the stairs to the temple and walk once around the outside of the temple (keeping your right shoulder toward the temple); you'll see the marble cutters working on the interminably unfinished carvings for the temple cornices.[4] In the back there is an oddly shaped mendicants' hostel (*upāśray*)—the plot of land is on a diagonal to the east-west orientation of the temple and the mendicants' hostel is packed in behind the temple—which is used both to house visiting mendicants and as a meeting hall for activities of the maṇḍaḷ (singing circle), congregational activities, and explicitly Jain celebrations and rituals. Near the entrance is a chalkboard announcing in Gujarātī the upcoming pūjās (formal liturgical worship performances) and programs and a painted board listing the year's major donors. The steps have a railing now, which was built after my first research trip, after Jyethiben had fallen on the steps in the rain. Enter through the center door.

The Ajitnāth Temple, whose construction was exclusively funded by a large donation from Jyethiben in the memory of her late husband, was consecrated in 1983. The central marble image (*mūḷ nāyak*) is Ajitnāth;[5] to his right inside the inner sanctum (*gabhāro*) are marble images of Ādināth and two of Mahāvīr, and on his left, Gautam Svāmī, Sīmandhar Svāmī and Pārśvanāth.[6] There are also several metal (*pañcadhātu*) images of Śāntināth, Ādināth, Mahāvīr and Pārśvanāth. In the two outside niches nearest to the inner sanctum are images of Mahāvīr and the old image of Kunthunāth, which was the central image of the house temple (*ghar derāsar*) at Savita's house across the street, where the Shivajinagar Jains worshipped before this temple was built. Kunthunāth's image was consecrated in 1938 after it was brought from Gujarat. The two guardian deities (*śāsan-devatā*) have small separate sanctuaries of their own: one is a marble image of Nākoḍā Bhairav and the other of Padmāvatī (see figure 1-3). There is a large silver chest (*bhandār*) a meter or so in front of the central doors to the inner sanctum, and to Padmāvatī's side is a circular, three-tiered silver stand (*samavasaraṇ*) with a metal image of Mahāvīr and a *siddhacakra* (a symbolic representation of the ideals of Jainism). Near Padmāvatī's shrine are piles of stavan books and rosaries in a small basket near the box of incense. Near the entrance doors are two niches without images in them. One holds a large number of religious books: guides to worship and fasts. The other holds tins of ghee, camphor, saffron, and various other items used in worship. There are always a few low tables on the floor near the entrance doors with rice and fruit offerings on them left by worshippers.

At any given time early in the morning, the temple may have between twenty and forty people performing their individual morning worship—a scene of chaos until you learn to maneuver in the movement, when the chaos becomes paradoxically peaceful. In the back of the room many women may be sitting behind the low tables reciting morning prayers (*caityavandan*) or singing stavan. One or two old men might be seated closer to the inner sanctum doors, counting out the Jinas' names on a rosary. If you sit quietly, the singing of the women who perform the morning worship in the inner sanctum blends with the recitations and the voices of the singers nearer to the back of the room. In the afternoon, fifteen to thirty women (perhaps in matching saris)—this would probably be the Śrī Pārśva Mahilā Maṇḍaḷ—may be seated in parallel facing lines singing and clashing short sticks while a few women

FIGURE 1-2. Ajitnāth Temple, Shivajinagar, Pune, January 1999. The contingent of mendicants and laity who walked with the Padmāvatī image from Mumbaī were having darśan at the temple. (Photo by Steven C. Runge)

FIGURE 1-3. Padmāvatī with *angī* (image decoration) by Arun Pandey during Paryuṣaṇ, Ajitnāth Temple, Shivajinagar, Pune, September 1994. Jina angīs differ in that they wear silver armor (rather than fabric) and like Padmāvatī's crown the armor is often covered with flowers and gems.

in fancy saris—but not matching—perform pūjā to a small metal image of Mahāvīr (see figure 1-4). As each person enters or leaves the temple, he or she rings one or two of the brass bells hanging near the doors. People leave carefully, often without turning their backs on the Jinas.

Jainism in Brief

Defining Jainism is a problem to begin with; it is one to which Jains have applied themselves throughout the ages. This entire book attempts to figure out how and why a certain group of Jains could and would deem another group of Jains to be not Jain. In essence, then, this book is one attempt to grapple with the definition of "Jainism" and who determines that definition on the ground, among the very real and very particular lives of living Jains. Individual experiences inevitably complicate a definition. I did not set out to complicate a definition, but this is what happened. I set out to explore women's singing and along the way the individual and collective experiences of several dozen Jain women in Pune somewhat confounded what I thought Jains believed and did, an experience paralleled by many scholars who set out to measure women's experiences against that which has previously been assumed to be paradigmatic.

In the meantime, some provisional summaries of those traditions spoken of as Jainism may prove useful. Jains are a minority religious community clustered primarily in Western India (from Rajasthan to Mumbaī) with a smaller cluster in South India (mostly Karnataka and southern Maharashtra).[7] The highest number of Jains is in Maharashtra, followed in order of decreasing numbers by Rajasthan, Gujarat, Madhya Pradesh, and Karnataka. There are two distinct mendicant lineages (and lay devotees who are associated with them) in Jainism, the Śvetāmbar (literally, "white clad") and the Digambar ("sky-clad"). Śvetāmbar Jains are identified with southern Rajasthan, Gujarat, and the Mumbaī area of Maharashtra while Digambar Jains are clustered in Rajasthan, southern Maharashtra, and Karnataka. There are Jains in most major Indian cities and also substantial communities in East Africa, Great Britain, and North America—especially the United States. The 1991 census of India gave the total population of Jains in India as 3,352,706 (0.4 percent of the total population). The 1991 census also provides totals for Maharashtra—total population: 78,937,187 and Jains: 965,840 (1.2 percent of the total population); Pune District—total population: 5,532,532 and Jains: 71,712 (1.3 percent); and Pune Municipal Corporation—total population: 1,566,651 and Jains: 33,918 (2.2 percent).[8]

FIGURE 1-4. Śrī Pārśva Mahilā Maṇḍaḷ performing the monthly Snātra Pūjā, Ajitnāth Temple, Shivajinagar, December 1993. Arun (the *pujārī*), in pūjā clothes on the left side, is applying the angī to the image in the niche.

The United Nations gives the 1996 figure for the area of Pune's urban agglomeration as 3.1 million people.[9] In 1994, several Jains I knew gave the offhand figure of one *lākh* (100,000) Jains in Pune (approximately 3 percent) in which they would no doubt include the noncorporate urban suburbs of Pune such as Katraj, Pimpri, and Chinchwad, which have growing Jain communities. According to a locally published stavan collection, *Surataru Sarīkhā Sāhibā* (1996), which gives the locations of all the temples in Pune so that one can make a complete temple circuit during the annual festival of Paryuṣaṇ, there are forty-three Śvetāmbar temples in Pune City, twelve house temples in Pune City, and fifty-nine Śvetāmbar temples in the Pune region—outside the Pune municipal area—broadly defined. Though a minority group in Pune, they are a significant, fast-growing, and established minority.

Jainism is a collection of traditions stemming from a religious movement which scholars date from approximately the sixth century B.C.E. (based on Buddhist references to a teacher contemporary to Gautama Buddha who appears to be Mahāvīr) or sometimes back to the ninth century B.C.E. (based on some suggestive but inconclusive evidence of a group that sounds like Jains) (Folkert 1993).[10] Jains see Mahāvīr as the most recent of twenty-four enlightened teachers (hereafter, Jinas) who have come to revitalize the Jain faith in this era. Jinas (literally, "victors" over the senses) are understood to have been perfect renouncers—definitively, human beings—and now transcendent, omniscient souls. Though there are twenty-four Jinas (all of whose names were known by most Jains I encountered), they are not equally prominent. The Jains I knew, the stavan, and the liturgies concerned themselves primarily with Adināth (the first), Ajitnāth (second), Śantināth (sixteenth), Nemināth (twenty-second), Pārśvanāth (twenty-third), and Mahāvīr (twenty-fourth). Although these Jinas are nontransactional—they do not accept offerings or return blessings (Babb 1996)—they are the objects of veneration and temple worship. Jains also worship a few other kinds of beings: guardian deities, such as Padmāvatī and Bhairav, who are understood to be lay Jains and therefore grant help to their fellow Jains; miraculous monks who are understood to do much the same (a dominant cultus in the Khartar Gacch); and various Hindu deities, such as Lakṣmī and Ganapati, associated with certain festivals and locations.

In the Śvetāmbar Mūrtipūjak Jain context, temple worship can be individual or congregational (formal pūjās), neither of which requires an intermediary between the worshiper and the temple image; any Jain—or any person actually—in a proper state of purity can perform Jain worship and come in contact with the Jina image. A central Jain event at which the community is reidentified is the annual festival of Paryuṣaṇ. The Jain community gathers for eight days of prayer, fasting, and worship, and it is the most important festival for Mūrtipūjak Śvetāmbar Jains in part because it is the only time during which all four groups in the Jain community (male mendicants, female mendicants, laymen, and laywomen) are gathered. Central to this festival are the reading of the Kalpa Sūtra, the garlanding of the fourteen dreams of Mahāvīr's mother, and the community's public confession. Jain worship includes much which is shared with other South Asian traditions: temple worship, domestic worship and rites, guru veneration, annual and monthly festivals linked to a lunar calendar, and pilgrimage. Jains also participate in the pan-Indian festivals of Dīvālī and Kartak Pūṇam in ways that can be understood to be Jain (Cort 1989; Laidlaw

1995).[11] Jains describe themselves as a fourfold community (*caturvidh saṅgh*) of male mendicants (*sādhu*), female mendicants (*sādhvī*), laymen (*śrāvak*), and laywomen (*śrāvikā*). The mendicants follow a strict regimen of asceticism modeled (more or less) on the accounts of the lives of the Jinas and the instructions for mendicants attributed to Mahāvīr with the goal of attaining *mokṣa* (total spiritual release from worldly bonds) if not now, eventually. The laity, especially women, also perform some comparable acts of asceticism, but these acts are understood to be aimed at well-being (*puṇya marg*)—a model of behavior encouraged in a multitude of religious narratives and in the very sermons given by mendicants.

Jains share in the pan-Indic concepts of *karma* and the transmigration of souls but understand the workings of these in a unique way. Jain karma is a material substance which binds to the soul when the soul is made sticky with passion or other strong emotions or attachments. This matter prevents the soul from rising to the top of the universe (*siddhalok*) from which it cannot return (mokṣa). Much of the Jain textual tradition is concerned with the workings of karma and the ways to avoid the accrual of karma and to destroy karma that has already bound with one's soul. Contemporary Jains speak of karma in the language of the path of spiritual liberation (*mokṣa-marg*), particularly when explaining the workings of mokṣa itself. In most of the conversations I had, when karma came up for discussion, it was more a question of good karma or merit (*puṇya*) and bad karma or sin (*pāp*). In the present era of spiritual decline (*duśama avasarpiṇī*) in which Jains believe mokṣa is not possible,[12] Jains work toward maximizing their merit while decreasing their sin, in hopes of both enjoying a good rebirth and facilitating the gradual progression of their souls toward mokṣa.

Jain Sectarianism

A few sectarian divisions are significant to this study. The largest is that between the Śvetāmbar and Digambar Jains; this division appears to have arisen as a result of geographic separation, which in turn led to differences in mendicant practice and conflict over the textual canon. This division was not cemented until the Council of Vallabhi in the fifth century C.E. (Dundas 1992). There were three primary differences between the two groups: (1) the Digambars rejected the Śvetāmbar claim that they had maintained the original texts spoken by Mahāvīr extant; (2) the Śvetāmbar mendicants argued that mendicants should wear clothing and, in a connected line of reasoning, that women can achieve (and have achieved) mokṣa (Jaini 1991); and (3) the mendicants disagreed on certain aspects of the nature of enlightened beings, particularly whether they eat (Dundas 1985). These divisions are significant to the mendicant community as a matter of practice, theology, and identification, but most of these issues have little or no direct relevance for contemporary lay Jains, though, again, these debates inform the mendicants to which they attach themselves. Both the Śvetāmbar and Digambar sects have had internal divisions as well; within the Śvetāmbars there are the image worshiping (Mūrtipūjak) and those who reject image worship (most significantly, Sthānakavāsīs). Among Mūrtipūjaks, there are several lineages of mendicants with two represented in Pune, the first being the majority lineage, the Tapā Gacch, and the second being the lineage popular in Rajasthan, the Khartar Gacch. There were three significant differences between these two lineages that mattered to the Jains I knew. First, Tapā Gacch mendicants were identified (rightly or wrongly) as Gujarātīs, and Khartar Gacch as Mārvāḍīs (Rājasthānīs). Second, the Tapā Gacch places a restriction on female mendicants reading certain religious texts and giving sermons. And third, the Khartar Gacch worship a group of miraculous (nonliberated) mendicant figures who have the capability of interacting with the worshiper (Babb 1996; Humphrey and Laidlaw 1994; Laidlaw 1995). The issue of mendicant practice which informed the sectarian and lineage divisions within Jainism was not central for contemporary lay Jains either in their theologizing or in their understanding of who these "other" Jains are. The divisions—when they were recognized—were more a question of a sociocultural identity; most Jains with whom I spoke had almost no sense of what those "other" Jains did or believed that was different, only that they were different.

In Maharashtra, the first Jains were Digambar; evidence lies in the various rock-cut temples found scattered around Maharashtra (Jain caves, Ellora; Mānmoda and Tulja caves, Junnar). There is still a large population of Marāṭhī-speaking Digambar Jains in southern Maharashtra and Karnataka,[13] but the Digambar community is small in Pune. In southern Maharashtra, where the Śvetāmbar community is expanding into previously Digambar territory and where the Śvetāmbars are gaining economic power, there have been several contentious legal (and political) battles over the control of several temples and temple sites (Carrithers 1988). Because the Digambar community is small in Pune and there are no contested temples anywhere nearby, and because the two groups had virtually no contact (social, religious, or economic) with each other, these conflicts only came up in conversation once when I was visiting Karaḍ—a city in southern Maharashtra on the edge of the region where these debates were going on. Although none of the Śvetāmbar groups are necessarily at odds with each other, they rarely celebrate holidays together—except for the temple visiting between Tapā Gacch and Khartar Gacch Jains at Dīvālī and Paryuṣaṇ and the mass "pilgrimage" "to the large Khartar Gacch temple "Dādāvāḍī Mandir," near the newer suburbs, to see the huge three-dimensional model of Śatruñjay on the day of Kartak Pūṇam—nor do they intermarry, do business together, or socialize outside of a few rare Jain contexts. Tapā Gacch Mūrtipūjak Śvetāmbar Jains are the largest community within Jainism today; this group is concentrated in Western India, mostly in Gujarat and Mumbaī (Carrithers 1991).

Because all Digambar and Śvetāmbar Jains agree that Mahāvīr's birthday is on the fourteenth day (of the dark fortnight) of the month of Caitri,[14] the Indian government declared that day the religious holiday to represent Jainism (to match the celebrations of Guru Nanak Jayanti, Christmas, etc.) in their effort to make the holiday schedule "fair." Though neither Digambar nor Śvetāmbar historically made much of the holiday within their own temples or homes, since 1979—when Jain community organizations tried to present a unified celebration of the 2,500th anniversary of Mahāvīr's teachings—there have been public displays of Jain unity on this day. In Pune, this unity was expressed in a large parade in the old city. The parade included groups from Gujarātī-, Rājasthānī- and Marāṭhī-speaking Jains, and Digambar and Śvetāmbar Jains; among the Śvetāmbar Mūrtipūjak Jains were both Tapā and Khartar Gacch. Each group had its own band and at least one float with a sign identifying the community to which each group belonged: Rājasthānī Digambar, Maharastrian Digambar, Sthānakavāsī, Mārvāḍī Śvetāmbar, and Gujarātī Śvetāmbar. The groups represented clearly articulated links between ethnolinguistic identity and the self-representation of Jain sectarianism.

My research was with Śvetāmbar Mūrtipūjak Jains and mostly with those who identified with Tapā Gacch mendicants and temple practices; only Tapā Gacch mendicants came to Ajitnāth Temple's mendicant hostel. The Jains I met divided their own religion into three groups: Śvetāmbar (by which they meant Mūrtipūjak), Sthānakavāsī (though technically Śvetāmbar, they were seen as totally distinct), and Digambar (about whose divisions they knew nothing at all). The Mūrtipūjak Jains were further divided by linguistic group: Gujarātī and Mārvāḍī. The division between the Khartar Gacch and Tapā Gacch was not the operative one, probably because the Khartar Gacch Jains were simply included as a subset of Mārvāḍī Jains. These other groups would inevitably have their own articulations of difference. The Khartar Gacch temple, Dādāvāḍī Mandir, was called "the Mārvāḍī temple" by everyone I knew. There were a few Mārvāḍī Jain families that worshipped at the temple in Shivajinagar, but most of the Jains in Shivajinagar were Gujarātīs and identified themselves as such. The philosophical distinctions between these groups were peripheral to how they described their divisions.

Gujarātī and Mārvāḍī Identity

Although by no means are all Jains Gujarātī, Gujarātīness has dominated Śvetāmbar Jainism in Maharashtra (Carrithers 1988). Most Jain texts, published in Amdāvād (Ahmedabad) and Mumbaī, are in Gujarātī language and script. The texts conform to Gujarātī aesthetics and the melodies draw from Gujarātī folk music. The conflation of ethnic identity with the religion is strong. Once, while I was walking with Ranjana's young daughter, Moni, she (Moni) explained to me: "I am a Gujarātī, so I don't eat those potatoes." Not eating potatoes is purely a Jain food restriction; it is not shared by Puṣṭimarg Vaiṣṇavs (the Hindu group in Gujarat with which Jains share the most religiously and socioculturally) or by Swāmīnārāyaṇs (the ascending Hindu group which draws its devotees from the comparable Hindu community in Gujarat), both of which do share the practice of vegetarianism and some further food restrictions (no onions) with Jains. The food, the dress, and the language become part of a whole picture of "Jain-ness" which is expressed in part through continued emphasis on Gujarātīness in Maharashtra. Although most of the temples in Pune are dominated either by Gujarātī or by Mārvāḍī Jains (with the Khartar Gacch temple as the center of Mārvāḍī Jains in Pune), the Ajitnāth Temple and the Pārśva Maṇḍaḷ are relatively mixed between the two groups, with between one quarter and one third of the members and the congregation being Mārvāḍī. This may stem from the presence at Ajitnāth Temple of a powerful image of Nakoḍa Bhairav—who was especially popular with many of the Mārvāḍī men. However, the Mārvāḍī speakers (and singers) have to work from texts and stavan almost always written in Gujarātī script and in Gujarātī language.[15]

Sheelu, who was one of the few Śvetāmbar Jains I knew who grew up with Marāṭhī-speaking parents, asked specifically to be married into a Gujarātī-speaking household in order to learn to speak it fluently. I found that the adult men spoke both Gujarātī and Marāṭhī, because their businesses were patronized by Marāṭhī speakers—though their business contacts were Gujarātī speaking—and their homes were Gujarātī speaking. Their languages were divided between home and work, suggesting a preference for speaking their "mother's" language when at home. One young man I knew insisted that his younger cousins always speak to him in Gujarātī at home, correcting them when they used Marāṭhī, despite the fact that he himself spoke Marāṭhī at work.[16] There is only one Gujarātī medium school in Pune, and only a few families I encountered could send their children there. (It is expensive and far from Shivajinagar—the school is near the Jain "ghetto" in Guruwar Peth in the heart of the old city.) Because the children in Pune often grow up going to Marāṭhī medium schools, I found that many stavan notebooks were written in a somewhat erratic Marāṭhī script—minus the top line—despite the fact that the language was clearly Gujarātī. The older women all wrote in Gujarātī script, if they wrote at all, but the younger women were mostly educated in Marāṭhī medium schools and wrote in a mixture of the two scripts. Despite Marāṭhī language education, the Gujarātī Jains in Pune retain a high level of Gujarātī fluency and preference after over 150 years or more in Maharashtra.

Although there were both Gujarātī and Mārvāḍī Jains at the Ajitnāth Temple, these groups had an uneasy relationship in most of the city, where they have divided into separate identities when building temples and supporting mendicant lineages. Likewise, these groups do not generally intermarry or do business together. The stereotypes reproduced by both men and women focused on the roles and expectations of women in the other group. Gujarātī Jains often commented in casual conversation that the Mārvāḍī Jains were conservative to the point of backwardness; there were references to the practice of Mārvāḍī women of covering their faces in front of everyone, including women (set against the Gujarātī practice of covering just one's hair, and that only in the temple and in front of older male affinal kin), the limits on their ability to go to events that would take them outside their homes or neighborhoods, and the relative preoccupation with caste (here, subcaste). Likewise, Gujarātī Jains attributed the preponderance of young Mārvāḍī women becoming mendicants to their fathers' assumed stinginess (i.e., they do not want to or cannot afford dowries) and/or fiscal irresponsibility (i.e., they give too much dowry). Mārvāḍī Jains spoke generally of the low level of propriety and honor shown in the Gujarātī community. This was evidenced by the apparent lack of respect Gujarātī women showed for their husband's family honor (e.g., they speak directly to elder affinal relatives and they do not veil in front of their mother-in-law or *jethānī*, the wife of the eldest brother of their husband, their daughters work outside the home, and their wives and daughters are all permitted to "wander around"). None of these stereotypes were ever invoked in front of or about women from the congregation whom the speaker knew; they served more as abstract in-group descriptions of how these two groups are different with attention to how one's own group is superior.

Brief History of Jains in Pune

Though I cannot say when the first Jains settled in Pune—there were already Jains elsewhere in Maharashtra earlier—it is clear that previous to 1750 they had a community large enough to support a Jain temple outside the city walls and of sufficient importance that the Peshwas granted the Jains land for temples inside the city at Guruwar Peth, near the present commercial center of Pune. It was at this time that the Jains built the oldest part of Goḍijī temple and the nearby Digambar temple; this temple complex remains the central Jain site in Pune. The 1885 *Gazetteer of the Bombay Presidency* (Campbell 1885) states that the Peshwas, however, were adamant that the temple should remain unobtrusive and invisible. It was, therefore, built underground: a striking metaphor for the Jain experience in Pune.[17] At the May 8, 1834, dedication of the Ādināth Temple—next to Goḍījī—there were said to be "10,000 śrāvaks"[18] (Campbell 1885, 341) which we can assume to be all Śvetāmbar, it being unlikely that Digambar Jains attended a Śvetāmbar temple dedication. At the time, if all these Jains were from Pune itself,[19] they would have comprised 10 percent of the city's population. The dominant image of Pune, reproduced by those living there, does not include a public acknowledgment of the Jain community. Despite the two or three centuries of Jains in Pune, the widespread knowledge of Goḍījī Temple (it is listed in every tourist guide book and on tourist maps as the Pārśvanāth Jain Temple), and the lavish and loud Jain parades for holidays and ordinations, most Marāṭhī speakers I met assured me that there were no Jains in Pune—that it was a purely Hindu city. When pressed, they admitted to communities of Muslims, Christians, Buddhists, and Sikhs, but never Jains. This is remarkable when one considers the public aspects of Jain worship, especially those large (and loud) parades. This invisibility may arise out of an impulse among Jains to keep a low profile in a city and region dominated by Hindu nationalist politics, and because Jains do not differentiate themselves in dress or any visual way from Hindus of the same ethnicity and castes.[20] The Marāṭhī speakers probably lumped all Gujarātīs (and perhaps, all Rājasthānīs with them) into a single group.

Dadaji (the late Shantilal Deepchand Shah) was the head of the household with which I was most closely associated, and the father-in-law of Lata, Hema, Ranjana, Nita, and Kavita. I was introduced to the maṇḍaḷ through his family, whose respectability and piety gave me, by association, access to many Jain events and households. He and his wife, Dadiji, excused certain lapses in the management of their household while their daughters-in-law helped me with my research. I present next a brief history—reconstructed from conversations with Dadaji, Dadiji and several other family members—of Dadaji's family to give a sense of how history contributed to the ways that this family ended up living in Shivajinagar. This history is not the same as those of other families but gives a parallel development of a family and the region.

Pāṭaṇ, a city in northern Gujarat with a large Jain population and central to Jain identity in the region, had already seen its political and economic zenith under the Caulukhya dynasty in the eleventh and twelfth centuries, though Jains did thrive economically—but not politically—under Muslim rule until the fifteenth century when the Muslims shifted the capital from Pāṭaṇ to Ahmedabad. By the mid-1700s it had long been in decline and was politically unstable; it changed hands between Muslim and Marāṭha rulers several times (Cort 1989). Gujarat (then a collection of states) was ruled by Marāṭha Peshwas from 1752 to 1818. In 1768, Pāṭaṇ was abandoned as capital by the Marāṭhas in favor of Baroda, and the city entered a precipitous decline. By the mid nineteenth century, Ahmedabad had British patronage, and much of the Jain-dominated trades were taken over by the British; the remaining trade was already controlled by Jain families from that city. In 1879, there was a devastating famine which drastically decreased Western Indian textile revenues (Bajpai 1989). In the late nineteenth century many Pāṭaṇ Jains left for Bombay and other parts of Maharashtra, and Mumbaī's oldest Jain temples date from this era of migration. A directory compiled by the Pāṭaṇ Jain Maṇḍaḷ in Mumbaī in 1982 listed 11,596 Pāṭaṇ Jains, most of whom live in Mumbaī. Some Jains have moved to Pāṭaṇ from other areas of Gujarat and live there now (Cort 1989).[21] In the late 1800s Dadaji's grandparents moved, along with the mass migrations, from Pāṭaṇ to Alandi—a town just eleven kilometers north of Pune in Maharashtra—and established a retail textile business there.

A series of monsoon failures (1896–97 and 1899–1900) brought famine to the Deccan along with a serious plague epidemic (in 1897 in Pune) which decimated the population of the region (Wolpert 1982). The beginning of the twentieth century found Maharashtra and the Deccan in weak condition economically and politically (Kaiwar 1994). Just as Dadaji's family was establishing a textile business in Alandi the plague swept through Maharashtra. Because people became wary of buying cloth (it was widely believed at the time to have carried the plague), the textile business could no longer support the entire family. Gautamlal—Dadaji's uncle—moved himself to Bombay and established his own textile business there, while Deepcand—Dadaji's father—kept the family store in Alandi. Deepcand had six sons and three daughters. When a second wave of disease hit around the end of the World War I (either the 1917 plague or 1919 influenza epidemic) Deepcand and his wife and one of their sons died from the illness and a second son was lost in the subsequent disruption of their family.

Because Alandi is too small a town to support many stores, Kantilal—the oldest son of Deepcand—soon moved to Pune to work, and once he had established his own shop he was followed by the two younger brothers. They had married their three sisters to men who lived in Pune as well. Dadaji remained in Alandi, where his six sons and two daughters were born. After a period of serious economic difficulty in the late 1960s during which one of Dadaji's sons died, he sent his oldest son to Pune to work for Kantilal, who had no children himself. When Kantilal died, the nephew inherited the store, and Dadaji's family resettled in a two-room flat in Shivajinagar in the neighborhood in which Dadaji's other two brothers lived. Soon after Dadaji's second son got a job in government service and moved away from Pune to Śirur (just about two hours away). In 1985, they moved into a larger five-room apartment in Shivajinagar. When Dadaji's first grandson married, the apartment was stretched to its limits, and after Dadaji's death in January 1997 it was decided that his youngest son and his wife, two children, and Dadaji's wife, Dadiji, should move into a small ground-floor apartment near the temple. This move both opened up space in the big apartment for the newly married couple and allowed Dadiji to live close enough to the temple (and on the first floor, as opposed to the fourth) to walk there with relative ease. The family has also retained the old apartment for the future expansion of the family after the six grandsons' marriages.

The first Jain men in Pune city were Gujarātī traders who settled in an area now called Guruwar Peth (Campbell 1885).[22] In 1714, the Peshwas declared Pune their home, and in 1750 it became the capital. The city grew quickly and many migrants from other states established businesses (Sawant 1978). When the center of the city (around Guruwar Peth) became overcrowded and fear of plague was rising, people began to settle on the other side of the river. Shivajinagar was a small settlement called Bharmudi, primarily of potters, across a seasonal bridge from the oldest part of Pune city. Shivajinagar developed in the early twentieth century; the first permanent bridge was built in 1919 (Sawant 1978). The neighborhood was primarily residential, but after the flood of 1961 (which devastated the low-income neighborhood of Kasba Peth) many low-income families moved to Shivajinagar. Many other Shivajinagar Jain families had also gone to an intermediate town in Maharashtra from Gujarat, and moved—often because of economic hardship—into Pune city later. Likewise, many, but not all, of the women who married into these families were born in Maharashtra. The Guruwar Peth area was long since well settled and the markets were in place; thus the newer migrants to the city settled in the outlying areas and opened stores there.

By the turn of the twentieth century there were several important Jain temples in Pune. Shivajinagar was settled by Jain families as early as the 1920s. Savita's husband's family settled into their house in Shivajinagar in the late 1920s and built a small shrine inside the house in the early 1930s. In 1938, the shrine was consecrated as a Kunthunāth temple and the local community of Jains began to worship there. Several Jains lived in Shivajinagar at that time and they worshipped at Goḍījī—a twenty-minute walk from Shivajinagar, once the Shivaji Bridge was completed in 1919. As population and traffic increased in Pune city, Goḍījī temple became increasingly difficult to get to (Karve and Ranadive 1965). The presence of the Jain temple in Savita's house made Shivajinagar more attractive to Jains, who, if possible, generally move into areas where there are temples.[23] By the end of the 1970s, Shivajinagar had a relatively large Jain population (according to Suresh Shah—Savita's husband; there are no population studies of Pune by neighborhood) and soon after a women's maṇḍaḷ was founded (in 1980 by Maluben), which performed pūjās and fast-breaking celebrations. When Jyethiben's husband died, she bought land in the area—although she did not live in that neighborhood—and built the Ajitnāth temple. When Jyethiben herself died in 1997, her family made a further large contribution which enabled (by 1999) the temple to buy land to expand its courtyard and to build the marble walls and gate.

Pune is still a receiver of migrant Jains who are gradually expanding the Jain community there. The recent construction of the Katraj Āgam Mandir temple complex just to the south of Pune city, under the enthusiastic direction of a charismatic mendicant leader, Daulasagarji, suggests a future for Pune as a local Jain center. By 1994 Katraj had already established itself as a pilgrimage stop for Jains traveling through central Maharashtra. In 1999, a huge, new Padmāvatī image was installed in this temple complex with the support of a large delegation of male and female mendicants (and lay devotees) who had walked 190 kilometers from Mumbaī specifically for this event. The Shivajinagar neighborhood still has a large Jain population, but several families have moved into fancier homes either in the nearby societies or downtown. The women who have moved often retain their membership in the women's maṇḍaḷ and in the congregation—they perform the annual rite of confession and expiation[24] at Ajitnāth rather than at the temple near their new homes, where they perform daily temple pūjā.

My summary of the history of Jains in Pune has been programatically brief; it provides a context of place and chronology in which one may choose to place the stories and discussions that follow, but once again I must draw attention to the radically different experiences of women. Such a history is problematic, if not inaccurate. The history of place cannot be substituted for the histories of these women, whose lives involve movement from town to town—from natal to affinal home every generation. To speak of the history of "Jains in Pune," as I have, is to speak of the history of Jain male lineages, not of the lives of the women who marry into the families (Kumar 1994; Scott 1988). To understand the roots of ethnicity and religion with regard to a specific practice or song, one must follow the women back home to their mother's homes and further follow their mothers back home to their mother's towns and so on. The history of how a Jain household is run, how the children learn about Jain rituals and beliefs, and the ways in which women construct their theological understandings all must be understood in terms of the continuities and discontinuities of women's lives. The problem, of course, is that their history is unwritten.

The women in the Pārśva Maṇḍaḷ came from all over the state of Maharashtra and some from Karnataka, Rajasthan, and, of course, Gujarat. As the Gujarātī Jain community continues to grow in Maharashtra, the women travel less and less far for marriage. Dadiji was from a village in Madhya Pradesh near the Maharashtra border (now ten hours by bus and train but much longer at the time of her wedding) and Hema's mother came from southern Uttar Pradesh. Most of the older women had come from Gujarat and Rajasthan when they married. The middle-age women were marrying on average only about four or five hours from their natal homes: Savita from Sangli (six hours by bus), Maluben from near Mumbaī (four hours by bus), Kavita from Kalyān (three and one-half hours by train), Lata from Kamshet near Lonāvalā (two hours by train and bus), Ranjana from Karaḍ (five hours by bus), though Pravina came from Amdāvād (twenty hours by train) and one of the Poḍwāl women came from near Udaipur (twenty-five hours by bus and train). The women marrying now often stay within the state of Maharashtra and many (like Monika and Reshma) are marrying within the Pune or Mumbaī districts. Vaishali came from Malegaon (ten hours) and Varsha came from Karaḍ (five hours); both are now married and living in Pune. Sheelu, married just four years ago, went to Sangamner (three hours by bus).

Even when a woman adopts the ways of her mother-in-law's house, the practices derive from a female source, which, if we are to establish an accurate sense of history, must be traced back through the geographically far-flung linkages of women's married lives. Among Maharashtrians, the concept of "home" presents a problem of place for married women who do not see any home as their own because of the inevitable movement they experience from one home to another through marriage (Glushkova and Feldhaus 1998). Women were expected to affect a complete transfer of their identity from their natal home and kin to that of their new affinal family. Sax (1991) speaks of the gendered differences in the understanding of a woman's relationship with her natal family and her natal location. The men—in their role as husbands—he said, see marriage as a complete break from a woman's natal family, whereas women said that maintaining their ties with their natal family is central to their happiness (and protection) in their married homes. Raheja and Gold (1994) speak of the centrality of the kinship ties of married women to their natal families and write of the stress and fear when those ties are challenged. In Rajasthan, Rajput women were expected to alter their religious practices—especially changing which lineage goddess they worship—as well as their clothing and food to match that of their husband's home (Harlan 1992). Jain women are likewise expected to become a part of their married lineage and location and to accept those transformations that are asked of her. (Most strikingly I think of one woman who had to change her name because one of the elder sisters-in-law had the same name and it was felt that it would be confusing.) Though women did resist this transfer in some ways—maintaining different dress, pūjā styles, devotion to particular deities or Jinas, and particular food preparations and preferences—it was just that, a "resistance" to social norms. Keep in mind that in the narrative literature discussed in chapter 2, women are revered for just such a resistance; the most virtuous women were those who remained devoted Jains against the pressures from their families, especially their affinal families. But that resistance is glorified only as it is in the name of the Jain religion.

The history of place, then, is germane only insofar as it illustrates the particular situation of a woman at a given time: a problem, also, even for the study of men, as it cannot account for the migrations and the long-standing transnational experience of many communities—Gujarātīs are certainly near the top of such a list (Ballard 1994; Banks 1994). Thus, for most of the women I knew, places were significant only insofar as they pertained to the women's lives and the network of lives established by the marriage practices they upheld. The histories given here set the stage for the lives of these women in their married homes, but what little record we have of Jains is exclusively male—except that the British officers and travelers briefly described the clothes, ornaments and skin color of the "wives" of Jain merchants in the nineteenth and early twentieth centuries, which at least tells us that they had their wives with them in Pune (Campbell 1885; Elwin 1907; Enthoven 1920–22). Some of this history could perhaps be reconstructed in part from either the copious records Jains often keep about temple activities or from accounts and oral histories retained in family self-representations. This kind of research has yet to be sufficiently done with Jain women—or any other Indian women, for that matter.[25] A feminist history of India would draw a different picture, one not based on single place but perhaps on a reconstruction of social and familial connections as the "place" of history.

A Profile of the Women in This Study

To set these conversations in the context of maṇḍaḷ membership and ethnic/linguistic identification, I include here a brief survey of those women with whom I spoke in more than passing conversations. There were sixty-nine women associated with Ajitnāth Temple with whom I regularly had directed and extended conversations, and many more women with whom I had occasional conversation. There were twelve maṇḍaḷ members (six active and six inactive) with whom I had virtually daily extensive conversations and twenty-two maṇḍaḷ members (twelve active and ten inactive) with whom I had these conversations at least once a week. (The active maṇḍaḷ members were those who went to maṇḍaḷ practice most weeks and performed pūjās with the maṇḍaḷ. All women who regularly went to the temple or performed more than the annual rite of confession and expiation—Saṃvatsarī Pratikramaṇ—with the congregation were considered inactive members of the maṇḍaḷ.) Of the fifty-eight women with whom I averaged two or more extensive conversations per month, thirty-one were active maṇḍaḷ members, twenty were inactive members of their maṇḍaḷ, and seven were completely uninvolved in maṇḍaḷ activities. There were an additional eleven women in active (four) and inactive (seven) maṇḍaḷ roles with whom I had regular short conversations but with whom I did not regularly have extensive conversations. In addition, there were twenty women who were never a part of the Ajitnāth congregation (often a maṇḍaḷ member's sister-in-law or niece) with whom I had fairly regular and extensive conversations (eight active in maṇḍaḷs in their congregations and twelve inactive). In total, I had ongoing discussions with eighty-nine (sixty-nine at Ajitnāth, twenty elsewhere) women. There was also a multitude of women with whom I had passing conversation or just one or two extensive discussions who also informed much of my understanding of Jain women's experience in a more general way. Moreover, there were twenty-one Jain laymen with whom I had regular conversations, providing comparisons and counterpoints which highlighted some of the gendered nuances of these women's experiences of Jainism.

Of these sixty-nine women from Ajitnāth, Shah (Śahā) was the dominant surname (forty-three in twelve families) followed by unknowns (three, each assumed to be Shahs based on their relatives), Poḍvāl (four in one family), Gandhi (three in two families), Solanki (three in one family), Osvāl (two in two families), Parekh (two in one family), Pungaliya (two in two families), Daga (one), Kapra (one), Khivansara (one), Mutha (one), Navalakha (one), Rathoḍ (one) and Shraph (one). Of these sixty-nine, fifty-two identified themselves as Gujarātī (Parekh, Shah/Śahā, Shraph, and Solanki) and seventeen identified themselves as Mārvāḍī or Rājasthānī (Daga, Gandhi, Kapra, Khivansara, Mutha, Navalakha, Osvāl, Poḍvāl, Pungaliya, Rathoḍ). This self-identification was expressed in terms of language—Gujarātī or Hindī/Mārvāḍī—more often than not. Even though families who are from the Visa Śrīmalī subcaste[26] (which includes most of the Shahs listed here) originate in Mārvāḍ (Marwar), they identify themselves as Gujarātīs, which Cort (1989) also reports in Pāṭaṇ. This, perhaps more than anything else, illustrates the tension between the contemporary Gujarātī and Mārvāḍī communities. There were twenty-nine Gujarātī and eleven Mārvāḍī active maṇḍaḷ members and sixteen Gujarātī and six Mārvāḍī inactive maṇḍaḷ members, and there were seven Gujarātī non-maṇḍaḷ members.

Jains are usually described as a middle-class mercantile community, a label they themselves reproduce. In fact, the maṇḍaḷ women came from a fairly wide economic class background. Though I was not privy to the actual financial status of these families, the kinds of houses they lived in, the amount of work performed by hired help, and the education and sometimes weddings of their children help illustrate something of their financial status. While I am dividing this into middle, upper, and lower-middle classes, the women's families' economic statuses are more appropriately thought of on a continuum. Most of the women (fifty-two in total, thirty-two active maṇḍaḷ members) lived in what I call middle-class families—a vague enough category—by which I mean that the family home (virtually always an apartment) had a separate bedroom for each married couple in a joint family and the family hired part-time help for washing (especially laundry and dishes) and had sufficient money both to invest in their family businesses and to have some disposable income. Most of these families sent their children (both boys and girls) to the local, but respectable, Marāṭhī medium school and college in Shivajinagar, and virtually all boys and some girls finished college. There were a handful of women (seven of the total, three active maṇḍaḷ members, mostly Mārvāḍīs) who came from upper-class families marked by fancy bungalows in suburban (or semiurban) housing developments. The men in these families often spoke English, but their wives did not; however, the women from these families were all literate. There was only one woman—a college-age, unmarried, young Mārvāḍī woman—who had any meaningful facility in English, but some of these families now send their children to English medium schools. In addition, there were a few women (ten in total, eight active maṇḍaḷ members) who came from families whose financial status was low by Jain standards (low or lower-middle class); their homes were often sections of divided houses and occasionally single-room dwellings. These families did not have any hired help or very minimal hired help, the women often did some kind of cottage industry work to help out with finances, and they married their children in money-saving group weddings sponsored by Jain social organizations. Sometimes these lower-middle class families were middle-class families who had fallen on hard times; if they were, these families used their family resources to educate their children (especially, but not only, sons) and to have separate and lavish (relative to their lifestyle) weddings. It was striking to me that the women in the maṇḍaḷ came from such disparate economic backgrounds and that some did not see each other socially except in the context of maṇḍaḷ and congregational events or group invitations extended to the maṇḍaḷ for weddings or other large, private events. Most women (except the eldest wife in the family who usually has control over the household budget) have little economic control (no money to call their own) and virtually all women are economically bound to the tides of their husbands' (and husbands' brothers') economic prowess. Just as it would be facile to equate religious authority with socioeconomic power—though among Jains there is a definite relationship between these two (Banks 1992; Laidlaw 1995; Reynell 1991)—it would be equally problematic to assume that their lack of socioeconomic power means that these women have no agency or meaningful authority.

Unquestionably, I spent most of my time with singers. When I went to someone's house, she sang for me and showed me materials related to my widely known interest. Women who were not singers or who were not interested in religion were not at the center of my research. But I talked to anyone who was willing to talk about singing, stavan, or laywomen's religiosity (*śrāvikā dharm*), as well as many conversations on related (and not so related) topics. My language training (in Hindī and Gujarātī) in part determined with whom I spoke; though there are some Marāṭhī-speaking Śvetāmbar Jains (most significantly for this study Maluben and Sheelu who spoke Gujarātī with me), I did not seek them out unless they worshipped at the local temple in Shivajinagar. Clearly, the women from whom much of my information came are those women who were most interested in the project; I depended a great deal on information volunteered to me without the initial prompting of questions or the frame of "the interview." These women did not have a lot of free time, but they did spend a good part of that time helping me do my research. These women were, for the most part, married women—though I did speak with unmarried young women, widows, and even one divorced woman. The dominance of married women reflects both that they were the majority of those who participated in stavan singing and that they were the women most socially comfortable with me—their lives were most similar to mine (I was there with my husband, Steve). They all worshipped (at least at one time) at the Ajitnāth Temple in Shivajinagar as their primary temple. Many other women contributed to the project in less central ways, and for the sake of readability, unless they are mentioned several times, I have not included their biographies.

Lay and Mendicant Interaction

Although each of the fourfold parts of the Jain comunity (male mendicants, female mendicants, laymen, and laywomen) is necessary for the community to be considered complete, the complete community is required only for a few major rituals, ordinations, and temple installations. Relationships between Jain mendicants and laity are less central to the formation of religious belief in Pune district than in major Gujarātī or Rājasthānī cities and pilgrimage towns, because their interactions are limited. The mendicants are only available extensively during the rainy season. Because there are relatively few mendicants in the region (and most of them stay near Mumbaī) and because these mendicants cannot remain in a single location for more than a few days except in the rainy season, the laity's relationship with the mendicants is, for the most part, not one from which the laity learn extensive theology.[27] I often heard that this type of learning was important in general, but I rarely heard any particular theological lesson or idea attributed to a particular mendicant. In general, mendicants in Jainism, when available, contribute actively to the normative models for the lay religiosity by writing manuals and devotional pieces and giving lectures encouraging pūjā and temple building. Lay praxis derives in part from these texts and lectures and in part from ideals arising out of the active and involved lay communities. Despite the privileging of mendicancy within most canonical texts, lay Jains are encouraged to follow a Jain path which includes asceticism (without renunciation), rituals of well-being, and the support of the mendicant tradition (Cort 1989).

The laity approach the mendicant community in two ways:[28] (1) auspicious vision (*darśan*) (the laity are blessed by their very attendance at rituals, including mendicant sermons, fast-breaking celebrations, temple image installations, major formal pūjās, and the celebrations surrounding initiation of mendicants) and (2) devotion (*bhakti*) (the laity become personally devoted to a certain guru allowing a longer, more influential relationship between the male and female lay devotees and the male and female mendicants; this type of relationship may be a source from which the laity acquire some theological knowledge). Dadiji—and subsequently the rest of her family to varying degrees—is devoted to a particular male mendicant, Viśvakalyāṇjī. Dadiji arranged to spend the rainy season in the same place as her guru several times. In 1994, when Viśvakalyāṇjī was spending the rainy season in Śirur, where Dadiji's second son lived, Dadiji also spent the rainy season there; twice, Dadiji (and Dadaji) spent the rainy season in Pālītāṇā when Viśvakalyāṇjī was doing so. After Dadaji died, the whole family (all the descendants of his father, Deepcand) went on a memorial pilgrimage to several new temples built in Maharashtra under the encouragement of Viśvakalyāṇjī, the pinnacle of which was when Viśvakalyāṇjī came to the family at the pilgrims' hostel to receive alms, to give a speech about Dadaji's devotion, and to give the whole family his blessing. The mantle of devotion to this guru has been taken up now by Dadiji's third son, who regularly traveled to see Viśvakalyāṇjī and to get his advice on issues of business and family. This son's visits, though, were limited by his obligations to the family businesses to those times when Viśvakalyāṇjī's mendicancy brought him within a few hours scooter-ride from Pune.

Although several mendicants stopped for a day or two at the Ajitnāth mendicants' hostel—it was just off the Mumbaī–Pune road—on their walk to the larger mendicants' hostels at Goḍījī or Ādināth Society, none stayed for the rainy season retreat. The Ajitnāth congregation was not large (or wealthy) enough to support a group of mendicants for the whole rainy season, because these mendicants depend exclusively on Jain food offerings. Thus, lay-mendicant interaction in the neighborhood was limited. Though several women went to Goḍījī to hear occasional sermons, to take classes in Jainism from male mendicants so they could teach religious education (*pāṭhśāḷā*) classes to Jain children, or to get advice and blessings from the mendicants, their religiosity flourished in an environment centered around other laity. In his research on Jain laymen, Cort (1989) argues that Jainism must be understood to have two thoroughly interconnected and acceptable modes: one based on mendicancy and renunciation and the other on lay life and well-being. Although the ideals for the layman differ from the ideals for the mendicant, both are expressed and explained in normative texts (Cort 1991b). When a lay Jain performs formal pūjās, he or she takes the role not of a mendicant but of Indra or Indrāṇī, the paradigmatic laypeople (Babb 1996). The temple practice of Jains is deeply informed by mendicants—despite the prohibition against mendicant participation in material temple worship (*dravya pūjā*)—and these mendicants are enthusiastic supporters of the laity's performing lay worship.[29] They do not, however, in my observations of contemporary interaction, insist that the laity should renounce—though they do see the renouncer's path as more suited to the pursuit of mokṣa—but focus their prescriptive advice on aspects of the lay path that the devotee should pursue. The mendicants particularly encouraged donation, fasting, temple building, and increased devotional activity.

Most Jain women choose to be laywomen despite certain religiously, socially, and intellectually appealing aspects of the renunciatory life of female mendicants (Holmstrom 1988; Reynell 1985a; Shanta 1985). There are more female mendicants than male ones, but, still, there were few occasions when female mendicants came to the Ajitnāth mendicants' hostel. When they did come (or when the laywomen went to other mendicants' hostels in Pune to see them), they gave advice to the laywomen on a variety of religious and social topics, including some long sermon-like lectures on themes brought up by the laywomen. When a female mendicant in Śirur finished listening to my recitation of the Navkār Mantra—something I was commonly asked to perform—she gave a forty-five-minute impromptu lecture on the meaning and efficacy of Navkār Mantra recitation (not only for me but for the thirty or so other women who had come to perform guru worship to the mendicants).[30] The distinction between the female mendicants and laywomen presents a challenge, as the divisions are often not as different in practice—many laywomen perform many of the same rituals as the mendicants do: confession and expiation (*pratikramaṇ*), meditation (*sāmāyik*), devotional prayers (caityavandan), guru veneration (*guruvandan*), and fasts (*tap*)—as they are different in status, education, and autonomy. I met several female mendicants with advanced degrees in Jain theology and philosophy, Jainology, or related topics. In addition, several had read extensively in Jain literature—some in Sanskrit and most in vernacular languages. In Pune, the female mendicants were treated with great respect by men and women alike. I did not see a wide differentiation between male and female mendicants with regard to general status—both were considered holy personages. Laidlaw (1995) discusses the importance of female mendicants as gurus among the Khartar Gacch Jains in Jaipur; Khartar Gacch female mendicants give formal sermons and thus may be in a better position to garner followers.

Though in 1993–1994 I did not hear any layperson profess a personal devotion to a female mendicant as guru (as they did with male mendicants), I did record several women speaking of a particularly charismatic female mendicant from the Tapā Gacch lineage, Padmarekhaśrī, who was considered very knowledgeable and "important." In 2000, I found a number of women who spoke of a particularly charismatic Tapā Gacch female mendicant, Divyaprabhājī, as their guru. Divyaprabhājī was born in Karjat (a town near Mumbaī) and had returned to her home region for the celebration of her fiftieth year since her ordination. This celebration, her sponsorship of an Updhān Tap in Katraj just south of Pune in the winter of 2000, and her subsequent acceptance of an invitation to stay at the Adinath Society temple complex in Pune for the 2000 rainy season gave her the opportunity to develop a cadre of followers among the lay Jains in Pune and allowed these followers sufficient access to her to lead them to accept her as a guru. In 1999 Divyaprabhājī spent her rainy season retreat in Kalyāṇ near Mumbaī; from 1986 to 1989 she also spent her rainy season retreats in Maharashtra, and followers from these previous rainy seasons were able to visit her in Pune where she spent the rainy season of 2000. By the summer of 2000, five women in this study were consistently giving Divyaprabhājī the kinds of devotional attention that I had previously only seen given to charismatic male mendicants.

Jain mendicants have created a body of literature called *śrāvakācāra*—lay manuals in Sanskrit, Prakrit, and now vernacular languages (mostly in Gujarātī, though there are one or two popular ones in Hindī)—in order to allow householders some access to an otherwise prohibitively demanding textual tradition. These lay manuals are more a series of rules to follow than theological treatises from which to derive Jain philosophy (Cort 1991b). I use only a few examples from lay manuals because women read few of these texts—they seem to read narrative and devotional texts rather than didactic texts—and because these texts rarely have advice addressing women; they are specific in their address of male Jains. Even though there is an assumption that in most ways Jains (male and female) are subject to the same expectations, the language and images of these texts are nearly exclusively male. In the most common lay manual, *Cālo Jinālaye Jaīe*, the only photos of women alone are those that show on which side of the Jina image women are supposed to stand and what kind of dress for women—who do not wear identifiable pūjā clothes as men do—is appropriate for the temple and reminders to cover one's head. In one case a photo of a praying woman is used to mark the section in which the manual speaks of menses restrictions.[31] This model was reproduced in all the lay manuals I saw. All of these mark women's religiosity as distinct only when it differs from male (rather than neutral) models of Jain praxis; there are no photos or sections that mark off differences in male praxis from a neutral model. More important, though, the women did not refer to these lay manuals when giving sources for their understandings and performances of worship; they named devotional, narrative, and liturgical texts and other women as their sources.

Laywomen's Religious Practice

Śvetāmbar Jain women balance their lives between received ideals of womanhood (Jain, Gujarātī, Indian, middle-class) and their own personal understandings of what it means to be a good Jain laywoman. Jain rhetoric and women intersect in several locations, particularly in the stavan, fasting narratives, saintly women's narratives, and the negative portrayal of women in mendicant-authored renunciatory texts. Balbir's 1994 article, "Women in Jainism," argues that source texts determine the view of Jain women that scholars encounter, specifically, that the most prominent image of Jain women is exclusively negative. The women, however, draw much of their rhetorical structure for "female-ness" from vernacular texts and images of women as devotees in the devotional literature. The lack of prescriptive advice expressly for women in the lay manual literature permits the laywomen to negotiate this terrain by articulating how they understand their own religious practice, usually by recreating Jain devotional narratives and songs. Despite laywomen's lack of direct access to the Sanskrit/ Prakrit orthodoxy, they build Jain theologies and transmit these beliefs and practices to their children (Reynell 1991)—the same children who may grow up to be the mendicants who write the prescriptive and devotional texts which then circle back to the women themselves.

To understand Jain lay religiosity, especially women's religiosity, one needs to examine the places where Jain laywomen negotiate the philosophical traditions in Jainism. The ways in which women I knew ran a Jain household— cooked, cleaned, went to the market, and raised their children—were partly determined by the direct or indirect influence of Jain normative ideals. A laywoman's facility with Jain food restrictions increased her family's reputation for being devout and made the complicated calendar of Jain fasts and feasts simpler (Mahias 1985). In my experience, all activities included food, or at least tea. Likewise, I found that not only the food restrictions the women themselves accepted but their competence at preparing the specialized Jain foods (minimally, upholding Jain precepts about food but also foods associated with particular festivals and fasts) was a source of prestige in and of itself; a reputation for upholding these rules strictly made a family a more likely candidate for feeding ascetics—a source of great merit. The piety of one woman often serves as a social gauge of the whole family's moral character (Reynell 1985a) and may directly affect the economic status of the male members of the family (Reynell 1987). Laymen are not expected to perform the same level of daily activities as women (Cort 1991b; Laidlaw 1995; Reynell 1987, 1991). Men were not directly responsible for the instillation of Jain values and identity in the next generation. Laywomen were responsible for the upkeep of a Jain household, including feeding Jain ascetics, maintaining Jain praxis in the family, and organizing social functions for women around Jain events, holidays, or values, in order to ensure that their children would be able to be married in, and accepted by, the Jain community. While men serve as public supporters of Jainism, women serve as public examples of Jain religiosity. Laywomen have full access to religious spheres of Jain activity in temples, homes, and festivals.[32]

Jain women's religious sphere encompasses congregational and daily individual pūjā, maṇḍaḷ activities, fasting, and participation in festivals and programs and pilgrimages. Women at Ajitnāth Temple performed daily worship and—as a sponsor, a maṇḍaḷ member, or an observer—participated in the performances of the formal pūjās. Formal pūjās were performed on the new moon day monthly, by specific sponsors on days deemed generally auspicious (e.g., New Year's Day or anniversaries of Jinas' auspicious events), or on days selected because of their relationship to the sponsor (wedding anniversaries, birthdays, forty days after a death in the family, inauguration of a new home). Formal pūjās were most often held in the afternoons after most men have had their tea and returned to work, leaving their wives relatively free to attend such programs. Most women participated in a certain amount of fasting, from involvement only on the Saṃvatsarī day (when fasting is the norm for all Jains) to extensive and repeated fasting according to their own choices. Virtually all the women I met had performed one extreme fast (usually the eight-day Paryuṣaṇ fast) and many had performed a variety of less extreme fasts as part of a program of maintaining the family's prosperity. Women attended the ordinations (*dīkṣā*) of mendicants whenever they could, fast-breaking celebrations, temple consecrations, and an assortment of religiously determined social activities (parades, Jain cooking lessons, the all-Pune women's maṇḍaḷs' gathering, maṇḍaḷ picnics and programs) and also those social obligations—which are not immediately religious—of familial or Jain community expectations (funeral gatherings, weddings, engagements, the seventh month of pregnancy celebrations and, sometimes, visiting).

Women (and men) participated in the Jain festivals at Paryuṣaṇ and Divālī, as well as the anniversary of the temple consecration at their own temple and the all-congregation feast. Almost all adult women had also gone on pilgrimage to Pālītānā, and most had gone to the other important Western Indian Jain pilgrimage sites of Girnār, Śankheśvar, Ābū, and Nākoḍā at some point in their lives. Although the women may have been to other pilgrimage sites and important temples (some women had traveled as far as Sammet Śikar in Bihar for important pilgrimages), these were the places they listed for me and which they showed me pictures of and souvenirs from, suggesting their central importance among the others. Whole families and whole congregations may go on long pilgrimages, while smaller groups may go on pilgrimage to local Jain sites. Every visit to a town included a visit to the Jain temple. Though these temples may not be of great religious, cultural, or historic significance, these visits are part of the pilgrimage ideal. Jain women's religious practice centers around activities organized around both the ideals of Jain religious orthopraxy and the sociocultural expectations of their Gujarātī Jain identities.

Stavan Singing and Maṇḍaḷ Singing

Women collectively dominated the Jain stavan repertoire and performances. Stavan singing is accessible to all women regardless of economic class and is portable to wherever the women are living. I have been told by Jain women in North America that before a temple was built in their city, stavan singing was doubly important because it served as a way to worship the Jinas when there was no temple. Stavan singing was tied to the Jain understanding of gender roles where—despite the fact that all Jains knew at least one or two stavan as a part of their daily worship—the primary singers, knowers, and collectors of stavan were women. Although many men (both mendicants and laymen) wrote stavan, the knowledge of them inhered primarily in women. Even in the temple in the morning, when the men were reciting mantras on a rosary, the women were singing. The texts of the stavan themselves recount the role of women as singers in the temple, as those who offer songs rather than the jewelry or flowers that men offer to the Jinas.

The stavan were sung as worship—they were not a genre for the expression of women's social commentary—but the texts of the stavan and the contexts of the stavan's performance do weave a theology which the women transmitted through performance and actively taught to the other women in their families, to the women's maṇḍaḷs, and to their children. The women purposefully organized their performances according to the stavan's meaning and the appropriateness of certain meanings to a specific context. The performances were determined by the women's thoughts about religion and theology far more than by their comments about women's status. However, this genre was a locus of women's sense of authority; maṇḍaḷs and stavan singing (and their related religious practices) were a place for asserting their expertise. Though there were other genres of religious literature with which the women were familiar—most important the liturgical texts and the fasting and renunciation narratives—stavan singing had the most fluid repertoire, one based on the interests of the women and the stavan's contextual usage. The understanding and use of religious authority illustrate the ways women used religion as a source of personal agency.[33]

All Jain rituals are accompanied by stavan singing. This ubiquity provided women with a forum in which to perform and learn stavan while affirming the orthodox values of the Jain community. Although stavan often accompany some other ritual, stavan singing itself should be seen as a Jain ritual both independent of, and in conjunction with, other ritual activities. Stavan singing is not just present in but central to several rituals. Morning worship includes a prayer series recitation. In the middle of that series, the worshipper sings a stavan. Stavan are also sung during the eightfold (*aṣṭaprakārī*) pūjā—the basis for morning worship. Stavan are of central importance in the transmission of Jain theology among the laity. Babb (1996) speaks of Jain worship as existing in a ritual culture—one that develops and surrounds a ritual complex—which is the context in which much of my discussion to come will take place. If a socioreligious culture develops in the context of shared beliefs and practices (Carrithers and Humphrey 1991; Jaini 1979), then rituals are loci around which the Jain community focuses and identifies its members. These rituals, by their public nature and community regulation, become models for orthopraxy (Cort 1991b, 1992; Reynell 1987). All rituals and texts accepted as normative, including stavan singing, must somehow fit into the system of Jain beliefs and practices in order to be accepted as normative.

Many women in Shivajinagar are involved in the Pārśva Maṇḍaḷ, which meets each Saturday to practice singing both stavan and the texts of the formal pūjās. This maṇḍaḷ is available for hire by other Jains for the performances of formal pūjās on special days or for housewarming rituals. Women sing stavan at these events as well as singing them as part of fast-breaking celebrations and as a form of entertainment. Stavan singing is done both singly as an offering to the Jinas and a form of meditation and as a maṇḍaḷ, in which case the stavan singers sing together as a central part of the production of the formal pūjās. In 1993–94 there were four men's maṇḍaḷs for the singing of stavan in Pune, but they were a minority: forty-eight of fifty-two maṇḍaḷs in Pune were women's maṇḍaḷs.[34]

Maṇḍaḷ singing is an urban phenomenon; Jains, as a historically urban community, have made maṇḍaḷ singing a part of the ritual specialist-for-hire system, which, for Hindus, usually involves brahmins (or sometimes, non-brahmin) priests and male singers.[35] Singer (1966) speaks of the communities that form around Vaiṣṇav singing groups in Madras; these communities are a result of the regular meetings of singers who do not share other social settings. Hindu women also use maṇḍaḷs to form social groups while performing rituals together (Flueckiger 1991a, 1991b). Women's maṇḍaḷs were central to the formation of women's socioreligious communities in an urban setting and were themselves shaped by the women's social worlds. Jain women joined the Pārśva Maṇḍaḷ because it provided a social outlet within the already defined community of Jain women in Shivajinagar. The community predated the maṇḍaḷ, though maṇḍaḷ events, especially the annual all-maṇḍaḷ picnic and the all-congregation women's party (snehasaṃmelan), redefined the community with the singers at the center (see figure 1-5).

The auspiciousness of women's singing is widely reported as part of the rhetoric of Indian religiosity in the scholarship on women's participation in Indian culture.[36] Among Hindus, maṇḍaḷ-style singing seems to be a locus of male religiosity (Lutgendorf 1991; Singer 1966; Slawek 1986). Hindu women sing at their festivals and familial celebrations, but scholars—especially, Flueckiger (1996), Henry (1988), and Tewari (1977)—suggest that public singing (except at weddings) is not a normative practice for Hindu women. Of course, context still affects the repertoire of the song performances, but Hindu women's choices—unlike the Jain maṇḍaḷ singers'—seem to be based in singing context and genre rather than in the theologies of the songs. However, I suspect that Hindu women's performances have more going on with regard to theology than is shown in the scholarship to date. Stavan performance by Jain women more resembles genres usually associated with male-centered performance.

The stavan singers' repertoire is constructed through rehearsal and discussions at maṇḍaḷ practice; it is not usually spontaneous. The women practice as a maṇḍaḷ-performing group and even come to formal pūjās in matching saris, but although the women are presented with a "gift"—often a relatively small sum of money, usually between 5 and 10 rupees each—they are not permanent and exclusive profes-

FIGURE 1-5. The 1994 all-maṇḍaḷ picnic in Alandi, July 1994.

sionals like those musicians hired to perform devotional singing (kīrtan) at Puṣṭimarg temples (Gaston 1997). Musically, stavan build on the folk music traditions of Gujarat and not, like Puṣṭimarg Vaiṣṇav's music (*havelī sangīt*), on classical traditions. Jain women are the locus of Jain devotional singing expertise—as Gujarātī Hindu women are the experts at Gujarātī devotional song to the goddess (*garbā*) singing (Thompson 1987; Vergati 1994)—and they have a certain level of prestige and authority, deriving from their special knowledge of singing and the rituals at which stavan are sung, over Jain ritual life.

The differences in stavan singing styles can be divided both by ethnic group and by gender. Gujarātī maṇḍaḷs (or those dominated by Gujarātī aesthetics) used Gujarātī language and *rās-garbā* melodies and instrumentation, while the Mārvāḍī men's maṇḍaḷ used Mārvāḍī and Hindī languages and Rājasthānī musicality. I did not observe any Mārvāḍī women's maṇḍaḷs in Pune. The relationship between Gujarātī-ness and Jain-ness illustrates the ways stavan were both a religious declaration and an ethnocentric dialect, where the group involved was aware of the music's role in ethnic identification (Stokes 1994). Though in 1993–94 there were four men's maṇḍaḷs, the most popular men's maṇḍaḷ was Mārvāḍī. In terms of musicality, the division along gender lines seemed less important than that of ethnicity: the two Gujarātī men's maṇḍaḷs I observed reflected similar (though slightly more complex) instrumentation and a similar repertoire to the Gujarātī women's maṇḍaḷs. The Mārvāḍī maṇḍaḷ performances were quite different from those of the Gujarātī maṇḍaḷs in terms of repertoire and musicality, which both derived from Rājasthānī musical context.

The overall divisions in musicality and location which Henry (1988), Slawek (1986), and others describe between men's (complex, virtuoso, public) and women's (simple, untrained, private) musical performances seem less pronounced within Jain devotional singing. The categories themselves seem to be based on an acceptance of the male worlds as the norm, a pattern that has been sufficiently critiqued by many feminist scholars (starting with Gilligan 1982). When men did perform stavan in a maṇḍaḷ, the performances differed mostly in their production—their use of amplification and electronic instruments and the absence of dance. Dance was part of the women's performances even in the one women's maṇḍaḷ I observed that had otherwise adopted a performance style associated with the local male maṇḍaḷs. Gujarātī Hindu devotional music—from which much of the stavan music is drawn—has a female/male distinction in the names of the genres (garbā/*garbī*) based on who is singing, which was also not reflected in the stavan repertoire (Thompson 1987). Men and women used similar melodies and vocal styles; men and women adhered to similar, though not identical, uses of stavan texts and melodies. The differing performances reflected their differing aesthetics and performance priorities.

Stavan as Text

Though stavan seem often to articulate devotional views and theological understandings seemingly at odds with the normative establishment, many of these stavan are written by male mendicants who also wrote more philosophical, prosaic texts. Stavan, a popular and pervasive genre of Jain literature, are a repository for the devotional theology of the Jain laity. Stavan describe and prescribe the Jain devotees' relationships with the Jina and the Jain religion rather than examine the specifics of Jain philosophy. When stavan writers are mendicants informed by the philosophical ideals and the previous devotional texts, their status lends a normative weight to these texts. The ways that stavan both reproduce and challenge normative models add texture to our understanding of Jain devotion and require a certain reformulation of these received categories of orthodoxy and lay religiosity.[37]

Stavan can be understood as the product of Jain devotionalism in the context of the bhakti movement in Western India in the medieval period. Hindu bhakti poetry is the focus of many Hindu religious practices, as some studies that focus on the contemporary uses and performances of Hindu bhakti poetry show.[38] Although there are numerous studies of Hindu bhakti, Jain bhakti—or devotionalism—is just beginning to be considered. Deriving from the medieval *raso* and *pada* literature, the modern stavan shares its roots with other devotional literature in Western India (including rās-garbā songs to goddesses and to Kṛṣṇa). The shared development can be seen with the form and musicology of garbā literature and songs as well as some less central relationships with Kṛṣṇa devotional song (*bhajan*) literature (Mallison 1983, 1989; Thompson 1987).[39] Though stavan were never closely tied to the court traditions (as opposed to the Aṣṭapad poets of Puṣṭimarg Vaiṣṇav Hinduism—though there were Jains writing raso poetry for the Solanki court at Pāṭaṇ), they still reflect certain aspects of *alankār* and *rasa* theories in their construction. However, the close performance link with Gujarātī folk music and primacy of oral transmission—through performance—over textual reproduction (though there are literally thousands of published stavan collections) shows the influence of Gujarātī folk culture on the stavan as well.

One must be careful not only to avoid limiting the notion of what can be a text, by narrowing the range of texts considered appropriate for analysis (O'Flaherty 1988), but also to understand that texts move between "fluid" and "fixed" collections (Doniger 1991). Jain stavan travel between women singers as oral texts, and they are collected in notebooks. Women use the notebooks as a mnemonic for stavan performances as well as an archive for future reference. The notebooks are not replaced by new ones or edited; new stavan are added to the end of the collection, and the more organized women add new titles to their tables of contents in the fronts of the notebooks. The notebooks are sometimes assembled into published collections and sold in the many Jain bookstores. The stavan from these publications are then copied into the women's notebooks. The texts go in and out of orality several times even in one year; how these collections function along with oral transmission in the spread of stavan is a project that this study can only briefly discuss (see chapter 3). The fact of a written text does not guarantee its stability over time, nor is the life of that text circumscribed by its published edition. Stavan texts must be seen as the totality of written and oral texts in performance in order to understand the stavan as an influential source for theological understanding (Graham 1987, 1989). Stavan collections—women's active repertoires, women's notebooks, and published collections—are fluid and multivalent texts.

Stavan are significant not only because of the unique theology contained within their lyrics but because of the way they are used. W. C. Smith (1989) writes that the study of Christianity would best benefit from the understanding of the use of the Bible, not only from the history of the compilation of the Bible or its ideas. Folkert (1989) reflects that Jain texts, especially the Kalpa Sūtra, are a challenge to the ideas of the canon which Protestant scholarship has imposed on other religions. Folkert (1989) proposes at least one division in canon, between texts which are vectors—belief determiners— and texts which are vectored—used to underline a belief. It is perhaps more useful to describe texts as acting as vectors or vectored texts rather than as being them; stavan act as both vectors for women's theology and as vectored texts when a performer determines the appropriate repertoire. Because we have no sources for the social role of stavan through history, the historical context of this study must be the present. The singing of stavan can only be understood by a thorough examination of the context of each stavan singer and her stavan choices and interpretations. A stavan itself has many meanings; I have tried to allow the stavan to be multivalent according to their ritual, performative and textual contexts. In addition, stavan performance has a "grammar" (after Abrahams 1976 and Ben-Amos 1976, 1982) which incorporates the previous uses of stavan and the components of past performances with the present performance moment: contextual harmonies are unavoidable (after Bakhtin, in Todorov 1984).

That I see stavan as carrying more than just devotional sentiments—I believe that much of Jain theology (as well as Jain sociocultural expectations) can be understood through stavan and other devotional texts—derives from studies of hymn singing in Victorian England and the United States (Adey 1988; De Jong 1986; Tamke 1978). Although the contexts of Victorian Christians and contemporary Jains in Pune are so different that the content of these articles bears little on the way I understood the actual stavan singing of Jains, the fact of their use of hymns to "read" theology made me able to see better the theology in Jain stavan. Victorian hymnody used communal production and hymnals to transmit normative values, but Jain stavan are collected individually by singers and performed by "experts" and nonexperts alike, without the exclusive authorized shared repertoire of the hymnal.[40] Jain women themselves control the stavan repertoires and thereby effectively control a significant part of the production of Jain devotional theology.

Knowing and Knowers

This book argues that Jain laywomen's theologies are developed in the practice and performance of stavan singing. Devotional songs articulate theology through their lyrics and through the contexts in which each stavan is sung, which themselves reflect the women's interpretations of these contexts and songs. Though there are other genres of religious literature with which the women are familiar—most important the formal pūjā texts and fasting and ordination narratives—stavan singing has the most fluid repertoire, one based on the interests of the women and their contextual usage. Stavan performers understand the stavan according to a complex relationship (like Heidegger's "forestructure," if you will) between received ideas and the singers' particular experiences. Stavan have a wide variety of poetic forms, musical styles, and content from which the women select those that best make a "fit" between the song and its performance. The use of stavan is tied to theological interpretation; performance contexts are chosen according to theological and musicological appropriateness. The usual performance pattern is broken specifically to infer theological critiques by juxtaposing two issues whose intersection reflects a particular question. Jain laywomen's expertise can offer us illustrations of the important questions that they ask about Jainism.

Jain laywomen are the experts at being Jain laywomen; not one tract instructs them on their practice. There are lay manuals specifically for laymen and for Hindu women but not specifically for Jain laywomen.[41] Textual scholarship using Jain materials,[42] though extremely useful for an overview of the normative traditions of Jainism, excludes most female mendicants and all laity from theological and philosophical discourse. This exclusion ultimately allows only one kind of Jainism to be "real" and sets scholars in the position of theologians—determining what is and is not "Jain." Recent ethnographic studies of Jain laity have challenged and broadened the available understanding of what Jains do and believe by including descriptions and discussions about Jain praxis and socioreligious culture.[43] This book examines the ways Jain laywomen recreate theology through the performances and understandings of stavan. To make sense of Jain laywomen's experiences of being Jain, one needs to study the "texts" that the women themselves recreate (Bynum 1987; Bynum et al. 1986), as well as the contexts in which laywomen use them. It is through devotional singing at gatherings that laywomen's theology develops and is broadcast. The choice of timing and repertoire for any particular performance reveals both individual singers' beliefs-in-context and the groups' normative ideas about which devotional songs and melodies and what behaviors (both ritual and nonritual) best reflect their orthodoxy.

When I asked theological questions at the start of my research on Jain laywomen's religiosity, the women, instead of answering the questions, handed me published tracts or brought me to Jain mendicants. When I insisted that I was interested in what the women felt about these questions, they repeatedly said, "these are questions mendicants think about." Fairly early in my research, while I was talking to a female mendicant in the Ajitnāth mendicant's hostel about my work, she asked me what Jain books I had read. I started by listing those canonical texts I had read—the Kalpa Sūtra, the Ācārānga, Sūtrakṛtanga, Uttarādhyayana Sūtras—and she raised her hand to stop me. She said, "You should not read those; those books are just for mendicants. I have read them, but those are not for laypeople. If you were studying mendicants it would be different."[44] She asked me to recite the Navkār Mantra,[45] explained the importance of the lay manuals and rituals for my research, and then explained to me about menses restrictions. This Jain mendicant reminded me, in sum, to keep my research focused on topics connected to laywomen's lives.

Thereafter, I was determined always to let the laywomen tell me what the appropriate questions were. This does not mean that I asked only comfortable questions but, rather, that the line of my inquiry was drawn from their idiom and the issues expressed by them rather than from questions I had encountered in academic texts. It would be a grave mistake to conflate the women's sense of a topic's irrelevance with a sense of incompetence. For example, men and women alike saw stavan singing as the domain of the women. In the context of stavan singing, the women were confident and competent to discuss complex theological questions which, because I had phrased them in terms (and literally using the terms in Sanskrit or Prakrit) of canonical theology, they had previously deflected. As my research time passed and I concentrated on understanding the questions and answers they presented to me as important, I found they no longer sent me to men for my answers; many times, the women stopped talking, turned to me and said, "Put this in the book." They came to understand that I was most interested in their own competencies. I came to understand that their questions (and answers) were equally important to—and more central to their religiosity than—the questions (and answers) I brought with me from the academy.

If we also accept epistomologically that women are "knowers" and have "knowledge" about certain areas, we are forced to see the ways in which women have power (after Foucault 1980). This model is not necessarily one of resistance; the problem with the fascination with resistance models is that they define women's power exclusively in opposition to "male" or "dominant" power (Abu-Lughod 1990b). When women's knowledge and authority can carry sociocultural prestige and it is acceptable within the dominant group for women to be experts—as is the situation among Jains—a search for modes of resistance would obscure the ways that power works for women within the Jain system of orthodox texts, ritual practice, and social expectation. Through their knowledge of stavan and the particular rituals of Jain worship and through their participation in singing, women gain prestige and socioreligious power within the women's community (and sometimes the men's). Both men and women perceived women as the "storehouses" of knowledge about lay religiosity and of the appropriate songs to sing in particular performance contexts.

Whereas the authority (arising from expertise) women hold within religious practice and women's social worlds does not necessarily give them prestige or economic power, it nonetheless is a central locus for women's reconstructions and expressions of agency through their explanations of how they make decisions about how to live their lives. To focus on only those relationships and social structures in which women are victims obscures the kinds of practices that maintain women as authorities. A scholar could mistakenly argue that Jain women waste much of their energy on religious devotion rather than concentrating on education, skills training, activism, and seeking sexual or reproductive freedoms or economic equality, but such a project would fail to see the ways in which Jain women's religious lives afford them creative expression, a community of women who often do help other women in times of crisis, and a genuine sense of authority.

Feminist scholarship which focused on the models of equality and values dictated by European and American (usually white, middle-class) feminists has come under considerable criticism for applying the western ideals of individual, socio-economic autonomy (after Rousseau) directly to women of the so-called Third World; this criticism points out that this scholarship recreates a colonial hierarchy by positing that Western women are the "knowers" and Third World women are those who "cannot represent themselves" (Abu-Lughod 1990a, 1993; Mohanty 1984; Spivak 1987). Likewise, the assumption of the greater importance of those areas over which women have little power subordinates women's agency to received (often from male-dominated rhetoric) ideals (Code 1991) and characterizes women's choices as somehow less "correct" than those the scholars might make. My aim has been to accept the Jain women's statements about expertise and authority and to examine the challenges to and theories about Jainism that Jain laywomen presented to each other and other Jains. By combining an analysis both of the texts of Jain devotional songs and the contexts in which the laywomen sing these particular texts with the women's theological understandings, their performances can be understood as the creative expression of their religious beliefs. Being wary of the private/public and lore/knowledge dichotomies which often deny women the status of knowers of knowledge, I read the women's devotional song performances and explanations as text and commentary in theological discourse which Jain women control.

The texts and theories—the theoretical models—in this book have a strong effect on the way I see the world. But this does not imply that they are a part of the world or of the thoughts of the women about whom I am writing, nor does this mean that these models are, by virtue of being from Europe or the United States, not a part of these women's discourse. Rather, it is inappropriate to assume that the Jains understand their lives and practices the way we may read them. It is this scholarly fallacy—a quite common one—that I hope to avoid here. The assumption that women do not know better than to follow societal norms or that they are operating on the level of "the unconscious" (for classic Freudians), of "false consciousness" (post-Engels Marxists), or other variations, which too often serve to explain why others might not accept the political and/or social values of the scholar, puts the burden of proof on the speaker rather than on the listener (scholar), where it properly belongs. The question is one of epistemology, ethics, and feminist theories. One way to avoid assumptions is to begin by accepting explanations given in conversations. If a woman states that she has "power" because of her religious knowledge, it is my job to identify why and how she is right. Certainly the scholar should identify other forces in these relationships, but the women's views should be considered as the valid subject rather than the obscure counterexample or curious variation.

Where the women's answers or questions have resonated with the questions asked in an academic or Jain normative source, I have included the appropriate theoretical discourse, but not otherwise. I am aware that this approach, too, may have pitfalls. Unavoidably, I have made choices about which materials and issues to include, but I attempted to work from those materials and issues the women themselves claimed as their own and as salient. I was clear about two things throughout my research time: (1) I was interested in what women said and deemed important about their religion and singing, sometimes to the explicit exclusion of male discourse; (2) I wanted to examine Jain singing, which Jain women in the United States told me was central to women's practice, and which had not been included in any scholarship—not even in a cursory way in any study of Indian religion, devotionalism, Gujarātī literature, Jain studies, Women's Studies, or social sciences—despite its ubiquity.

I approach my research as a "student" of Jain laywomen rather than an "expert" on Jain laywomen. This reversal of authority derives from the reflexive anthropology movement (Behar and Gordon 1995; Clifford and Marcus 1986) but differs from it in that I believe that the reflexive moment should not be located in the act of writing, but much earlier—in the very basic questions of who has the authority to be "knowers" and therefore has the position of determining what knowledge is during field research.[46] It is not that I, as a scholar interested in their knowledges, necessarily "empower" the women but that I accept their own statements of power and authority. The problems of feminist ethnography are the subject of substantial debate over the whether such a project is possible (Abu-Lughod 1990a; Visweswaran 1994; Wolf 1996) and about the intersection of these issues with class, race, and nationality (Patai 1991) and discussions about the risks of self-aggrandizing on the part of the author or, more disturbingly, the risk of the (accidental?) exploitation of the author's now admittedly personal relationships with women they "studied" in the context of "friendships" (Stacey 1991). Occasionally, women scholars speak of themselves as having a self-proclaimed ungendered Western female identity in their research communities. The intersection of class and its attending issues of being associated with ex-colonial powers presents an interesting challenge for women scholars, but when identity is seen as "ungendered," it appears to be more a question of which of one's identities is taking the primary place (Babiracki 1997).

My study does not claim to present a definitive answer to these challenges; rather, I have tried in my own research and writing to avoid the objectification of these women by not foreclosing the possibility of my learning from their expertise, while also acknowledging that women who did or did not talk with me chose one or the other in particular contexts—often for my project and sometimes in confidence—which determined the places these conversations have (or don't have) in my publications. I also understood that all the women would and should determine the extent to which they participated based on informed decisions. I made it quite clear that I was writing a book I hoped to publish in the United States, Europe, and possibly India. After much discussion during the initial research period and subsequent research trips, the only limitation these women have placed on this book, in fact, was to require that I not include a clear picture of a Jina image; one cannot be sure that all possible readers know better than to commit some act of disrespect, like eating meat while leafing through the book. Some women did, in one way or another, refuse a prominent place in the book either by not seeking to invite my presence or, perhaps, by downright avoiding me.[47]

I have also used the past tense in this book rather than the "ethnographic present" because of my discomfort with the implication of timelessness that the ethnographic present carries and because the lives of these women have even in this relatively short time changed—some women and some women's husbands have died, some have moved, sons have married, daughters moved away to their husbands' house, new families have moved to Shivajinagar—and with these changes the very personal expressions of faith have, no doubt, changed. It is in this that I attempt—we leave the reader to judge its success—to acknowledge and honor what Visweswaran calls the "tools" of feminist ethnography: "shifting identities, temporality, and silence" (Visweswaran 1994). I shelved many of my own questions because of the abundance of questions presented by the women, and because of my commitment to the belief that these women were best qualified to identify the central issues of their own practices.

The structure of the book itself draws much of its inspiration from the reflexive anthropology movement. My privileging of the laywomen's ideas in my book derives from feminist scholars' attempts—often in the genre of life histories—to listen while these women being "studied" articulate their agency themselves (Abu-Lughod 1986, 1993; Behar 1993; Kendall 1988; Narayan 1997). I know that, of course, these women articulate their agency whether or not I listen (Spivak 1988), but actively listening is central to the success of this kind of research. The epistemological question of who is capable of knowing arises out of a political one (Code 1991) which not only informed the basic way I conducted my field research but also the way I have written this book. Extending Heidegger's "forestructure" from the field researcher to the writer demands that the writer acknowledge those ways in which we order what we see and how we write about it; in a sense, the ways that we order our writing—even when seeming to let it order itself—comes from our sense of how things must be. It is this sense of order that we must struggle to dismantle. This kind of Heideggerian thinking presents a critique of the idea of objectivity and therefore the history of writing about "others" (Said 1978).[48] The very form of representation used for academic writing has altered under the pressures from the reflexive anthropology movement's growing challenges to obscuring of authorial power.

This book has no final statement of how these chapters should ultimately be understood and will no doubt seem to the academic reader somewhat jarring in its finish. Instead of providing a conclusion at the end—an intrusion of authorial power into a discourse that seemed adequately to provide its own forcefully stated argument—I address at the close of this introductory chapter some important resonances to listen for which bind this book together and provide fruitful possibilities for thinking with and about the questions these laywomen presented. My intention is that the reader will be prepared—having accumulated enough information about the women's expressive modes through the following chapters—to understand the theological and social challenges expressed by the conflicts and debates in the final two chapters and the "past-lives" of stavan singing, formal pūjās, stavan repertoires, and the ways the women used these practices to articulate their theology. I end instead the way many Jain congregational events during my research time ended: with a stavan that was in many ways the most popular of them all.

The ubiquitous academic abstraction, summation and concluding arguments lend an omniscience to the author which ultimately reproduces the colonial writers' penchant for order and control and the perceived superiority in knowledge of the subject—often "male"—who writes of the female (often "Third World") object (Mohanty 1984; Ong 1988; Said 1978). In addition, it creates a false sense of completion or closure (Mariniello 1998), especially in light of the continued lives of these women. The privileging of theoretical discussions is a form of objectification of friends and colleagues; one cannot transform people into data without essentializing and fixing those people into classifications. To preserve the subjectivities of the women with whom I lived for a year, I have simply continued to treat them as the friends, and in some ways colleagues, they have become. As the women did not speak, read, or write in English (though a few can read it), I know most of them will never really read my books. That does not, however, give me license to subordinate their own ideas of self and belief to some discussion with academic currency of which they are not a part.

Although I made recordings and took notes, I always asked the women, "May I put this in the book?" and I asked whether they wanted to choose pseudonyms for the book rather than using their own names. After explaining that I would have no control over (and no idea of) who might one day read this book, they still wanted their names used. When Jains sponsor events, complete fasts, give donations, or sponsor text publications, they attach their names to these offerings; in my book, the women attach their names, likewise, to their offerings. The writing of a book is a contract between us: I must use their names and I must not include that which they specifically asked to be excluded. The women chose their words carefully and I too choose mine. It is my obligation to earn their trust of me as a person while writing for the academic audience. There is no real conflict; if I write in a way that breaches our mutual trust, I will have learned nothing from them.

Resonances

Within the chapters to come are a few themes I think are significant for those who study religion in South Asia, women and religion, performance theory, and the role of text in theologizing. Basically, the book asks, "What will we hear if we listen to women in the Jain tradition?" The epistomological shift from Sanskrit and Prakrit textual traditions, mendicants, and men toward vernacular textual traditions, laity, women, and the institutions that matter to these women (primarily maṇḍaḷs) challenges much of how and what we think we know about Jains. This representation of these women says much about performance theory and theology making; the use of the stavan texts tells us much about the way that stavan are understood and the way the context is understood. Moreover, these women's stavan performances reformulate a theological statement about the nature of the Jinas, the relationship between intention and action, what it means to be a Jain, and how individual Jains site themselves within their tradition. For scholars of devotional literature and devotional movements, it serves as an analysis of a previously unexamined genre of devotional literature suggesting—because of those features that make Jainism unique—new ways of understanding devotionalism in general. It explores the way grace works in a tradition in which grace is impossible and articulates a rationale for devotion for its own sake. In the Jain context, these women are understood to be the very ones qualified to make these judgments and are the primary performers and storehouses of stavan, other theological genres, and ritual expertise; for scholars of women and religion, I suggest reading this book as a way of seeing how a community of women can and does see itself as a community of experts with the authority to make substantial judgments about religious thinking and identity, and how we might be able to listen to those claims.

My intention in the ordering of these chapters goes as follows: I want the reader to begin with the kind of general contextualizing information that answers the preliminary questions that journalists are always enjoined to answer: who, what, where, when and why. The next chapter is concerned primarily with the way that women are created and self-created as icons of Jain religiosity. Many of the debates and issues within Jain religiosity are argued and acted out upon the images of women. We must see the ways in which women participate in that icon making and some of the ways in which they understand that very process. It also looks at the two most public presentations of Jain women as icons of Jain piety: fasting and the ordination of female mendicants. Men can and do participate in both of these presentational complexes as icons (Laidlaw 1995) and when men participate there is considerable prestige attached, because both of these pious acts are seen as beyond the usual expectations of men. That the bulk of these presentations are of women points to the ways in which women serve as the primary icon for Jainism. Public presentations of women are also performed by and for women in the Jain community, which challenge the equation of all women's spaces with privacy. Presentations of women's piety for women are inarguably public; I have attended programs with anywhere from ten to more than one thousand women attendees. The key distinction between this kind of public and the other is the presence of male onlookers (such as in the ordinations and fast-breaking ceremonies) unrelated—and unacquainted to—the women in question.

The third and fourth chapters first introduce readers to stavan: What are stavan? Where can I find them? What do they say? And what do they sound like? And then help them to see how stavan are understood to fit under the rubric of religious knowledge and are accorded the same kinds of veneration as the canonical texts, though to a lesser degree. The texts are examined for the ways in which the stavan use poetics and performative aesthetics to contribute to Jain religious experiences by creating a proper tone and sonic counterpoint to the enactment of Jain theology. For, once we see the context of Jain stavan in knowledge making and veneration, we see how the expertise of the women who control this genre is a locus for theologizing.

So what happens when we look at the times and places where these stavan are sung? In chapters 5 and 6 we look at the places where stavan are sung both as a devotional genre and as specific stavan chosen for specific performative contexts. In both chapters the stavan's contents are examined in light of their performative context. The particulars of the choices tell us something of the choosers' theologies. The presence of stavan is fixed, but the choices are utterly fluid, suggesting that this is a particularly fruitful place to look at individual theologizing. First, we need to understand something about the ways Jains understand pūjā and the relationship between the three locations of ritual theologizing: the constitutive rules, the regulative rules, and improvisation. All three loci for making theological decisions in pūjā performance are clearly present in the ways that daily worship is performed. This examination of daily worship sets the stavan in a context where the reader can understand that the stavan's use is both an ubiquitous part of Jain worship and must fit within the regulative rules of Jain worship. In the latter chapter formal pūjā performances and the ways that the pūjās themselves were understood in a ritual context are complemented by the stavan that were chosen to accompany each pūjā. These choices were clearly negotiated at maṇḍaḷ practices and even sometimes in performance and thus can be read as a provisional statement of the maṇḍaḷ's theology. In the former chapter we see the ways in which stavan which articulate a theology of grace become central for women; each woman's individual devotional sentiments directly affected which stavan she chose, because the meanings spoke of religious hopes not voiced in other genres.

Women privileged their own praxis when they made their own theologies. Because women had fewer opportunities to win at the game of prestige they were far more interested in developing the kinds of expertise that could lead to an authority which could compete—at least within the ritual culture of Jainism—with prestige practices. This was a powerful model for women who rarely have authority in the world of prestige. Likewise, many of the women in the maṇḍaḷ came from families in which financial realities prevented them from becoming the kinds of donors who gain that kind of prestige. But more than a desire for authority, there was a strong sense that while prestige practices were acceptable (and financially important), financial offerings to the religion cannot replace daily practice and its accompanying merit or, better still, decrease in karma. This challenge echoes through my discussions in chapters 7 and 8.

The final chapter describes a particular pūjā performance and the ways that the issues of theology, orthopraxy, authority and stavan singing are navigated and negotiated by women in the Pārśva Maṇḍaḷ. The conflict over the efficacy of a particular Vāstuk Pūjā asks theological questions about the primacy of right thought (*bhāv*) and right knowledge (*jñān*) over right action (here, especially *dān*—religious gifting). It was at this performance that the Pārśva Maṇḍaḷ expressed through their choices of songs and other less subtle cues that the sponsors of the pūjā were not only impious but perhaps not even Jain. The women reconstructed this theological argument from a belief that they had both the authority to make a theological critique and a valid understanding of Jainism that derived from their own experiences. The women who are actively involved in devotional activities and daily worship in the temple privilege their own practice but do so by using shared (by women) normative models for Jain praxis.

I want readers to come away from this book with a greater understanding of the possibilities for understanding women's religiosity, for understanding Jains, and for trying new ways of doing religious studies research. If one allows oneself to listen to theologies that come in forms that may not carry the stamp of authority for which we so often look, one might hear, in fact, what may be more central to the ways people (especially laity) theologize within their own traditions. That these women have complex theological understandings of the tradition that they negotiate every day should not be a surprise. If one thinks that these women, because they are not versed in the subtleties of the orthodox textual tradition, are not theologically sophisticated, then some of the most nuanced and most relevant theologies to every day life will be overlooked. This book asks readers to listen attentively to the everyday statements of belief expressed in stavan and other areas where women speak and sing religiously.

*2

Hero Mahāvīr, Triśalā's son! Hero Mahāvīr, Siddharāth's prince!
On the thirteenth day of the month, Caitrī, the hero, Lord Mahāvīr was born!

In Kuṇḍa, every house was full of bliss because of the prince's birth.
Indra and Indrāṇī massaged him. On Mount Meru, everyone bathed him.

Gods and goddesses bow. Kings and people sing of his good qualities.
Mahāvīr is always seen with his brother, Nandivardhan; and there too is Mahāvīr's wife, Yaśodharā.

In the fullness of youth, this Jina became an ascetic and walked the path of restraint.
Every year remember this king and do fierce penance.

Candanbālā was a princess who did the three-day fast.
Bring lentils in the winnowing fan! That alms-giver, Mahāvīr, and that trader's wife all three attained liberation.

Transcription and translation of recording of performance during an interview in Pune, Maharashtra, on 25 October 1993. Courtesy of Ranjana Satish Shah.

Idealized Women

This popular stavan, "Hero Mahāvīr!," was written to a catchy Hindi film melody ("Ek do tin") for Paryuṣaṇ in 1993.[1] It was so well liked that the maṇḍaḷ immediately worked it into the repertoire. Because it tells of Mahāvīr's birth—an event reenacted in the Snātra Pūjā—it was often sung during pūjā performances. However, the combination of its telling of Mahāvīr's later life and the focus on fasting in its text suggest its origins as a fasting song (tapasya gīt) from Paryuṣaṇ, an eight-day festival culminating with the annual confession and expiation of sins and fast (pratikramaṇ) on Saṃvatsarī Day. Paryuṣaṇ is the zenith of the Jain religious calendar; the festival includes the annual rite of confession and expiation, the recitation of the Kalpa Sūtra, the celebration of the birth of Mahāvīr, and the height of religious observance, especially regarding food and fasting.[2] Likewise, Saṃvatsarī Day was the most common day for the completion of fasts. The completions of fasts are accompanied by fast-breaking programs where many stavan such as the one above are sung to celebrate the fast and to restate the orthodox focus on austerities highlighted during this festival. This stavan includes several paradigms of Jain women: Triśalā, the mother of Mahāvīr (a Jina Mother); Indrāṇī, the paradigmatic worshipper; Yaśodharā, Mahāvīr's wife before he renounced his worldly life; and Candanbālā, one of the *Satīs*[3] (the sixteen virtuous women whose edifying stories are often retold) known especially for her fasting. Here Triśalā and Indrāṇī have brief roles mentioned in the stavan: Triśalā as Mahāvīr's mother, and Indrāṇī's presence and participation in Mahāvīr's first bath. Yaśodharā is hardly mentioned, as reflected by her cursory status in the canonical literature as well.[4] The final verse tells an abbreviated version of the story of Candanbālā, the Satī, who was responsible for Mahāvīr's breaking his long fast.[5]

Candanbālā was a beautiful princess who was jailed and then released into a merchant's family as a maidservant. The merchant's wife was jealous of her beauty, and when the merchant went away on business, she shaved off Candanbālā's hair (hair being a common symbol in India of a woman's sexuality) and bound her in chains. The merchant's wife left her for three days without food when the merchant returned. He was horrified and released her. There were only black lentils (*uḍad ḍal*) in the kitchen, which he offered her, but she wouldn't eat until she had offered alms to a male mendicant. Candanbālā sat at the house's threshold reciting the Navkār Mantra and sorting lentils. Then Mahāvīr passed by the house, having been fasting for five months and twenty-five days. No one had met his conditions for fast breaking: that an unmarried girl from a royal house who now was a servant, having had her head shaved and fasting for three days, would be sitting in a threshold sorting lentils, saying the Navkār Mantra, and weeping. Candanbālā fulfilled all these conditions but was not weeping. When he passed by and wouldn't accept her alms she began to cry. Mahāvīr came back and took alms from her (see figure 2-1). Candanbālā's hair immediately grew back and she forgave the merchant's wife who had by her cruelty allowed Candanbālā to give the fast-breaking alms to Mahāvīr. Later Candanbālā became a female mendicant ordained by Mahāvīr, and she attained mokṣa.

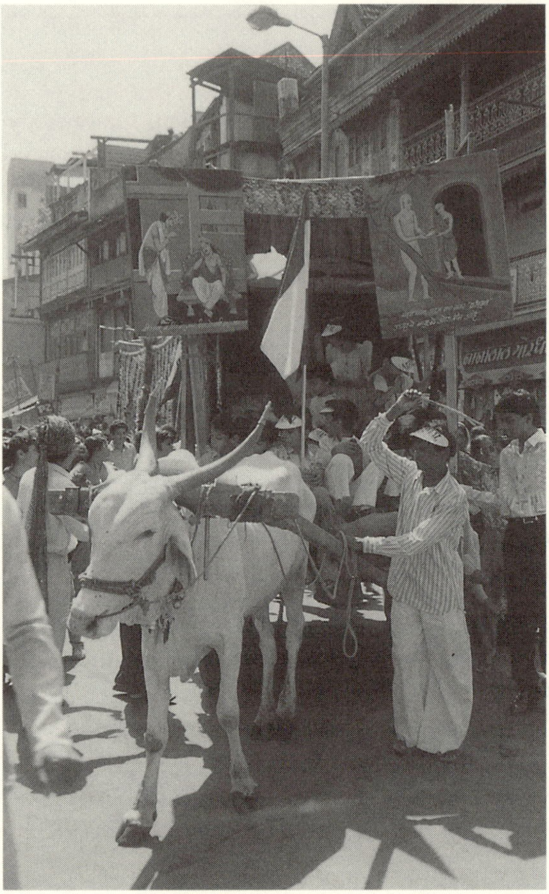

FIGURE 2-1. Poster on the right depicts Candanbālā narrative. The Mahāvīr Jayantiī parade in Guruvār Peṭh, Pune, April 1994.

The stavan's abbreviated version of this narrative reminds the hearer of the full details of the narrative in a succinct form. It suggests that torments may offer an opportunity for great merit. In fact, the stavan, through its call for practicing extreme fasting, suggests self-imposed austerities modeled on Candanbālā's self-imposed fast (or at least self-imposed after the merchant's return). The stavan shows one way that normative stories and ideas are worked into vernacular devotion texts. Stavan and the vernacular literature give Jain women a variety of models on which to pattern their piety. Women use and modify these normative narratives, recreating them in ways which both resonate with ideas and descriptions which make "sense" to the women and which further the prestige of the models of behavior that favor women's participation. The images of ideal Jain women are reflected in Jain women's actual practice and in the rhetoric which represents Jain women.

The study of the rhetoric about Jain women began only as seen through the eyes of those male mendicants whose writings were deemed worthy of study. Women are vilified in those texts that serve to instruct the male mendicants—perhaps most strikingly in the Sūtrakṛtanga—or those that are based on these texts. Even those texts which serve as didactic models for male behavior from the *Yogaśāstra*—purportedly written for layman-king Kumārapāl by the great Jain scholar-monk, Hemacandra—to contemporary tracts which use pictures of women to illustrate their lists of the sixteen faults primarily associate women with sin or as a locus for these sinful acts. The image derived from these texts implies both a contempt for women and a sense of the male-centeredness of Jainism which is not entirely reflected by the contemporary lay community or for that matter the normative traditions of texts written by male mendicants for other purposes. Although in his *Yogaśāstra*, Hemacandra includes in his argument for celibacy that it is "better to embrace a burning iron pillar than to approach the thighs of a woman which are the door to hell" (*Yogaśāstra*, II, 82 trans. by Gopani 1989),[6] Hemacandra also collected many of the virtuous woman narratives that set the backdrop for this chapter in his *Triṣaṣṭī-śalāka-puruṣa-cāritra* (Deeds of the Sixty-three Illustrious Men). Although I would not say that the Jain laywomen are given the same degree of authority or power as Jain men or that the female mendicants are as prestigious as the male mendicants, the degree of subordination is far less in reality than these texts suggest. Likewise, much of the vernacular literature describes the right actions for women through the illustration of the lives of pious women. Within the sum total of texts I encountered in people's homes (more than a hundred), there were a plethora of images of women and most of them were considered virtuous.

Scholars of Jains have often, like many scholars of Indian culture, relied on those texts which are in the light, displayed proudly by Jains themselves, translated by European scholars and deemed representatives of a "pan-Indian" Sanskritic tradition. Balbir argues what may be a regrettable truth, that all the texts we, as Jain scholars, read are written by and for men except only a few recent accounts in which female mendicants have spoken of their lives and beliefs (Balbir 1994). This exemplifies a problem for the study of women who are not permitted out of the "dark rooms" of understudied vernacular and oral literature into the "well-lit" place under the streetlight of male-dominated Sanskrit literature (Ramanujan 1990). Lay (and increasingly mendicant) Jains' access to these texts is limited by their lack of training in classical languages (Sanskrit and Prakrit) which prevents them from reading or writing these texts. Women are doubly restricted by the prohibitions—especially in the Tapā Gacch (the dominant lineage of the mendicants with whom Pune Jains associated themselves)—against any women even reading these texts.[7]

However, there are a variety of ways to work with the problem of texts for the study of Jain women. First, find out what texts are written by women and read them. Second, look at the way women use and understand the texts written by men. Third, look carefully at which rhetoric the women accept and, perhaps more important, which they ignore or outright reject. And, last, look at the ways women re-create their own traditions by analyzing the relationships between their self-representation, praxis, and texts. Let us not simply measure women's representations against an assumption that the male mendicants' voices are the exclusive normative voices in Jainism. This view not only disregards what is repeatedly referred to as the majority of practicing Jains, Jain women, but likewise limits the scholars' ability to see how Jainism evolves and eliminates many of the valid and fruitful ways of studying Jain men as well. This is not to suggest that these mendicants' texts have no effect on Jainism but, rather, that their effect is indirect, filtered, and selective. Rather than lamenting that Jains, particularly male mendicants, do not study the Sanskrit and Prakrit texts the way scholars would like them to, let us look at those texts that directly influence contemporary Jains. For a remedy, I submit the bulk of my book as an attempt to see a more complex account of Jain laywomen, which refocuses the questions of where Jainism as a normative textual tradition and Jainism as a religion of people who have practices and beliefs which sometimes derive from and sometimes create these texts, can be found.

Jain laywomen, like women in Hindu traditions, derive much of their theological knowledge from vernacular (often oral) sources rather than from the Sanskrit tradition.[8] Ramanujan (1991) shows that there are two kinds of women's tales: those that tell stories about women and those told by women. Both of these contribute to how folk narratives give a "voice" to women's experiences and theories about their experiences. This chapter seeks to see how these vernacular texts give not only a voice but present role models for women to consider. When one looks at vernacular normative and devotional literature, Jainism suddenly comes alive. Literally filled with narratives of holy people, stories of where others have gone astray, and suggestions for the best way to live one's Jain life, these materials are a fruitful source for the study of contemporary Jainism.[9] Perhaps most important for this study, these materials open a door into the rhetoric of what it means to be a Jain woman.

From the representations of the Kalpa Sūtra through Western scholarship to brand-new stavan, Jain "women" are recreated in an image. For the most part, women are described in ways that support the male writers' views of women and the arguments they wish to forward. For example, Jaini (1991) illustrates the ways that mendicants' debates over the relative merits and appropriateness of the various schools of Jain mendicants are couched in terms of women's salvation; these debates about women's access to mendicancy and hence access to salvation center around the acceptability and necessity (for women) of wearing clothing but function primarily as a thinly veiled discussion of male mendicancy. These debates are easily seen as one in which women are used as the battlefield for the argument over whether the male mendicants should or should not wear clothing, which in turn is a debate over whether the Digambar male mendicants or the Śvetāmbar male mendicants are correct in their practice. Whereas the Śvetāmbar stance may well be a cause of the increase in female mendicancy for Śvetāmbars and a decrease for Digambars or a source of Śvetāmbar laywomen's and female mendicants' sense of religious self-esteem, it is not primarily an issue of women's religious salvation (Jaini 1991). It is interesting to note that in spite of the fact that neither men nor women really look to the Jinas directly as religious role models,[10] the frame of these debates directed many scholars to assume that women did. This use of women as counters in an argument is not present only in the mendicants' debates; women are also "constructed" by male (and sometimes female) voices within normative texts as examples to be evaluated or as a method of evaluating the correctness or efficacy of Jain belief and practice. The representations of Jain women's behavior and possibilities become a fruitful place for understanding the project of representing Jainism but not necessarily a fruitful place for understanding women themselves.

The debate over women's mokṣa (spiritual liberation) was not part of either the common rhetoric or the popular religious texts I was continually being given to read.

For a long time, I would question virtually every woman I met with regard to this debate: What do you think about Mallināth (the nineteenth Jina, who Śvetāmbars believe to be female)? I was interested in this question because of the unique situation of Śvetāmbar Jain women who are theoretically spiritually equal. Just before going to India, I interviewed a Jain woman from Bombay, Niruben, who was visiting relatives in the United States. Niruben stopped our discussion about laywomen's practices to say, "You know that one Jina was a woman, Mallināth; Jain women can achieve mokṣa." I was not surprised to hear her invoke Mallināth in her justification for Jain women's importance; I had expected this debate over women's mokṣa—guided as I was by the feminist literature about female imagery and earlier scholarly literature which suggested the centrality of the Jinas as role models—to be very important for Jain women. In reality, Niruben was unique. Never again did a woman seem motivated by Mallināth's example. I asked most women about Mallināth and they would say "Mallināth is the nineteenth Jina," and if I pressed the issue they would say that Mallināth was born a woman because in a previous incarnation the Jina-elect had performed a secret extra fast—a deception, albeit a devout one—which caused a female birth. But the deception was not one that could prevent the next birth from being one as a Jina; thus Mallināth the Jina had been born as a woman, reconstructing, of course, the female birth as punishment for sin. In addition, Mallināth also attained omniscience (*kaivalya*) before she reached puberty and thus never really became a woman. One day when I asked Ranjana why Mallināth's image looked like a man, Ranjana, almost dismissively said, "A Jina is not really a man or a woman, a Jina is beyond the specifics of its [the word here is declined to match the word 'birth,' not 'Jina' in Gujarātī] birth." If Mallināth was not the source of the laywomen's self-perception within the religion, I knew the search for the other "role models" would have to continue.

Many scholars of women's religiosity looked to the presence of goddesses and goddess imagery to redress imbalances of male authority.[11] Although the Jain goddesses may be a source of Jain women's sense of power—through the pan-Indic understanding of power (*śaktī*) as feminine, especially within reproduction and running a household—the goddesses were not named in the conversations I had with the many Jain women with whom I worked, except as intercessionary forces. I never saw any real identification between the laywomen and these goddesses as role models; these goddesses remain in the place of indirect influence. Instead, Jain laywomen commonly named two female role model types derived from the normative literature, with respect to their own religiosity: the Jinas' mothers (*Jinamātā*s) and the virtuous women (*Mahāsatī*s). These Jain women are responsible in a characteristically Jain self-help way for their own well-being and success, which result from their devotion and austerities.

The Jina Mothers are Jain laywomen—queens, but human. The role these women play in the literal reproduction of Jainism is central and indispensable. Hymn after hymn sings the religious success stories of these women. Śvetāmbar women proudly told me that the first person ever to achieve mokṣa was Marudevī, the mother of Ādināth.[12] The idea that a laywoman could attain mokṣa is powerful and is repeated again and again. The stories of the Jina Mothers' pregnancies (with the Jinas) are the focus of much of the devotional literature about the Jinas, and are told with realistic detail. The Jina Mother and her baby are an image virtually all adult Jain laywomen can relate to and sympathize with and identify with. The narratives of Jina's births make pregnancy—at least pregnancy with a Jina—a holy state. Though the Jina will someday become a mendicant and leave the home, the devotional narratives center around the celebration of the conception, pregnancy, birth, and upbringing of an extraordinary son. These mythic laywomen are responsible for running a Jain house and raising the ultimate Jains, thereby guaranteeing the continuity of their own religion.

Most women were familiar with the rich and extensive virtuous women and renunciation narrative traditions in which the Jain layperson—virtually always female—renounces the world (Granoff 1998; Reynell 1985a; Shanta 1985). As opposed to Hindu traditions, where female renunciation is neither socially acceptable nor necessarily a viable option (McDaniel 1989; Ojha 1981), Jain women can and do make a basic decision regarding their life goals: whether to be a female mendicant or to be a housewife.[13] The fact of choosing—even if there is pressure to do one or the other—may well contribute to the fundamental well-being of the many Jain women I knew; I suspect that this choice, especially in a culture where women's choices are often curtailed, gives a sense of real agency. Most Jain women choose not to be female mendicants; they choose to follow the path of their mothers and get married and have children. The reasons for becoming a female mendicant are usually a combination of a variety of socioeconomic conditions, the personal ambitions of the woman, and her attitudes toward and prospects of marriage (Holmstrom 1988; Reynell 1985b; Shanta 1985). The virtuous women narratives illustrate the ways in which renunciation narratives both exemplify an alternative to being a housewife and give the women a way of situating their personal renunciations (usually fasting) in a narrative structure (Kelting, forthcoming).

Fasting: A Locus of Ideals

A Jain fast is a public event monitored and supported by the community, starting with the family's approval. A fast cannot be done secretly; it must be undertaken with the consent of a mendicant symbolized by the formal statement of intention (*paccakkhāṇ*).[14] Though I found fasting to be an important part of women's religious autobiography, it did not play a leading role in their daily lives. Only during the Āyambil Oḷī, the period leading up to Paryuṣaṇ, and during a young woman's marriage negotiations did women talk to me about fasting—unless they were showing me their photo albums, which often had some pictures from a fast-breaking ceremony. Reynell's research in Jaipur suggests that fasting and fasting groups are central to women's practice and that they fulfill many of the same social roles as I found maṇḍaḷs to fulfill (Reynell 1985a). This is not to suggest that fasting is not important as a reaffirmation of Jain values and a locus for prestige but to counteract the heightened focusing on women's fasting in scholarly works on Jainism. This focus on women as fasters and on men as donors creates a false dichotomy between men's and women's practices as men did fast—even beyond the nearly definitive Jain fast at the Saṃvatsarī which virtually all Jains do—and women did donate.[15] While these practices were publicly displayed (for mixed-sex groups of Jains and for non-Jains) as male (donation) and female (fasting), this dichotomy may be most significant in its reflection of the gendered expression of public Jainism. That being said, a look at the rhetoric about fasting illustrates the way women serve as a public symbol of Jain values.

During my research, women used three words to generally name fasting: *vrat*[16] (for Hindu fasts) and tap or *upvās* (for Jain fasts). Tap was used as a more generalized term referring to all austerities but most commonly to complex series of fasting. Upvās referred specifically to fasts during which one takes no food or water (*caũvihār upvās*) or one takes only boiled water (*tivihār upvās*). These fasts are sometimes linked to a chain of fasts (which the women and the fasting manuals called tap): two and a half days (*aṭṭham*), eight days (*aṭhṭhaī*), and one month (*māskhamaṇ*) being the more commonly spoken of upvās among the women I knew. Many Jain fasts are actually restricted eating (rather than no eating), which are called *beāsan* (two sittings a day), *ekāsan* (one sitting a day), *nokārsī* (not eating from sunset until forty-eight minutes after sunrise), and *āyambil* (eating bland food). These restrictions were usually organized into series of fasts sometimes alternating with upvās (which were also called tap) which were each said to have areas of particular efficacy. The way Jain laywomen in Pune categorized these fasts differs slightly (mostly in lumping all the restricted eating fasting together) from other accounts of fasting categories (Cort 1989; Laidlaw 1995; Reynell 1985a).[17] I also found that for the most part women did not speak of the particular kind of fast (except for āyambil) but rather named the fast series (tap) they were performing. This is reflected in Reynell's use of tap names to refer to fasts women performed (Reynell 1985a, 1991). Of these, there were Jain fasts, which women said they performed for familial well-being (*saubhāgya*), and others, which women spoke of in terms more closely tied to Jain mokṣa marg (the path directed toward the attainment of liberation as opposed to puṇya marg—the path of well-being) ideologies of karma destruction (*karma haryu*); however, all the Jain fasts—perhaps because of the statement of intention (paccakkhāṇ)—were seen as a locus of karma reduction.

Unmarried women may perform Hindu (as well as Jain) fasts for a good future husband. When we were in Karad in May 1994, the unmarried (now married and living in Pune) daughter of the middle-class Gujarātī family with whom we stayed was fasting every Tuesday for a speedy and good marriage. Varsha was 25 years old—older than most of the unmarried girls in the neighborhood—and was the last of her girlfriends to be married. Her fast consisted of taking only two meals on Tuesday, both of which seemed to consist entirely of tapioca—a common fast food in Maharashtra (McGee 1987). This was a common fast among Hindu women and it did not have any overlay of a Jain narrative or morals. There was no recitation of the paccakkhāṇ—the intention to perform a fast—nor was it a prescribed fast, nor did it include any Jain prayers or the confession and expiation (pratikramaṇ). Likewise, when I asked the story of the fast, the women in her family just said "it helps her get married well." This fast might be accompanied by a Hindu narrative in the Hindu context, but the narrative was not translated into this Jain context as the particular food restrictions of the fast and its particular locus of efficacy were.[18]

There are also several Jain fasts that a woman might do to fortify her position as a married woman and to protect her (male) children. This is a distinctly worldly matter—often in contradistinction to the orthodox narratives that accompany the fast. I found that women spoke of the Āyambil Oḷī as a married woman's fast though there were men who performed it—often at the urging of their wives who are following the example of the fasting narrative. This fast is also linked to a virtuous woman narrative—that of Mayṇāsundarī whose fast and related pūjā are directly responsible for the well-being and recovery of her leper husband, King Śrīpal, who himself went on to become famously devout and wealthy by following his wife's example. According to Cort, one woman listed the Aṭhṭham (no food and sometimes no water for three days), the Āyambil Oḷī (eating bland foods at one sitting daily, usually for nine days), the month-long fast of Māskhamaṇ (only water for thirty-one days), and the Rohini fasts as those performed for familial well-being (Cort 1989).

The Aṭhṭham Tap is also a famous fast performed at Śankheśvar in imitation of its performance first by Kṛṣṇa in order to free his arm from a curse (Cort 1988). In the beginning of this chapter, I tell the story of Candanbālā and the clearly orthodox bent to the narrative of her three-day fast (also the Aṭhṭham Tap). Now many Jain women perform this fast for familial well-being, rather than for expiation. The Candanbālā Tap is a version of the Aṭhṭham Tap in which the faster performs several rituals in direct imitation of Candanbālā's three-day fast where she gains both a worldly reward symbolized by her hair growing back (a return to householder's life and sexuality) and spiritual result (the acceptance of her faith by the town) and her ultimate attainment of mokṣa. The most striking and public feature of the Candanbālā Tap is the performance of the fast-breaking: the faster is dressed in white clothes and her hands and feet are bound, while she makes an offering to a Jain mendicant before accepting food herself. In Pune during the 2000 rainy season, a group of young marriageable women performed the Candanbālā Tap, which suggests a link here between the fast for the well-being of married women and both the public statement of a young woman's marriageability and the private concerns during a time when a young woman's marital future is being planned. Dadiji had performed the Navpad Oḷī fast (where one does the nine-day Āyambil Oḷī fast every six months nine times and a second fast of 108 days of alternate-day fasting) as her husband was becoming increasingly unhealthy, suggesting that this fasting was expected to help his health (and also providing a way for her to articulate her concerns about his health through her austerities). Often women explained their reason for fasting to me as increasing their sense of peace (*śānt*), which, although not explicitly an agenda of familial well-being, reflects those concerns that more often than not were at the heart of women's explanations of why they felt their lives were not peaceful.

Not only does fasting gain a woman merit, protect her family from harm or illness, help her get a good husband, assist her family in financial success, gain prestige for her family, or prove her (and her daughter's) honor but it is also an important way for a woman to attain some of the perfection usually reserved for female mendicants or for the virtuous women in mythology. A Jain woman can, through her austerities, become a powerful force in the sustaining of her family and its prosperity. In addition, it is a way for women to be sociable in an utterly acceptable forum. Likewise, fasting puts a woman at the center of attention and may—in a more strenuous fast than the Akṣaynidhi or Oḷī fasts—give her leave from her normal daily work. The monthlong fast—a strenuous thirty-one-day fast with no food, only water—is widely pointed to as the ultimate Jain fast. It customarily earns the woman performing the fast enormous merit and removes a huge amount of built-up karma, but it also was reported to Reynell to prove unquestionably the virtue and piety of any woman who completed it. Reynell describes how the performance of the monthlong fast is portrayed as proof of the continued sexual honor of the married woman performing the fast and thus is performed to protect the honor of her unmarried daughters (Reynell 1991). While virtually all the women with whom I have spoken had performed the eight-day fast with only water, only about one in four of the older woman had attempted the longer fasts such as the monthlong fast. Many older women would show me the photo albums of their monthlong fast, which were displayed as an extension of their wedding photos.[19] When the women pointed to this fast they were reaffirming the role this fast has in defining extreme piety versus simply being a good Jain laywoman. It is through this fast that a laywoman achieves a degree of karmic perfection (in the sense of the mokṣa mārg ideology) not usually attainable in her ordinary household life or through devotional activities.

With women's performances and understandings of fasting rituals and narratives, we see the personal reasons and interpretations of this kind of piety; this is contrasted with the public displays of generic Jain piety which mark the fast-breaking celebrations. The Akṣaynidhi fast[20] is a Jain fast with distinctly worldly expectations; it is associated with gaining or restoring wealth. Nita and Ranjana (co-sisters-in-law in a middle-class family), an upper-middle-class Mārvāḍī woman (middle-age) and her two unmarried daughters (both in their late teens), a newly married upper-class Mārvāḍī young woman (early 20s) and three upper-middle-class Gujarātī women (two in late middle age and one early middle age) had all decided to perform this fast together. In 1994, the group was performing the last of the four years' fasts. The fasting narrative is the story of a king who was banished from his kingdom and lost all his money. After performing the Akṣaynidhi Fast, he had gained so much merit that when there was a trial in which an elephant chose the next king, the elephant chose the ex-king. He was once again king and regained his wealth (Reynell 1985a). When I asked why the women were performing the fast, they answered with a vague reference to the ascetic values of Jainism and the merit to be gained. Perhaps whatever reason prompted the women to take on this fast four years ago is either somehow so embarrassing they cannot mention it—poverty is quite embarrassing for many Jains who often equate economic success with religiosity—or the reason is simply forgotten or less central now. Of the women who performed this fast, the one woman and her two daughters, who performed the fast together, were explicitly concerned with the arrangements of the elder daughter's upcoming wedding, with its challenge to find a suitable (read "prestigious enough") groom for their socioeconomic position whose dowry requests would not impinge on her second daughter's dowry. All the women, though, shared an understanding that it was a "good" fast. The good fasts were often described as those that achieved the stated intention of the faster—efficacious; however, the woman were often hesitant to share their intentions for fasting except in the most general terms: to gain peace (sometimes in the face of familial tensions, exams, worries about marriage), because it is good for oneself, because the fast is "good." It was clear that one should not perform fasts (especially Jain fasts) exclusively as bribes (either coercive fasting to get the attention of the gods or as fulfillment of contractual vow taking); the language of vernacular fasting narratives clearly states that the sentiment or intention of the woman performing the fast could adversely affect the outcome of the fast and thus women, at least publicly, resisted any language of intention beyond the very abstract.

During the fifteen days of the fast, each woman's family would sponsor a midday meal at their house after the special pūjā. On September 2, 1994, the women participating in the Akṣaynidhi fast came for lunch at Nita and Ranjana's house. Unlike the Oḷī fast, where the food must be special āyambil food, or fast-breaking ceremonies, where special party foods are served, here the women ate a spruced-up lunch. The women were there for about an hour or so and there was a lot of talking and socializing while they ate. The women spoke of many things going on in their families, debated the relative merits of the men's maṇḍaḷ that was playing that night in the temple, and discussed the details of the Pārśva Maṇḍaḷ's program coming in three days. Their talk was not focused, as it had been at the Oḷī fast, on the details of the fast and pūjā. Here it was a group of female friends.

Before the women left to go home, they each received a present from Nita and Ranjana of plastic food storage containers. At the end of this fast, as well as at the end of all organized fasts, gifts were given to each of the fasters by each of the other fasters. In this case, the fasters were also given a gift at the end of each of their lunch gatherings; Ranjana pointed out that these gifts were actually *prabhāvanā*—a gift to show appreciation for right conduct always given to all attendees at the end of a Jain ritual. The gifts were not given at the temple; they were given after lunch. Nor were the gifts given out when the group did not meet to lunch; thus it was the eating together which marked the end of the daily fasting pūjā. At the end of the pūjā, the fasters also sponsored a feeding of the entire congregation as directed by the fast's instructions in the fasting manual itself. In a sense, the commensality of eating together was central to the performance of this fast. There are varying degrees of the use of religious rhetoric and justifications for the different fasts, suggesting that these performances can be understood both in the context of orthodox understanding and in the ways in which the women use fasting as part of their sociocultural practices.

The larger and more strenuous Jain fasts (usually of the third category of fast: the predominantly orthodox) end with a public feeding of the fasters and are celebrated with large parties to accompany the fast-breaking. Fast-breakings involve several events, each "packaging" the Jain women as the personification of Jain religious values. The fasters are taken on a parade through the center of the city (near the central temple), their photographs are published in the local newspaper with an explanation of their achievement, and at the party itself the women are set into a space decorated like the couch of a queen. At the party the women perform all the singing and dancing, facing the faster in much the same way they would perform stavan and dance in the Jain temples in front of the Jinas. Fasting songs are sung during the parties and often accompanied by Gujarātī folk dancing. The female relatives began to practice fast-breaking songs for the event. One popular fasting song which Ranjana, Nita and Kavita sang for Hema's fast-breaking describes the excitement of going to the fast-breaking parties:[21]

The fast-breaking day draws near
Now a full year has passed.
Lord Ādi did this fast,
Śreyās made the fast-breaking day complete.
Padmarekhaśrī did the one-year fast,
Inside the city of bliss, everyone is excited
Oṃ Karśrījī gave the blessing
The guru compassionately made the fast complete.
Full of devotion and worshipful restraint,
The glory of that fast's crown keeps shining.
For twelve months, you have been fasting,
Today everyone keeps asking about the fast.
The Pārśva's women's maṇḍaḷ sang songs
Hereyu kept dancing from joy.

Though the fast-breaking party in this stavan celebrates the completion of the year-long fast (*varsītap*), the components are the same. These programs are an important part of the social season during the rainy season, when there are no weddings, and offer a time when the whole family gathers together.

Hema (a middle-aged, middle-class woman) began a month-long fast on 11 August 1994.[22] After a few days she became extremely weak.[23] Hema's son, a doctor, spoke with her after the seventh day, and they decided she should end her fast on the eleventh day. Invitations were immediately printed and sent out to invite people to the fast-breaking program. Although Hema ended her fast prematurely, her program resembled both those programs I have subsequently seen on videotape and the one I observed at the close of Paryuṣaṇ in 2000 which ended the planned eleven-day fast of Pushpaphoi (an older, middle-class woman). To give some idea of these programs I will transcribe directly from my fieldnotes the fast-breaking program in Śirur on 24 August 1994.[24]

> We had arrived in Śirur at 9 in the morning, too late to see the male mendicant bless Hema; he had come several hours earlier than expected. Once there we quickly changed into fancy saris and went in to feed Hema spoonsful of mung beans and sugarcane juice. Hema was seated with her two daughters behind a low table with a large design drawn around the table and her. Everyone wanted a picture taken of Hema being fed by him or her. She looked rather weak and as soon as we all had fed her, she went to her bed to lie down. Her bedroom was decorated with a number of saris I recognized to be Ranjana's fancy saris, and Dīvālī decorations.

The morning event was mostly for family and her closest friends. They would gain the most merit for feeding her. Women from Hema's maṇḍaḷ came by to see her and to wish her well. The young girls were asked to sing fasting songs (*tapasya gīt*) because it is widely believed that hearing these songs give women the strength to finish a fast. (Though Hema had eaten, the fast would not really be done until the afternoon program was over.) Later, at the afternoon program, the rest of her community (her friends, neighbors, and relatives) came and performed for her, and a certain number of women would come to the afternoon program to have darśan of her before returning home. The afternoon program was a display of Hema as an ideal Jain laywoman and a chance for others to gain merit through the appreciation of her fast. Fast-breaking parties have several features that resemble a formal pūjā as performed in front of a Jina in the temple. The description from my notes continues:

> Hema's son and nephews went to the hall to decorate the area where Hema would sit. Hema was dressed in a very heavy brocade sari and lots of gold jewelry and helped to walk the block and a half to the hall; she lay down as soon as she got to the cushions they had set up for her. The women of the family sat in front on Hema's right side. Then other women came and sat at the back of the room with a handful of men from her family in the far back. Hema's maṇḍaḷ sat directly in front of Hema. Ranjana started off the program with a stavan. Hema's maṇḍaḷ sang a few stavan while Sveta, Sangita, Soni and Aparna [Hema's two daughters and two nieces] danced Gujarātī folk dances (garbā and *dāṇḍiya-rās*). Hema's youngest niece sang a fasting song she had written herself. The niece's performance was so popular that she was asked to sing again later in the program. The local girl's maṇḍaḷ performed several folk dances and Hema's daughter Sveta danced the winnowing basket dance. Then the maṇḍaḷ finished up the program with a few more stavan. As people left they each gave Hema a present or some money and she would give them a small steel dish. Her maṇḍaḷ

FIGURE 2-2. Fast-breaking gathering. Hema (the garlanded faster) is seated in a "throne" while her maṇḍaḷ performs fasting songs, Śirur, August 1994. (Photo by Steven C. Runge)

FIGURE 2-3. Fast-breaking gathering. Hema (the garlanded faster) dancing dāṇḍiya-rās with her family. Śirur, August 1994.

> gave her a set of steel canisters. Then the boys put on cassettes of Gujarātī folk music (rās-garbā and *dhamal*) and the family danced a Gujarātī stick dance (dāṇḍiya). Hema got up and performed a minute's worth of this dance with Ranjana and then went to lie down again. When everyone got tired we cleaned up and returned to Hema's for a snack and returned to Pune.

In the afternoon program Hema was being worshipped as an ideal of Jainism. The women came and sang many stavan for her while the girls danced for her. They were lined up in front of her the same way they would line up in a temple with Hema in the place that the Jina usually is (compare figure 2-2 to figure 1-4). Surrounded by a canopy of saris and seated on cushions, her fancy clothes made her look like a queen. In the photo albums and in the videos, the fast-breaker's dancing is a common thread of the fast-breaking parties (see figure 2-3). I suspect it was to prove that she was so strong that even after her fast she was capable of dancing for joy like Hereyu, in the fast-breaking stavan described previously. The distinctly fast-centered parts of the day—the feeding of the faster, the dancing in front of her which mimics the dancing in front of the Jinas that are part of the formal pūjā performances, the fasting songs, and the exchange of gifts mark this celebration. The celebrations I saw in the photos and in one video were similar, but the fact of the fast being broken early and the ill health of Hema meant that the whole program was on a smaller scale. Many times the women who complete the strenuous monthlong fast are brought in a parade around the center of town. Lay Jains will come for darśan (auspicious viewing) of the women and to see the Jina images and the dancing. Loud marching bands gather the attention of all the people in the neighborhood. In many of the photo albums the women were shown on procession to local pilgrimage spots. The women are a symbol of Jainism expressed to the other people in Pune—Jain and non-Jain—by their processions. Surprisingly, for a community that prides itself on its women's chaste reputations, they publish their photos in the Mumbaī newspapers, parade their fasting wives and daughters through the streets of the old city, and invite everyone to watch. Perhaps these displays are encouraged by a combination of the celebration of what is "good" and the belief that a woman who has completed a great fast or—as we will see later in this chapter—who is going to become a female mendicant is so pure that she cannot be tainted by the eyes of the public.

When a Jain encounters those things worthy of approval, it is his or her duty to honor them through *anumodan* (the appreciation or celebration of the correct acts of others). This is most tangible in the public celebrations of women as a Jain ideal. When the women had completed a major fast, usually the eight-day Paryuṣaṇ fast or the longer thirty-one-day fast, the families often put an advertisement in the newspaper listing the fast among the women's good qualities. Reynell's work suggests that the women's participation in fasting is a symbol of their piety and therefore religious purity. She likewise suggests that the celebrations themselves serve as a location for ostentatious charity and donation, which show the "creditworthiness" of the Jain businessman (Reynell 1991). Though fasting is not easy, it is a religious break from work in the home—most fasters are given some leeway within the work schedule. From December 1999 through half of January 2000, Ranjana, Nita, and Soni performed an Updhān Tap at a temple complex in Katraj (just south of Pune) which involves living like a Jain mendicant for forty-five days; on top of the standard austerities of Jain mendicants, it includes additional food restrictions and fasting. This fast took them (three out of the five women in the household) away from home for a month and a half, but rather than seeing this as shirking their household duties, it was understood to be part of their job as women. Those performing the more difficult fasts are often completely released from work, and if possible a family may hire in a cook or cleaner for the time being. Likewise, at the end of a fast a woman receives a certain amount of gifts (often jewelry) and the fast-breaking party includes all of her relatives who come to see her. All these sociological elements certainly come to play in the decision to perform a fast.[25] I would like to suggest further that Jain women are symbolically representative of the lay path and that Jain laity have consistently celebrated their own path within Jainism. These women represent both how women are pious in themselves and also how they are no obstacle to Jain male piety. The women both accrue merit and gain prestige through both the fasting and the general "fame" among Jains.

The external asceticisms—those visible to observers (*bāhya-tapas*)—are primarily focused on fasting and encouraged for both men and women. Likewise, many of the orthodox texts do not describe a laywoman's path, expecting her to follow the same path as men, if possible. Because women do seem to be more involved with fasting than men, fasting has been deemed the primary expression of Jain women's piety. But my research suggests that the centrality of fasting in the rhetoric of women had more to do with what the public—especially the male public—wishes to display as Jain piety. Whereas most women saw fasting as a good thing to do for a variety of reasons and they acknowledged that men did far less fasting than women, they did not ever suggest to me that it was *the* area of female religious expertise. Reynell's research looks at the role of fasting as a public display of laywomen's morality (Reynell 1987) while the social aspects of participation in fasts are rightly placed alongside attendance at sermons and other places that women link religious practice with their social lives (Reynell 1985a, 1991).[26] Laidlaw writes of how fasting illustrates the ways in which Jainism is acted out on the body (and here he draws our attention—through his discussion of two Jain laymen who are revered as paragons of Jain extreme asceticism: Śrīmad Rajcandra and Śrīman Amarcand-ji Nahar—to the forms fasting may take when acted out on the male body) and thus the display of this body demonstrates the moral qualities of the individual (Laidlaw 1995). While the rhetorical equation of women's religiosity with fasting was an important icon for Jains, it may limit our understanding of the totality of Jain lay religiosity. The tendency to define women in what is a clearly orthodox and self-denying model structures the way men (and women) create religious autobiographies (Kelting 1996) and in turn the women's sense that they need to perform a certain amount of fasting in order to be respected, particularly unmarried women of marriageable age. The more ambiguous aspects of women's Jainism have an uneasy place in the public expression of what Jains do. Fasting rituals and the public display of female piety have a message of laywomen's piety that—while asserting liberation-centered ideologies about the centrality of austerity—mark these women as laywomen and publicly illustrates piety within the lay life. As a counterpoint, it is useful to look at the other primary public display of female piety—the ordination of a (usually) female mendicant. Although men do perform most of the same rituals at their ordinations, men comprise a smaller number of those ordained and their piety was not described as the shadow narrative to weddings and lay life in the way that women's ordinations most certainly were.

The Ordination Ritual as Icon Making

Nowhere during the ordination rhetoric is the image of the *dīkṣārthī* (the soon-to-be female mendicant) as queen and bride more pronounced than during the parade of the dīkṣārthī through the streets of the city (see figure 2-4).[27] The ordination parade is a popular feature of the ordination process. The day before the ordination and again on the morning of the ordination, the dīkṣārthī is paraded through the streets, dressed in wedding finery (including the henna designs on her arms and feet)[28] to give away her wealth in imitation of the ordination story in the Kalpa Sūtra when Mahāvīr distributes his wealth (*varṣīdān*). The parades may include the woman (and often her sisters as well) on her carriage, the male mendicant who is performing the ordination (*dīkṣāguru*) and his entourage, a marching band, dāṇḍiya

FIGURE 2-4. The pre-ordination parade of a female mendicant, Guruvār Peṭh, Pune, February 1994. The soon-to-be mendicant (dīkṣārthī) is throwing rice, coins, and flower garlands to the crowds on the street. (Photo by Steven C. Runge)

dancers (all men, mostly young unmarried men from her family and congregation), a cart with a Jina image being worshipped by her parents, and the bidder who has won the right to carry the basket that contains the clothing the new female mendicant will wear. Because the ordination parade is very public and because it is the perfect icon of Jain orthodoxy, the ordination rituals focus on the high-profile virtues displayed in these events.

The parade and the many events surrounding an ordination highlight the image-making role of these public celebrations of the Jain ideal and the way that women are both excluded from, and perhaps a little cynical about this image making. After the ordination parade (on February 18, 1994), the dīkṣārthī (an unmarried Mārvāḍī young woman in her late teens) was garlanded and many photos were taken and she was led into a hall. There were strikingly separate events in one room. The twenty or so men in the front were giving speeches and singing a song written for the ordination over and over again through their microphone. They were standing in a circle around the girl and her parents. In the rest of the room roughly two hundred women sat crowded together and sang songs about leaving home and wept. One or two women were reciting rosaries but the rest (who could not have really seen the whole event up front for the standing men) were singing, crying, and clapping. Even when the man sang his song through the microphone, the women did not stop singing their own songs. There seemed to be no relationship between these groups. While the men in the front were unambiguously celebrating a Jain ideal as an icon and taking pictures of the beautiful dīkṣārthī,[29] the women were singing, clapping, and weeping as they might at the departure of a bride at a wedding. This weeping was mixed with pride in both this woman's decision and the ultimate fulfillment of their religious tradition. This complex experience of weeping can be seen, in part, as a formalized act which may serve to prevent suggestions that the family wanted their daughter to take ordination and as an expression of affection for this young woman as a daughter. At the same time, the dīkṣārthī becomes, for men, an icon made material in the proudly and emblematically displayed laminated photos of the dīkṣārthī they all were wearing. These very photos became a certain currency at the ordination the next day when they allowed the wearers—all of whom were granted the status of "official"—to go on to the platform. Notably, the women on the platform (who were a mix of female mendicants and her relatives) were not wearing their passes, but all the men—except her father—were.

The next day, February 19, 1994, the dīkṣārthī came in a procession, much like her parade the day before, to Dādāvāḍi Temple where she did pūjā (offering dravya pūjā for the last time). Then she was carried by her brother from the cart to the platform for the ordination. The ordination guru was there as well as several other male mendicants. The young woman's closest family members and a variety of "official" men (wearing their passes) were seated on the platform stage on the sides and a Jina image was set up in the middle. Most of the ordination was performed by the male mendicant, who recited the initiation (*pravrajyā vidhi*)—which could only be heard by those closest to him—to the dīkṣārthī. Then her family, one by one, marked her forehead with vermilion powder and wept again—here, in a direct parallel to the moment when a new bride leaves her natal family, at which time she is likewise marked on her forehead with vermilion powder before leaving the house. After some more recitations, the ordination guru tossed the broom into her hands and she danced, spinning with the broom above her head (*rajoharaṇ*)—having symbolically accepted her renunciation—while everyone stood up clapping and singing. Everyone began to throw rice and sandalwood powder at her; she renounced the world. It seemed to me at the time and upon reflection, confirmed by Cort's research as well (1989), that the rajoharaṇ dance was the most important part of the ordination. It was at that very moment that the whole crowd leapt up cheering and that the dīkṣārthī began to be treated as a female mendicant. Sandalwood powder and rice offerings are also the way that Jains worship Jina images that are either dressed in silver ornaments or covered with flowers, and the way that all photo images were worshipped. The new female mendicant was now utterly worthy of worship. The female mendicants (including the newest one) then left to perform the hair removal and to accompany her to her meditation. Holding her cloth broom aloft, she was carried out—so she was untainted by the ground—to the cart one last time by her brother. While she was gone, the laymen took over the stage and auctioned off the privilege of performing various acts (including giving extra clothing and a staff to the new female mendicant) that are associated with the new mendicant, each of which accrues merit for the performer. Those who made the highest bid won the privilege of being the first to perform mendicant veneration (*guruvandan*) to her. When the auction was finished, the auctioneer gave the microphone to the same man who had sung at yesterday's post-parade program. When the man began to sing the same stavan as the day before, the woman next to me rolled her eyes and said, "This terrible singer, give a man a microphone," and everyone around us laughed. In the crowd, many women were singing stavan in small groups, and occasionally a cheer would spring up from some group of women.

About an hour later, the new female mendicant returned on foot, with the other female mendicants, dressed in her white clothes. The men very officiously made a barrier to keep people from crowding the new female mendicant. This barrier is a common part of public interactions with mendicants in many regions (though I only saw it invoked with dīkṣārthīs). However, this barrier is more a symbolic barrier; no one even attempted to move near her and would certainly not have touched her now. Throughout the whole proceeding there were many photos taken. My husband, Steven, whose camera was the largest at the ordination, was dragged onto the stage to record the whole event. There were also two professional (male) photographers. The image—both literal and metaphoric—of this woman's choice of renunciation was collected, presented, and worshipped. Though the fasting gatherings involved recordkeeping for the family through photos and videos, the ordination was recorded by many people who were not related to the new female mendicant. The dīkṣārthī's image is edifying as an example of the pinnacle of female piety (see figure 2-5). Likewise, it was important that she was beautiful and hence marriageable; as one man told me (in English), "She could have had any husband, but see, she is too holy." These ordination images are then framed and hung up in houses both of the relatives and of others connected directly with the ordination. These photos often hang on the walls next to the photos of deceased members of the family, hinting at some of the language of "social death" arising from ordination which much more clearly marks Hindu initiation.[30]

When a middle-age Gujarātī woman in Katraj became a female mendicant in the presence of her whole family, the women I knew felt she was lucky that her husband's family let her do this. Even if the middle-age woman might have been taking ordination in order to get out of an unhappy marriage, no one speculated out loud that she was escaping family troubles or that her husband's family "made" her do it. If they thought this, the pressure to uphold the Jain ideal of an ordination as life goal was enough to keep them from sharing the thoughts with a scholar. Any real speculations were usually focused on the ordinations of the young people, because it seems that they were the ones with the most to lose. Because of the relatively low status of women (especially as a new daughter-in-law) and the anxieties

FIGURE 2-5. The ordination of a female mendicant, near Dādāvādī Temple, Pune, February 1994. The new mendicant is performing prayers after she returns from pulling out her hair and changing into her mendicant clothing. (Photo by Steven C. Runge)

about marriage (the family's about dowry and the girl's about moving to a new family and town), there are sometimes speculations about whether the girl was encouraged by her family because they could not marry her well—she may also be considered ugly, deformed, or too tall, or she may be one of many daughters in a family who cannot support yet another dowry.[31] Although doctrinally acceptable as a reason for taking ordination (Dundas 1992), it becomes an abstract criticism of the other Jains who "dump" their daughters. Among the Gujarātī Jains, it was often said that Mārvāḍīs force their daughters to take ordination to avoid dowry costs, but I never heard it said by a Gujarātī about any Gujarātī Jain women who took ordination. I did notice that none of these critiques were said after the ordination had taken place and never about anyone known to the speaker. I suspect that it was a way to explain what makes a young girl choose to be a female mendicant instead of choosing a family, but it was also a criticism that it was unthinkable to voice about one's own community. Although in Pune Gujarātī and Mārvāḍī Jains saw themselves as having more in common with each other than they perceived themselves as having with other groups in this region, there are substantial socioeconomic and ethnic differences that are sometimes expressed by one community in direct criticism of the other's behavior (often focused on behavior of or toward women). The way in which the criticism was directed at the other dominant ethnic group among Pune Jains also points to the welling up of the uneasy relationship between Gujarātī and Mārvāḍī Jains. In addition, I never heard a woman specifically critique a female mendicant as not really religious. Regardless of whether the ordination watchers believe in the young woman's piety or pure intentions beforehand, the normative models of the ordination proceedings, put on stage and worshipped, preclude even covert doubts. For the laywomen, the female mendicant's break from the family and the cycle of labor in exchange for religious merit was both daunting and liberating as an image.

In some practical ways women also gain from taking ordination. A dīkṣārthī is the center of a lot of positive attention, which culminates in a rise in status leading ultimately to the worship of her. From the time that the woman decides to be a female mendicant until the day of her ordination, her family and her congregation show her all that she is renouncing. The dīkṣārthī sees all her relatives, she is in parades, she travels to sites she may not see after her ordination and she is doted on—perhaps even more than a bride, who at least will occasionally return home to visit her natal family—until the day she renounces the worldly life (Holmstrom 1988). Reynell lists several other reasons that ordination may be very appealing for Jain women: intellectual fulfillment and study, the company of a community of women, and an escape from a life of (potentially) dull labor (Reynell 1985a). I must concur with Reynell that these mendicants saw their choices to be mendicants as fulfilling ones, not as a last refuge. Among the Terapanthī Jains (and the Sthānakavāsī and Khartar Gacch Mūrtipūjak), there seem to be many chances for the female mendicants to continue their education (Holmstrom 1988), but within the Tapā Gacch, the female mendicants have fewer opportunities for extensive study—though I did meet three female mendicants who had completed advanced degrees (two master's degrees and one doctorate) in Jain theology before becoming female mendicants—because of the Tapā Gacch restrictions on which texts female mendicants study;[32] the female mendicants are, however, both permitted and encouraged to study the narrative and devotional literature. Further, there is some time allotted for study each day, which could be used by a female mendicant to further her studies.[33] Within the Tapā Gacch there are also injunctions against women giving public sermons, but Khartar Gacch female mendicants are commonly known to give sermons (Laidlaw 1995). Being a Jain mendicant may afford women a life where their own religious success is at the center of their efforts. In the social reality of a new daughter-in-law, in most of the Jain families I met, ordination is a true alternative to many years of hard work and relatively low status. Reynell (1985a) quotes a proverb a Jain pandit told her: "If you want to be like a queen, then go to Nemināth and become a nun. But if all you want to be is a servant, then go and get married."

While these virtues and their narratives were cited and applauded by the women themselves, they were only part of what women could achieve. Jain men and women whom I questioned virtually always agreed that the women are more observant than the men in their Jain praxis.[34] Likewise, it was often said that women are more adept at fasting and the performance of the high-status austerities—though Laidlaw found that all of the extreme self-destructive fasting was performed by men (Laidlaw 1995). It was widely felt that women were better at being devout, a pan-Indian stereotype reflecting the levels of religious practice and interaction seen in the public eye. While the "worship" of women's piety can be seen in Hindu practices—especially those associated with weddings or the worship of young virgins (*kanyā pūjā*) (L. Bennett 1983; Leslie 1989; Raheja and Gold 1994)—the public display of women's piety seems to take a central place in Jainism. At certain events (usually surrounding the practice of fasting or at ordinations) women's piety is displayed quite prominently. Although not all Jain public displays were exclusively of women, the public display of Jain women at all was unique among Pune religious communities. Except during the pilgrimage to Pandharpur, it was unusual to see Hindu women in a public parade and in the Pandharpur group the women are not explicitly displayed. Likewise, Hindu women's photos were rarely displayed in newspapers or books. In the rhetoric of what makes a good Jain woman, there have always been two basic paths: the female mendicant and the laywoman. Both of these paths have long and popular narrative traditions which help formulate what "good" is and what is worthy of celebration. Through the rituals surrounding fasting and ordinations we can see how the "good Jain woman" is produced, packaged, and displayed for the public.

3

You are the ocean of compassion, mercy's storehouse.
You give knowledge. Coming to your door, I accept you as my protector.

In the eyes, your affection rests, on your face, the empire of peace,
In your chest, non-violence dwells, on your lips, the royal truth.
The moon's light, the sun's rays, they are not like the light of knowledge.
In all times, at any time, no sky can compare to you.
In this world you are matchless, Great Soul, Mahāvīr.

We are passengers seated in a boat, Excellent Jina, you are the boat's shore.
We wander on life's path afraid, without you, the way is so difficult.
A day's pain, the poor man's labor; who has the strength to get by without you?
The path is made, the way is shown, yours is no one else's fate.
You are the highest soul, the highest Lord, transcendent Lord of the Jinas.

Transcription and translation of recording of ritual performance in Pune, Maharashtra, on 11 November 1993. Courtesy Monali Satish Shah.

Religious Knowledge and Stavan Collecting

For Jains, Jain stavan collections fall under the greater category of Jain religious texts and are thus considered worthy of worship. Women often have stavan diaries in which they have copied the words to stavan they are singing in their maṇḍaḷs or ones they particularly enjoy singing. If a woman is in a maṇḍaḷ, these collections become the performance source for the active and inactive stavan repertoires. Women, when they collect stavan into diaries, are participating in a Jain practice of text compilation, copying, and collection: practices usually associated with the canonical Āgam literature.[1] The ultimate statement of text worship may be the Āgam Mandir temples like those in Katraj (just south of Pune) or the famous Āgam Mandir at the base of Śatruñjay Hill in Pālītāṇā. Here the Āgam texts themselves are carved and painted on the walls of the temple and the inside of the temple wall. In a reform movement in the late nineteenth century, the Jain Śvetāmbar Conference and several influential male mendicants started a large cataloguing effort to organize the various Jain libraries from western India while compiling the eleven *aṅga* texts (Cort 1992). As a result of this general movement toward Āgam text veneration there were several Āgam Mandirs built: the first in Pālītāṇā in 1935 and the second in Surat in 1948. There is another at Śankheśvar which was not completed at the time of Cort's 1992 article. The temple at Katraj, near Pune, was built several years before my initial research trip in 1993–94 but the Āgam tablets are still being carved. There are devotional texts written to address jñān or the Āgam texts (as in the Forty-Five Āgam pūjā), but no one I asked either knew these by heart or had ever performed this; so although pūjā and stavan text veneration may differ from Āgam text veneration, the modes of veneration seem to be parallel. Both are to be worshipped as part of the worship of religious knowledge and to be treated with special respect and veneration; they serve as generic loci of knowledge.

Folkert challenges the equation of Jain scripture with the Jain Āgam in Sanskrit and Prakrit because this narrow definition of scripture is insufficient for explaining which texts are important to Jains and in what ways they are used (Folkert 1993). Cort also challenges the view that the Forty-Five-Āgam-texts limit on Jain scripture excludes texts which are inextricably linked to the Āgam texts (Cort 1992) and thereby overlooks the importance of these paired texts for Jain praxis. I too propose that for the Jain laywomen with whom I did my research, this notion of text would be extremely limiting and not representative of which texts were central to their understanding both of Jainism and of religious texts. For example, the pūjā liturgies were clearly seen in the context of other texts performed with them—stavan and prayers. Likewise, the bulk of the texts the Jain laity owned, read, or worshipped were not the Āgam texts but the vernacular texts with which they had greater familiarity and greater understanding: the fasting and ordination narratives, the life histories of the Jinas, the formal pūjā liturgical texts, vernacular lay manuals, and the stavan collections. Although both laymen and laywomen had access to these texts, it was primarily women who read, studied, and memorized these texts. It is important to recall Folkert and Cort's expanded notions of scripture in order to see the workings of knowledge worship (jñān pūjā) within the Jain tradition. Scripture includes Āgam texts, other mendicant texts, vernacular prescriptive texts, lessons of the mendicants, devotional literature, and often any text which addresses Jain concerns. However, the Āgam texts are not seen as acceptable for study by lay Jains, nor are they linguistically accessible to the laypeople; though it is good for the laity to venerate these texts, the laypeople's religious knowledge comes from other "scriptures." The varieties of religious veneration directed toward texts other than Āgam texts illustrates the lay perception of scripture, religious knowledge, and the centrality of these other texts.

Knowledge Worship and the Goddess of Knowledge

The worship of knowledge is part of the yearlong praxis of Jains, but it culminates yearly with the festival of Knowledge Fifth (Jñān Pañcamī—five days after the new moon in Kārtak which marks the center of the Dīvālī festival and the New Year), where knowledge is the sole object of worship. During Knowledge Fifth, a temporary shrine was built in Ajitnāth Temple's mendicants' hostel and the temple's books were placed on bookstands inside the shrine. The central books (at Ajitnāth, three Kalpa Sūtras and the Sūtrakritaṅga Sūtra) were covered with sandalwood garlands along with the other hardcover books from the temple, including fasting manuals, formal pūjā texts, the Jain rite of confession and expiation (pratikramaṇ) texts, and a stavan book. With the books, a *sthāpanā*—a bundle wrapped with five cut shells inside representing the lineage of the guru—was included in the knowledge worship. Each person who came in put a coin in the metal plate and sprinkled sandalwood powder (*vāskep*) on the books. Aside from this, the worship varied—from children who did three prostrations (praṇāms) to women who performed ten-minute homages to knowledge. Two women came and sang stavan that praised knowledge.[2]

Many Jains attempt to worship five kinds of knowledge in five locations on this day (Cort 1989). Though most of the women I knew only performed knowledge worship at Ajitnāth and in their homes, many of the men went to temples downtown to perform guru worship to mendicants. Many of the students were encouraged to bring their notebooks to the mendicants' hostel and write homages on the top of the first page to ensure good results in school and on state exams. I was even asked to take my field notes out of my bag and told to write "Śrī Mahāvīray Namaḥ" (Praise to Śrī Mahāvīr) on the inside cover, which I did. On Knowledge Fifth, the women who sang stavan either sang stavan addressed to Mahāvīr or Ādināth or sang from printed texts to melodies with which they were familiar; they did not appear to know knowledge stavan by heart.

Although Knowledge Fifth is the most important day for knowledge worship, it is by no means the only performance of book and knowledge worship. At other times, when we went to visit a *Guru mahārāj* (chief mendicant of a group) at Goḍījī Temple in Guruwar Peṭh, we first had to perform knowledge worship to one of the miniature books in a plate next to the male mendicant before we could perform the Guru worship. In Amdāvād, one could purchase small (2 by 1 inch) copies of the Kalpa Sūtra and other important texts (including the Bhaktāmara Stotra) which, because they are too small for regular reading use, are used as "representatives" of the textual tradition for the purposes of knowledge worship; in home shrines, these books are covered with accumulations of sandalwood powder from the family's knowledge worship. The presence of the Kalpa Sūtra in a household shrine, a mendicants' hostel, or even a bookstore is a material marker of Śvetāmbar identity (Folkert 1989). All acts which are appreciative of Jain knowledge are considered part of a Jain's knowledge worship—the sponsoring of text recitation or publication, the academic programs about Jainism, virtually all interactions with mendicants, and virtually all books. When I met with a women's study group of students from Poona University's Jainology Department, one woman said that instead of merely performing temple worship these women were engaged in daily knowledge worship through their studies of Jain philosophy.[3] Jain religious texts are the object of considerable Jain devotion, exemplified by the ritual of knowledge worship on Knowledge Fifth,[4] but knowledge worship is also central to many Jain religious rituals and praxis as we can see in the Kalpa Sūtra worship as part of Paryuṣaṇ, the worship of knowledge as part of the siddhacakra, the location of Sarasvatī in the Jain context, and the worship of the ritual texts themselves as part of the Akṣāynidhi Tap.

During Paryuṣaṇ, the Kalpa Sūtra[5] reigns as the text to be worshipped; the text is publicly recited (and in many congregations the manuscript is paraded around the neighborhood) and worshipped similarly to the way texts are worshipped on Knowledge Fifth: with sandalwood powder and flowers. During the bulk of the year the women's direct interaction with the Kalpa Sūtra is limited. The Paryuṣaṇ Kalpa Sūtra recitations are attended by many women who use the recitation as a time and place for meditation. The very hearing of the Kalpa Sūtra is considered edifying. The Kalpa Sūtra is scripturally important as a source of basic theology, as it contains the basic life histories of Mahāvīr, Pārśvanāth, Neminātb, and Ādināth. However, the versions of these stories that women told were based on versions found in the devotional literature more than the relatively bare-bones narratives in the Kalpa Sūtra.

The focus on the Kalpa Sūtra recitation during the central Śvetāmbar festival of Paryuṣaṇ reaches its peak at the celebration of Mahāvīr's Birthday (Mahāvīr Janam Dīvas) where the privileges to carry and to garland each of the fourteen dreams, to be the first to rock the cradle of Mahāvīr, and to take Mahāvīr home for three days were auctioned off. Once the auction was over, each of these sections of the story of Mahāvīr's birth was reenacted. When the section was read telling that Mahāvīr was born, pandemonium broke loose: Coconuts were broken of the floor, men and women rushed forward to rock Mahāvīr's cradle, and everyone threw rice, reliving the experience of the birth of Mahāvīr as told in the Kalpa Sūtra.[6]

During the Akṣāynidhi Tap, the women performing this fast met in the morning at Ajitnāth to do pūjā. For each of the fifteen days of this fast, the collective group of the women who were performing the fast placed a different text on a bookstand in the center of the large silver plate and offered milk and water by pouring them in a circle around the base of the bookstand. The text varied each day from a copy of the Kalpa Sūtra one day to the Laghu Pūjā Saṇgrah—the most common Gujarātī pūjā manual[7]—to the fasting text which guided them through their pūjā. All these texts were seen as worthy of worship as examples of the "wealth" of knowledge Jainism has to offer. Each day the women returned to the side shrine where they had set the Kalpa Sūtra on a bookstand surrounded by pots of rice with coconuts on top. This stand and the manuscript were draped with a sandal garland and worshipped with sandalwood powder each morning; they became the focal point of the fasting pūjā. During the fasting pūjā and on Knowledge Fifth, the devotional activity was directed at the texts available in the temple for use; no special effort was made to obtain Āgamic texts for either pūjā.

The Navpad Olī fast is connected to the worship of the siddhacakra, whose nine positions each represent a different aspect worthy of Jain worship: the Five Highest Ones: the Liberated (*arhat*), the Perfected Ones (*siddha*), the Mendicant Leaders (*ācārya*), the Mendicant Teachers (*upādhyāya*), the Mendicant (sādhu); and Right Faith, Right Knowledge, Right Action, and Right Austerity. The Navpadjī Pūjā by Padmavijay, which accompanies the completion of the Navpad Olī fast, speaks extensively about the virtues of knowledge. Each of the nine points (*pads*) represented on the siddhacakra is given a special worship; the seventh is knowledge (jñān). While each of the pūjās include comparisons between knowers (*jñānī*) and unknowers (*ajñānī*) of Jainism, the jñān pad pūjā focuses on knowing knowledge. The jñān pad pūjā (within the Navpadjī Pūjā) includes the following couplets:

> The nature of lives of knowledge is that they illuminate themselves.
> This lamp of knowledge is undiminished, so we bow to our beloved religion.
>
> Ten million years waste away, and the unknowing gather so much karma.
> But with every breath, the knowledgeable wear away their karma.

Through knowledge of Jain religious belief, text, and practices the Jain devotee does not accrue as much karma as does the nonbeliever, even in the very act of living. Knowledge in itself makes one do the correct actions. The pūjā states: "Compassion arises only out of knowledge." The importance of gaining knowledge through the association with Jain worship is central to the explanations of the efficacy of Jain pūjā. Later I discuss the interconnectedness of knowledge and the ability to perform meritorious acts, but here we see the elevation of knowledge within Jain practice as an expression of a central tenet (one of the "Three Jewels of Jainism") of that practice. I spoke in chapter 2 of the worldly results of these two fasts (Akṣāynidhi Tap and Navpad Olī Tap), but they also carry a strong sense of the worship of knowledge as a central part of the ways to attain well-being. The fasting instructions for the Akṣāynidhi Tap ask the faster to recite daily: "Without knowledge, there can be no wealth and without both of these no happiness" (*Śrī Taporatna Mahovidhi*, 1989). Omniscience (*kevaljñān*) is the ultimate state for a living Jina before mokṣa; available only to a select few, it is, nonetheless, the highest attainment of the living.

With the Jain attention to the worship of knowledge and to knowledge as central to one's ability to be a good Jain, it is not surprising to see Jain worship of the goddess of knowledge. Sarasvatī is well-known as the pan-Indian goddess associated with learning and the arts. Jains can be counted among her followers. Sarasvatī, Śāradā, or Śrutadevī (as she was usually called by the Jain women) is the guardian of Jain knowledge.[8] She is not attached, as the guardian goddesses are, to a particular Jina but, rather, protects the whole textual tradition. She is the granter of Right Knowledge; daily worship and knowledge worship are supplemented by reciting prayers and mantras to Śrutadevī. Śrutadevī worship is a part of Śvetāmbar Knowledge Fifth worship and part of Śruta Pañcamī—the Digambar equivalent to Knowledge Fifth worship (Cort 1987). Tiwari (1985) attributes Sarasvatī's worship to her connection with the scripture around 100 C.E., and S. K. Jain (1985) also puts this beginning in the Kushan period. The earliest sculptural depiction of Sarasvatī in any religious tradition is the Mathura Jain Sarasvatī from Kankali Tila (132 C.E.) in which she is depicted carrying a manuscript. As the keeper of knowledge, Sarasvatī is a natural patroness of libraries and universities. Sarasvatī has a long history of worship and praise within the Jain religious tradition, represented by her presence in temples, literature, and places of education.

Sarasvatī's Jain character is shown by her position in the rituals of Jain worship. She is called on to guarantee the Jain community a way and a chance to propagate their teachings. It is only through Sarasvatī's grace that a Jain can learn and perform Jain rituals correctly, understand the teachings, and therefore attain mokṣa. Jain worship puts Sarasvatī in a powerful position; she controls, through her power, those individuals who succeed in perfecting their state. For Śvetāmbars, like many Hindus, she is also associated with music (in addition to knowledge), and her descriptions include musical imagery. The lay manual, *Jindarśan* by Bhadrabahu Vijay, includes a prayer to Sarasvatī at the end:

> O Shrutadevi; O, renowned one!
> O Scriptural Deity! Saraswati!
> Bestow upon us your blessed boons;
> Fill the flute of our life
> with the miraculous tunes of radiant faith.
> Kindle the light of true knowledge in our minds
> and dispel the dense darkness from our minds.
> O mother!
> Show us the right path of life, so that at anytime,
> we may not wander blindly, aimlessly;
> and so that we may not forget or lose our way. (Bhadrabahuvijay, his own translation)

Sarasvatī is first the guardian of Jain scriptures but then gives knowledge, keeps a Jain on the Jain religious path, and brings the Jain back to the "faith." Although I did not hear women sing to Sarasvatī as part of daily pūjā or knowledge worship, I did find a stavan to Śāradā in *Śraddhanuṇ Sangīt Yane Samskar Śibir* (a stavan collection from Sangli):

> O Śāradā Ma
> Give us a message to take us from ignorance.
>
> You are the goddess of sound, this music comes from you
> Each word is yours, each song comes from you.
> We are lonely, we are incomplete
> In your refuge, you give us a mother's love.
>
> The mendicants are your company, the meritorious your beloved
> In the language of peace, in the voice of the Āgam,
> We are also your company, we are also your beloved
> Allow us to have knowledge.

You are pure white, seated on the lotus
In your hands is the vina, a crown sits on your head
From our hearts, remove all darkness
Give us that family of lights.

This stavan suggests her role not only as the protector of the Jain knowledge but also as the creator of the stavan themselves. The collection from which it comes is one based on giving directions for performing various Jain pūjās to be used for teaching Jain religious education.

Sarasvatī is also invoked in the context of teaching and learning Jainism; her picture was taped to the wardrobe closet which contained all the Jain texts in Ajitnāth Temple's mendicants' hostel and is included in Knowledge Worship pūjā. The goddess of knowledge is invoked at the opening of the *Śrīpal Rājā no Rās* (as well as many other devotional texts), and in the annual rite of confession and expiation a special prayer is said by women to Śrutadevī.[9] As the embodiment of Jain knowledge, Śrutadevī is separate from the other guardian deities who protect the Jinas and the Jain temples, and the family deities who protect certain lineages; she is the guardian of the light of knowledge, giving grace in the form of access to knowledge. In sum, those texts which are central for Jain laypeople cannot simply be classified in the contexts of (or subordinated to) that which is canonical in the Āgam tradition. The laity brings within its compass a wide range of texts (pūjā manuals, fasting manuals, confession and expiation texts, devotional narratives, stavan) which address issues central to the lay mode and which themselves becomes objects of veneration.

Collections and Collecting as Jain Values

Jains have a long history of collecting manuscripts in libraries—often more like subterranean warehouses—for the protection and preservation of their religious texts. The collections' numbers, not surprisingly, reflect the use-dynamic of the various texts. In his article about Jain libraries (*jñān bhaṇḍār*), Cort (1995b) writes that these libraries will have multiple copies of manuscripts which are either ritually or authoritatively used (Āgam, devotional, narrative, and mendicant praxis texts) rather than philosophical treatises. At Ajitnāth (as I suspect they are elsewhere), the Āgam texts, though there were not many to be found, were disproportionately represented at the Knowledge Fifth worship because of their centrality to the "idea" of Jain texts more than because of their level of use. At Ajitnāth Temple's mendicants' hostel, there is a wardrobe closet filled with religious books: mostly fasting manuals, pūjā manuals, copies of the formal pūjās, confession texts, and *devvandan* (a series of prayers each dedicated to one of the twenty-four Jinas) texts. The temple closet also held three printed copies of the Kalpa Sūtra, the Sūtrakṛtaṅga, and a few other texts reserved for study by visiting mendicants. Inside the temple itself, a stack of fasting texts, pūjā manuals, stavan books, and a separate pile of copies of the *Śrī Sudhāras Stavan Saṅgrah* (the most popular stavan collection) were mixed in with rosaries. The personal collections of the many families did not include any of the Āgam texts, except for the miniature versions used for knowledge worship; instead, they were comprised of fasting texts, stavan books, narrative literature about Jinas and other pious Jains, and a handful of vernacular lay manuals interpreting Jain philosophical ideas into how to live a Jain life. Although the texts of the modern temple collection and the personal collection of a contemporary family differ in scope and purpose from the texts within the famous Jain libraries, the practice of collecting and worshipping Jain religious texts continues in lay practice.

There are two ways of "knowing" a Jain text—through writing (*lakhvu*) or through memorization (*kaṇṭhasth*, literally "in the throat"). *Vacana* denotes the councils of the Jain mendicants; it comes from the word for recitation. Though the recitations could have been like the modern *vacan*, where a text is read from a manuscript while others listen, these recitations were at least supposed to serve to strengthen the mendicants' knowledge of the Jain texts and purportedly to check these mendicants' recitations for errors. Jain textual history focuses on the loss of certain Jain texts by lack of memory and calamity. The very philosophical debates about Jain "canon" are based on whether or not the original texts have been remembered. It is a small wonder that Jains would turn to manuscript collections to protect their religious knowledge, as they have been taught that the oldest texts were nearly (or completely, as Digambars believe) lost through the years.

The idea of stavan collecting as a devotional act reflects a long-standing relationship between the collection and veneration of devotional texts and Jains. The copying of texts for mendicants to use was a great source of merit for laymen[10] in the medieval period and an expected form of devotion to the mendicant community (Cort 1995b). The stavan diaries are themselves manuscripts filled with Jain devotional literature. Likewise, on several occasions several women spoke to me of the merits gained from "writing" (lakhvu)—which I later clarified to mean writing down or copying stavan (though women also composed new stavan lyrics)—as an act of knowledge worship. Thus a stavan, by passing through the woman who writes it down, enters her and increases the merit of her act. Thus the maṇḍaḷ diaries become copies of a sacred text. This text, though, is a part of the greater collection of all the stavan of the temple, of Pune, and of Jains, being at the same time the personal "text" of the individual woman. The restrictions surrounding physical contact with texts (during menses or after childbirth or a death) are extended not only to religious texts, including the stavan books, but to the maṇḍaḷ diaries themselves, whereas women would during these times read nonreligious texts and newspapers and young women did their homework for school with the books and notebooks they always used.[11] Even my field notebooks were subject to these restrictions because, as Soni said, "They are filled with stavan and your sketches of the temple." The collections of stavan created by women are sacred texts, though lacking the exalted authoritative status of texts written or collected by religious leaders (ācāryas).

Women's stavan diaries serve as an ever-expanding total repertoire. However, a stavan's entrance into the diary does not guarantee a place in the women's or maṇḍaḷ's active repertoire. Because the women's maṇḍaḷs have a continuous supply of stavan collected and written by their members and because they do not publish stavan books, the maṇḍaḷ's repertoire is easily modified and remains a fluid text (Doniger 1991; Flueckiger 1991b; Rosenberg 1980). A stavan does not have to be removed from the collection; it is merely allowed to drift out of use. The women's collections are far larger than either the maṇḍaḷ's or any individual's active repertoire. While the maṇḍaḷ's active repertoire included about forty stavan,[12] the collection of stavan which had been brought to the maṇḍaḷ over the fourteen years must have been considerable. Not all women copied down every stavan that was presented to the maṇḍaḷ, but even a stavan that did not ever reach the active repertoire could appear in several maṇḍaḷ singer's notebooks. The stavan that were used by the maṇḍaḷ appeared in more of the notebooks—not unlike the multiple copies of useful texts in libraries and temple collections mentioned previously. It should be remembered that in 1994 even Sheelu, whose collection was new and still relatively small, had collected more than one hundred stavan, while Ranjana had collected more than seven hundred stavan. Though Ranjana's collection was large, her active repertoire was closer to seventy-five. The active repertoire consists of those stavan the women sing in the course of their worship, pūjā programs, and social programs. The total repertoire would be those stavan the woman could sing, with the lyrics (and perhaps the melody name) in front of her. A stavan whose melody no one can remember is inactive until it is reset in a new tune; in this way, stavan go in and out of active repertoire from the diaries and from published collections (Flueckiger 1991b).

Women often used stavan books or their stavan notebooks to aid in remembering the lyrics exactly, which easily doubled their working repertoires. During morning worship one day in Śirur, several women were singing a stavan from the *Śrī Sudhāras Stavan Saṅgrah* as they flipped through the pages of the stavan books looking for the page. One woman finally found the stavan as they started the last verse. I observed this on countless occasions during maṇḍaḷ performances, morning pūjā, and even while making recordings of individual singers. The collections often serve as a reminder of the specific words or melodies for songs women do not sing often, and perhaps for the songs they often sing it is a source for the "correct" words. The older women who could not write (or for whom writing was slow and tiring) retained their repertoires primarily in their extensive memories. The size of their repertoires was not hindered much; these women had extensive collections of stavan (more than one hundred) at their disposal. However, once a woman uses a stavan notebook or published stavan books, her repertoire is easy to expand.

Stavan books are both a source for new stavan and a repository for old stavan. A stavan book can be a representation of a total repertoire for a maṇḍaḷ, a particular festival, or a community. Several stavan books were created solely for use during Paryuṣaṇ; the repertoire may only be for the singular performance during Paryuṣaṇ, but for that evening that stavan book is the repertoire. There are two major kinds of stavan books: the locally produced, usually Paryuṣaṇ-specific collections, and the collections that have become a loose center for the "canon" of stavan.[13] At Ajitnāth Temple there is, as there was at every Jain temple I entered, a pile of stavan books and pūjā books available for worshipers to use. In September 1993, this one included one copy of the Jain Yuvak Maṇḍaḷ's (Pune) Paryuṣaṇ 1993 collection, one copy of *Bhakti Gīt Māḷā* produced by Jain Bhakti Seva Maṇḍaḷ (Pune) for Paryuṣaṇ 1979, three copies of the *Ādarś Stavanāvali* (Pune) from Paryuṣaṇ 1993, one copy of *Śraddhānu Sangīt Yāne Saṃskār Śibir* (Sangli) with no date, and nine copies of the *Śrī Sudhāras Stavan Saṅgrah* (Amdāvād).[14]

The *Śrī Sudhāras Stavan Saṅgrah* was represented in all stavan book collections I encountered in temples.[15] As well as being available in every Jain temple I visited, the *Śrī Sudhāras Stavan Saṅgrah* was carried in the pūjā box[16] of most families. Because of its position as a "vectored" and "vectoring" text (after Folkert), the *Śrī Sudhāras Stavan Saṅgrah* collection serves a neocanonical text; it is an undisputed source for stavan with impeccably Jain lyrics. The texts, written mostly by male mendicants, are a source for Jain idiom, especially in stavan writing, and articulate Jain devotional theology which challenges—by their focus on grace (*kṛpā*) or compassion (*dayā*) from the transcendent Jinas—Āgamic textual traditions but which have themselves become normative. The stavan books also serve an important purpose in creating a shared repertoire; whenever Jains sang informally in large groups the stavan were chosen from this collection.

The stavan books, like the *Śrī Sudhāras Stavan Saṅgrah,* themselves represent the work of stavan collectors. The edition of the *Śrī Sudhāras Stavan Saṅgrah* in vogue during my 1993–94 field research for this study was published in Amdāvād and distributed through its editors at the Śrī Jain Prakāśan Mandir in Dośīwāḍāpoḷ. The first thirty pages of the *Sudhāras* collection are prayers (*stutis* and caityavandans) to specific Jina images.[17] These are followed by forty-eight stavan. Then the collection is rounded off with shorter prayers (*chand*s and stutis) and instructions for performing a pilgrimage to Śatruñjay. This collection was available to buy in Pune at the Jain Pustak Bhaṇḍār in Guruwar Peth, as well as in every other Jain bookstore I saw and at roadside shops in Pālītāṇā. It does not include any advertisements or pictures; it has no lists of donors or even contributors. The stavan writers' names may be embedded in the final verses of the stavan, though not always. There were seven writers who had more than one stavan included in the collection,[18] the most prolific being Padmavijay with eight stavan attributed to him. Of the remaining stavan, six were anonymous and the rest were from single-entry writers. That the *Śrī Sudhāras Stavan Saṅgrah* is an authoritative stavan text, however, should not be taken to imply its stability. The volume has grown considerably even in just the last six years. The text itself is expanding, but in 1994 still only a few of the stavan from this text were part of the active repertoire of the maṇḍaḷ (two) or of the women I knew (six); these stavan were used in performances when the group did not have a large shared repertoire or when a Jina being addressed was one for whom the singer did not know any other stavan. There were exceptions, such as the widely popular "Śrī Śantināth Stavan" and the "Śrī Śankheśvar Pārśvanāth Stavan," which many people sang (male and female, maṇḍaḷ or non-maṇḍaḷ members) and which were commonly reprinted in the many local collections.[19]

The most common local booklet in Pune in 1993–94 was the *Ādarś Stavanāvali* produced by the Śrī Ādarś Men's Maṇḍaḷ. They had produced a smaller plainer stavan book (no color photos, twenty-nine stavan) the year before, but had recently produced a slick stavan book (in 1994) that included 111 stavan. This is the largest local collection I found. Most of the stavan were written by six members of the Ādarś Men's Maṇḍaḷ, including the deceased man to whom the collection is dedicated.[20] Aside from the stavan, it included the text of the caityavandan and the Snātra Pūjā in the beginning of the booklet. It includes four black-and-white photos—two of dancers, one of an important male mendicant, and one of a deceased member of the maṇḍaḷ to whom the collection is dedicated. It also includes a colored cover with two pictures of the entire maṇḍaḷ (inside covers), another of the deceased man (back cover), and a Jain montage (front cover). There are also three maps of important Jain pilgrimage sites in Northern and Southern Gujarat and Rajasthan. There are fifty-eight advertisements and a list of donations as well—some of which include the cost of the advertisement. The listing of the donations—a common feature of Jain practice—shows the reader which people would receive the merit of putting out the publication and who has money to give in donation, thus establishing class prestige and creditworthiness (Laidlaw 1995; Reynell 1985a).

As the copying of Jain texts becomes less central to Jain rituals (Cort 1995b), and printed versions are more widely available, the publication of stavan collections serves as a "field of donation" for lay Jains wishing to fulfill their "duty" of giving money for religious causes, supplanting, perhaps, the sponsorship of copies of Āgam and other orthodox texts.[21] Most stavan collections are funded through extensive advertising, but a few have no advertisements, and a single donor—often pictured in the front with a biography—may donate the entire expense. Many of these collections are published in the memory of a deceased relative and the merit of this act is transferred to that relative (Cort forthcoming).

The commercial cassettes available to women in Pune include those locally produced as well as those produced in Mumbaī, Amdāvād, and Delhi. The few cassettes I saw or heard in homes were produced locally or in Mumbaī, the most popular being those sung by Sheela Shethiya, available in Pune at the Jain Pustak Bhaṇḍār. There were also locally produced recordings of some of the prayers recited in the temples, most popularly the *Bhaktāmara Stotra* recited by Anuradha Pauḍvāl. Although there were cassettes available in Amdāvād, Pālītāṇā, Śankheśvar, and other Jain pilgrimage sites, no one to whom I spoke had brought tapes home from any of these places; they had either purchased the tapes from the Jain bookstore in Guruwar Peth or acquired them from relatives and friends. Still, even in Amdāvād, Pālītāṇā or Śrāvan Belgola, where I saw the largest collections of stavan cassettes, they numbered only between ten and twenty different tapes, as opposed to the thirty or so Ganapatī bhajan tapes I saw in Lenyādri, or the multitudes of Kṛṣṇa bhajan tapes I saw in Jaipur and Udaipur.

In 1993–94 two Mumbaī-produced cassettes sung by Sheela Shethiya were especially popular with a few members of the Pārśva Maṇḍaḷ. Once, when Sheelu and I were in Guruwar Peth, she recommended that I buy two tapes by Shethiya. The cassettes had several stavan which were performed by the Pārśva Maṇḍaḷ: "Śankheśvar Pārśva Prabhu," "Just Once, Lord Pārśva," "Little Bird," and "Whoever Goes to Pālītāṇā." But the movement of the stavan may not be as simple as this implies. For example, Ranjana brought "Whoever Goes to Pālītāṇā" back with her from Karaḍ. She had learned it from one of her sisters-in-law there. When I brought the tape over to her house, she had not heard it before and was surprised to hear that stavan on the tape. With the Mumbaī- and locally produced tapes, it is not that difficult to imagine the movements back and forth between the "published" world of these cassettes and the informal oral channels of stavan. The locally produced cassettes can be seen as a source for new stavan, as well as a crystallization of the popular canon in a region, city, or neighborhood, suggesting that the popular stavan cassettes may reflect the local repertoire rather than always be the source of these stavan.

The cassette tapes tend to have a variety of "standards,"[22] such as the "Śrī Śāntināth Stavan" from the *Śrī Sudhāras Stavan Saṅgrah*, and also have a selection of new stavan.[23] Prayers set to music are also scattered throughout most recordings. The tapes often start with the "Navkār Mantra," which is sung or recited at the start of all Jain rituals and thus is a fitting start to one's recording. In fact, during several of my recordings of women singers (Sheelu, Pramila, and Ranjana) the singers started by singing the "Navkār Mantra" for me. The inclusion of other stotra and prayers on the cassettes can be seen as an attempt to make the cassette a "complete" Jain meditation (sāmāyik). I was also struck by the almost universal use of women singers on the most popular stavan tapes. Though there exist stavan recordings sung by men, I only once saw one in a family's cassette collection. This certainly reflects the belief (of both men and women) that women's singing is auspicious (Flueckiger 1996; Gold 1988; Henry 1988; Narayan 1986). The primary market and audience for these cassettes were men, perhaps because these men had access to money to purchase cassettes but did not have ready access to stavan singing.

The stavan cassettes do not have a large market, nor are they a central source for Jain religious music. I heard Jain devotional cassettes played twice during Jain festivals. The first time was at the Kārtak Pūṇam festival at Dādāvāḍī Mandir, when a cassette with a mix of stavan and Jain cheers was played over one sound system while another system simultaneously played the live performance of the Ādarś Men's Maṇḍaḷ. Adding to the tumult, women sang their own stavan in various rooms and shrines and a man auctioned off the parts of the pūjā over yet another public address system. None of these were especially discernible in the din, but the loudest upstairs was the live maṇḍaḷ and downstairs the auctioneer. The second time occurred during the 1993 Digambar Mahāmastikābhiśekha (Great Head Anointing) festival in Śrāvan Belgola, where a recording of the "Navkār Mantra" was blaring out of speakers that lined the climb to the temple. It is perhaps significant that the pilgrims climbing the steps did not audibly join in the recitation but, rather, initiated jubilant cheers: "Say the name, Mahāvīr" or "All praise to Bāhubali." Cassettes are far from replacing Jain singing in the pūjā contexts. At Hema's fast-breaking gathering after the maṇḍaḷ left, her family put on a cassette of Gujarātī folk music (rās-garbā) for dancing. Here the cassette replaced hiring a live band to perform party music; for the Shivajinagar Jains rās-garbā is seen neither as religious nor as devotional music even though the lyrics are usually devotional lyrics to the goddess Ambadevī in Northern Gujarat.[24]

Stavan Learning through Women's Lives

While stavan singing is certainly not overtly discouraged among boys (in fact, women sometimes would tell me that so-and-so's son was a great singer), the environment that fosters stavan singing and stavan acquisition is the women's sphere, and men (and adolescent boys) are not generally a part of that sphere. When boys and girls are young, they learn stavan from their mothers and aunts. Often when I was making a recording of a stavan singer, her children—and sometimes her nieces and nephews—would sing along while she sang for me. These early stavan are often the ones that remain in the singers' personal repertoire throughout his or her life. These early stavan dominate the boys' personal repertoire because their opportunities to learn new stavan later—unless they become active in one of Pune's four men's maṇḍaḷs—are limited. The primary difference between boys' and girls' stavan learning is that when a boy reaches 12 years old he is not encouraged to spend as much time as girls with the women in the temple (or at the social gatherings where stavan are exchanged) and his worship is expected to become "male." This distinction was pointed out to me by several Jain laymen to explain the importance of formal education in Jainism for boys. In his 12th year, Ranjana's son Nilesh went to Jain camp during his Dīvālī break to learn how to be a Jain layman (śrāvak) and to recite his prayers (not to sing songs) and thereafter was expected to perform his pūjā alone. Superficially, this education focuses on those prayers men say and women don't (certain *mantra*s and certain parts of recitations), but more deeply this education focused on a difference in worship priorities and styles and Jain identity. For the girls there is no formal training or break in religious practice; they remain at their mothers' side where they learn what it means to be a Jain laywoman (śrāvikā). For Ranjana's daughter, Moni, age 9, learning all the words to her first stavan—"Knowledge Is Given," which heads this chapter—from her mother was a source of great pride, and she sang the stavan every morning in the temple from then on. It marked the beginning of her life as an independently practicing Jain laywoman; she could then perform a pūjā by herself. This compares with Tushad, age 7 (Moni's brother), who came home from informal Jain school and recited for me his first memorized prayers or Nilesh, age 12, who returned from Jain camp proud of being a new layman; their "coming of age" into Jainism hinged on recitation.

As girls grow older they are encouraged to participate in their mothers' maṇḍaḷs either in the singing women's maṇḍaḷ or with the young unmarried women who perform dance for maṇḍaḷ programs, while their brothers are encouraged to help out in the ubiquitous family business. Once they stopped going to college, Soni and another young unmarried woman began to memorize lengthy recitations by sitting with Dadiji for an hour a day and repeating after her key Jain texts (such as the "Moṭī Śanti") whose memorization would mark these young women as quite knowledgeable. Among young women at Ajitnāth, Manisha, Sheelu, and Doli joined the women's singing maṇḍaḷ. Manisha was an active singer—from the age of 16 until she was married in 1995 (she does not participate in a maṇḍaḷ in her new home)—with the women's maṇḍaḷ, performed much of the unrehearsed dancing that happens at Snātra and other pūjā performances, and led the young unmarried women in their dancing group. In Shivajinagar, Sheelu had done some dancing with the maṇḍaḷ's young unmarried women's group at festivals but was not an active singer, and she had a relatively small collection of stavan when she left for her husband's village. Though she had been somewhat involved with the maṇḍaḷ in Shivajinagar, which her mother had founded, she was not a regular participant in the women's maṇḍaḷ in Sangamner. Doli was involved in the young unmarried women's maṇḍaḷ at Ajitnāth but not the women's singing maṇḍaḷ. Recently married (and now living in her husband's town) she had not decided whether to become involved with the maṇḍaḷ at her husband's temple. As new daughters-in-law with young children they had less freedom to go to maṇḍaḷ practices and programs.

During her youth, a girl is encouraged to participate in Jain activities as a part of her identification as Jain and as a sanctioned social life. As her marriage time comes closer, the girl's attention may shift from performances with the young unmarried women to the collection of stavan and the activities of the women's singing maṇḍaḷ. In Karaḍ, Varsha, her sister and her cousin (all unmarried Gujarātī women) were all involved in the women's singing maṇḍaḷ. Maṇḍaḷ involvement before marriage is a place for young women to meet and to publicly express their piety. Their involvement provides a forum for learning the religious practices of married women while showing that they are "good" prospective brides. As the expectation that their behavior will conform more closely to that of married women increases, their involvement provides an outlet for sociability that is acceptable to their parents and above reproach. Many women first began their stavan collections as they reached marriageable age. Sheelu said that as her parents began to look for a suitable husband, she realized that soon she would not have regular access to her mother's extensive stavan collections; she began her own collection by copying over stavan from her mother's maṇḍaḷ notebook and then attending the maṇḍaḷ practices. In Karaḍ, Varsha was at one time preparing her dowry for her prospective wedding, meeting prospective families, and rapidly and pointedly filling her diary with good stavan. During each day she would go through the various stavan diaries of the women who were visiting Varsha's home—including my field notes—looking for stavan she liked and did not already have. Maṇḍaḷ participation at this time is a way to display the potential bride to women who—although they all probably know the girl—must begin to see her as a woman. The active participation of young women in women's maṇḍaḷ activities (and other practices associated with women rather than girls)—unless they are very interested in singing or dance, as Manisha is—signals the approach of marriageability.

Pune's Gujarātī Jains generally married their daughters to fellow Jains from another town (or even another city or state), but this arises from the smallness of the marriage pool in Maharashtra rather than from a belief in village exogamy.[25] Because Śvetāmbar Jains are still relatively few in Maharashtra (outside of Mumbaī), Jain women are still married over considerable distances. However, it is now increasingly common in Pune and Mumbaī—where there are large enough marriage pools—for women to marry someone from the same city. After marriage, the women I knew moved promptly into their husband's family's house but visited their mother's home for long periods in the hot season and otherwise for all important family events (fast-breakings, weddings, births, deaths, etc.) Except for the oldest women (who were often married quite young, between 11 and 18 years old), most women I knew were married between the years of 18 and 25. It is now considered mandatory to educate one's daughters to get them good marriages—aside from the real interest in education itself that many men and women expressed—which means that the young women are usually in school until they are at least 17. After completing their studies, the young women now spend a few years learning household skills, as they were too busy studying to have become proficient in them, and participating in religious activities: maṇḍaḷs, fasting, and study groups.

After marriage, a woman moves to her husband's house, and many of the new brides are brought to the maṇḍaḷ practice by their mother-in-law or sisters-in-law. Young brides rarely have the free time or the option to come to all maṇḍaḷ events, but maṇḍaḷ programs and pūjās are often given higher priority by their mothers-in-law than is visiting; for those who can get permission for maṇḍaḷ activities but not for visiting, maṇḍaḷs are the center of their social life. Some new brides are encouraged to join the maṇḍaḷ to help them adjust to their new home (and make friends) and as a sign of a family's propriety (and prosperity). Within the Pārśva Maṇḍaḷ, there were two women who were childhood friends who had both been married to men in Pune. Even though neither family still lived in Shivajinagar, the two women retained their membership in the Pārśva Maṇḍaḷ, I suspect as a way to see each other more often without difficulty. Reynell (1985a) speaks of Jain rituals and fasting as social events for the Jain women in Jaipur who are otherwise discouraged from leaving their homes. The presence of women who were not interested in singing at maṇḍaḷ activities may be a product of the important social and emotional support of the women's maṇḍaḷ for these women.

Women's Lives, Stavan Collection, and the Maṇḍaḷ Repertoire

The Pārśva Maṇḍaḷ has two concentric groups: active members, which includes all the women who come to maṇḍaḷ practice and those who participate in maṇḍaḷ pūjā performances, and inactive members, which includes all the women and (girls) associated with the temple—in effect all the reasonably observant women in the congregation. Aside from the performances of pūjās, the maṇḍaḷ sponsored an all-maṇḍaḷ picnic; an all-congregation women's program on Mahāvīr Nirvāṇ (during Divālī) with stavan singing, dance, dramas, speeches, awards, and snacks; and a monthly program whose activities vary from games to cooking lessons. During the all-congregation women's program, the maṇḍaḷ's officers are chosen for the next year; however, according to Maluben, most women reelect the incumbents unless someone resigns. The active members are primarily the organizers of these activities as well as many of the other non-maṇḍaḷ congregation events, such as the annual confession and expiation of sins at the Saṃvatsarī, the congregation feast, and the rainy season religious education program. Maṇḍaḷs provide both a primary nonfamilial—though there are usually some other women from one's family—social life and a place for the practice of their singing and collecting efforts while they gain religious merit for themselves and their families. Maṇḍaḷs are religious organizations and a woman's interest in singing is rarely curtailed (though it must not seriously interfere with her housework). Being religious is seen as part of a woman's job, and the maṇḍaḷ is an enjoyable and serious way to be religious.

Pramila, Ranjana, Savita, and Sharmila brought in the stavan for the maṇḍaḷ to learn during the year I was doing my research. The first three women are central members and officers of the maṇḍaḷ; Sharmila was a newer member (then a recent bride in a Gujarātī middle-class family) whose extensive knowledge and involvement probably signal her future in maṇḍaḷ administration.[26] Their level of participation consolidates their positions in the maṇḍaḷ and also raises the expectation level of what these three women should be accomplishing. When a new pūjā is being prepared, new songs are often needed. These songs were solicited from the more active singers who would either suggest a song from the repertoire or discuss possible sources for brand-new stavan. For example, right before the first performance of the Navāṇu Prakārī Pūjā (a longer pūjā requiring more songs), Maluben asked Ranjana and Savita to prepare more songs to teach the maṇḍaḷ for that pūjā. Often after maṇḍaḷ practice during the officers' meeting or over tea, Ranjana and Savita would discuss possible stavan and sources for new stavan.

On several occasions I listened while the officers figured out which kind of new stavan were needed. When a particular stavan was needed it was usually either Savita or Pramila who brought the new stavan to the maṇḍaḷ, whereas Ranjana and Sharmila were guided more by their encounters with other stavan singers than by the immediate needs of the maṇḍaḷ. This is not to suggest that the needs of the maṇḍaḷ did not direct Ranjana's attention to particular kinds of stavan. For example, when Ranjana was seeking fasting songs right before Paryuṣaṇ, she did not say, "Teach me fasting songs." Rather, she asked what the women were singing these days, which, because of the season, was likely to be fasting songs. Which stavan were incorporated may be the result of a variety of factors about the contributor and timing: the prestige of the singer bringing the stavan to the maṇḍaḷ, the singer's ability to present the stavan to the maṇḍaḷ well, and the likelihood of the presenter leading the stavan in performances. The quality of the stavan itself can affect its fate: good words (*kāvy*), good melody (*tarj*), good meaning (*arth*), and the stavan's overall usefulness (or the need for a stavan that fits the same general description or purpose). These qualities can all convince the maṇḍaḷ to include it, as might a stavan's singularity—if there is only one fasting song presented it is more likely to be included in the repertoire than if it is one of four fasting songs being presented. The majority are either commonly known or new enough to the repertoire that the singers in the maṇḍaḷ still remember who was responsible for finding the stavan. The women's stavan diaries often have stavan after stavan with no identified source or melody, making it quite difficult to trace sources. Even when I was able to find other versions of a stavan it was hard to find out the particulars of its transmission. The stavan moved quickly through the conduits of women's visiting and maṇḍaḷ participation, illustrating the importance of the particular lives of women for understanding the genre.

Stavan learning, and thus the conduits of stavan transmission, is tied partly to the shared experience of Jain women as "migrants" to a new town and partly to the specific conditions of their lives in their new homes. Ranjana's daily life passes in the context of a large joint family. Ranjana is married to the third of five brothers who lived together in one house—though one brother and his family have lived elsewhere because of his job in government service for twenty years, and in 1998 the youngest brother and his family moved into a separate apartment. She grew up in a large joint family as well. When I was in Pune, her workload was heavy in spite of being shared with three other daughters-in-law and her time alone was limited to a few rare moments when, for one reason or another, everyone was out. In her family, the women were each given a day off—usually coinciding with their husband's day off. Ranjana chose to take Saturday off rather than Wednesday (her husband's day) in order to guarantee her participation in the maṇḍaḷ. She scheduled her work week around maṇḍaḷ practice, programs, and pūjās. If there was a pūjā or program during the week, Ranjana was virtually always able to go—though it may have meant getting up earlier in the morning to finish her work. Ranjana and her co-sisters-in-law were all usually permitted (and often encouraged) to attend many maṇḍaḷ programs and performances, and Ranjana attended them all. Ranjana's involvement with the maṇḍaḷ demanded frequent short visits with maṇḍaḷ members to give messages, pass on materials, or ask questions. Likewise, she had a sister in Guruwar Peth in Pune's old city and a niece in Pimpri (a suburb of Pune) whom she visited whenever she could. Visiting—primarily familial—made up the bulk of women's nonreligious social activity: there are long hot season visits to their mothers' houses (usually from two to six weeks), shorter visits to their mothers' houses for special events (up to a week), short visits to natal relatives—especially to sisters' houses at special events in the sister's husband's family (one or two days), short visits to one's husband's relatives as part of special events or when they need some household assistance—after a birth, death, operation, etc. (up to approximately two weeks except under the most serious conditions), and brief visits to relatives and friends for tea. Visiting was the primary source of stavan learning for most of the women I knew.

The ways that women move from house to house for visits—often long visits which few men take after they are adults—facilitate stavan collection and transmission by putting women in contact with a large group of other singers not in their own maṇḍaḷ. On July 31, 1994, when Ranjana and I were in Śirur visiting Hema, her co-sister-in-law, Ranjana asked Hema to teach her a new stavan. Hema sang two or three stavan and Ranjana said that the third one was pretty and wanted to learn it. While driving out to a picnic spot, Hema sang the stavan over and over (on top of the Hindī film music blaring from the jeep's stereo) and Ranjana sang along. When we returned to the house, Ranjana had Hema show her the lyrics in her notebook and she copied them over. Hema had recently returned from a visit with her mother, and because she lived in a different town, Hema's maṇḍaḷ had a unique repertoire to examine.

In late May 1994, during my visit to Karaḍ—where Ranjana's mother lived and where Ranjana had already stayed for a week before my arrival—I was surprised to discover the extent to which the visit was punctuated with stavan learning. Ranjana had brought her stavan diaries with her to Karaḍ. When my husband and I arrived we sat down for tea and the unmarried daughters and their maternal cousin sang us the new stavan they had learned from Ranjana's sister, who was also visiting the house. Then the unmarried daughters sang a stavan that their maṇḍaḷ was performing those days. I am aware that in part this particular performance was done for our benefit because we were first-time guests—deserving of special entertainment—and because I was doing research on stavan and was also known to be a singer. This knowledge was certainly a catalyst for stavan performances, but I found any gathering or festive visit was an opportunity for stavan singing and its accompanying dāṇḍiya rās dance. Later that day, I found the unmarried daughters all peering into Ranjana's stavan notebooks, copying lyrics into their own new notebooks and asking her to sing the melodies over and over until they had them right. Her visit gave them all an opportunity to learn stavan from Pune to add to their collections from Karaḍ.

Later in the night, after most of the family had gone to sleep, some of the women were keeping me company as I boiled my drinking water for the next day, and it was Ranjana's turn to learn a stavan. Her oldest sister-in-law sang a stavan and Ranjana asked her if she could give Ranjana the lyrics to it and repeat the melody. When Ranjana returned to Pune from her stay in Karaḍ (a shorter visit than usual—only fifteen days) she brought several new stavan with her ("Whoever Goes to Pālītāṇā,"

"Kesarīyā O Kesarīyā," "Jingle Jangle," and "Money or God"), and many of the stavan from her new collection had made their way into the collections of the women and girls who were in Karaḍ. Ranjana's stavan, which were added to the unmarried nieces' collections, would soon travel to yet a third location after their marriages. During these visits Ranjana collected many stavan from her sisters, sisters-in-law, other visitors (including the sister of one of her sisters-in-law), and other women she knew in Karaḍ. She learned from the occasional maṇḍaḷ meetings and performances of the maṇḍaḷ in her mother's town. One can perhaps appreciate the impossibility of tracing origins of stavan in personal collections.

Ranjana also looked for new stavan at singing programs. On September 3, 1994 (during Paryuṣaṇ), the Ādarś men's maṇḍaḷ from the old city came to sing at Ajitnāth Temple at night; they distributed a few handouts of the stavan they were singing, and Ranjana made sure to secure herself a copy. During the whole performance she followed along in the handout and sang along carefully, learning the melodies that went with each of the stavan. I left before I could see whether any of these stavan was included ultimately in her repertoire, but she did say to me that they were Mārvāḍī melodies and the primarily Gujarātī maṇḍaḷ would not know them. Second, for a large maṇḍaḷ program for Makar Sankranti (January 14, 1994), a downtown maṇḍaḷ hired a male stavan singer from Mumbaī to perform solo on stage. During the program, Ranjana listened to one stavan and explained to me, "This melody you know from the stavan, 'Knowledge Is Given'; we sing different words but it's the same melody (tarj)." She either knew the stavan or sang a different stavan to the same melodies of all the stavan the singer performed. At the end she said, "It was a good program, wasn't it? We know the stavan though. Nothing new, but he sings well." For an active collector like Ranjana, all stavan singing performances or occasions are a possible source for new stavan. For Ranjana the internalization of the words and melodies from other singers' performances formed the core of stavan learning.

Savita's free time was limited, even by Indian standards, by the structure of her family. Her husband's brothers have divided their house into separate homes where the wives are individually responsible for the full cycle of daily work in each house—cooking, some laundry, cleaning, most of the shopping, and ironing—whereas in a joint family division of labor and the presence of other workers sometimes frees up time. Two of her three brothers-in-law and her father-in-law died young, which put additional pressure on the already strained divided resources of the family. To decrease the financial strain, Savita did piecework in her home—making bags and decorations for celebrations: weddings, engagements, and pregnancy celebrations. Savita's home was quiet and for the greater part of the day she was working alone in the house. She told me the quiet made it easy to concentrate on singing. However, the family's organization meant that Savita had less free time to go visiting other women—she also had no family in Pune to visit. Savita's home was across the street from the temple, but even so she sometimes had to cut short her time at maṇḍaḷ practice or not come at all because of her duties at home.

Savita's primary sources for learning new stavan were books. Her home had been the location of the Jain temple for forty-five years before the new temple was built in 1983. With the new temple came new books and Savita's family was left with an extensive collection of devotional literature. It was not easy for Savita to go visiting or to see other maṇḍaḷs performing because of the expectation that she would be home, but Savita could take a few minutes and page through her family's books (which remain in her part of the divided house) to see what she could find. Savita commonly brought new stavan to the maṇḍaḷ practice that she had found in the extensive stavan books and pūjā manual collection of her family. She would either set them to the tune suggested in the book or find on her own a melody which suited the rhythms of the poetry. (It seemed she drew melodies from stavan cassette recordings but she herself did not have a cassette recorder—perhaps there was one in another section of the house.) Her focus on the stavan books as a source for new stavan allowed her to focus her collection to fit the changing needs of the maṇḍaḷ. For example, as Paryuṣaṇ arrived and the maṇḍaḷ was preparing to perform at fasting gatherings, Savita searched for good fasting songs (tapasya gīt) and was able to bring several to maṇḍaḷ practice at that time. Thus her style of stavan collection was conducive to a pointed reformation both of the active repertoire of the maṇḍaḷ and of her own.

Pramila also brought most of her stavan to the maṇḍaḷ from stavan books. Her collecting was pointed toward the specific needs of the maṇḍaḷ's upcoming performances. She was less confident with melodies, which may have reflected her lack of access to other singers or cassettes for repeated practice. Pramila lived near Goḍījī temple and performed her morning pūjā there. However, she remained a member of the Pārśva Maṇḍaḷ, which she had joined when her family still lived in Shivajinagar. After her husband died, the family moved to a new apartment, though they maintained a store near Ajitnāth Temple. Pramila was involved in the family businesses—a sari shop and a Jain bakery—which occasionally cut into her maṇḍaḷ activity time. Likewise, because she lived in another neighborhood she was not a part of the daily give and take between other singers who exchanged ideas on the bench in front of the temple. Pramila brought stavan after stavan to the maṇḍaḷ that she found in her many collections, but few were incorporated into the repertoire. Her stavan were far less likely to be included in the maṇḍaḷ repertoire or to be copied into the stavan notebooks, probably because she did not campaign for her stavan, as both Ranjana and Savita did, and because her singing was less confident than theirs.

Writing and Publishing Stavan

Many women at one time or another wrote stavan. There are two types of songs written: devotional songs focused on the qualities of the Jinas or aspects of Jain worship and songs to commemorate specific events. The second type is more common. Sheelu wrote a stavan in memory of her aunt who died; Hema's niece from Junnar wrote a stavan in honor of Hema, who had completed an eleven-day fast; and Ranjana wrote one to wish me well as I was leaving Pune in 1994 to return to the United States. These were written to already existing stavan melodies, some with the poetic structure of an already existing stavan. Among the collections of stavan in stavan books available from the Jain Pustak Bhaṇḍār, virtually every stavan was attributed to an author, and most local collections name Hindī film melodies for some stavan, and thus date the stavan by the corresponding film's release date. The use of existing melodies presents no problem for the stavan writer, collector, or singer; in fact, it presents a valuable tool for expanding the repertoire quickly (Henry 1988; Manuel 1993).

Writing stavan combines an act of devotion with an expression of the woman's or man's creativity. Sheelu was an active stavan writer. When discussing stavan with her during an interview on March 29, 1994, during one of her many stays at her mother's (Maluben) house, Sheelu was paging through her maṇḍaḷ notebook. She was still quite young, 28, and had a relatively small stavan collection. At this time she had been married 1 year (at 27, a later age than most of the other women in the maṇḍaḷ) and unlike Manisha, another young woman, Sheelu had not been a very active singer before she was marriageable. In her maṇḍaḷ diary were several stavan she had written, though she believed most of them were not very good. There were two she liked a lot and permitted me to record them. One had been written for a fasting gathering to commemorate her mother's fast-breaking and the second was a welcome song (*svāgatam gīt*) to celebrate her aunt and uncle's wedding anniversary by describing their good "qualities." A fasting song (tapasya gīt) may be both commemorative—of the particular faster—and religious—as an expression of Jain ideals. She sang me a third song she had written to commemorate the death of her aunt and to include in a family booklet compiled in her aunt's memory. This third song was for the family, and she did not sing that for the maṇḍaḷ, nor did she expect to. When I told her it was a lovely song—its lyrics were quite moving—and suggested she sing it for Ranjana, Sheelu said, "It's not for the maṇḍaḷ though, just for my family." The other two she had written that year were appropriate for the maṇḍaḷ and the fasting song had been used by the Pārśva Maṇḍaḷ while the welcome song was sung by her new maṇḍaḷ in Sangamner. Most of these gīts were written for a specific event[27] without the idea that they would become a part of the repertoire—even that of the song writer.

When a woman writes a song, she may not intend the song for a wider audience than the group attending an event. When Ranjana wrote a welcome song for me, she sang the song at a party at my house where there would only be about eighteen women from the maṇḍaḷ (see figure 3-1). The song was never intended for a greater audience and, I expect, it would not ever be sung in another context. Likewise, the song Sheelu wrote for her aunt's death commemorated a singular event and she had no intention of singing it for anyone else.[28] The fasting songs or the welcome songs were both written with a larger audience in mind, and Sheelu performed them at the original functions and after some encouragement brought them to her maṇḍaḷ in Pune or Sangamner.[29] The audiences of stavan can be seen as embedded in concentric groups: self, family, the maṇḍaḷ for events in closed settings, the maṇḍaḷ for possible inclusion in repertoire, as a part of pūjās performed by the maṇḍaḷ, for those who hire maṇḍaḷs and attend formal pūjās, and as a part of maṇḍaḷ programs. Male singers may enter singing competitions and are more likely to participate in stavan book publication, both high-prestige activities. Once the stavan has been incorporated into a maṇḍaḷ's repertoire, the performances of the stavan are no longer directly linked to the singer. When a stavan was performed in a pūjā or program, the author was never mentioned—even with the more published maṇḍaḷs such as the Ādarś Men's Maṇḍaḷ. Yet the women's reserve about solo performance or stavan introduction in general prevents most of them from bringing their own stavan to the maṇḍaḷ's attention.

This reserve does not impede the distribution of some stavan across wide geographic areas. Women performed stavan in situations that encourage stavan learning and exchange: with other individual women seeking new stavan, with other maṇḍaḷ

FIGURE 3-1. Core members of the Pārśva Maṇḍaḷ at tea in our flat, Pune, August 1994.

groups in their towns, their mother's towns, and surrounding towns, on pilgrimage to distant towns, and at large gatherings (e.g., fast-breakings and weddings). The movement of a stavan from one maṇḍaḷ to another involves several stavan performances: the original singing heard by a collector from a different maṇḍaḷ, the repeat of the stavan with its accompanying lyrics learning—usually by one representative of the original maṇḍaḷ for the collector—and then minimally the final performance by the collector to teach the new stavan to the second maṇḍaḷ. In addition, the stavan may have other performances (the collector singing the stavan for a friend or relative to ask her opinion, the preview performance for lead singers in the maṇḍaḷ), and it may be that the collector learns the stavan from a third party in neither of the two maṇḍaḷs that perform the stavan. All these exchanges take place in a sturdy network that distributes information quickly through the bonds of families, friends, and motivated singers. This is not a public versus private issue, because these women do perform in public spaces for audiences (but those audiences are women), but simply a difference between one network of knowledge transmission and another of display: performance-as-information-distribution versus performance-as-spectacle.

The process of learning, collecting, and writing stavan highlights the roles that women may adopt during the process of stavan transmission. The women's repertoires expand with new stavan learned from family, friends, and maṇḍaḷ singers and still more stavan reconstructed from published stavan collections. The intersection of the women's social worlds and stavan collecting fuels the interconnectedness of stavan singers. Participation in maṇḍaḷs and maṇḍaḷ performances serves as a social and religious activity and as a focal point for a woman's creative energy; women have a group for whom they collect stavan and an audience for the stavan they write themselves. The maṇḍaḷ is a "safe" place for Jain laywomen to express their desire to be "heard."

In the sphere of stavan book publishing, men are more commonly found as the authors of stavan. The dominance of women in the performances of stavan and the dominance of men in the stavan books is worth noting. The stavan singing of women is given less prestige at temples where there are men's maṇḍaḷs. This reflects the preferential treatment of men's public culture and men in general commonly found in India. At medium and small temples, where there were no men's maṇḍaḷs—in fact at all but three of Pune city's forty-three Mūrtipūjak Jain temples[30]—the women's maṇḍaḷ's repertoire of stavan is often the only active stavan repertoire. Perhaps the women's maṇḍaḷs do not have access to the business contacts which sell advertisements, making such publication possible, or perhaps the women are not as interested in the wider male affirmation of their piety or stavan-writing skills; they seem to get plenty of public affirmation from women.

Although one might expect the circles to continue to widen to a published sphere after the circle of maṇḍaḷ performance, they don't. Though it may seem as if recorded cassettes are the next concentric circle, they really are not, because they are unrelated to the network of associations women themselves mark as significant. In June 1994, Maluben suggested that I put together a recording of the maṇḍaḷ singers and lined up a few recording sessions, but the women were hesitant or uninterested in being recorded for a cassette and Maluben abandoned her project. It is significant that gestures toward high-prestige activities (as is discussed further in chapter 7) often seemed to start from Maluben's initiative. As most women draw their personal repertoire from the stavan they learned in their social worlds rather than from stavan books, it may be that the local stavan books carry less prestige among women than they do among men, for whom they seem to be the major source of stavan learning. There were a few stavan books written and published by women. *Bhakti Prerṇā* was one I found in an Amdāvād bookstore. The book itself had no list of donors or advertisements; it was sponsored by the members of a women's maṇḍaḷ in the memory of the founder. The collection had several blank pages at the back for the book's owner to add her own stavan to the collection, reflecting the differing understandings of stavan collections between the more "fixed" stavan book of men and the more open-ended women's stavan notebooks.

As well as being performers of stavan, Jain women can be seen as collectors and creators of this genre. Even though many stavan are written by male mendicants and laymen, Jain laywomen are the primary transmitters of stavan to other women—who are the primary performers of stavan. Women learn new stavan, create collections of stavan for their own use and for the use of their maṇḍaḷs, and write stavan as an expression of piety and creativity as well as a source for new stavan. Although men are involved with the publication of locally produced stavan collections and are the editors of the more widely distributed collections, the world of devotional singing and stavan in Pune is dominated by women and women's stavan repertoires. Because stavan and other devotional texts with which the women have expertise are understood to be knowledge—especially in the context of lay religiosity—these women can be seen as the primary source for important knowledge about being Jains. The dynamics of stavan collection and transmission are understood best in the context of the Jain woman's daily social life, which is as varied, complex, and multifaceted as the genre of literature they continue to create, modify, and widely disperse.

*4

O compassionate Lord, your compassion has no end,
O destroyer of troubles, is there no end to your mercy?
My sin is this, I forgot to do your worship.
O forgetter of my forgetfulness, is there no end to your mercy?
I knew inside that I was playing crooked games.
O Lord who makes the crooked straight, is there no end to your mercy?
O merciful Lord, I have drunk the glass of poison,
But you turned it from poison to nectar, is there no end to your mercy?
There was no shore to the sea of my ignorance, O my shore, from where have you come?
O my true savior, is there no end to your mercy?
My life is so sad, take me into your protection, O immortal one.
You are in my heart, O delightful one, is there no end to your mercy?

Transcription and translation of recording of performance during an interview in Pune, Maharashtra, on 23 August 1994. Courtesy Savita Suresh Shah.

The Shapes and Categories of Stavan

According to both Śvetāmbar and Digambar traditions, stavan derive mythologically from the king of the gods', Śakra's, praise of the Jinas (Jaini 1979), which has become the Śakra Stava. The Śakra Stava is recited as part of the daily morning prayers and is memorized by all observant Jains:

> Praise to the arhats, the Lords, who cause the beginnings, the *Tīrthaṅkaras*, who by themselves have attained enlightenment, the best of men, lions among men, excellent lotuses among men, excellent perfume elephants among men, the best in the world, lords of the world, benefactors of the world, lights of the world, illuminators of the world, givers of freedom from fear, givers of insight, givers of the path, givers of refuge, givers of enlightenment, givers of dharma, expounders of dharma, leaders of dharma, guides of dharma, the best world emperors of dharma, possessors of the irrefutable best knowledge and faith, freed from bondage, the victors, the conquerors, who have crossed over, who bring others across, wise, enlightened, liberated, who liberate [others], omniscient, all-seeing, who have attained the place called *siddhigati* which is beneficent, firm, inviolable, eternal, imperishable, undisturbed, and from which there is no return; praise to the Jinas who have conquered fear. In this threefold manner I praise all the siddhas, those who have been, those who will be in a future time, and those who are in the present. (Cort 1989, 351–52)

The text provides a litany of stock epithets for Jain devotional literature while also giving that literature a mythological pedigree. Because this and other texts recited as part of the morning worship are memorized by many Jains—more often than any other long text—these images are formative in the understanding of who the Jinas are and what a Jina can do.[1] Jain women sing a variety of genres as part of their religious practice: stavan, *gīt*, and the formal pūjā texts. The first two, stavan (devotional songs) and gīt (songs either secular or addressed to laity or mendicants) are the genres from which women choose their personal repertoires. In looking at the development of stavan (a task which, in its entirety, could take a lifetime in itself) one is faced with a confusing array of names (*stavan*, *stava*, *stotra*, *stuti*, *sajjhai*, etc.) sometimes used interchangeably, poetic forms that derive different elements from different traditions and religions, and thematic and syntactic motifs that allude to or derive both from the diverse Jain literature and from the Western Indian milieu.

There are couplets in many stavan that suggest origins in other non-Jain genres. For example, in "O Compassionate One," the stavan which starts this chapter, the couplet—or at least the specific image—below is clearly borrowed from the lyrics of Mīrābāī:

> O merciful Lord, I have drunk the glass of poison,
> But you turned it from poison to nectar, is there no end to your mercy?

Mīrābāī tells the story of how the king sends poison in a cup to kill her and how Kṛṣṇa saves her life over and over in her poetry. (Harinārāyanji 1968; Hawley and Juergensmeyer 1988; Kishwar and Vanita 1989; Mukta 1994). In one famous poem she writes: "The king sent me a cup of poison, but when I drank it, you turned it to nectar."[2] In the stavan lyric there is little attempt to make a Jain couplet of it; the image of the compassion is enough to justify its inclusion in the stavan. With couplets that appear to derive from Muslim devotional lyrics (*gazals*), there is a stronger urge to frame the couplet in a Jain context. In the "Śrī Ajitnāth Stavan" the devotee is "addicted" to love—an image more appropriate to the love imagery of gazals than to the detached equanimity of Jainism—but still turns to the "Giver of Liberation" to be sure it is meritorious love:

> Am I addicted to the work of Love, oh Invincible Bliss of the Jinas?
> Without God in my heart, not even one moment is beautiful.

In another stavan the Jina is uniquely called the tower (*mināro*) to which the devotee retreats from worldly troubles. It is a unique image I haven't found elsewhere, but the use of the Muslim image (and language) here and in other stavan may reflect the realities of Jain-Muslim interaction in literary—as well as social (or work)—contexts. All this may suggest either a non-Jain source for the couplet or, more subtly, the deeper incorporation of Persian and Urdu motifs and ideas into Jain poetry.[3] Much like borrowed melodies which are discussed later in this chapter, the Jains have not rejected external sources for devotional materials; however, most lyrics based on another song are thoroughly "Jainized" before being sung as stavan.

The lines of influence are unclear and the obvious changes in taxonomy obscure any sense of linear development; the process seems to be one of an agglomeration of elements of poetry, music, and dance which find their way into the contemporary Jain performances. Of course, anyone who has sat through a Mārvāḍī (Khartar Gacch) Jain men's maṇḍaḷ performance in a predominantly Gujarātī (Tapā Gacch) temple, of stavan (written in Braj Bhāṣā) set to a Hindī film tune with its roots in a now popular form of Muslim devotional music (*qavali*) should not be surprised by such agglomeration. In his article focusing on the Jain scholar-monk, Hemacandra who collected many devotional narratives, Tubb (1998) argues that Hemacandra's "amalgamative approach" to text collection is characteristic of the approaches of Jain scholars of poetics on the whole, suggesting possibilities for seeing this amalgamative or agglomerative impulse as part of a Jain aesthetic surrounding texts more generally. The agglomeration itself may be a source for understanding what a Jain performance is and how it is created. The women in the Pārśva Maṇḍaḷ used the English word "fit" (*fit karvu*) many times with each other and with me to describe the meshing of lyrics, melody, dance, stavan content, and performance context. The use of various poetic, melodic and rhythmic styles for a performance illustrate a Jain aesthetic which privileges a "fit" between context, text, tune, gesture and poetics over the use of a specific genre, school of music or "Jain" source materials.

There are several words used to denote hymns within the Jain tradition: stavan, stuti, and stotra (and colloquially in Rājasthān, bhajan). Despite a confusing history of usage, these terms were each used differently among the contemporary Jains I knew. A stotra was a prayer to be recited or chanted, not sung; a stuti was an old prayer usually in Prakrit or Apabhraṁśa, which could be chanted or recited; a *sūtra* was usually a "fixed" text (which the reciter could never amend, append or emend—such as the Kalpa Sūtra or more humbly the two-line "Khamāsamāṇo Sūtra") recited often from memory; and a stavan was a devotional song.[4] The prayers for recitation within the caityavandan were usually referred to individually by their first lines; collectively they were the caityavandan (Cort 1995d). These prayers were called sūtras. Even the "Śakra Stava", which is mythologically and taxonomically seen as a stavan, was called the "Namotthuṇam Sūtra" by Jains I knew. The women did know, though, that the "Śakra Stava" and the "Namotthuṇam Sūtra" were names for the same text. The taxonomy is further complicated by the use of terms differently within the texts themselves; for example, caityavandan refers both to the short prayer recited at the beginning of the series of prayers recited in the daily worship and to that series of prayers as a whole.[5]

Jaini (1979) names three stava[6] among the canonical texts: the "Śakra Stava," which was spoken by Indra (Śakra) to praise a series of good qualities shared by all the Jinas; "Nāma-Jina-Stava," the "Caturviṁśatistava," where the twenty-four Jinas' names are recited; and "Śruta-Stava," which praises the canon and the Jinas. Williams (1963) includes all the sections of the caityavandan (daily prayers) as stava, though in contemporary usage the prayers were called sūtras and the songs, stavan. Though the stotra may have their origins as populist texts, as Jaini suggests, the stotra—mostly in Prakrit, Sanskrit and Apabhraṁśa / Old Gujarātī—are now as far beyond the comprehension of ordinary people as the canonical texts had been earlier. There are certain stotra which are widely read and recited, most notably the Bhaktāmara Stotra, but the bulk of devotional texts and hymns are the stavan. The Bhaktāmara Stotra is recited as a devotional act. I heard this stotra recited by an informal gathering of men and women (though mostly women) every morning at sunrise during Paryuṣan in 2000 and by a group of women during a bus pilgrimage in 1997. In 2000, Dadiji started reciting the Bhaktāmara Stotra each morning during her meditation. In his thesis Cort (1989) mentions the Bhaktāmara Stotra as a text men recited while performing pūjā. He found that many female mendicants also performed the Bhaktāmara Stotra. This stotra was not recited daily by most laywomen I met; it may be that—except for the eldest women—laywomen did not have enough time to recite the stotra during their worship. The Bhaktāmara Stotra is also ubiquitously reproduced in stavan collections, in the tiny books for receiving knowledge worship, in cassette recordings, and in illustrated texts, usually with photos of many of the particularly popular Jina images from various pilgrim destinations. Jaini (1979) explains that stotras—hymns of praise addressed to one or more Jinas—are the source for the lay understandings of Jain doctrine since only mendicants read canonical materials. Then Jaini goes on to explain several works and the ways that they popularize the "cultic worship" of the Jinas. In much the same way that he describes these stotra as functioning—dedicating verses to each Jina while explaining a philosophical point—several stavan I collected served both as a mnemonic explanation of Jain theology and as a source for an emotional tie with the Jina (often with a specific image in a particular location). The devvandan ritual (a recitation of a series of prayers dedicated individually to each of the twenty-four Jinas) probably derived from the caityavandan prayers (Cort 1989), and the stavan sung as part of the devvandan are a source for stavan stylistics and form. The devvandan's shorter stavan texts are more like the Śakra Stava in form, but each is dedicated to a specific Jina. The poetics, form, and content of the stavan seem to indicate that they derive in part from stava—such as the "Caturviṁśatistava" and the "Śakra Stava." These stava texts are recited as part of daily worship by Jains today.[7]

The term stavan first appears in early Gujarātī texts to refer to extended stotra-format devotional (more than didactic) literature written in the medieval period (eleventh to sixteenth century).[8] Krause (1952) examined seven of these early texts in late Apabhraṁśa or early Gujarātī called stotra, stuti and stavan. These seven devotional texts take their form from the stotra literature. Six of Krause's texts are addressed to a specific Jina (Munisuvrat, one; Pārśvanāth, two; Mahāvīr, two; and Sīmandhar Svāmī, one), and one lists the various pilgrimage sites. Two are addressed to site-specific Jinas: Śankheśvar Pārśvanāth and Varakāṇ Pārśvanāth. These texts begin with interchangeable descriptions of the Jinas. In later texts, we see the particularization of each of the Jina praised. Finally, the later texts also address location-specific Jina images. The use of the form to address specific Jinas, Jina images, and male mendicants is clearly illustrated in Nāhṭa's important collection of medieval Jain poetry—excerpted from various poetic forms of the same period (Nāhṭa 1975). There were a large number of anonymous (the author did not use a signature line) stavan and other devotional prayers (chand, *kalaś*, stotra, gīt, *phāgu*, etc.) collected in Nāhṭa's manuscript collection as well as a handful of songs written by laymen (*bhakt śrāvak*) dedicated to their gurus (Nāhṭa 1975); writing songs (especially, welcome songs to one's guru or to male mendicants spending the rainy season at one's temple) is still a common practice today. The use of the multitude of specific forms—like kalaś for the bathing of an image—suggests the use of these songs during Jain worship, much as they are used today. Stavan becomes a term used for the devotional songs addressed to Jinas themselves, and other genres (such as gīt) become differentiated; the language of these stavan shifts from generic praises of the Jinas to praises directed at specific Jinas and specific Jina images.

Given the confusions inevitable in taxonomic references across genres, let me take a moment to clarify what I mean by stavan.[9] Stavan are devotional songs sung by Jains. Among Pune Jains, stavan were usually sung in Gujarātī (and sometimes Mārvāḍī, Braj Bhāṣā, and Hindī); for the purposes of the discussion, I include two types of gīt in this study: tapasya gīt (fasting songs) and sādhu svāgatam gīt (male mendicant welcome songs). They are musically and poetically indistinguishable—in spite of their different subject matter and performance contexts—and the women I knew mixed the two types together in their collections of Jain songs. However, they were always taxonomically marked as gīt rather than stavan, probably because they address living (and not liberated) humans rather than Jinas or other perfect aspects of the Jain religion. Formal pūjā liturgical texts, which accompany extended formalized worship performances, are also sung, though they include chanted sections and mantras, too. The liturgical texts are usually sung by maṇḍaḷs, whereas the sponsor performs the pūjā. The written texts of these pūjās do not include stavan, but the maṇḍaḷ appended at least one stavan to each section. Thus both stavan and liturgical pūjā texts are part of the sung repertoire and should be seen as linked texts in the pūjā context. To understand the ways in which stavan are categorized by these Jain women, to highlight the multiple factors in stavan choice in performance contexts, and to give the reader a sense of the sound of these stavan genres, I turn to a discussion of stavan poetics and musicality.

Stavan Poetics

The poetic form that most closely resembles the modern stavan is the *pada* form. In performance, particularly popular couplets or the whole stavan were sometimes repeated. Likewise, the pada usually have four to seven rhyming couplets which use the first or second line of the whole poem as a refrain throughout. Following Jayadeva—and the South Indian bhakti poetry style which influenced Jayadeva—padas are usually marked also by the poet's name in the last line (Stoller-Miller 1977); the poet's name is included in the final line of some of the older stavan, but it has been dropped from use in many of the newer ones. Garbā poetry, which accompanies garbā dance at Nāvrātrī, is also in pada form. Stavan draw much of their imagery from these garbā poems—probably in part from the popular celebration of goddess festivals and worship—and the two traditions share certain performance aspects based in music and dance, as well. Thus the pada becomes a part of how one writes a devotional lyric. In addition, the reuse of the same melodies across the many traditions is simplified by using the same general poetic syntax.

The medieval period is marked by the rise of bhakti devotional poetry in North India. Vaiṣṇav poet saints dominate the historical studies of this literary period: Mīrābāī (in Braj Bhāṣā), Sūrdās (in Braj Bhāṣā), Tulsīdās (in Avadhī), Jñāneśvar (in Marāṭhī), Tukaram (in Marāṭhī), and Narsī Mehtā (in Gujarātī). Despite the extensive study of bhakti poetry in Hindu studies and the Jains' participation in the bhakti school (Dundas 1992), Jain poets remain mostly unstudied by Western scholars.[10] The importance in the poet-saint model of the authors as individuals (particularly with regard to the resistance of social norms) is central to the scholars' examination of the creative individual, but it elevates the writings of these named poets above that of unnamed writers in other forms and runs the risk of focusing on the works of a single poet with little reference to contemporary poets. These hagiographies—quite interesting and instructive about what a "saint" is supposed to be like—have made for exciting studies about various forms of Hindu religion.[11] However, it has left the Jain devotional or bhakti literature outside the discussion, the conference, the collected volume, and the classroom, thus reproducing the marginality of the Jain texts which are, at the very least, a parallel development in the medieval period that has continued to evolve to the present.

The Jain bhakti poets seem to have made little effort to individuate themselves and were anything but resistant to cultural norms; most of the poets were male mendicants—who are determinant in the development of Jain morality—and the poems are reproduced in volumes often edited by the present-day mendicants. (The collections do not have, then, the cachet of having once been rebellious.) These poets suggest ways that bhakti can work within the Jain system. Stavan suggest—through the texts and the obviously normative roles of the poets themselves—that bhakti-style devotionalism did not suggest the social upheaval in the Jain tradition that it did in much of the Hindu tradition (Chitre 1991; Hawley and Juergensmeyer

1988; Mukta 1994; Ramanujan 1973). Jain devotionalism, therefore, took a different color. The inward focus of Jain orthopraxy—where it is the soul that is purified more than the god who is pleased—made stavan more likely to focus on a celebration of the Jina's moral characteristics rather than his "play" or "sport" (*līlā*). The content of stavan is quite different from Hindu bhakti poetry even when using similar poetic strategies and forms. Moreover, Jain poets did not develop the kind of personae that the Hindu poets did. Even the standard use of the poet's name in the final line of the pada poetic form is often dropped in Jain stavan.[12] A stavan is not an artifact of a particular saint, and the singers are welcome to change radically the lyrics and the melodies of stavan to fit their performance needs.

Stavan vary from poetic to prosaic, from beautiful lyrics to songs resembling treatises more than poems. The lyrics can be examined through Sanskrit-based schools of aesthetics as well as through the aesthetic judgments of the women who sing them. Sanskrit poetics are split into two major paradigms: alaṅkār and rasa (Dimock 1974). The alaṅkār (or ornament) devices include both metaphors and the music of the poetry. Thus, under this heading one sees the analysis of a simile as well as a study of rhyme. Rasa poetics is a theory of mood with regard to the eloquence of a poem's evocation. There are eight rasas (love, humor, pity/compassion, wrath, heroism, terror, disgust, and wonder) which one might evoke in a piece of poetry as outlined in Bharata's *Nāṭyaśāstra*. The stavan—addressed to the detached Jinas—should not even desire to evoke these moods in the moodless Jina; clearly, it is the singer and listeners whose proper sentiments are to be evoked through the stavan's poetry. Udbhaṭa (a rasa theory author of the early ninth century) added, to Bharata's eight rasas, the ninth rasa of calm or peace (śānt) to which most stavan aim their poetics.[13] While there are a few devotional lyrics in the stavan which seem to aim for the rasa of love or the rasa of compassion, the bulk of the stavan address the rasa of peace and thus attempt to evoke peacefulness in the listener. The writers achieve this peaceful effect through a variety of poetic devices that calm the listener. The alaṅkār devices discussed next illustrate the ways in which the words themselves and the words within their lines evoke certain moods and sentiments that contribute to a work's rasa. In doing this, I do not conform entirely to rasa theory, which focuses on the whole work or major section as having a single rasa rather than the line or stanza. The whole work must reflect a single mood. Stavan, on the whole, aim for this through the use of a single motif, either in imagery or in poetics.

The importance of erotic love (*śṛngār*) and parental love (*vatsalya*) in the Vaiṣṇav poetry is not really an appropriate rasa for Jain male mendicants to evoke without the subsequent reversal to renunciation that so characterizes Jain erotic or romantic works (Ryan 1985, 1998). These poems, then, may have been overlooked simply because they lack, programmatically, several thematic elements that attracted the Western or Western-educated ear to their contemporaries—indeed, much of the criticism directed at the Jain aesthetic has focused on what it is not, and when it has attempted fleeting positive critiques, it has labeled it "didactic" and moved on.[14] Stavan, though they use and refer to the rasas of love and heroism, focus on the rasa of peace or compassion, more "Jain-like" both in devotional style and in aesthetic value. Stavan are not didactic poems negating worldly attachments (as represented in most of the classical Jain literature); they are the positive lyric models for Jain poetry affirming Jain devotion to the Jinas and Jain ideals.

The aesthetics of stavan also draw from the alaṅkār school of poetics. One focus of the alaṇkār school of poetics is simile. The most prevalent simile in the stavan was the *rūpaka*, identification of image and subject, and its most common use was didactic. One form of rūpaka, a kind of extended simile in which constituents of the two image sets parallel, appears in "Knowledge is Given," where the various parts of the Jina image are described as containing the various ideals of Jainism:

> In the eyes, your affection is seated, on your face, the empire of peace,
> In your chest, non-violence dwells, on your lips, the royal truth.

In a sense Jainism is the Jina image. Throughout this stavan the Jina is identified with a variety of objects: gold, a boat, the shore of the ocean, a carrier, and the helmsman. The image of water—the sea of worldly emotions and attachments—is pervasive in Jain stavan.[15] Aside from the epithet of the Jina as the "ocean of compassion," the Jina is identified also with the method of crossing the water or in the image of the shore (where the boat is usually the Jain religion); the Jina is the still boundary of the sea of emotions. Likewise, in the stavan the Jain religion is described not as a "path" (as one finds in Jain didactic literature) but as a boat, sometimes with the Jina as the helmsman steering the devotees across the ocean of life, suggesting that there is more to Jain devotion to Jinas than following in the Jina's footsteps. Many of these images illustrate requests from Jain devotees not for a role model to emulate but an active agent of some kind of grace.

By examining the use of imagery in one stavan, we may see how stavan both articulate Jain theology and practice and reflect the singers' experiences of Jain devotion. The stavan "My Golden Throne" illustrates, through its method of description, the movement of the devotee from the initial dazzle of the golden throne to an intimate vision of the Jina. The devotee first encounters the opulence of the temple and the assembly hall/ throne (samavasaraṇ):

> In my temple there's a golden throne, O God, your image looks beautiful.
> The diamond-covered dome, the jeweled dome, the handsome mountain frames you.

The jewels and the gold show the grandeur of the Jina and the high level of spiritual donations to that Jina. There are two levels: (1) the Jina in his cosmic glory and (2) the Jina image in the devotee's temple. Thus the throne in the stavan can be both the throne-like stand in which the Jina image is placed for formal pūjās and the assembly hall that the gods build around the Jina whenever he stops to preach. The Jina's jewelry and ornaments can be seen as literally the jewels of the Jina image decoration (*angī*), and thus the generous gift of a wealthy devotee to the temple:

> Your heavy gold crown sparkling looks so very beautiful
> Your armbands and bracelets look so very beautiful
> In your ears, the shining earrings look so very beautiful
> The pearls in your nine stringed necklace look so very beautiful.

These ornaments may also be read as symbolizing, in a more abstract way, the good qualities of the Jina and his teachings. In the fasting song, "Fast-Breaking Day," the woman is said to wear her fast like a crown: "The glory of that fast's crown keeps shining." The gems the Jina wears are more glorious but may be the beauty of his acts or nonacts as well as the more material understanding of these ornaments as the image's decoration. Likewise, the flowers used to worship and decorate the Jina are described:

The campā, roses and jasmine flowers look so very beautiful
Like going to the jasmine bush, you look so beautiful.

When the images are decorated, the flowers, instead of being distinct entities, meld into a flowery texture of a single basic color. The effect can be overwhelming, as the Jina image and its surroundings are designed in stripes of yellow (*campā*), red (roses), and white (jasmine). The devotee finds the Jina within all this opulence and then has darśan of the Jina. Paradoxically, the devotee has to wade through the worldly offerings—which alone lead to "real" darśan—in order to see the Jina himself.

The moment of darśan is made palpable by a change in the line length of the lyrics and the rhythm and melody of the music. Suddenly everything is different. The Jina's darśan gives the devotee the chance and the confidence to ask for the Jina's attention:

O God, your face is beautiful.
Will you ferry us across the sea of emotions?
O God, accept our request, O Lord
Cut off our sorrow and give us the joy of liberation.
The maṇḍaḷ sees your greatness, we came to you Lord
O the Pārśva Maṇḍaḷ sing songs, today show yourself.

Asking for the joy of liberation, the devotee may be asking that these be the result of the "real" darśan found at his face. The request that the Jina "show" himself, an act the Jina is not going to do because he has transcended the mundane world—even the mundane world of the Jain temple—is all the more a statement of faith. The stavan has the maṇḍaḷ looking through all the materiality—the pomp and grandeur—for the Jina himself, obscured in a way by the very attempts to encounter him, and made plain again through metaphor. In this way, metaphor itself becomes a vehicle for the problematic duality of Jain pūjā: material image/nonattached Jina. Reflecting the process of darśan, in which a physical image leads one to (transcendent) understanding, the singing of the image's physical attributes ends with a renunciation of those material attributes.

Many stavan, such as the one examined previously, are written around extended metaphors as a link from verse to verse. In others, the repetition of whole phrases in a stavan tie the text together. The repetitions take two forms; in some stavan the refrain comes after each line. In "Mahāvīr Śrī Bhagavān," the refrain is also the name of the Jina and serves as remembering the name of God (*nām smaraṇ*) as well as holding the text of the stavan together:

We are filled with your glance,
  Mahāvīr Śrī Bhagavān
You give darśan, you cut away sorrow
  Mahāvīr Śrī Bhagavān

The repetition (the melody of the refrain is unvarying) has the effect of making the stavan seem chant-like and hypnotic. From line to line there is not as much concern for rhyme because the refrain dominates the poetic language. When the refrain is used more like a chorus is used in English songs, the effect is simply to tie the many verses together. There are other stavan which have a line repeated after each couplet. This form instead provides a background against which the verses stand out as if in relief; the music of the refrain is often in a somewhat different rhythm. In the pada form (in which most stavan are written) the standard refrain is one of the lines from the first couplet, which is then repeated throughout the stavan. An example from the "Śrī Śāntināth Stavan" shows how the refrain makes the whole stavan into a repeated request for the Jina's attention:

Accept my praise, King! Excellent Lord Śānti!
O Acīrājī's son, we came lovingly to you for darśan.
O Lord whose faith delights us, our devotion brought us to you.
Accept my praise, King! Excellent Lord Śānti!

Your promise is to reduce sorrow, our hope is the same as yours.
You are passionless and free, what is the state of our consciousness?
Accept my praise, King! Excellent Lord Śānti!

The use of the repeated refrain serves to tie the whole song together and usually has its own musical refrain as well.

Whereas the musical component of language (*śabda-alaṅkār*) was seen by the alaṅkār poets as less central than figures of speech (Dimock 1974), the poetic devices of alliteration, rhyme, and meter are central to the effectiveness of the stavan as songs. The poetic devices most often used in the stavan are rhyme (both end rhyme and internal rhyme) and alliteration. Because of the grammatical structure of Gujarātī (subject-object-verb), which it shares with the Sanskritic languages, end rhyme is not difficult. If the subject remains the same in number and gender, the verbs will make the lines end with a rhyme over at least two syllables. An example, though there are hundreds, from "Kesarīyā O Kesarīyā"—a not especially poetic stavan:

Tara Gīto Hu Gāu, Manmandir Padh<u>arāvū</u>
  Tarī Mudrāo Vārī <u>Jāū</u>, Vārī <u>Jāū</u>
Jal Kalaśā M<u>arāvū</u> Snātra Vidhīye K<u>arāvū</u>
  Mārā Antarnā Mel Dho<u>varāū</u>

Thus, the kind of polysyllabic end rhyme which is so difficult in English is simple in Gujarātī and Hindī. Perhaps because of the influence of the gazal poetics, the lines often end with a repeated word (*Re* or *Lol* are the most common), with the rhyme including the repeated phrase and the word before it; here is an example from the stavan "Śankheśvar Svāmī":

Dukh Sankaṭane K<u>āpo</u>, <u>Svāmī</u>!
Vānchītane <u>Āpo</u>, <u>Svāmī</u>!

The effect, despite its ease, is to solidify the pattern of the song, which makes it easier to remember, to sing, and to anticipate the coming lines. The music of the rhymes, because they are linguistically natural, prevents some of the chimey nature of mediocre rhymed verse in English.

Alliteration is the most often used poetic device after end rhyme. It is used in two ways: first, by repeating initial consonants or vowels and second, by using different words which share the same root, which gives a kind of alliteration and assonance that makes the line both meaningful in the sense of carrying meaning (the meanings of the words that are part of the alliterative pattern are conjoined) and nonsensical, in the sense that the repetition of the same two or three consonants almost dissolves into vocables. The effect can be both overwhelming and almost mantric, as it is in this example from "Say the Navkār":

Jāp Japo Japate Raho, Dipak Jalape He.

The final example alternates a long ā and a short a, creating an echoic effect. This device can be used throughout a stavan, changing the pervasive consonants in each line or couplet.

The stavan that begins this chapter, "O Compassionate One," is the best example (that I collected) of the use of these poetic devices in creating a composed and beautiful lyric. I give this stavan in transliteration so that someone without Gujarātī might be able to appreciate the sound of the lyrics:

He Karuṇānā Karaṇārā, Tārī Karuṇāno Koī Pār Nathī?
He Sankaṭanā Haraṇārā, Tārī Karuṇāno Koī Pār Nathī?

Me Pāp Kavyā Che Evā, Hu Bhūlyo Tārī Sevā
Mārī Bhulonā Bhūlanārā, Tārī Karuṇāno Koī Pār Nathī?

Hu Antarmā Thaī Rājī, Khelyo Chu Avḷī Bājī
Avaḷī Ne Savaḷī Karaṇārā, Tārī Karuṇāno Koī Pār Nathī?

He Param Kṛupāḷū[16] Vhālī, Me Pīdhā Viṣnā Pyālī
Viṣane Amaṛut Karaṇārā, Tārī Karuṇāno Koī Pār Nathī?

Mane Jaḍato Nathī Kināro, Māro Kyāthī Āvyo Āro
O Mārā Sācā Sevanhārā, Tārī Karuṇāno Koī Pār Nathī?

Che Māru Jīvan Udāsī, Tu Śaraṇe Le Avināśī
Mārā Dilamā He Ramaṇārā, Tārī Karuṇāno Koī Pār Nathī?

The repetitions within each line of the same vowels and consonants gives this stavan an especially lilting sound. Likewise, the internal rhymes expand on the sense of the verses as connected by musicality. The end rhyme is subordinated to a rhyme pattern based on the internal rhymes of the first line and the way that the second lines of each couplet rhyme with each other. This results in a rhyme pattern if divided by quarters (rather than lines) of AB, AB| CC, AB| DD, AB| EE, AB| FF, AB| GG, AB|. In addition, if one only looks at the vowels without the consonants in the rhymes, the repetition is increased, with most of the quarter lines ending in the vowel pattern a then i—though one verse has ā then o (*Kināro/Āro*) and another e then ā (*Evā/Sevā*) to close the quarter lines. The slant rhymes, particularly those in the initial quarter of each line, hint at an initial rhyme without actually making one:

Mane Jaḍato Nathī Kināro, Māro Kyāthī Āvyo Āro
O Mārā Sācā Sevanahārā, Tārī Karuṇāno Koī Pār Nathī?
Che Māru Jīvan Udāsī, Tu Śaraṇe Le Avināśī
Mārā Dilamā He Ramaṇārā, Tārī Karuṇāno Koī Pār Nathī?

The initial rhymes are reflected in assonance through the verse, an assonance used lightly and effectively in this stavan. In a more heavy-handed line, the alliteration works against the repeated line by suggesting a connection with the p sound in the refrain:

He Param Kṛupāḷū Vhālī, Me Pīdhā Viṣnā Pyālī
Viṣane Amaṛut Karaṇārā, Tārī Karuṇāno Koī Pār Nathī?

The assonance of the p against the v sound creates a sound like a singer breathing. The stavan uses repeated opposing consonant sounds throughout the lyrics, giving the song a "living" quality not reflected in those lyrics where the lines use primarily related consonants (p with b and m, for example). The use of oppositional content as shown in the second verse bring out further alliteration and assonance by using the same verb stem:

Me Pāp Kavyā Che Evā, Hu Bhūlyo Tārī Sevā
Mārī Bhulonā Bhūlanārā, Tārī Karuṇāno Koī Pār Nathī?

My sin is doing this, I have forgotten to do your worship.
O forgetter of my forgetfulness, is there no end to your mercy?[17]

Throughout the stavan these quarter lines become epithets for the compassionate Jina, and the effect is a litany of the compassionate acts of the Jina. The stavan as a whole uses alliteration and assonance to create a feeling of the breathing of the singer. The images show the Jina's compassion and the singer's humility. The close melding of the poetic music, the uses of repetition, and the content of this stavan made women repeatedly name this stavan as a favorite.

Although the foregoing discussion of stavan poetics helps to situate stavan poetry in a relationship to Sanskrit aesthetic theory and Hindu devotional poetry, it does not represent the ways in which Jain women spoke of stavan aesthetics. The women's conversations about stavan aesthetics were set squarely in their understanding of how to organize and when to perform stavan.

Categorizing Stavan

In most published stavan collections the stavan are not divided into any categories, nor were they organized in any explicit order. In 1995, the ubiquitous *Śrī Sudhāras Stavan Saṅgrah* came out with a new edition (Śankheśvar 1995) in which stavan are divided (for the first time) into two categories: stavan and *bhāvnā* (devotional) stavan. The first category—the unmarked stavan—includes most of the stavan found in earlier editions of the *Sudhāras Stavan Saṅgrah*; the second category includes primarily popular stavan which the women with whom I spoke called "good for performance." None of the bhāvnā stavan were included in the earlier versions of the *Sudhāras Stavan Saṅgrah* I examined and they have not acquired the neocanonical status that the stavan in the previous editions have. I suspect that the separation of the stavan and the bhāvnā stavan serves two purposes: (1) to include the new stavan that are most popular, thereby both increasing sales of the *Sudhāras Stavan Saṇgrah* and preventing people from turning to the newer publications, which include almost all new stavan; and (2) to clearly demarcate the old and proven stavan from the new popular ones. This distinction was unnecessary for the earlier editions of the *Sudhāras Stavan Saṇgrah*, in which the "stavan" category (as organized in the 1995 and 1998 editions) was synonymous with the *Sudhāras Stavan Saṇgrah*'s repertoire of stavan and all those stavan called bhāvnā stavan (in the 1985 and 1998 *Sudhāras Stavan Saṇgrah* editions) were only to be found in the newly published stavan collections.

The women I knew divided the stavan into three categories: good meaning (*saro arth*), beautiful (*sundar*), and good for maṇḍaḷ performance (*maṇḍaḷī*). These categories reflected the contexts in which the stavan would be best performed. When categorizing stavan, women made decisions that were based on both content of the lyrics and their aesthetic judgment about the sound of the stavan as sung. Like decorated Jina images (Cort 2000), stavan can only be fully understood if the Jain devotee's aesthetic experience (here, the sound of the stavan) is brought to the discussion. The choices for the general performance context and for the taxonomy of stavan are largely made on these aesthetic grounds. Loosely, the "beautiful" stavan category shared much with the *Sudhāras Stavan Saṇgrah* category of "stavan," while the "good for maṇḍaḷ performance" category resembled that of that book's category of "bhāvnā stavan." These were not hard-and-fast categories; several stavan could be primarily in one category and yet be used along with those of another. These categories themselves as categories seemed fairly stable, but the repertoire of stavan included in each category was less so. Likewise, not all women put the same stavan in the same category and an individual woman might not always categorize a stavan the same way over time. Briefly here, the "good meaning" stavan tended to be those stavan whose content was either explicitly didactic or whose content suggested the stavan's use for learning. The "beautiful" stavan were most often those written to older "Jain" melodies, whereas the "good for performance" stavan were, more often than not, new stavan written to existing melodies drawn from either Hindi film music or Gujarātī rās-garbā music and which lent themselves to group performance. For a few more organized collectors these categories were reified by their use as organizing principles for stavan notebook collections.

A further look at the three categories illuminates some of the rationales behind the use of particular stavan and the ways that stavan repertoires are controlled. The "good meaning" stavan are primarily those whose theological or instructive messages are both clear and normative. The stavan in this category were the most clearly delineated in my discussions with contemporary laywomen; it was this category they most commonly offered without any prompting or questioning. This kind of stavan was the least commonly performed, though it is widely collected. These stavan's meaning and educational potential made them stavan one might include in one's collection, even though these stavan were often particularly stilted poetically and musically. However, that they were collected at all points to the importance of "meaning" in the collection of stavan.

"Good meaning" stavan often celebrated the orthodox values of Jainism through glorification of fasting or through the abstract concepts of Jainism. Many women showed me the words to these songs in their notebooks, saying that they had "good meaning" (*saro arth*) and would be a good place to learn the meanings of Jainism. In their lyrics, the abstract stavan focus on the ideals of asceticism, knowledge, and merit rather than the more devotional aspects of Jain theology. If I asked for a stavan that explained Jainism, I was always shown one of these didactic stavan—despite the fact that they were rarely sung. In the role of "teacher of Jainism," women chose these stavan; when they were in the role of singer or devotee, they chose other stavan—usually ones with smoother and more "beautiful" or celebratory poetics or musicality.

This idealization and abstraction extends also to those stavan that celebrate practices illuminating normative ideas, such as in "Pūjā Sandalwood," where the daily pūjā is described as directly contributing to one's spiritual liberation: "In the sandalwood for sandalwood pūjā is the light of liberation, but in the sandalwood of the world is man's darkness." This stavan gets at the transformation of an object through its association with pūjā; the "nature" of the sandalwood is altered by being used for worship. In the stavan "Say the Navkār," the meaning and efficacy of the Navkār Mantra is described. The mantra itself tells us that it destroys all sin, but the stavan expands to include some of the other beliefs about the power of the mantra: that it can protect the speaker from sin (many women also said from evil), that it brings happiness, and that reciting the mantra itself helps one gain knowledge:

> Saying the Navkār Mantra, everyone is happy.
> In life, one's body and mind are always filled with sorrow;
> In the garden of the heart, the flowers of joy bloom.
> Saying the Navkār Mantra, everyone is happy.
>
> It has sixty-eight syllables;
> He who concentrates on it, his sorrow disappears.
> The five highest ones are purifying, and
> The Navpadjī[18] is also pure.
> Say the names, keep saying them and cut the binds of karma!
>
> From sin one is saved and protected.
> Sorrow comes but we endure it laughing.
> One should protect the Navkār;
> These are the nine praises of the Arhats.
> Say the names, keep saying them and destroy all troubles!
>
> When someone is angry with us,
> The hearts duel and one abandons the relationship;
> Don't take this sadness in your soul.
> Keep the name of the great lord in your heart.
> Say the names, keep saying them and light the lamp of knowledge!

The "Navkār Mantra" is believed contemporarily by many Jains to have magical powers, a belief also illustrated by the earlier miracle narratives about the mantra's recitation. The stavan puts into verse a central principle of jap (name recitation): If one continuously says a God's name, one's mind is concentrated on that God; it is believed that this concentration leads to well-being. "Say the Navkār," like "Pūjā Sandalwood," was occasionally sung as a part of the longer formal pūjās but neither was very popular. In addition, the "good meaning" stavan were rarely sung as women's personal stavan; I suspect the abstract nature was not especially moving and the poetry and music were usually awkward at best. In a sense, this category justified the collection of stavan that were neither "beautiful" nor good for maṇḍaḷ performance yet seemed worth collecting. These stavan serve as occasionally sung sources for learning and reminders of the efficacy of Jain practices. Likewise, these stavan would remind the singers and hearers of the normative understanding of a particular practice.

The other two categories were much more difficult to delineate partly because the nature of the categories was aesthetic and there was no completely uniform view of aesthetics. Here I reconstruct the categories from stavan selected as particularly well suited for each category. The "beautiful" were those in which poetics and musicality were more central than didactic messages. There were four stavan widely named as beautiful: "Śrī Śantināth Stavan," "Mahāvīr Śrī Bhagavān," "O Compassionate Lord," and "Look at Śrī Pārśva." These four were among the most commonly sung stavan I heard; they were widely known and sung both as personal stavan choices as part of one's daily worship and as congregational stavan at gatherings or on pilgrimage. However, none of these was commonly used in the context of the formal pūjās or maṇḍaḷ performances. Likewise, when I asked women to sing a stavan informally or formally—when I was recording—these were among the most commonly sung, which may stem from the women's comfort level with the stavan, the stavan's potential for beauty particularly in terms of a singer's virtuosity, and their place as women's favorite stavan.

These four stavan, along with others in the beautiful stavan category, share several features which seem to mark them as a category. This category, even more than the other categories, depends on an understanding of the "family resemblance" between the various selections. The following description is less a framing of the category of beautiful stavan than an outline of some of the reasons women deemed a particular stavan beautiful. The features that marked the four foregoing stavan included the melody, the poetry of the lyrics, and the sentiment (*bhāv*) of the lyrics. The sentiment of the stavan's lyrics was sometimes included by women when they explained why a particular stavan was beautiful. In much the same way that a particular image, temple, or image decoration can be said to carry miraculous or magic power (*camatkārī*) or can inspire intense devotional sentiments (Babb 1996; Cort 1988, 1989, 1997, 2000; Laidlaw 1995), particular stavan were said to evoke the devotional sentiment in the singer more effectively than were others. Usually this evocation occurred because the stavan effectively provoked an emotional response in the singer (*rāsik bhāv*). For the more elusive response of memory, women also spoke of how a stavan reminded them of a particular temple or pilgrimage and the beauty of the location was transposed onto the stavan that reminded them of the location. The four stavan listed above shared a few sentiments. The Jinas are described as an active agent of grace: giver of liberation and well-being, giver of darśan and blessings, destroyer of troubles, giver of peace, protector of the devotee. While the

Jina as an agent of grace may appear in the "good for performance" stavan, it was a less common motif; in the beautiful stavan it is a dominant motif. The Jina as an agent of grace is discussed further in the context of daily pūjā. However, not all stavan with a grace theme were seen as universally beautiful, nor did every beautiful stavan include a Jina as an agent of grace. The "beautiful" category can be seen as primarily an aesthetic—rather than theological—category with its focus on the musicality and poetics of the stavan.

The poetry of the "beautiful" stavan was again marked by more alliteration and often a more consistent poetic meter and rhyme scheme. Earlier I discuss the poetics of two stavan regularly referred to as "beautiful" stavan: "O Compassionate Lord" and "Mahāvīr Śrī Bhagavān." The other stavan called beautiful usually shared the overall effect of good poetry. However, the successful link of the poetic meter of a stavan to a complex melody was the most consistent feature of those stavan called beautiful. The melodies of the beautiful stavan were often those melodies that were seen as "Jain" and were slow and complex. The exception to this was a stavan "Rock Mahāvīr's Cradle," which, though uniquely (for the beautiful stavan) written to a Hindi film song melody, was called beautiful too. However, the melody when examined included many of the same features as the "Jain" melodies: the slow uneven rhythm, a complex melody based on a fairly wide tonal range; it did not rely on the standard timbre or arrangements of Hindi film music. This melody was used as a lullaby in the film context (and perhaps was borrowed from a traditional lullaby or Kṛṣṇa birth song for the film) and was reproduced as a lullaby stavan for the celebration of Mahāvīr's birth and was sung at a naming ceremony in June 2000. Many of these were associated with older stavans (though occasionally a new stavan was written to a Jain melody) and were some of the most widely sung during personal worship. They were among the most often called "beautiful" by the women themselves and they were the more difficult melodies women sang. The aesthetic of the Jain stavan melodies with their slow but clear movement and the flexible line length were considered good for introspection and meditation. The Jain melodies dominated the solo stavan singing and were described to me many times by different women, as "beautiful" (sundar) and "religious" (*dharmik*). The solo singing does not rely on unison singing and the use of percussion to guarantee an orderly performance. It is here in the women's morning worship that one sees virtuoso singing. The singing is still relatively unornamented, but timing is fluid and key phrases in the stavan text accented.

The "good for performance" stavan dominated singing in formal liturgical pūjās and devotional singing sessions (bhāvnā) in homes, in temples, and on pilgrimage. Those stavan, which were named as "good for performance," were the largest group named—probably because the bulk of the women I knew were maṇḍaḷ singers and because maṇḍaḷs change their repertoire more frequently than individual singers do. This was the most publicly negotiated category as well because it was often in the context of maṇḍaḷ practice that the women would hear a "good for performance" stavan and there they would, by their enthusiasm, discussions, or dismissal, rate a stavan in terms of its performative value. Thus not only were these stavan rarely present in the active repertoire of women who did not presently sing in a maṇḍaḷ, but judgments about them at maṇḍaḷ practice accentuated their visibility as a category. Within the "good for performance" stavan there were groups of stavan considered good for performance in certain contexts. These stavan were virtually all written either to Gujarātī folk dance melodies or to Hindi film song music melodies; virtually none written to Gujarātī folk dance melodies or Hindi film melodies were included in the "beautiful" category. This clear distinction reflects the impulse of the maṇḍaḷ to both entertain and articulate the celebratory nature of the pūjās as much as of the individual to privilege the more difficult-to-perform "Jain" melodies used for "beautiful" stavan. The "good for performance" stavan were virtually all marked with an upbeat tempo, a steady rhythm facilitating group singing, lyrics generally focused on devotional (rather than didactic) themes, and a melody with an easily recognizable "hook." When stavan from the "beautiful" category were performed in the context of these devotional singing sessions, their musicality was restructured to conform to the "good for performance" musicality: even line length, steady and pronounced pulse, lines repeated in a call-and-response format, and sometimes the addition of pūjā performance instrumentation—drums, hand percussion, and clapping.

Making Choices about Stavan Performance

The Śrī Pārśva Mahila Maṇḍaḷ met (and still meets) at the Ajitnāth mendicants' hostel every Saturday afternoon. Maṇḍaḷ practice was (and is) a primary locus for stavan learning. Most weeks, one or two women came with a new stavan for the maṇḍaḷ to try out. The collector sang the stavan for the maṇḍaḷ once through. Then the women all sang in a "call-and-response" format through the entire stavan. If the stavan was received enthusiastically by the singers, the maṇḍaḷ sang it several more times until the women had a comfortable familiarity with at least the melody and chorus. If a stavan was not liked by anyone, it usually died in the first run-through; whenever that happened I never heard the stavan again at maṇḍaḷ practice.[19] If a stavan was worked on beyond a single run-through, the maṇḍaḷ would eventually learn (usually either that day or in the next couple of weeks) the stavan, and at the end of maṇḍaḷ practice, the women copied the lyrics from the original diary into their own stavan diary. Often, other women in the bringer's family or a close friend had already copied the lyrics into their diary, and there would be several copies to work from. This preview of the stavan (which leads to the other copies) was also where the women tried out their stavan to see if others thought it should be brought to the maṇḍaḷ. Several times when Ranjana and I stopped by Savita's house after morning pūjā, Savita showed Ranjana the lyrics to a new stavan she had found. Savita asked whether Ranjana thought it would be a "good" one. If Ranjana said yes, Savita sang the verse and chorus through and they would chat about the stavan for a bit. Ranjana then copied the lyrics into her diary (if she had it with her). At maṇḍaḷ practice Ranjana sang along with Savita on the choruses. This would be especially important for the less secure or central singers in the maṇḍaḷ. For the less confident singers, it would also give them another voice or two to sing with while presenting the stavan, to avoid a solo singing performance. If Ranjana and Savita—the two strongest singers in the maṇḍaḷ—agreed, this almost always guaranteed the stavan's place in the repertoire.

The maṇḍaḷ's learning of a stavan does not guarantee it a spot in the active repertoire; ultimately, someone must be willing to sing the lead, the stavan must fit into a performance context, and it must acquire a finalized performance style. Two negotiations at maṇḍaḷ practice over the presentation of a stavan highlight the dynamic of stavan introduction: the first, on January 15, 1994, and the second several months later on the June 18, 1994. On January 15, Pramila (the maṇḍaḷ president) introduced a new stavan, "Let It, Let It Be." After one run-through solo and one pass as a group, Savita questioned the phrasing of the line; she thought it should be less plodding.[20] Manisha, Pramila's niece, suggested another way of phrasing the line—with a lighter accent on the rhythmic pulse—and the maṇḍaḷ tried it. Savita interrupted the singing, because she was not satisfied with Manisha's phrasing. Pramila suggested that if the drum rhythm were steady, Manisha's phrasing would work and suggested an alternative rhythm. Savita did not agree and gave a rephrasing of the melody (in a syncopated rhythm) and the maṇḍaḷ acquiesced. Then Ranjana suggested a clapping rhythm and they tried it. At this point, at the other end of the maṇḍaḷ's facing parallel lines, women began to chat. Pramila suggested a clapping rhythm which changed the singing rhythm back to her original phrasing, but it was rejected by Savita. The maṇḍaḷ then tabled the stavan for next week, signaling temporary abandonment; a few weeks later Pramila began singing this stavan during a pūjā performance and the maṇḍaḷ joined in. She sang the stavan in the way that she had originally introduced it (but had obviously practiced enough to be confident in her singing), and the singers accepted her version. The stavan was then incorporated into the active repertoire.

In the Pārśva Maṇḍaḷ, Savita and Ranjana are the strongest singers and also officers of the maṇḍaḷ. This does not give them unlimited influence, but to override one of their suggestions is difficult. Pramila was the president of the maṇḍaḷ but not as strong a singer; in fact, she does not often lead stavan in pūjās or practice. Because of this, Savita and Ranjana felt comfortable taking over the stylistic presentation of the stavan. When Manisha—a young unmarried woman and an excellent performer with very strong opinions about stavan singing—tried to support her aunt's interpretation, her youth and relative newness to the singing maṇḍaḷ made her opinion easy to override. However, when Pramila—the president of the maṇḍaḷ—argued her own case, she was given the opportunity to be heard. In the end, when Pramila suggested another rhythm and Savita rejected it, the stakes became to high for this stavan and it was temporarily abandoned. In the maṇḍaḷ practice, Savita's equal authority meant the maṇḍaḷ would have to "take sides." Pramila's later reintroduction during a pūjā was a democratic demonstration of her stavan's acceptance. In the pūjā context, everyone joined in on the song, suggesting that they liked the song—in fact, it was a very popular stavan for the rest of the year. Savita joined in the singing as well—a signal that she accepted Pramila's performance style and the conflict evaporated—as she could have "sat out" the performance of this stavan. In 1999, Ranjana's daughter, Soni, introduced a new stavan during maṇḍaḷ practice. Savita questioned Soni's phrasing and set out a new timing. Ranjana reintroduced Soni's version and it was accepted fairly quickly, suggesting that a young age and new status in the maṇḍaḷ makes it harder to introduce new stavan and/or the particulars of performance of the new stavan.

On June 18, 1994, Ranjana introduced a new stavan, "Whoever Goes to Pālītāṇā," which she had learned during her visit to her mother's house. While debating the way to sing this new stavan, Kanchanben insisted that there was a longer pause between the verse and the refrain. No one listened to her, and she said, "I have a cassette where the song is *correct.*" Kanchanben used the English word, "correct," for emphasis here. Maluben rolled her eyes, and Kanchanben's suggestion was overruled. Kanchanben's attempt to boost the strength of her suggestion by citing a recording failed partly because Maluben does not particularly like stavan cassettes which often use Hindī film melodies. Maluben was the only member of the Pārśva Maṇḍaḷ who had shown resistance to the use of popular Hindī film song melodies, a resistance she showed primarily by not singing them. As the founder of the maṇḍaḷ and a strong and opinionated woman, Maluben's rejection carried a fair amount of weight. No one wanted to have a conflict with her; there were times when Maluben voiced sentiments that others thought (and may have discussed with her) but would not have said outside private conversation. Second, because Kanchanben's suggestions on the whole carried little weight—perhaps from her relatively lax attendance of maṇḍaḷ events or from a view that she was not much of a singer—it was quite easy for Maluben to dismiss her version in favor of Ranjana's version. To continue with the account of this stavan, later, when Ranjana tried her clapping pattern again, Savita suggested a more graceful snapping pattern in the same rhythm. Sheelu suggested a different clapping pattern with a slightly different rhythm and Kanchanben jumped in with her original timing. The maṇḍaḷ without pause started out with Sheelu's pattern, which they ultimately adopted. Later I told Ranjana that I had a copy of the cassette that Kanchanben mentioned and she asked to hear it; she said she liked the version that she learned in Karaḍ better. The maṇḍaḷ's performance of this stavan finally resembled the cassette version only in the basic lyrics. Inclusion on a commercial cassette did little in this case to establish an authoritative style of performance; only once did I hear a stavan sung in the style of the commercial tapes (by a hired solo male singer at the Makar Sankranti program). The maṇḍaḷs' access to recorded authoritative cassettes is relatively new. However, in 2000—six years after my initial research—cassettes had hardly made any inroads into the learning and transmitting process. It will be interesting to see whether the influence of recorded materials changes as it becomes a habitual medium. While women may have differing versions of the same stavan, the version that ultimately succeeds is the one preferred by the woman willing to lead the stavan in performance. Thus, the strong singers generally carried more weight in style decisions—especially those decisions made during a performance, but here, too, Sheelu's pattern, which seemed to highlight the melodic "hook" to the stavan, was settled on for the performance, suggesting the equal participation of aesthetic judgment in the assessment of how stavan should and will be performed.

Jain Aesthetics

The agglomerative nature of the Jain tradition is illuminated by a look at the history of the Jain devotional poetry genres and taxonomy. As discussed earlier in this chapter, stavan draw primarily from the stotra literature for their lyrical quality and from the pada tradition popular with the Vaiṣṇav poets as well for the form. In the production of Jain devotional performance genres, the importance of any particular form seems to be subordinated to a selective use of the available and applicable popular media. How is it, then, that we can know a Jain performance when we see or hear it? While it freely borrows from other traditions to such an extent that its "Jain-ness" might well be obscured to the casual observer, there is something in the "fit" of poetics, music, and performance that suggests the Jain ideals of restraint and precision.

The performance of stavan illuminates the desire for unity in performance while offering one's best (virtuosity). The poles of virtuosity and unity are central to pūjā performative aesthetics. These three aesthetics of poetry, music, and the "fit" of stavan to performance context shared the value placed on unity—rather than, for example, counterpoint. Symmetry is central to good form. Women usually arrive at pūjā performances in matching saris with matching dāṇḍiya sticks and maṇḍaḷ bags and always sit in straight lines facing each other directly in front of the image being worshipped (see figure 1-4). As worship, these Jain laywomen perform complicated combinations of singing and dancing in unison with a group of other Jain women. Their precision shows other Jains that they have spent a lot of time concentrating on Jain devotional praxis. The carefulness and symmetrical unity of the pūjā performance are valued as a statement of Jain religious values expressed through Jain performative aesthetics. Because stavan cannot be used to evoke a response in the Jinas, it is important to look at the sentiments that arise within the singers and the other listeners. The listeners include the gods and goddesses who give prosperity to those whose praises of the Jinas please them. Further unification is achieved through fitting the performance style of each stavan with the context of the surrounding pūjā liturgy into which it is inserted in performance. The repertoire of pūjā stavan was based in part on the text of the pūjās themselves, as you will see in chapter 6. The maṇḍaḷ women were quite familiar with the pūjā texts and the meanings of the poetic sections of the pūjā liturgy; stavan were chosen to fit into the pūjā. The "fit" of the repertoire was a reflection of the topic of the pūjā liturgy and the text and tone of the accompanying stavan.

Stavan, as well as sections of the formal pūjās, were often performed to popular rās-garbā melodies. The stress on dance during the pūjās made these choices especially popular. The swing—created by the syncopation of the melody and the rhythm—and the upbeat tempo were considered especially appropriate for the celebrations of the Jina's lives. These melodies are popular and were recorded on several dāṇḍiya-rās and garbā cassettes.[21] Rās-garbā music is familiar to and very popular with the Jains I knew—of all ages. Though rās-garbā is associated with a seasonal festival for Hindus, it is the standard dance for Gujarātī Jain celebrations in Pune, all weddings, fast-breaking parties, formal pūjās, and plain evening entertainment. Because the women all knew most of the melodies by heart it was relatively easy to sing new words to an old melody. The singers are assumed (usually rightly) to know the melodies of these folksongs and to be capable of converting the lyrics to songs, though in reality some practice is required for the maṇḍaḷ to perform the pūjās well. Garbā songs are sung quickly and with a lot of syncopation. Hindi film song melodies are recognizable generally by the Western style of long chorus passages between the verses, the small tonal range, and the steady and simpler rhythm. Among the stavan singers I met, Hindī film music melodies were considered good for performance settings focused on liveliness. However, they were not considered especially holy. Jain literature has many such conversions and conglomerations; as people are constantly converted within the narratives, the melodies and poetics are likewise converted to Jainism. In this instance, the secular (and perhaps downright racy) suggestiveness of Hindi film song lyrics that a film melody carries with it are overridden by the appreciation of the melody for the purposes of maintaining a steady rhythm and providing a widely recognizable melody. A maṇḍaḷ can coopt the melody of these film melodies (e.g., "Tu Chīz Baḍī Hai," popular in 1994) to Jain ends.

The aesthetic sensibilities of the unified shared production by maṇḍaḷs of the formal pūjās means all the singers sing in unison and that this togetherness itself is a sign of virtue. The instrumentation of stavan singing was remarkably uniform. A solo singer in the temple—man or woman—always sang unaccompanied in my observations, whereas group singing was accompanied by a variety of percussive instruments.[22] Usually one woman played a steady beat on a double-headed drum and the rest sang, marking the more complex rhythms with sticks, snapping and clapping, hand cymbals, or tambourines. The most rhythmic stavan were accompanied with the stick-clashing percussion, but group singing was accompanied by steady percussion on the strong pulse at all times; the more rhythmically irregular stavan were generally reserved for solo singing. The women all sang with a minimum of ornamentation and nasality, and the stavan were pitched at the range of their natural speaking voices. The timbre, if altered from the natural timbre of their speaking voices, derived more from the throaty, unornamented tones of rās-garbā and dhamal singers of Gujarātī folk music[23] than from the falsetto of Hindī film music[24] or classical singing.[25]

Women singing formal pūjā texts and stavan use dance as percussion. Seated in facing rows, the women sound the rhythm of the music with hand gestures; each stavan has a particular set of gestures that the women practice to go along with it (see figure 4-1). These hand gestures are unrelated to those used to keep *tāla* at Indian classical music performances. They are not a system of keeping the rhythm; they *are* the rhythm. These gestures are either a series of repeated sticking patterns similar to dānḍiya rās or hand patterns drawn from garbā. The sticking patterns made by the clashing of sticks were less similar to dānḍiya rās; the clashes were made not only with the facing person but with her diagonals and neighbors. As discussed earlier, the maṇḍaḷ would rehearse the dance part of the music, which also served as the bulk of the percussion, over and over until the pattern they chose "fit" the music and the tone of the stavan or pūjā section. The seated versions of these dances dominated the women's maṇḍaḷ performances and were one way people would identify a performance as "Jain." Dance was considered an inextricable part of the Jain pūjā—both the formal pūjās and daily pūjā.[26] Carefully synchronized dance, like song, is an effective means of under-

FIGURE 4-1. Pārśva Maṇḍaḷ performing seated dāṇḍiya-rās as part of housewarming (Vāstuk) pūjā, Pune, June 1994. The pūjā sponsor is standing next to the assembly hall stand (samavasaraṇ) with the pitchers for bathing the image.

standing the Jina, staying on the religious path, and displaying the kind of precision expected of Jains.

There are three other dance performances I saw associated with Jain worship, and both were performed by a solo dancer who faced the Jina image. The most difficult was the lamp (*dīpak*) dance, where the dancer has a burning oil lamp in each hand (and sometimes arms, feet, shoulders, and top of head) which she waves while dancing in front of the Jina image in the temple. It is perceived as an extension of the lamp offering (dīpak pūjā). The dance must be done with extreme concentration to avoid dropping or blowing out the ghee lamps and to avoid burning oneself in the process. This dance is usually a solo performance (although Soni and Moni performed the lamp dance as a duet at the 1998 Mahāvīr Nirvāṇ program), and like the solo singing, allows a place for virtuosity within the structure of the unified pūjā. It is here that the best dancers in a maṇḍaḷ can make a "better" offering with an individual expression. However, this individuated performance, like the solo singing, still adheres to the Jain aesthetic of Śānt rāsa and carefulness. In fact, this dance is quintessentially careful and precise.

Near the close of the formal pūjās, a dance was performed with a tambourine. The tambourine dance was usually a very simple affair, danced solo by a maṇḍaḷ woman with little enthusiasm. However, in both 1994 and 2000 at the evening singing sessions during Paryuṣaṇ at Ajitnāth Temple, groups of young women performed more complicated tambourine dances whose choreographies were based on garbā dance (see figure 4-3). In both the formal pūjās and the daily pūjā, women performed the *cāmar* dance, in which a flywhisk (*cāmar*; a yak tail flywhisk and a sign of royal authority) is waved in front of the image of the Jina. This was not usually danced with much enthusiasm or grace and lasted only for a brief moment—clearly performed perfunctorily and symbolically.[27] However, at one pūjā performed and sponsored by the Kacchi Maṇḍaḷ, when an older woman was performing the flywhisk dance, she seemed to become either possessed or hypnotized. She whirled around several times and fell to the floor of the temple and writhed. Once the music stopped, she got up, returned the flywhisk to its place hanging on the temple wall, and sat down as if nothing had happened. I asked the women around me what had happened, and they said, "Oh, she is dancing for the Jina." No further comment. I asked whether she might have been possessed, and they said, "No, we Jains don't do that." Privately, after the pūjā, one woman said to me that the performing maṇḍaḷ was from another part of Gujarat and did not know how to behave. The implication was that her behavior had probably been possession, or at least very odd, and it was seen in a disparaging light both by her maṇḍaḷ—which claimed it did not happen—and the outsiders watching, who said it was not Jain. To lose control was unacceptable and doubly so inside the Jina's temple.[28]

There was a seeming exception to this restraint in the dāṇḍiya-rās dancing as part of the formal pūjās and evening devotional singing sessions (bhāvnā) when, to the accompaniment of stavan singing (either a maṇḍaḷ or a hired professional singer), Jains would dance in the temple (see figures 4-2 and 4-3). This dance would sometimes be fairly fast and enthusiastic—though more often when done by the young men than anyone else—and seemed to contrast with the stately and reserved performances of the seated dance that the maṇḍaḷs perform, the lamp offering dance, the tambourine dance, or the flywhisk dance. I did notice that the performances of dāṇḍiya-rās at housewarming pūjās, fast-breaking parties, and other events (not in the temple) were more spirited even than the most spirited dancing I saw at an evening stavan singing session, suggesting a certain restraint imposed by the location. It seemed that this dancing was a place where the Jain celebration was the central focus; perhaps most important, here the "offering" is the happiness of Jains at being Jain rather than the offerings of lamp or the cāmar.

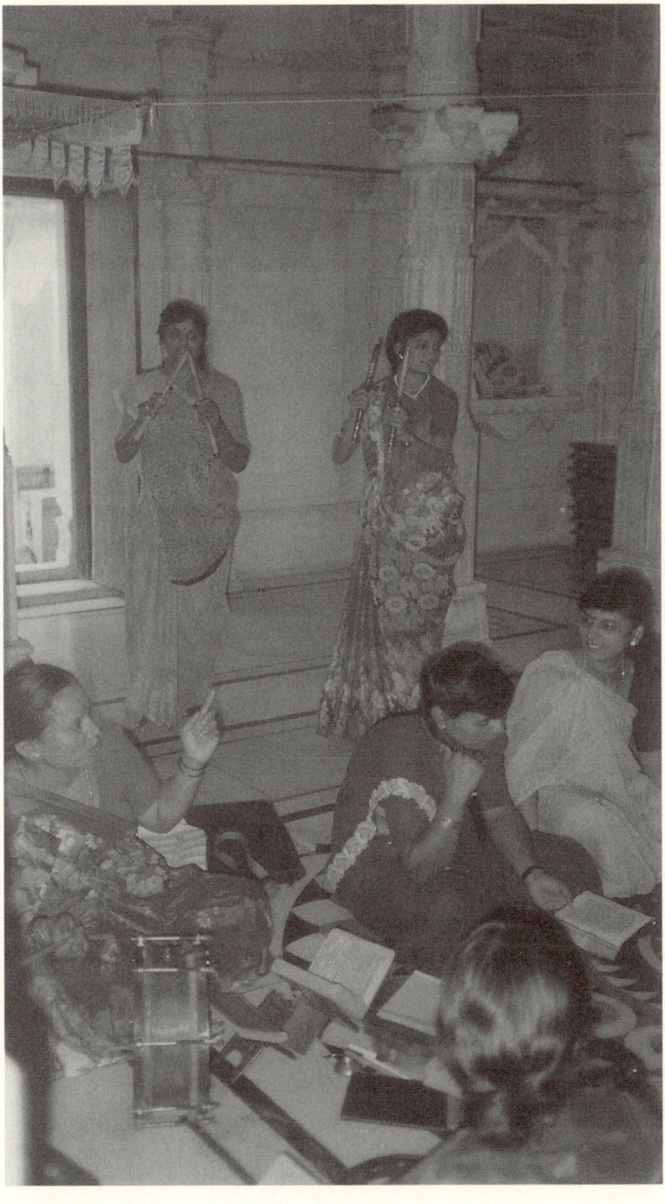

FIGURE 4-2. Dāṇḍiya-rās dance as an offering during a Pañcakalyāṇak Pūjā, Ajitnāth Temple, Shivajinagar, Pune, 1994.

FIGURE 4-3. Young girls performing dance in the temple during Paryuṣaṇ 1994, Ajitnāth Temple, Shivajinagar, Pune.

While there was nothing explicitly referred to as "Jain" about the aesthetics of the stavan performances, certain aspects of the performances illustrate a difference between the Hindu world and the Jain world of religious performance. Above all, when people discuss Jain music and dance, they speak of the restraint (sometimes pejoratively) and calm of the performances. The abandon of the Hindu religious performances, with wild dancing, possession, and loss of emotional control, does contrast with the reserve shown in the Jain performances. For a Jain to lose control is not merely a social impropriety with which Jains would feel uncomfortable but also a breach of the Jain ethic of control of action. The gracefulness is more a reflection of the care to do the act correctly. These precise and careful movements are definitely reflected in the ways Jains dance in the temples. The whirling I saw in Kṛṣṇa *kīrtan* performances would likely seem like violence through nonattention to most Jains.

The precision of the Jain dances—especially the seated dance—and the music reflect less a lack of enthusiasm for the performance than an adherence to a Jain understanding of worthy devotional behavior. The release from behavioral restrictions which is celebrated in the bhakti tradition (and by its scholars) would be a failure to maintain Jain standards of behavior. Devotion that is violent is no devotion. The importance of the teachings as an object of devotion means that a rejection of their values is ultimately an act of disrespect for the religion—a major source of sin.

However, the match of the song and its melody, the dance moves, and the rhythms shows *attention*, which is, in itself, proof of devotion. It articulates the women's time spent at practice, which, in a Jain understanding not unlike "practice makes perfect," shows the dedication of the women to their spiritual progress. The more conscientiously the women perform the pūjās, the closer to having only good karma they seem to be. Their sense of Jain devotional behavior is all the more devoted to the Jinas for being precise.

5

Am I addicted to the work of Love, O Invincible Bliss of the Jinas?
Not even one moment is beautiful without God in my heart.
Passing time in meditation, will I feel love
As the clouds clear, O Giver of Liberation, Vehicle of Grace?

Maddened by love, my heart, God, remains unashamed.
Body, mind, and wealth, from all of these, my God, see this:
My support is you, Lord of the People,
Inner Lord, previously, I say, it was secret.

Lord, make the truth known to the whole world,
Make it easy for your devotee to do the correct work,
It's like this, how do I keep doing the right thing?
Your promise is to be that floating ship to carry me.

Deliverance is within you, it listens with your ear.
I have come to see your compassion for the sick and the poor.
Attending to your grace is my business.
Can we be persuaded, before having knowledge, to be merciful?

Through this vision of compassion your devotee rises
Feelings of fear, troubled thoughts are broken, at the moment of devotion.
My heart's desires are fulfilled, I rest with you
Making a pair, the enchanted one says, see the color of my heart.

Transcription and translation of recording of performance during an interview in Pune, Maharashtra, on 25 October 1993. Courtesy Ranjana Satish Shah.

Daily Worship, Improvisation, and Individual Devotion

In Shivajinagar, I heard the "Śrī Ajitnāth Stavan," set out above, sung as the darśan stavan; not only does the stavan address the central Jina at the Ajitnāth temple, but it is also found in the ubiquitous stavan collection, *Śrī Sudhāras Stavan Saṅgrah*. The Ajitnāth stavan describes the devotee's relationship to the Jina and to those characteristics of the Jina that make the Jina so acutely important to the devotee's spiritual progress: grace, protector, supporter. Through Jain devotion the Jain devotee hopes for the Jina's grace, which in turn gives the devotee the inspiration to continue the hard "work" of being Jain. The stavan asks: "How do I keep doing the right thing?" The reply is implicit: by "attending" to the Jina through meditation—in a more generalized understanding than the formulaic meditations of Buddhist or Yogic practice—and keeping God in the heart. Keeping God in the heart is akin to the practices of repetition of a mantra (*mantra-jap*) and remembering the name of God—essentially repetition of the name or names of God (*nām-smaraṇ*). Jains, as do many in other Indic religions, use repetition of names as a meditation strategy.[1] This stavan asks for the devotee's full concentration on the Jinas, or in the words of the women who sang it, devotional sentiments (*bhakti bhāv*). Bhakti means devotion and can refer to devotional practices within a tradition and also to the dominance of devotionalism in certain religious movements. Bhāv was usually used by laywomen to mean one's emotions, attitude, or intention in performing worship. Often the word bhāv alone was used to denote bhakti bhāv—a devotional disposition toward the Jina; one either has bhāv or not. The women believed that the intention of one's pūjā had a direct relationship to the efficacy of worship. If one has the wrong sentiment—usually described as wanting just worldly things—worship does not bring about spiritual progress, nor does it help with prosperity, as prosperity is granted only by the guardian deities who are pleased by Jina worship.[2] Jina pūjā is more than karmically meritorious; it is the medium for Jain devotion. My field research was punctuated by constant reminders that pūjā was the important topic and that without an understanding—and a daily practice—of pūjā, one could not possibly understand Jain religiosity.[3] In addition, the rate of contemporary temple building and image installation suggests a view that pūjā and temple worship are still seen as a central good and the sponsorship of temple building and pūjās, a duty of lay Jains—usually laymen. It is only through pūjā (material and mental worship for laity, mental worship alone for ascetics) that one can express the devotional sentiments so important for the cultivation of inner purity and merit (*puṇya*). Jain worship includes a variety of actions performed as part of daily worship, various devotional acts performed throughout a Jain year, and formal pūjās (in the Jain context, liturgical performances).

Daily worship is focused on two locations: the household shrine and the neighborhood temple. In 1993–94, in the household shrine at Dadiji's home, there was a small unconsecrated metal Pārśvanāth image in the center,[4] and behind this three other metal images of Pārśvanāth, Gaṇapati and Lakṣmī. There were two small medallions of Bhairav with betel nut offerings and several framed or laminated pictures of Pārśvanāth, Śankheśvar Pārśvanāth, Śatruñjay Ādināth, Gautam Svāmī, a map of the Jain cosmos, and a silver commemorative coin impressed with an image of the local Ajitnāth temple from the temple installation ceremony. Above the box in which the shrine was situated were several more pictures, including two pilgrimage maps of Śatruñjay. Underneath were the supplies for household worship: a silver lamp and incense holder, as well as a tin of sandalwood powder in front, and to one side was a water pot with a coconut on top. There were several rosaries and bookstands scattered underneath the shrine. The shrine itself sat on top of the wardrobe closet in which were stored religious books and other supplies for special religious observances (mats, brooms, extra handkerchiefs, unused men's pūjā clothes).[5] For most women, morning worship in the house was participation in the lamp offering or offering incense, and if they had enough time, meditation (*sāmāyik*) or mantra recitation. Reynell (1985a) speaks of the majority of the older married women she surveyed (40 out of 54) as performing meditation every morning, but few women I knew had time—before they reached the age of their grandchildren's marriages—to perform meditation daily. During the rainy season (at least until Paryuṣaṇ) or during Paryuṣaṇ, women often made a special effort to perform meditation daily, making time by getting up yet earlier to do household work or by foregoing their rest in the afternoon. There were a few women who I saw perform this kind of meditation every day—Dadiji, for example—but the few other women who said that they did perform meditation, did so very early in the morning and I did not observe it. Many mornings, while waiting to go to the temple, I watched as the men in the family performed darśan, a short meditation, or mantra recitation in the shrine room before heading to the temple for darśan or worship. In the evenings, the whole family—whoever was home—offered a lamp to the images in the shrine as well.[6] This shrine was used for all but the largest household festivals (if there were too many people to fit in the shrine room, at the opening of accounts at Dīvālī, blessing of fasters or wedding couples, etc., the images would be installed in the larger living room area for the purpose of performing pūjā), and the room itself was used by everyone as a place for quiet reflection and a rest from family life.

Temples have similar variation in images for worship. The first and most visible are the Jina images such as those named in my earlier description of Ajitnāth Temple. They are supposed to receive worship before anything else (I never saw anyone skip the Jinas' worship, even if they did it quickly), and they dominate the central spaces in the temples. At Ajitnāth Temple, there are nine consecrated stone Jina images and twelve consecrated metal images including the image in the "assembly hall" pūjā stand. There is also a stone image of Gautam Svāmī (a disciple of Mahāvīr—now a Siddha representing the path of mendicants as a guru of sorts)—who is worshipped exactly as the Jinas were even though he is not a Jina, two metal plates with the eight auspicious symbols on them (*aṣṭamaṅgalam*), and four *siddhacakra*s (a symbolic representation of all worshipful things).[7] In addition, there are images of the guardian deities in their own side niche-shrines: a stone image of Nākoḍā Bhairav and next to him a small silver plaque with his image on it, and a stone image of Padmāvatī with a small silver plaque with her image on it.[8] Although many temples have paintings or maps of Jain pilgrimage sites that receive a certain amount of devotion—stavan singing and incense, usually—Ajitnāth congregation only displays their map of Śatruñjay on Kārtak Pūṇam, at which time it is worshipped with sandalwood powder, incense, and lamps and rice, money, fruit, and sweets offerings. The many objects receiving devotion are organized with a certain amount of hierarchy, placing the Jinas at the top, but all these objects (as well as Jain texts) are worthy of worship. The ways in which the lay Jains organized their worship to reflect the hierarchy while adjusting the worship to suit their personal devotion is part of the negotiations between "correct action" in the correct order and a spirit of devotionalism which justifies all these practices.

Humphrey and Laidlaw's theory of ritual action, derived from their study of Khartar Gacch Jain laity in Jaipur, suggests a useful heuristic for understanding the fluidity of Jain daily worship. Rather than looking for set discursive models to be reproduced as ritual with varying degrees of success, they speak of the idea of the Jain devotee (or, in their terms, celebrant) entering into a "ritual commitment"—a state of intending to perform the ritual or worship quite similar to the way Jains with whom I spoke used the term *bhāv*—which marks all actions during the time of ritual commitment as pūjā. Humphrey and Laidlaw are careful to outline a set of actions which count as pūjā acts and it is these acts alone that actually constitute pūjā once one has entered into this ritual commitment (Humphrey and Laidlaw 1994). In this chapter I discuss primarily the borders of what is acceptably called pūjā: (1) the role of devotionalism generally in the Jain tradition; (2) where the women work from discursive models of ideal worship as a tool in teaching pūjā; (3) where women saw the limits of individuation in pūjā, I call this (after Humphrey and Laidlaw) "getting it wrong"; and (4) where these women's personal style and understanding of devotion are articulated in their choices of devotional songs. In sum, I address some key places where pūjā in particular practice intersects with and pulls against pūjā praxis.

Jain Devotionalism

Cort has already convincingly argued that bhakti as devotionalism is a central part of Jain practice.[9] The Tattvārtha Sūtra—a text belonging to the third century C.E. of Jain textual tradition (accepted by both Digambar and Śvetāmbar Jains) includes a general discussion of the daily obligations of the mendicants (*āvaśyakas*). The six daily duties of a mendicant include meditation (*sāmāyik*), the praise of the twenty-four Jinas (*caturvimśatistava*), worship of mendicants, especially gurus (*vandana*), confession and expiation of sin (*pratikramaṇa*), renouncing doing anything for a time (*kāyotsarga*), and renouncing certain things such as food, travel, and so on (*pratyākhyāna*). Although these are expressly for mendicants, the medieval manuals for behavior of laymen are based on this model. The daily obligations (*āvaśyaka*) literature (most important to Śvetāmbar mendicants, the Āvaśyaka Sūtra) includes the hymn venerating the twenty-four Jinas (*caturvimśati-stava*) as one of the daily obligations for the mendicants. Later Jain texts use the term *bhakti* to describe Jain devotionalism. Likewise, books of devotional hymns account for the greater part of Jain library collections. The abundance of Jina images and the descriptions of image worship suggest the long-standing centrality of temple worship (Cort n.d. b; Folkert 1993).[10] Though some earlier scholarship (Jaini 1979; Schubring 1962) has argued that Jina devotionalism was a residue of Hindu-Jain interaction and "merely" the province of lesser Jains (the laity), the previous evidence shows the active role that the male mendicants—who wrote most of those texts and who must be present for the installation of a new Jina image—have in the reproduction of Jain devotion. The assumption that asceticism and devotionalism are mutually exclusive is contradicted by the Jain model of devotion, where the devotion to Jain mendicants and to asceticism itself—there are huge numbers of fasting songs—plays a central role in Jain practice (Cort n.d. a). However, for the Shivajinagar Jain laywomen, the appropriateness of devotionalism was unquestioned; their concerns centered on how best to express this devotion and how to maintain devotional sentiments in a world of distractions and household duties.

The nature of devotional sentiments in a Jain context and its centrality becomes clearer in contrast to the devotionalism (also called bhakti) of Hindu worship. In Babb's work on Jain worship, he explains the fundamental difference between Jain worship and Hindu (particularly Puṣṭimārg Vaiṣṇav) worship as the differences in the relationships between the worshipped and the worshipper (Babb 1996). As the Jinas are "nontransactional" beings—they do not receive or return the offerings—the worshipper is making offerings in imitation of the Jina's rejection of worldly materials. With Puṣṭimārg Vaiṣṇav worship it is of paramount importance that the inhabited Kṛṣṇa image (*swarūp*) be comfortable and happy; in hot weather cooling offerings are made and in cold weather the offerings include warm clothes.[11] Although Jains do offer cooling substances during worship it is not varied according to the season; it reflects rather the Jain focus on "cooling" the passions.[12] Neither are any of the aspects of the Jain worship significantly altered according to the season—except the singing of season-specific stavan during worship (like "Dīvālīnu Stavan" or "Śrī Paryuṣaṇānu Stavan"). It does not seem that the stavan repertoire is altered to "please" the Jina. Although the Jains do have devotionalism and they do express a belief in grace, this grace does not come from the Jina's pleasure but from his compassion. The offerings made to the Jinas are not there to "please" the Jinas but rather to remind the worshippers of the qualities of the Jina and the Jain religion. Thus, there is no question—as there may be in Hindu worship—of whether the Jina would prefer certain gestures or whether stavan singing must accompany, for instance, limb pūjā. There are normative descriptions of how daily worship should be done in lay manuals and there are local traditions and understandings of worship, but the individual worshipper is relatively free to choose her worship actions from a wide array of acceptable gestures (Humphrey and Laidlaw 1994).

Puṣṭimārg Vaiṣṇav devotionalism is based on the emotional attachment that either Rādhā (Kṛṣṇa's beloved) or Yaśodā (Kṛṣṇa's mother) have for Kṛṣṇa. Dimock lists the relative sentiments or emotional relationships appropriate for a Kṛṣṇa devotee in the Bengali Vaiṣṇav tradition: peacefulness in the face of Kṛṣṇa's supremacy (*Śanta-bhāva*) and after this the sentiments of a servant (*dāsya-bhāva*), a parent or brother (*vātsalya-bhāva*), a friend (*sākhya-bhāva*), or a lover (*mādhurya-bhāva*) of the deity (Dimock 1966).[13] Śanta bhāva is most similar to the Jain relationship based on the role model of the Jina but without carrying the element of helplessness; a Jain can attempt to reach perfection even if she cannot reach it in this era. The paradigmatic Jina worshippers are Indra and Indrāṇī, who accept the Jina as their Lord rather than as a beloved. However, the efficacy of the parent-like devotion (*vātsalya*) is demonstrated in the stories of the Jina mothers—especially of Marudevī's mokṣa—and are important sources of identification for Jain women. The Jain pūjā alternates between the idea of the postpartum bath of a well-loved (royal) child and the anointing of a king.

Barz (1976) writes of the difference according to Puṣṭimārg Vaiṣṇavs between Puṣṭimārg worship (called *sevā*) and other Hindu worship (called pūjā), stressing that sevā, translated literally as service, is focused exclusively on doing service to the deity with no expectation of reward whereas pūjā is focused on the isolated individual performer. Jain worship is by this division rightly called pūjā—it is an act necessarily focused on the pūjā performer because of the Jina's transcendence; however, the implication that the pūjā performer is expecting a reward does not carry over to the Jains. Instead, the Jain devotee's devotion is a way of making actions "good" and a way of reorienting one's mind toward the "good." One enters into the ritual commitment (Humphrey and Laidlaw 1994), but doing the ritual must include doing it with devotion; in the language of laywomen, one must have more than the intention of performing pūjā—one must also have the right sentiment, that is a devotional sentiment, which was part of their descriptions of doing pūjā correctly. Where Puṣṭimārg grace comes from Kṛṣṇa's recognition of the devotee's love, Jain devotees must perfect themselves—even when looking for grace. As Kṛṣṇa iconography attempts to bring the devotee closer to the intimate particularities of Kṛṣṇa (Aslet 1993), Jain iconography reminds the Jain devotee of the Jinas' shared experience of a perfection that inhibits emotional intimacy.

Stavan singing becomes an expressive tool—almost an inevitable one—for an individual's devotion. The "Śrī Ajitnāth Stavan" (which begins this chapter) portrays a model of devotion which clearly shows the centrality of devotion to the Jinas:

> Deliverance is within you, it listens with your ear.
> I have come to see your compassion for the sick and the poor.
> Attending to your grace is my business.
> Can we be persuaded, before having knowledge, to be merciful?

Thus, through the prayer and this stavan (as well as many others) the laywomen are reminded daily of the importance of the sentiment they bring to do pūjā. Stavan singing as a manifestation of devotion is a part of the normative models of Jain pūjā. The relationship between a Jain devotee and the Jina is theoretically one in which the Jina is a role model to be emulated by the devotee, and Jina pūjā is justified by saying that through pūjā one gains insight into the Jina's nature, and that through pūjā one's mind is focused on the correct path. Women did give these explanations to me. One Tapā Gacch female mendicant staying in Śirur for the 1994 rainy season explained Jina pūjā to me as the importance of keeping the Jina "near" oneself:

> If you put a magnet against iron for a long time, slowly the iron becomes magnetic, the iron becomes a magnet. This happens because they are near each other and soon the iron absorbs the magnet's qualities. So if I am near her [the female mendicant leader—on whose feet she then placed her head], near her everyday, perhaps I will absorb some of her good qualities. If I am in her proximity, I will retain just a tiny bit so I try to be near her everyday. The less I go away, the more will stay with me. Like the magnet I'll have some of her qualities someday. If you go to the temple everyday and in front of the Jinas say the Navkār, then maybe some of their qualities will stick to you. The more times, the more will stick to you.

The very interaction between a devotee and the Jina image, like a magnet, will cause good Jina qualities to be absorbed into the woman. Thus, practice—without, necessarily, study—will give the Jain access to some (even a tiny bit) of the Jina's nature. This version of the role-model efficacy bridges the gap between the utter self-help depictions in Āgam texts and in the many lay manuals and the idea of Jina's grace represented in many of the stavan texts.

The idea that the Jinas hear the prayers of the devotee was explained by several laywomen by the Jina's omniscience. The desire for "true darśan" or another tangible response from the Jina pushes at the limits of what one can ask for from a Jina. The stavan "Just Once, Lord Pārśva" asks for a momentary grace which is acknowledged tacitly, by the humility of the requests, as more than it is really appropriate to ask:

> Just once, Lord Pārśva, Come to my temple!
> Come to my temple, that's my request.
> My request is that you come, I beg you to do this.
> That is my song's devoted wish.
> Dark and daylight, my heart is large,
> Thus, I came respectfully to you.
> With the flowers of the soul, I spoke to you.
> Take these flowers and bring back your precious ones.
> In crushing illusion, one is your name
> One is your name, Saying it is my work.

Stavan do not represent anger at the Jina's aloofness or attempts to use leverage to attain grace (as one sometimes sees in Hindu devotional literature), just a wish for the Jina to help make being Jain easier.[14] Jains themselves perceive their religion as very difficult, and the stavan repeatedly ask for help in order to keep "doing the right thing." Humphrey and Laidlaw introduce the idea of "getting it right" in ritual activity in particular arising out of their own experience of being taught pūjā by Jains with whom they were doing their research. Here they found getting it right to be more a question of not getting it wrong (Humphrey and Laidlaw 1994). It is, however, useful to look at the way pūjā is taught with the idea that those statements of correctness can tell us something about the frame within which the pūjā actions are located.

Negotiating Ideals in Teaching Pūjā

The Sanskrit and Prakrit lay manual texts were sometimes familiar to the women by name, though not one layperson (male or female) I asked could tell me anything about the actual contents of these Sanskrit and Prakrit lay manual texts.[15] Women do have access (if they can read, which many older Jain women and virtually all younger women can do) to vernacular lay manuals (mostly in Gujarātī), which are written by both monks and nuns to instruct laity how to be Jains in a very formal and philosophical sense. Rarely do they address the more practical issues of Jain households.[16] These books are filled with special prayers and stavan and the proper way to perform temple prayers, mendicant homage, and ritual confession and expiation of sin (especially at Saṃvatsarī). Only once did a laywoman, Maluben, show any specific knowledge of a lay manual's contents (Hemaratnavijay's 1993 text *Cālo Jinālaye Jaīe* intended for daily pūjā instruction) and she showed me this text. This manual is intended for teaching pūjā especially in children's religious education (pāṭhśāḷā) and is divided into sections in which suggested recitation couplets are linked with various acts, all within the frame of pūjā. These kinds of couplets (there are many versions of them) were recited by some women I observed while they were worshipping the central image—Dadiji, Maluben, Nita—but not all. Each section is followed by an exposition on the "meaning" of each action and the text winds up with a series of narratives of religious lay Jains. There are other books that outline the practice, history, and special prayers of a wide variety of fasts as well. But this information does not only appear in books; women learn pūjā and fasts when they do these pūjās and fasts with others. Women's most important source for knowledge of worship is, in fact, the other women in their lives.

There were a few occasions on which women (Dadiji, Ranjana, and Maluben) specifically intended to teach me how to perform pūjā rather than simply bring me along on their morning pūjā.[17] When looking at teaching worship, it is important to remember that the women may have adjusted their worship for the purposes of showing me the "correct" way to do the Jain pūjā—compared with the examples of daily pūjā given later in this chapter. In a sense, each woman was condensing what children learn over years of doing pūjā with their female relatives in an attempt to teach pūjā in a single temple visit or perhaps a few visits. The most important difference was their impulse to be sure that all parts of the pūjā were done in an ideal order based on the ordering of each action that falls within the eightfold pūjā, plus the additional actions of offering the flywhisk, fan, and mirror. Common practice did not seem to insist that a worshipper perform all aspects of the pūjā on all days; the women's reconstruction of the perfect and complete pūjā, which has all aspects in the ideal order, is more a reflection of their ideas of what pūjā could be than what it is or needs to be. Nearing the end of my research I realized that I had never performed morning pūjā with Maluben, who was central to my research on formal pūjās. She took the opportunity then to make sure that I did not return to the United States to write this book with imperfect knowledge of daily pūjā. Following are my notes from that experience.

PŪJĀ WITH MALUBEN

On August 19, 1994, I arrived at the temple alone and met up with Maluben. I asked her if she would bring me through the pūjā today, and we headed over to where the sandalwood paste is made. Arun was still scraping the sandalwood block to make sandalwood paste, so we put our silver plates down and headed back inside to say the darśan prayer in front of Ajitnāth. Maluben said Jina-specific prayers in front of each of the images of Ādināth, Mahāvīr, and then Pārśvanāth. We made a bow in front of Padmāvatī and then in front of Bhairav, where Maluben said a prayer. Then the sandalwood paste was ready, and Arun filled our small silver bowls on the plates.

Maluben passed her silver plate over the incense and entered the inner sanctum. There were many people in front of Ajitnāth—the central image—so she went to Ādināth, the image on the left, first. She pointedly told me that the Jina should only be touched by the ring finger of the right hand and that putting one's hands on the Jina's knees, as some people do, was wrong.[18] She said a prayer[19] and then applied the sandalwood paste to Ādināth and then put her silver plate down. She then asked me to do the same. Together we placed a flower on Ādināth's foot. She moved around, doing sandalwood paste pūjā to each of the images. When we were at the central image she told me to move over to the right to be on the women's side of the image.[20] When an image had side images Maluben put sandalwood paste on the right foot of each one. Maluben did the worship of the siddhacakras as she met them and then applied the sandalwood paste to the outer Jina images.

Then she entered Padmāvatī's shrine, put a dab of sandalwood paste with her ring finger on the Pārśvanāth image at the top of the guardian goddess' image, then dabbed with her thumb Padmāvatī's forehead on both the marble and the silver images and then each of the snake's heads in Padmāvatī's snake hood.[21] Maluben filled a vial[22] with the milk-water which had been used to bathe Padmāvatī and then, dipping her finger in the bucket, put a dab of the milk-water on both her eyelids and in the part of her hair. We cleaned our silver plates and our hands and went to the center door where she offered incense and a lamp (on her own pūjā plate) and waved the flywhisk and finally the fan and mirror.

We sat and made the rice designs—the extended svastik (*nandyāvart*).[23] After correcting my design, saying it needed to have nine clear corners, we added almonds to the top part of the design: a curved line opening toward the top with a dot in the center of the arc. Maluben wanted to show me the "correct" offering, so (since we had no sweets ourselves) she grabbed two sweets from a neighboring table. A woman insisted that we take two new ones from her and placed one piece of the rock sugar on the center of our extended svastik. We picked up and replaced the almonds at the top while saying a prayer. After three prostrations, Maluben recited the morning worship prayer series (*caityavandan*) in the middle of which she sang the "Śrī Śāntināth Stavan." After the prayer series, she told me to sit peacefully while she sang "Look at Lord Pārśva" quietly to herself and said another prayer. Then we said the final prayer of the prayer series and tossed a handful of rice each onto the rice board where we had made our drawings and offerings. Then Maluben went to have another darśan of Padmāvatī and Bhairav. Finally she rang the bell, and she said, "That is how pūjā should be done."

This was Maluben's reconstruction of how the perfect pūjā should be done. She was paying much more attention to what I was doing than she would have normally while doing pūjā; theoretically one's own pūjā should be the focus of one's attention, not the people who are doing pūjā nearby. The fact that Maluben took the sweets from the other table and—because she felt the chronology had been skewed by the confusion of the sweets offering—that we performed the offering of the almonds twice was unusual for Maluben's or any woman's daily pūjā; this level of attention to chronology and completeness is not seen as necessary for correct or effective pūjā and in fact the reofferings of the almond and the sweets were not acceptable (because once something has been offered it becomes *dev dravya* and does not belong to the Jain whose offerings must be her own) and the other woman insisted on giving us new ones. Teaching pūjā is a place where it was widely accepted that one has to make sure that the learner is doing everything correctly—especially if the learner could inadvertently perform an unacceptable act.

On many occasions, I watched as women taught their children different aspects of pūjā. In one very intimate style of teaching sandalwood paste pūjā, the mother (or aunt or sister) would first put sandalwood paste on the toe of the Jina and the child would follow the example. This would continue throughout the whole sandalwood paste pūjā. The child would be lifted to reach the Jina's head and forehead. As the children became adept at sandalwood paste pūjā, the mother would teach them the prayers by reciting them as they both did sandalwood paste pūjā; this was the same way the gestures were taught, but much more quickly, so that the prayers covered both of their actions. In learning sandalwood paste pūjā, the repetition is over many days; as a matter of common practice, the women would not do sandalwood paste pūjā or a morning worship prayer series more than once a day. Finally, the children would be free to perform those parts of the pūjā that they could do independently before meeting up with someone who could show them how to do something or recite a prayer for them.[24]

Often with the darśan prayer, making rice offering designs, learning a stavan, or other repeatable ritual acts, the learner would be asked to repeat the ritual over and over until she got it right or until the teacher got tired of waiting. On November 10, 1993, when we made our rice offerings, Ranjana decided to teach her daughter, Soni, and me a new rice design. First, she made the four piles of rice at the top of the table and spread the rest of the rice in a circle. She waited while we did the same on the tables next to hers. Step by step (not unlike the way children are taught how to perform sandalwood pūjā) she showed us how to make the rice design out of the rice circle. She would draw a line and then wait for us to do so. If we didn't do it right, she would make us both start from the beginning. After several restarts we both got the rice design right. Then Ranjana went on to recite the prayer series. In a similar way, children learn daily pūjā by observation and imitation of older women. This did not vary between girls and boys until the boys were about 12 years old and were expected to do pūjā with men or alone—not with women. This is not to suggest that children never went to the temple with male relatives, just that these male relatives left the teaching of pūjā to the women.[25]

There was a difference in the approach to the morning pūjā when the women I was with perceived the pūjā as a "learning" experience for me. Once the women were comfortable that I knew what I was doing, they would return to their usual practice. I do not want to imply that they adopted the normative model for pūjā at the expense of their usual practice, more that when the women felt they were instructing me they went much slower than usual and were careful not to forget even the most optional of acts, to ensure that I had the full range of the pūjā actions to select from. As an extreme example, when Ranjana taught me pūjā on my first day at the temple, she moved very slowly through the individual acts, naming each act and the items used to perform it. On another day, Dadiji spoke all the words to the pūjā and the prayer series very slowly, out loud, so I could hear and understand all of them. On later days, neither of these women took special care to instruct me and therefore moved quickly from one act to the next, reciting the prayer series at its normal breakneck speed.

Daily Pūjā as an Improvisational Practice

Daily worship includes the daily temple worship (be it *darśan*, *agra*, *anga*, or *bhāv pūjās*), worship done at home, and the individual practices which loosely mark off the time and space of the day: morning meditation, morning pūjā, evening darśan, evening *āratī*. All the women I knew performed daily pūjā of some kind, unless they were experiencing their menses.[26] Among the women with whom I felt comfortable enough to ask, they did not perform anga pūjā (or enter the inner sanctum) for an additional three days after their menses were completed.[27] Jains with whom I spoke usually categorized temple worship into four general sets of actions: darśan, anga, agra, and bhāv pūjās.[28] Darśan (seeing) usually involved coming into the temple and reciting a prayer in front of the Jina (and sometimes singing a stavan), leaving some kind of offering—in the abbreviated version usually a coin or a small rice svastik—and performing three prostrations before leaving the temple. This becomes a combination of part of the agra pūjā and the bhāv pūjā; it was not very different from what these same Jains did when visiting non-Jain temples for darśan except that it was widely held that one should not do more than two prostrations in front of any image except a Jina image, and the prayers (if they knew or spoke any) were obviously not the same. The anga (limb) pūjā includes those actions performed on the Jina image: bathing the image, anointing the image with sandalwood paste, putting flowers on the image. The agra (in front) pūjā includes the offerings of the fan and the mirror, the flywhisk (cāmar), incense, and lamps in front of the image and also the offerings of rice, sweets, money, and fruits on a table in the main section of the temple. The eightfold (aṣṭaprakārī) pūjā theoretically includes bathing, sandalwood paste, flowers, incense, lamp, rice, sweets, and fruit, but in actual practice it referred to a combination of at least some actions from each of the four groups of actions described previously. Bhāv pūjā is performed while seated behind the table on which one has made these offerings (see figure 5-1). Bhāv pūjā includes the caityavandan series of prayers and gestures plus any additional meditation, mantra recitation, and stavan singing one might do at the temple; in short, any pūjā that does not involve physical or material worship is called bhāv pūjā.[29] It is the meditative manifestation of the material worship of the Jinas. If there are several temples being vis-

FIGURE 5-1. Pūjā offerings: twenty rice svastiks and one rice nandyāvart with an apple on top share a low table with a second offering rice svastik covered by a coconut. Kārtak Pūṇam 1993, Dādāvādī Temple, Pune. (Photo by Steven C. Runge)

ited on a single visit (as there are near Goḍījī temple in downtown Pune or on pilgrimage) bhāv pūjā (including any prayers said to accompany other pūjā acts) is only performed at the central and first temple. In a sense, bhāv pūjā sets the proper sentiment for the pūjā as a whole by establishing the sentiments at the first temple.

Morning worship may vary from a short darśan visit—fairly common with young men and children—to full eightfold pūjā. The women rarely performed only the short darśan pūjā, preferring at least an abbreviated version of the longer agra or eightfold pūjā. This may reflect the way that pūjā serves as a rest from the work and duties of home and as an opportunity for women to control the pacing of their own worship according to their own wishes.[30] The time spent at pūjā varied from woman to woman and also from day to day; Nita usually spent close to an hour at the temple each day while Lata usually spent under twenty minutes at the temple each morning. In addition, when women did not perform the anga pūjā—such as in the three days after their menses—they often spent more time singing stavan or performing mantra recitation, highlighting the women's sense of time ownership while at the temple.

The particular social realities and the temperament of the women performing pūjās have a great effect on the actual ways in which they practice Jainism. Within the frame of those actions that can comprise pūjā, the women improvise based on their own understandings and constraints: time, access, knowledge, and style. Following are three descriptions of three women's morning temple worship. All three sets here are women who regularly performed the full eightfold pūjā. These women came from a single joint family, which accentuates their variation and suggests something of the individuation of daily worship.[31] Variations between their pūjā styles show the latitude of the orthopraxy, which allows all three to be expressions of appropriate Jain pūjā.

PŪJĀ WITH DADIJI, 78 YEARS OLD

On April 9, 1994, I walked down to the temple with Dadiji. We went right over to Kavita—her youngest daughter-in-law—who was doing mantra recitation, and collected flowers from the family pūjā box. Then we went out on the porch, tied our handkerchiefs over our mouths, and got our silver plates (only silver should be brought into the inner sanctum) with sandalwood paste and put our flowers on the silver plate as well. Going first to the center door, Dadiji said the darśan prayer and then three times said: "It is abandoned" (*ṇisīhi*).

Starting with the central Jina image she dabbed the sandalwood paste on the image with her ring finger while saying a prayer for each limb.[32] She did the pūjā of the central image quite slowly and ended with placing the flowers on the Jina image's hands. Dadiji applied sandalwood paste to all of the smaller Jina images attached to the central image. After this she went and did sandalwood paste and flower pūjā to all the images in the inner sanctum, followed by the two Jina images outside the inner sanctum. Finally, she applied the paste to the image of Mahāvīr and the siddhacakra (a *yantra* used in Jain worship with the five worshipful things and the four components of praxis—in sum, the central tenets of Jainism—represented stylistically) that are in the assembly hall pūjā stand in the main part of the temple.

We put our silver plates on a shelf of the assembly hall pūjā stand and we sat down to make our offerings—rice designs (svastiks)—and to recite the caityavandan prayers. Dadiji was interrupted in the recitation by a woman who was making an offering at the assembly hall pūjā stand and needed a prayer recited that the woman did not know.[33] After Dadiji had said the prayer for the woman, she returned to finish the prayer series.

Arun, the pujārī, had finished cleaning off the image of the guardian goddess Padmāvatī, and it was time to perform the ritual bath (*abhiṣek*) of her image.

We stood up and a woman handed us barās—a watery mix of pleasant-smelling woods in a camphor base—to apply to Padmāvatī's image and then we went out of her shrine and got our silver plates. We applied sandalwood paste with the ring finger to the image of Pārśvanāth at the top of Padmāvatī's image and then with our thumbs to Padmāvatī's forehead. Then we went out, took off our handkerchiefs, and went to clean our silver plates. After cleaning the silver plates, we sat down at our rice table.

Dadiji handed me a rosary and told me to say the Navkār Mantra while she did mantra recitation with two rosaries.[34] The first was a 108-bead rosary for which she said "*Namo Ajitnāthāy*" (Praise to Ajitnāth) for each bead; the second was shorter and she said a mantra that her guru, Viśvakalyāṇjī, a local male mendicant leader, had told her to say—which she was not supposed to tell me. After mantra recitation we left the temple, ringing the bell first, and walked slowly home. Before having her hot milk, she changed out of her pūjā clothes and said three Navkār Mantras; the morning pūjā was completed.

On this day she did not make the offerings of incense and lamp that she did on virtually all other days. Still, Dadiji's morning pūjā was relatively long (over an hour), but among her peer group (grandmothers and widows) spending a long time performing pūjā is common. Because these women have stopped most of their household work—passing it onto the daughters-in-law[35]—they have more time to devote to temple worship. Frequently, the older women spent entire days at the temple. Difficulties in walking justified spending a large part of the day in the mendicants' hostel talking or reading, especially if the women knew they would be returning to the temple again later that day. During the Āyambil Olī fast the older women performing the fast were at the temple complex for most of the day. Dadiji was accepted at the temple as a very devout and knowledgeable Jain. Her pūjā, which I just described, was complete in the sense that she did all the pieces of a pūjā, but you can see that the ordering of the pūjā acts was very fluid, allowing Dadiji to improvise according to the particular rhythm of that day's worship. Ideally, the pūjā of Padmāvatī would have been done immediately following Jina pūjā. Likewise, the prayer series was interrupted to help the other woman with her prayers, and the bhāv pūjā was interrupted for Padmāvatī's pūjā. The fluidity of Dadiji's pūjā and her flexibility mark her confidence as a laywoman. In contrast, a certain rigidity highlights the concerns of her teenage granddaughters, who had recently started doing their full morning pūjā (especially the prayer recitations) without older female relatives on hand to assist them.

PŪJĀ WITH SONI, 16, AND SVETA, 17

During the Dīvālī school holiday (November 16, 1993), Sveta (Hema's daughter and Soni's cousin) was visiting. Soni, Sveta, and I went to the temple together. We entered the temple after dabbing a dot of sandalwood paste on our foreheads and had darśan of the Jinas, beginning with the darśan song and then proceeding around to each image. Finally they sang the prayer to Padmāvatī together. We went to get sandalwood paste, which Soni poured from the bowl into our silver bowls and we went to the central door to the inner sanctum.

The images—starting with the central image of Ajitnāth—were dabbed with sandalwood paste on the nine limbs of the Jina with the ring finger. During the whole sandalwood pūjā, Sveta sang stavan aloud. These stavan did not necessarily match her actions; while she was doing pūjā to Mahāvīr, she was singing a stavan to Pārśvanāth. Then they went and applied sandalwood to Bhairav on his forehead.

We then went to the image of Padmāvatī. They applied the paste with their thumbs to her forehead and then to her attributes (the noose and the goad) and then, pulling aside the edge of Padmāvatī's sari, Soni put some sandalwood on her right toe. A woman came and corrected her, saying, "You do not do that." We went out, washed our silver plates and hands, and then got a rice board.

Before sitting down, Soni and Sveta offered the incense. Then I picked up the mirror to hand it to Sveta and she said that the flywhisk came first, so we waved the flywhisk and then the fan and mirror. There was no available lamp at the time, but a woman lit one and handed it to us to offer. We sat down to make rice svastik and Soni practiced the new round svastik she had just learned from her mother (Ranjana) and showed Sveta how it was made. Sveta made a fancy rice drawing shaped like a clover leaf (*śrīvatsa*—one of the aṣṭamaṅgalam). Then Soni recited the prayer series and Sveta chimed in the first line of the next section whenever Soni lagged. In the end they sang a stavan together. Then we went back to their house changed and had tea.

Soni and Sveta were still young enough that they were learning to perform pūjā without their mothers' help. When they recited the prayer series, they would prompt each other on which section came next. It was of paramount importance to the Jains I knew that they recited texts correctly. The formal Jain school exams involved writing down the entire morning worship prayer series (and later, pratikramaṇ) series from memory without mistakes.[36] The informal Jain schools include memorization of key texts as well. It is important enough to say one's prayers correctly that it was acceptable for the other woman to interrupt Dadiji during Dadiji's own prayers. A request for prayer recitation was the most common reason Dadiji's worship was interrupted by others; otherwise people generally treated pūjā as inviolable. With Soni and Sveta, who were still learning their pūjā, the prayer series recitation was a time when they were both especially careful and corrective. For them as learners, the differences between their pūjā styles was a mild source of tension, as they would correct what they saw as each other's (and my) "mistakes." Likewise, the woman corrected Soni's putting sandalwood paste on Padmāvatī's foot—a gesture reserved usually for Jinas—which no one critiqued when done by a grown and devout laywoman like Nita, in the following example.[37] Although it was not a mistake to skip a particular part of the pūjā (except the Jinas in general), neither of the girls applied sandalwood paste to the side images on the Jina images or to the siddhacakra as their mothers did.

I never saw anyone correct the daily pūjā of an observant adult laywoman except for correcting misspoken words during a recitation.[38] Nita was an active participant in the maṇḍaḷ and, like most women in Shivajinagar, she went to the temple every morning. Nita's daily worship was more introspective and quiet—as was she herself—than the women whose pūjās I have described. I include her pūjā to give an example of a less interactive style, which was common among the younger and middle-aged married women.[39]

PŪJĀ WITH NITA, 31

On January 17, 1994, I went to the temple with Nita. We went to the central door and sang the darśan prayer and then performed a bow to each of the Jinas. We put on our handkerchiefs and after getting sandalwood paste in her own silver plate and silver bowl, Nita did sandalwood pūjā to every single Jina image in the inner sanctum—not just the toes of the side images (as Dadiji did) and not excluding the small Jinas on the brass images—singing stavan while she worshipped Ajitnāth and Mahāvīr. Then she applied sandalwood paste to the forehead of Bhairav and went over to Padmāvatī's shrine.

At Padmāvatī she applied sandal paste to the forehead, attributes, and right foot on both the marble and the metal images; Nita also sang a stavan to Padmāvatī while doing her worship [unlike in the previous two examples]. We took off our handkerchiefs and washed our silver plates and went to do the prayer series when Nita saw that there were flowers. After putting our handkerchiefs back on, we took flowers and placed one on each of the large Jina images. Outside the inner sanctum we offered incense, the lamp, and then the fan and mirror.

Then we sat down with the rice boards. Nita made one fancy svastik and four smaller ones around it. She recited the morning worship prayer series and sang the "Śrī Śāntināth Stavan" as she flipped through the pages of the *Śrī Sudhāras Stavan Saṅgrah*. While she was reciting the prayer series, her husband and daughter came in for pūjā. Rashmi, age 6, went with her father for darśan, and then, as he did sandalwood pūjā, she went to get incense and light it at the lamp next to the "assembly hall" pūjā stand. Rashmi carefully covered her mouth while offering the incense to the Jinas and then after offering it to Padmāvatī, waved the incense in front of her mother and I. Nita corrected her and told her the incense was not for people, only for God (*Bhagavān*) and must also be offered to the Jinas first.

A group of women went to the assembly hall pūjā stand and we got up to join them. There were so many women that Nita could not get her hand in to help while they bathed the image, so when they were done, she poured the *pañcamṛt* (the milky mixture) and then water ablutions over the brass Mahāvīr and the siddhacakra. Then she did seven circumambulations (each separated by a prostration) of the "assembly hall" pūjā stand—turning as she passed in front of Padmāvatī so she did not have her back to this goddess. Then we left the temple and went to the mendicants' hostel, where there were four female mendicants. Starting with the female mendicant leader she performed four guruvandans (sets of prostrations and prayers to the teachers)—one for each female mendicant. Nita briefly explained who I was and then we left. We split up at the temple, as I had to go directly home that day.

Nita performed both the circumambulations (*pradakṣinā*) and the bathing or ablutions (*abhiṣek*) of the Mahāvīr image in the pūjā stand daily. She came earlier than many women did and rarely missed the ablutions of the central Jina or Padmāvatī, either. Nita also performed most of the gestures available for pūjā virtually every day. Her daily pūjā was based on her internalized sense of ideal pūjā. The order of the acts, too, was loosely based on this ideal, but as the previous example shows, the particular details of the day—that she could not do the ablutions with the other women—meant that she worked around these obstacles to the order.

Nita's pūjā was single-minded and solitary. Her style was less fluid than her sisters-in-law, who each spent less time in the temple than she did and were therefore faced with decisions of priorities. Her sisters-in-law each had a somewhat different approach to temple worship: Lata, as the eldest sister-in-law (*bhābhī*), had more work at home and felt obligated to return to the house quickly and performed sandalwood pūjā and morning worship prayer series at a breakneck speed; Ranjana often sang extra stavan and sang them quite loudly; Kavita did several rounds of mantra recitation each morning. Each woman's devotional sentiments determines what style her daily pūjā takes. Women's pūjā varies as widely as the women's personalities. For Ranjana and Nita, pūjā seemed to provide a place to be alone, as I suspect it does for other women who live in joint families. For other women, it was a respite from the endless work at home. Without a doubt the meditative elements of pūjā and the attention to worship gave many women a sense of peace and pleasure; there were innumerable times when women of many families expressed great sympathy when for some reason a woman could not do her pūjā (menses, birth or death in the family, serious personal illness) or if it was curtailed by work.

While the workload in the home may affect the timing and the length of a woman's visit to the temple, a "good Jain" family would be pushing its luck if it totally prevented women's worship. Among the observant families of Shivajinagar it was expected that all members of the families would visit the temple every day.[40] Almost every visit I made to the temple included a discussion about where so-and-so was. After pūjā, when the women had their tea, they would invariably report on where the other women were; it seemed not to be gossip but an exchange which ultimately let the women know what was going on in the lives of the women of their congregation.[41] That a family would prevent her pūjā was so unthinkable that I never heard it as a suggestion or even a jest.

For the women whose families had strict limits on social visiting, temple going (and all temple or maṇḍaḷ sponsored events) was very important socially; it was those women's sole sense of a community outside the house. If a family can allow fairly extensive visiting because of the number of women doing the work, the women may still have very little time for introspection; in a large joint family with too few hands, quiet and solitude are a rare commodity. Ranjana used the time at the temple as an uninterruptable time to be alone. Even the walk to and from the temple was part of her time, though many times the walk presented an opportunity for her to stop briefly and talk with a friend on the street.

Rarely did anyone have the time to linger over every aspect of the pūjā—though if the time was available to the women they seemed to take the opportunity. For example, when women were in their mother's home or often when they had my "education" to accomplish, they spent much more time in the temple doing pūjā and in coming and going to temple than they did otherwise. However, with Kavita or Lata, I was occasionally rushed along—I moved very slowly in the temple even compared with then 9-year-old Moni—so they could get back to the house and finish their morning work. I feel certain that one reason for the number of times I was brought along was that because my research had been widely approved in Shivajinagar as Jain appreciation and glorification (*prabhāvanā*), the women were given a bit more freedom to linger, go visiting, or take a break from work to help me. Most women did this infrequently enough to uphold the sense of a vacation. At the end of my research, I went to thank Sheelu for all the help she had given me during the year and her response was to thank me for the opportunity to gain merit through helping me work on my book which she felt—I hope rightly—would ultimately add to the greater general knowledge and appreciation of Jainism. Perhaps because of this belief and the perquisites of extra freedom, rarely did I feel that my presence was a serious irritation.[42]

In many ways the women's temple worship resembled the men's, except for the amount of attention men often paid to Bhairav.[43] Because Bhairav took a vow of *brahmacarya* (a complex celibacy vow), I was told that laywomen can only put a sandalwood paste mark on his forehead; Maluben and Dadiji, who themselves had taken a vow of brahmacarya, omitted even that. The Jinas' gender neutrality is illustrated by the fact that a woman with a vow of brahmacarya still performs sandalwood pūjā to the Jinas, while Bhairav is still decidedly male.[44] Bhairav received complex and extended attention from several men in the congregation. One Mārvāḍī layman came across town daily to perform pūjā, image decoration, and āratī of the Bhairav every day. The Bhairav image was often decorated with a design of dabs of sandalwood around his chest and face, and special trident-shaped rice designs were drawn in front of his image. Padmāvatī was somewhat less specifically gendered in her appeal—both men and women offered her prayers and āratī. However, women were more involved in the daily worship of Padmāvatī; the women bathed her, marked her with sandalwood paste, and offered saris to Padmāvatī far more than any of the men did (except Arun, the *pujārī*, who regularly offered coconuts to Padmāvatī).[45] The gendered focus of devotion to the these two guardian deities was marked when, at a large evening singing session in January 1999, the Bhairav āratī was performed by a crowd of men while the Padmāvatī āratī was performed by a young couple accompanied by a crowd of women.

The differences between men's and women's practice was more in the style and focus of the pūjā. Men rarely sang stavan during their worship—they often recited additional prayers (and sometimes litanies) instead—and were more likely to perform the angī—dressing of the Jinas or guardian deities in silver armor or special clothes (see figure 1-3)—and the āratīs. These latter two are acts which must be sponsored and paid for, and women did not have access to the money required. Men, however, did not have the time away from the stores (until they retired) to go to the afternoon programs—sermons and pūjās—which form a large part of the women's practice. In fact, for a working adult man to do so often could lead to criticism about whether he was doing his part for the family or whether he had sufficient ambition. Because of the relative brevity of men's morning pūjā, they did not perform the time-consuming prayer series, circumambulations, and other additional pūjās (like the daily ablutions or Snātra Pūjās) that some women performed. Because women performed most of the fasting, they also performed most of the fasting pūjās. Women's work (though extremely rigorous) was somewhat time flexible—if the women in the house were cooperative—and the women's practices reflect this nonfixed timing throughout their praxis. There were several men in the Ajitnāth congregation who had adjusted their work schedules so that they could do eightfold pūjā every morning, but even those men who wished to perform the eightfold pūjā daily voiced time concerns: men who had the economic authority to sponsor special acts rarely felt they had the time flexibility and those of more limited resources often felt that they could not risk opening their stores (or going to work for someone else) late every morning to perform the longer pūjā.

For the Jain women of Ajitnāth congregation, there was a wide variety of ritual actions from which they could make their choices. However, these acts were determined within overlapping spheres of normative values. Women construct their daily pūjā from a menu of ritual acts, all of which are considered pūjā. They learn these acts primarily through repetition of pūjā with older female relatives. As adults, these same women teach Jain practice to the children in their households. Although there is formal Jain religious education where some children learn their prayers and edifying stories, the basic understanding of what constitutes Jain pūjā—and by extension what it means to be an observant Jain—is learned at home. The occasional Jain boy may gain some knowledge of Jain theology from residential Jain camps, but for the most part theological questions are left to the individual to sort out. The only source for that kind of discussion is lay manuals, which are mostly helpful in terms of determining what is "wrong" rather than what is "right." No one source, then, is ultimately authoritative in determining the form and structure of pūjā.

Limits of Individuation

Despite the basically improvisational nature of Jain daily pūjā, the acts that can be performed in a temple are circumscribed by a shared understanding of what it means to "get it wrong."[46] There are several limits to the fluidity of Jain pūjā which seem to arise primarily from two frames: the idea of faults (*āśātnā*), which arise out of carelessness or a lack of respect, and the hierarchy of images worthy of worship, which ultimately becomes an issue of respect for that hierarchy. For example, when one offers anything to any image that is not a Jina, that offering cannot be reoffered to the Jinas. Thus, if one wants to offer a stick of incense to both the Jinas and the guardian deities, it must be offered to all the Jinas first and then, after offering it to the guardian deities, it must be left in the guardian deities' incense holders—so it could not possibly be offered to a Jina. This is true of all offerings. The importance of a devotional attitude cannot override what is seen as carelessness (*pramāda*) or a disrespectful act (*āśātnā*).

In the *Yogaśāstra*, Hemacandra gives a list of ten faults or acts which are disrespectful to Jainism and therefore should be avoided by all Jains: sleeping, laughter, sporting, quarreling, spitting, evil gossip, and eating any of the four kinds of food and drink. In time these shift from generally bad things to do to things especially to be avoided in the temple (Williams 1963). If a woman (or man) wore shoes to get to the temple—Maluben, Savita, and others living nearby came on bare feet, while Ranjana, Nita and others who came from further away wore sandals—these shoes were left to the side of the temple entrance stairs along with any other inappropriate items such as bags for purchasing vegetables, umbrellas, canes, and so on. The things that were left outside reflected a contemporary understanding of faults. Nemicandra's list of eighty-four faults is primarily an elaboration on the themes presented in the ten faults listed by Hemacandra but with more of a focus on things to avoid during religious activities; he specifically includes leaving shoes and umbrellas outside the temple (Williams 1963). The list also includes an injunction against wearing a tiara in a temple, but during the Snātra Pūjā, the pūjā sponsors are commonly encouraged to do just that. In all the lay manuals, the pūjā sponsors are invariably dressed in fancy jewelry and wearing crowns or tiaras. The injunctions, then, not only do not directly instruct Jains who have not read the original texts but also do not rigidly define the contemporary understandings—or probably those of any time period—of faults.

Śāntisūri lists injunctions with regard to books: one should not touch a book with one's foot, drop a book on the ground, eat near a book, or express disapproval toward sacred knowledge or books (Williams 1963). Keeping books, rosaries, and, in fact, any objects associated with Jain knowledge or Jinas themselves off the floor, taking care not to drop them, and to not touch them during menses was—for the women I knew—a part of the way they expected everyone to behave, not a special consideration like some of the more complex and esoteric restrictions on actions in the temple. They were seen as examples of minimal respect, the sort of practices even rather lax Jains performed. At a Vāstuk Pūjā, several maṇḍaḷ women voiced concerns about whether the sponsor's intentions were bad enough to counteract the good effects of the action of sponsoring a formal pūjā. To sponsor a formal pūjā with a lack of respect (the women especially pointed out that the sponsoring family was gossiping throughout the pūjā—a fault according to every list I encountered) was perceived as a greater sin than not to sponsor a pūjā at all.

In a relatively popular lay manual, *Cālo Jinalaye Jaiye*, each description of the proper performance of a part of Jain pūjā is followed by precautions pertaining to the particular pūjā. For example, when discussing the importance of a pre-pūjā bath and the particular way it should be performed, the precautions which follow say, "When bathing before worship, keep absolutely silent. These days youth sing film songs while bathing, this is not okay" (Hemaratnavijay 1993, 28), extending the restriction against nonreligious behavior back to the point of the pre-pūjā bath. Many Jains I knew did not participate in any nonreligious activities from their bath until they had finished their pūjā. Hemaratnavijay gives extensive restrictions about performing each act of the pūjā based on the lists of the eighty-four sinful acts. Maluben drew the line at any non-pūjā specific talk in the temple—as most women did—and insisted that even information about the maṇḍaḷ must be shared outside the temple—often on the side porches. One woman, however, did not hesitate to discuss inside the temple (as I was leaving on three occasions) my coming to tea and what I did or did not eat. While Ranjana would go out on the porch to have extended discussions of any kind during the morning pūjā, she was quick to pass around photos before a formal pūjā and comment on them. In a skit that acted out different examples of having the wrong sentiments in the temple, Kamalben mocked the women who talk about nonreligious topics in the temple. She pretended to be chatting about the latest gossip—including discussion about possible available girls for her son's marriage—in between sections of her morning prayer recitation.

While the pūjā space can often be most clearly marked by the lack of idle conversation and the items left outside (and, of course, the pūjā rituals themselves), the demarcation of pūjā time is most clearly represented by the donning of pūjā clothes. Because anga pūjā (that part of pūjā that takes one inside the inner sanctum) cannot be performed in regular clothing and because of the restrictions surrounding keeping pūjā clothes pure, anga pūjā is always framed by the change into and out of pūjā clothes—and further still by the donning of the handkerchief over the mouth and nose, which is also required to enter the inner sanctum.[47] It is at the changing of the clothes that the mind becomes focused on pūjā. Because of its framing role it behooves us to look at the clothing and its restrictions to see what is required for a Jain to enter into pūjā. Nothing should be done that will interfere with one's devotional attitude from the time of donning pūjā clothes until they are removed. One morning while I waited for Soni to go to the temple with me, I saw Rashmi, her youngest cousin-sister, nearly hit Soni. Rashmi's mother grabbed her and said, "Can't you see Soni is wearing pūjā clothes? What kind of sin (pāp) do you wish for?" and Rashmi fled the room, distraught. Although she may not have understood the theological implications of her mother's scolding, the ultimate lesson—that someone in pūjā clothes cannot be disturbed—was painfully clear. Hitting her sister in pūjā clothes was like hitting her in the temple.

Pūjā clothes are kept "ritually pure" through adherence to a series of restrictions about the activities that can be performed in the clothing. During my research time, I was periodically stopped from certain acts when I was in pūjā clothes. I was first told that I should never put on my pūjā clothes if I was not freshly bathed. When in these clothes, I was not to take food or water[48] or ever enter a toilet, much less use one, and during menses I was not even to touch the clothes. While wearing pūjā clothes, according to Dadiji, I should not have idle conversations or do work, though I often saw women finish up a last-minute chore before heading out the door to go to the temple. According to Maluben, one should do nothing except pūjā in the clothes; she would not even chat outside the temple as other women did. Even though there was a strong negative relationship between pūjā clothes and eating, it was common for the daughters-in-law to buy vegetables on their way home from the temple, which saved them time in going from their house to the vegetable sellers, who were nearer to the temple. Some women, like Savita, were very particular about having any nonreligious interactions while in their pūjā clothes; Savita could afford to be particular, though, as she lived quite close to the temple and the vegetable sellers. But others, like Lata, often had errands to run on the way home. Almost every morning either she or Ranjana would have to stop on the way home and purchase the vegetables for that day's midday meal.[49]

Pūjā clothes are also protected from impurities when they are not being worn. They were not always stored in isolation—though in Karaḍ two of the daughters-in-law did store their pūjā saris separately from their cupboards in hard suitcases—but most women I knew tried to keep the pūjā saris separate within their cupboards in spite of the fact that these women did not touch any of the fabrics in their cupboard at all during their menses, asking other women to pull out the clothes needed. Likewise, pūjā clothes were not washed separately in Dadiji's house, as they are in Puṣṭimārg Vaiṣṇav houses,[50] but those clothes worn during menses were washed separately. Pūjā clothes included undergarments as well, but jewelry was not seen to carry pollutants with them and were worn whenever and wherever. When a place is deeply polluted after death or a birth, it is not enough to have the pūjā clothes out of sight and contact; after Sheelu had just given birth to her baby I was not permitted to enter her house (by Maluben, her mother) because I had my pūjā clothes in a bag with me. She said, "It will make them unclean" and thus unsuitable to wear to the temple.

For men, pūjā clothes—a white or cream-colored *dhotī* and *khes*—were easily identified as pūjā clothes, but for the women it was usually one of the saris they had set aside for pūjā. Often women were aware of which saris, especially in their own families, were pūjā clothes. However, there were other signs, besides sari recognition, that identified a woman on her way to do pūjā. A woman would not be carrying her purse, she would be carrying a box or bag full of rice and often a handful of flowers from her garden, and she would also be subdued and single-minded about the way she walked to the temple. The young girls and unmarried women often wore their new clothes for pūjā before the clothes were relegated to regular use—except for clothing that had a black base color because of the seemingly universal belief that black is inauspicious and never acceptable for temple worship. Sometimes, as in the case of Soni and Sveta, the young girls were given special dresses and traditional Gujarātī outfits (*caṇiyā-colīs*),[51] which they wore for pūjā on special days. These special pūjā clothes remained pūjā clothes until they either did not fit or were intentionally worn as fancy clothes to an event that included eating. Sometimes—like the young women and their fancy caṇiyā-colīs—a middle-age woman would save a special sari for pūjā; when I gave Ranjana a sari from Pālītānā, it remained one of her permanent pūjā saris. After some time, most pūjā saris were used for regular wear.

In *Jindarśan*, Bhadrabahusūri writes about temple precautions against faults (āsātnā). He writes a lot about dress, as pūjā clothes express a commitment to Jain ideals, and I include here a few examples:

> Do not wear indecent dress and decorations. The temple is not a fashion-show gallery. . . . Ladies and girls should never enter the temple wearing modern fashionable dress. . . . When you go to the temple, it is not proper to use any cosmetics to decorate yourself or add beauty to your appearance. (*Jinadarśan* 1991, 55–56)

Although the lay manuals stress the importance of plain and simple clothing in the temple, the women often wore their best saris to the temple. Reynell discusses this conflict of proper restraint and ostentatiousness between the ideals of the Jain religion and social practice with regard to women's dress (Reynell 1985a, 1985b). However, Norman (1991) sees Reynell's critique as a conflation of lay and ascetic practices of nonattachment (*aparigrah*). Neither scholar encountered the kinds of articulations of complex theological rationales for this "fancy dress" that seemed to be woven into the fabric of Shivajinagar's Jain women's identification with Indrāṇī or other queens as part of their worship and as part of being lay Jains. Although there were critiques of ostentatiousness among Jain women (during the maṇḍaḷ picnic to Alandi, Kamalben's skit satirized a woman doing her morning prayers while she keeps looking around to see if anyone has a nicer sari than hers), many women explained to me that to offer one's finest clothing to the temple counteracts the sin (pāp) of pride.[52] For example, when I arrived in June 1997 with saris for all the women in the Alandikar family, they saved the saris to wear first at a Snātra Pūjā while on pilgrimage later that month. Likewise, Soni's new clothes were always worn at least once as pūjā clothes before she wore them as regular clothes. This in effect makes all clothing first an expression of faith, and thus encourages a detachment from the pride of wealth and beauty. On Mahāvīr Janam Dīvas, the women all wore their fanciest clothing and were clearly participating in a visual statement of their family's and the community's success; as opposed to the wearing of fancy clothes for pūjā, at this event there was a sense of pride.

The women, in dressing up for pūjā—especially for special pūjās like the Snātra, Pañcakalyāṇak, and Vāstuk Pūjās, are identifying with Indrāṇī (Queen of the Gods) as the ideal worshipper of the Jina (Babb 1996). In fact, as part of the Dīvālī season, an all-Pune women's maṇḍaḷ fancy dress contest is held.[53] During Paryuṣaṇ in 1994, when another all-Pune contest was held for which maṇḍaḷ could perform the perfect Snātra Pūjā, I helped Ranjana dress in pūjā clothes to perform the Snātra Pūjā (as it involves touching the image during the eightfold pūjā section, pūjā clothes were required). While she was choosing her sari and jewelry she sought out her fanciest jewelry and borrowed the best pieces belonging to her co-sisters-in-law (see figure 5-2, Ranjana is wearing the crown). When I helped her put all the jewelry on before the competition she asked me: "Do I look like a queen?" Even Maluben, who made a point of wearing simple cotton pūjā saris every morning, dressed up in a fancy silk sari for the Navānu Prakārī (99 Offerings) Pūjā that the maṇḍaḷ sponsored during the rainy season.

Even pūjā clothes themselves, a relatively unquestioned aspect of daily pūjā, when explored can demonstrate the conflicts and individual resolutions of the Jain laywomen with regard to normative texts and each women's personal expression of her devotion to the Jinas. For the women who are involved in the daily worship of the Jinas there was no dichotomy between devotionalism and correct worship; as long as the pūjā was not "wrong" it was meritorious. Humphrey and Laidlaw articulate a useful distinction between the constitutive rules—those that govern what is considered to be pūjā—and regulative rules—those that govern what is the proper way to perform pūjā. The distinction becomes clear when one looks at the results of a transgression against the rules; if one does not follow the constitutive rules the

FIGURE 5-2. Pārśva Maṇḍaḷ doing the Śānti Kalaś during the 1994 Snātra Pūjā Competition, Goḍījī Temple, Guruvār Peṭh, Pune. The woman in the center is performing the Sānti Kalaś. Behind her, the woman dressed as a queen is reciting the text that accompanies the ritual. Behind the reciter is the rest of the maṇḍaḷ in matching saris and to the right is the young women's maṇḍaḷ.

act is simply not an act of pūjā (and therefore not a source of either merit or sin), whereas if one does not follow the regulative rules the act is a source of sin (pāp) (Humphrey and Laidlaw 1994). However, the women with whom I spoke included having any sentiment other than devotion as a transgression against the regulative rules. A lack of devotion sometimes (in conversations with these women) denoted that the pūjā was done disrespectfully (with inappropriate materials, in clothes worn during acts of violence or uncleanliness, with disregard for possible violence) and thus displayed the pūjā performer's lack of concern about the regulative rules. At other times this lack of devotion denoted that the pūjā performers who did pūjā had incorrect intentions (only in order to gain wealth or prestige, in order to gain the attentions of others for gain), usually evidenced by either acts of disrespect or a lack of enthusiasm for their worship.

The women at Ajitnāth seemed reluctant—when questioned—to make sentiment or intention the sole determiner of the meritoriousness or sinfulness of an act but voiced their belief that intention was sometimes more significant (in determining the karmic results) than the details of an act. The women's ambiguity here mirrors an issue for the development of Jain karma theory. The earliest Jain teachings of karma (the *Sūtrakṛtanga*), explain that negative karma accrues through even involuntary and unintentional acts of violence; this idea is later expanded in the *Viyahapannatti* (*Bhagavaī*—one of the twelve anga texts) along more compromising lines to state that the acts unintentionally committed by Jain mendicants in the process of religious activity have only momentary effects. Later still, Jinabhadra (sixth century) articulates an intention-based understanding of sin which allows the mendicants to continue to perform life-sustaining and religiously sanctioned actions while acknowledging the inevitable injury to the omnipresent souls (Dundas 1992). Cort looks at intention particularly in the context of what Jains argued to be the right sentiments to have during worship and how those sentiments either increase or decrease the possible effects of destroying karma or gaining merit (Cort 1989). Humphrey and Laidlaw (1994) speak of the ongoing presence of this debate in contemporary Jainism which becomes the terrain for Jain negotiations between belief in the primacy of action and that of the primacy of intention; laywomen with whom I spoke in Pune were also struggling with these same questions in the context of their devotional praxis and in the context of maṇḍaḷs—the latter of which we turn to in chapter 8. In the frame of this discussion of daily pūjā, the women wondered whether small transgressions of regulative rules in the acts of pūjā may be overlooked if one's intention was good and whether seemingly correct actions in pūjā are meritorious if the performer's intention transgresses the regulative rules.

Stavan Choice and Personal Devotion

The centrality of the sentiment of the worshipper is a "great equalizer" for women who rarely had the authority to completely determine the time they could give for worship or the amount of offerings—both money and material—they could bring. At daily pūjā, the details of the individual worship may represent what the woman feels she can best perform, but the overriding consideration for the women as a whole was that they brought themselves to the temple to do pūjā (similar to

Humphrey and Laidlaw's idea of ritual commitment) and that proper pūjā would arise organically from devotional sentiment. This idea reflects the doctrinal ideal of the stages of spiritual development (*guṇasthānas*) where each stage leads the devotee from that initial insight of right faith to correct knowledge which leads to right action or proper conduct (Jaini 1979). It is important to remember that the ways these women defined right knowledge and right action differ somewhat from the mokṣa-oriented ascetic definitions according to the stages of spiritual development in the orthodox mendicant texts. The Ajitnāth stavan that starts this chapter asks: "Can we be persuaded, before having knowledge, to be merciful?" The question here is one that matters to Jain laywomen who focus on practice as the primary constitutive act of being Jains. As we see later, maṇḍaḷ women sometimes saw correct practice as the automatic result of correct belief; they wondered, for example, If people do not have knowledge of correct practice, could they possibly have correct belief? It was a strong assumption among the maṇḍaḷ women that anyone with correct belief and proper devotional sentiment would necessarily be interested in knowing how to perform Jainism. But the rationale for performing pūjā—that by being close to the Jina as a role model will cause some of the Jina's good qualities to attach themselves to the devotee and thereby make the devotee more devoted—given to me by the female mendicant and discussed earlier in the chapter challenges this linear model of religious progress from faith to knowledge to action.

The Jain laywomen in Shivajinagar were engaged in their own expressions of Jain piety and devotion. Daily pūjā was a time and place where they were relatively free to individuate their practice. It was then that women sang stavan that personally affected them, and at that time they could choose which particular manifestation of Jain devotion suited them best. While the women performed the eightfold pūjā, they often sang stavan quietly to themselves. Some recited texts as they performed their pūjā to the central image, but afterward they would switch to singing a stavan while doing sandalwood pūjā to the other images in the temple. During the morning worship prayer series—which requires a stavan to be sung in the late middle of the recitation—women usually sang their favorite stavan, often ones with slow and beautiful melodies. Between the rapid recitation and many postures of the prayer series, stavan singing provides a break, as one is supposed to be seated comfortably and with eyes on the Jina while singing. It is the only slow part of the morning pūjā. Virtually all of the morning pūjā repertoire stavan, in fact, are slow and languorous, with many verses. For women who were less involved in the singing of stavan and for men, when they sang rather than reciting an alternate prayer, the stavan sung here was usually one from the Sudhāras collection. This was a time that most women sang favorite stavan to themselves, with virtually no concern about context. A woman with a large repertoire of stavan may choose stavan appropriate to the various Jina images; Dadiji would sing a stavan addressing the Jina in front of whom she was seated in the temple. As opposed to the performances of stavan where the audience (perhaps, including the Jina) must be entertained with auspicious songs, the singing in morning pūjā was more an act of personal introspective devotion, and the singer's particular style of devotion mattered more than the appropriateness of the aesthetic "fit," the worthiness of the content (as in fasting songs) or the quality of her performance "style." The release from performative critiques—

which were definitely present at prepared performances—allowed the singer to sing for the Jina's sake and as a creative expression of her devotion.

Most of the time women did not sing stavan unless they were at home sitting for meditation, at the temple or on pilgrimage.[54] There is a strong belief that the stavan are for the Jina. When I was interviewing and recording Savita's singing in August 1994, she insisted that we go into the temple room in her house where, she said, the sound was better. Although it was certainly true that the sounds of the pressure cookers, children, and birds were plentiful in the outer room and the shrine quiet, there seemed to be more to it than that. In 1999, when there was a stavan singing program in Ranjana's house, the singing was stopped while someone fetched a picture of Pārśvanāth and placed it in front of all the singers, after which the singing could proceed. When I asked whether they sang stavan when they worked, Dadiji said that the stavan should not be sung while one might be committing violence. This precluded singing while cooking or washing—times when Christian hymns or spirituals have often been sung—and left only nonwork time—a rare commodity for most women. Whenever women gathered for a religiously sponsored event, they would sing stavan. When we were driving to Alandi for the maṇḍaḷ picnic, the older women in the jeep began to sing old stavan. They first sang the "Navkār Mantra" (sung at the beginning of every religious event and recited whenever groups set out to travel) and then went on to sing stavan for the forty-minute drive. The fact that it was a maṇḍaḷ-sponsored trip seemed to make it a religious event and justified the stavan singing, in spite of the potential violence of the jeep's motion. In June 1997, the women started one bus pilgrimage with the "Navkār Mantra" followed by five stavan and then, ultimately, followed with a recitation of the *Bhaktāmara Stotra*. All this was sanctioned because it focused the pilgrims' minds collectively on the purpose of their travel, while also insuring a safe journey.

Stavan singing is part of pūjā and part of what one does as nonaction, which precludes their use as work songs. However, because all the homes I went into had a small house shrine, a woman could go there and sing, as Nita often did. Nita said she went to sing in the shrine room—which also happened to be her bedroom—when she wanted peace (and quiet). She would sing either "Mahāvīr Śrī Bhagavān" or "O Compassionate Lord" while there. This was a rare time just for herself away from the business of housework. Savita, too, found her household shrine to be a retreat within her home. When the women wanted to go to the temple, it required more time, but during the day they could take a few minutes in the shrine room. Solo singing provides a private time for "communion" (even if theoretically one-sided) with the Jina and establishes a sacred "place" which serves as a respite or religious retreat for women.

Stavan choice reflects a person's temperament as well as her style of devotion. For most of the women I knew, the stavan they sang for themselves or as part of their daily worship were categorized as "beautiful" stavan. A discussion of three of these favorite stavan illustrates the relationships between singers, their personal understandings of Jain devotion and Jain theology, and personal stavan choice. All three examples that follow have a few things in common; they are considered old stavan and are sung to slow and traditional melodies. They focus on the relationship between the singer and the Jina they are addressing. For two of the women, their favorite stavan actually addressed their particular favorite Jina.[55]

Nita is married to the fourth brother in a joint family. Her husband is losing his sight, and they have only one child, a daughter. Nita herself lost her mother at a relatively young age but has a very close relationship with her mother's sister, who also lives in Pune. She often must be extra flexible and resilient in the face of her dependence on others for the present and future well-being of herself, her husband, and her daughter. Nita, whose daily pūjā included the humbling practice of no less than eleven circumambulations and prostrations, asking the Jina for forgiveness, often sang the following stavan. In her choice of a favorite (*manpasand*) stavan, Nita picked one that described the proper humility of the Jain who desires nothing so grand as mokṣa but simply a blessing from the Jina:

We are filled with your glance,
 Mahāvīr Śrī Bhagavān
You give darśan, you cut away sorrow,
 Mahāvīr Śrī Bhagavān
I am the humbled student at your lotus feet.
I do prayers of salutation to Mahāvīr.
Have mercy and accept our devotion,
 Mahāvīr Śrī Bhagavān
Distressed I went to your door, O Mahāvīr,
Give me your blessing, take us into your heart, O Mahāvīr,
Helmsman, make it successful.
 Mahāvīr Śrī Bhagavān
Listen to your devotee's pleas, O Mahāvīr,
Let me live in your courtyard.
 Mahāvīr Śrī Bhagavān

When I first started my research, Nita, who was usually very reserved, told me to bring my tape recorder to her house so I could record this stavan from her. She told me this was the best stavan for peacefulness. Later she said of this stavan: "I sing this stavan when I am sad or upset and I have peace again." Nita was a very private person; she sang under her breath while she performed her daily pūjā. In general, she was more likely to hope for help than to demand it. This particular stavan was one of the two most popular for personal singing. "Mahāvīr Śrī Bhagavān" and "O Compassionate Lord" (Savita's favorite) were sung by most women at one time or another. Likewise, they were often chosen when women were singing several stavan, particularly for me. Both of these two stavan had especially beautiful melodies and very humble lyrics.

Ranjana, 38 years old, is married to the second brother in a joint family with two sons and two daughters. She also came from a close-knit joint family where she returns for at least six weeks every year and where she is the youngest child (four brothers, three sisters) in her generation. Ranjana's favorite Jina was Pārśvanāth, as Nita's was Mahāvīr. Their choice of songs reflected either the previous interest in the particular Jina or that the choice of favorite Jina evolved from the song. Ranjana's favorite stavan, "Inner Lord, Hear My Song," addresses the Jina, Pārśvanāth:[56]

Inner Lord, hear my song, the glory of the Three Worlds is yours.
Hearing you, I came to your door, carry me across the sorrow of birth and death.
 Do this for your servant, O King, give us the joy of liberation!
You fulfill all the heart's desires and you destroy all worries.

Such is your promise, O King, but why do you stay so far away?
  Do this for your servant, O King, give us the joy of liberation!
Seeing your servant so restless, will you never hold me in your heart?
How are you called the ocean of compassion, will you never do me this favor?
  Do this for your servant, O King, give us the joy of liberation!
O Gem of Śankheśvar, Sāhib, pay attention to this request.
Jinaharsa says: rescue me, your servant, from the sea of emotions,
  Do this for your servant, O King, give us the joy of liberation!

Ranjana sang this stavan most mornings as part of her morning worship. It was her favorite stavan for two reasons. She loved the melody—an "old" stavan melody—and she said the words had good meaning (*sāro arth*). Ranjana was a very confident singer and was sure of her position as a devout Jain laywoman within her congregation. Her daily pūjā, involvement in the maṇḍaḷ, and marriage into a very observant family were external manifestations of her religious history and practice. Ranjana was comfortable singing loudly in the temple while she performed her pūjā, reflecting her forceful character. Where Nita's favorite stavan asks for grace from the Jina, Ranjana's makes demands that sound almost impertinent. Nita's requests—"Let me live in your courtyard"—are for acceptance in the presence of the Jina; Ranjana's for direct intercession: "Do this for your servant, O King, give us the joy of liberation!" Ranjana's favorite is a song which, while humble in its assessment of the devotee's ability to achieve equanimity on her own, is quite assertive in its requests for the attentions of the Jina, showing an assertiveness also in keeping with Ranjana as I knew her.

In orthodox theological texts the Jina is completely impervious to the demands of devotees or any other worldly activity. "For the fordmakers to be so gratified by praise and worship directed toward them that they would grant the request of a devotee would imply that they have not cast away the passions and are in some way physically present" (Dundas 1992, 180). Normatively, the Jina will not answer a request and the Jain should never make a worldly request of a Jina, but Jains frequently ask for "real" darśan—a vision of the Jina that would give them the motivation or strength to follow the path of Jainism. In spite of colliding headlong with the orthodox tradition, the stavan abound with these requests. The Jain devotee is walking the fine line between prayer or request (*yācnā*) and faults arising from worldly desires (*nindā*). This distinction, however, shows that not all requests or prayers represent worldly desire. The Jina cannot act on his knowledge—because of his lack of the passion necessary to will an act to happen (*vītarāga*)—and the Jain devotee cannot make worldly requests. However, what is worldly for a Jina (any action at all) is not necessarily worldly for the laywoman. For a laywoman to ask for help in being a better Jain is not considered a worldly act but rather the opposite; it is considered a piously religious act. The conflation of what is appropriate for a Jina (or for a mendicant) with what is appropriate for all Jains is not only misleading (Babb 1996; Cort 1989, 1991b, 1998; Laidlaw 1995) but greatly narrows the possibilities for understanding Jain religiosity and devotion.

Although I found that Ranjana knew of this philosophical conflict (between the vītarāga Jina and the devotee's devotion) for Jains—clearly articulated by her within the area of what is appropriate to ask for from a Jina (one must not ask a Jina for worldly help as a Jain would not even attempt to involve the Jinas in the imperfect world)—she also was aware of this theological conflict between devotion and the Jinas. Once I asked Ranjana, "Why do you sing in the temple?" and she said, "To please Mahāvīr." I asked, "Can the Mahāvīr image 'hear' your singing?" She told me, "No, the image is just stone." Then I continued, "If Mahāvīr cannot hear you sing, why do you sing for him?" She replied, "Because he knows I am singing." The Jina's omniscience (*anantajñān*) means that, of course, the Jina would know that she is singing; the laywoman's ability to "please" a Jina whose bliss is already unending (*anantānanda*) is more complicated. The stavan clearly ask the Jina to do more than "know" that the devotee is devoted. The stavan "Just once Lord Pārśva" states the devotees' wishes quite directly:

> Just once, Lord Pārśva, Come to my temple!
> Come to my temple, that's my request.
> My request is that you come, I beg you to do this.
> That is my song's devoted wish.
> With the flowers of the soul, I spoke to you.
> Take these flowers and bring back your precious ones.

I found this kind of theological ambiguity common among the women I talked to. Whether because they, too, saw the conflict between the detached Jina and their devotions or because they did not understand the conflict I tried to present, the women would not let the conversation stay on this track. This model Ranjana presented was a compromise; the omniscience of the Jina was a vehicle for expressing devotion.

Women often explained to me that the external acts of devotion were an extension of the internal state of devotion. Thus, if you are so devoted inside that you sing loudly in the temple, your devotion is understood by Mahāvīr, even though he is unaffected. That being said, in this stavan it seems clear that the singer is asking the Jina to be affected. The stavan is addressing a Jina who is still capable of compassion and mercy. Though the request is for liberation from the "sea of emotions" into the "joy of liberation," the Jina is asked to "hold in his heart" the devotee and to "rescue" the devotee. There are several requests and questions asked that are not merely rhetorical. They are calls for grace from the Jina. The desire for assistance or a kind of divine intervention from the Jinas permeates many of the stavan which people sang independently. The stavan which women sang morning after morning sought this personal interaction with the Jina—requesting, sometimes on the behalf of all Jains, that the Jina come and help them achieve mokṣa.

The stavan that portray the Jina as an agent of grace tell of the Jina's compassion, often to the exclusion of other Jina attributes. These are especially popular stavan to sing during the prayer series in the morning pūjā. The "Śrī Ajitnāth Stavan," which starts this chapter, states:

> Deliverance is within you, it listens with your ear.
> I have come to see your compassion for the sick and the poor.
> Attending to your grace is my business.
> Can we be persuaded, before having knowledge, to be merciful?

That deliverance is said to "listen" is significant; Ajitnāth is pictured as compassionate and listening—a direct reversal of the model of laity as those who listen to the Jinas, and even to the mendicants. If the Jina listens to the sick and the poor, perhaps he'll listen to the devotee's conundrums over the difficulty of following the lay path and the challenge of daily confronting (during pūjā) her own imperfection in the presence of the model of perfection. It is the devotee's job to find the Jina's grace within the many aspects of life: "Attending to your grace is my business." However, this grace is not a direct source for liberation but more a sense of peace, the strength to continue being Jain, and a vision of the correct path; the devotee is still responsible for following the Jina's example.

This focus on the devotee's limitations and the Jina's compassion is best articulated in the popular "Śrī Śāntināth Stavan":

> People say: "Don't go before God with demands."
> But the child speaking does not understand how else to approach the beloved.
> You are so kind and powerful, Lord, how can I do less than obey?
> O Jewel of the mind, I am bound in a knot with you, whose work is whose?

The two Gujarātī words for grace, *kṛpā* and *dayā,* were ubiquitous in the stavan texts. Rather than dismissing them as un-Jain, I propose that the understanding of Jain devotion be altered. Though it was clear to women that it was not appropriate to make a worldly request of a Jina, there did not seem to be any hesitation to ask for religious things. Usually the stavan ask for grace in the form of help on the religious path or in the less direct requests which ask for darśan—a vision of the Jina—which would give the devotee the devotional inspiration she wants. These stavan do not ask for prosperity or good marriages but perhaps more radically ask for the Jina to respond to devotion at all—a challenge to the individualistic understanding of Jain religiosity which separates each "soul" from the possibility of interaction in a spiritually efficacious manner.

Savita, in her early 40s, was married to the third son in a family which had broken up into several family units. She had an unmarried son and a married daughter. Savita's workload was especially heavy, as her husband's family had separate apartments—though in the same building—and she earned extra money sewing bags piecemeal and making decorations for special programs. She had to squeeze out time for religious activities. Her apartment used to be Shivajinagar's Jain temple before the new temple was built, and I suspect she missed its presence. "O Compassionate Lord" (which heads chapter 4) was Savita's favorite stavan. It was said to have been written by a female mendicant from Sangli—the town in Maharashtra in which she grew up. It was very popular as a personal stavan and was even included in stavan collections produced in North America. She sang this stavan for me at her home, as I had not been able to hear her sing the stavan in her morning worship; Savita, like Nita, sang very quietly during her morning worship. She told me she sang it every morning.

> O compassionate Lord, your compassion has no end.
> O destroyer of troubles, there is no limit to your mercy.
> My sin is doing this, I have forgotten to do your worship.
> O forgetter of my forgetfulness, there is no end to your mercy.

This stavan asks for the endless forgiveness for the frailties of humanity. It is especially poignant as a request of the Jina to forgive the women for the times they cannot come to perform pūjā. The women singing this stavan are the agents of their sin and the Jina is the agent of grace. The last verse asks the Jina to protect the singer whose life is so difficult and sad.

> My life is so sad, take me into your protection, O Immortal One.
> You are in my heart, O Delightful One! There is no end to your mercy.

The presence of the Jina in the heart gives the women the strength to get through the many challenges of their lives. The stavan don't express an expectation of an answer to these requests: in fact, Jain pūjā is predicated on there being no answer.

The message of these stavan reconstructs the Jina as imminent and compassionate. The image of Jain theology as cold and distant is clearly not drawn from the devotional tradition. The Jinas of the stavan are often compassionate and responsive to the requests of the devotees. When the Jina is not responsive, the devotee may, as in the "Śankheśvar Pārśvanāth Stavan," complain "when will you . . ." Of the stavan women sang in the morning, there is an attachment to those stavan that provide a relationship with the Jina. These stavan still aimed for goals considered appropriate as goals of Jain worship: equanimity, mokṣa, mukti (liberation), and peace—even though they often seem to emulate the beseeching tone of the sometimes problematic earthly requests directed toward the guardian deities. The women did not have the kind of control over their time or the families' resources to determine the kind of offerings they could make at the temple. Likewise, they did not choose how much time they could spend there. All the women—except the oldest women who no longer did work at home—said they wished they could spend more time at the temple but that their time was not their own. The temple was an escape from work and a place that offered both solitude (during worship) and sociability (during maṇḍaḷ activities or formal pūjās). A Jina who grants grace may come to a woman who cannot always come to the Jina.

When women sang by themselves during their morning pūjā, they sang their favorite stavan, reflecting aspects of their understandings of Jain devotion, their personal history, and their personal style; devotion and personal style are central to the actual practice of the rituals of daily pūjā. Daily worship involves an improvisational practice deriving its actions from a set of gestures called pūjā. Their daily worship is learned primarily from women in their own families; those reading the occasional lay manual are already familiar with how to do pūjā and thus lay manuals form more a source for interpretations of their actions than a guideline for how to do pūjā. Women are familiar with—to borrow the terms from Humphrey and Laidlaw (1994)—both the constitutive rules for pūjā (what acts can be considered pūjā) and the regulative rules that prohibit acts that are faults arising from a lack of respect (āśātnā) which could make pūjā sinful instead of meritorious. Within these frames, women's daily worship took its particular form and balance from the women's own relationship with the Jinas (particularly their understanding of devotionalism) and style of devotion reflected in part by their stavan choices. Daily worship provides a ground on which women can develop their own understandings of the tricky and inevitable theological questions of a Jain lay path. Whereas these frames also apply somewhat to the formal pūjās (discussed in the next chapter), formal pūjās, as practiced and negotiated performances, depend more on a shared understanding of the proper form and feel for these developments.

*6

I sing your songs and go to my beloved temple,
  I go to each of your images.
Tipping the water pitcher, I bathe you, and
  Clean the dirt inside me.
I bring the gold grindstone, and I prepare sandalwood for pūjā.
  Kesarīyā, may I gain liberation at your feet.
I bring flowers, and with an expensive garland I dress you.
  I yield, with love, to the exquisite scent of your soul.
I bring the incense burner, otherwise I will gain nothing.
  I go to you, Lord, who have attained equanimity.
I light the lamp, waking the flame of devotion.
  I go to the flame of your brilliance.
I make a rice svastik, create the Three Jewels.
  I go to overcome the mountain of the Siddhas.
I always offer sweets, with love I cook special treats.
  I go to become a non-eater myself.
I bring the fruit of Indra's tree and place it at your feet.
  I set my mind on the devotion to liberation, and so I am devoted.
I make noise and sing auspicious songs,
  Through dancing, I gain the feet of the Jina.

Transcription and translation of recording of ritual performance in Pune, Maharashtra, on 21 June 1994. Courtesy Śrī Pārśva Mahilā Maṇḍaḷ.

Formal Pūjās and Stavan Repertoires

The formal pūjās themselves are constructed experiences (Bauman 1986)—from the expansions of the eightfold pūjā written in the pūjā texts, to the particulars of the stavan adjusted to include local names. In addition, as Ben-Amos suggests about the communicative roles of folklore, they have their own "grammar" articulating the place of meaning in the performance (Ben-Amos 1976, 1982). The meaning, here theological, has much to do with the context of the text (in performance) and the intention of the performer; the text cannot be separated from the performance. The most common religious performances (excepting daily worship) for Jain laywomen are the formal pūjās—the Snātra (Bathing) Pūjā, the Pañcakalyāṇak (Five Auspicious Moments) Pūjā, the Vāstuk (Belongings) Pūjā, and the Antarāyakarm Nivāraṇanī (Soul-blocking Karma Removal) Pūjā. The Snātra Pūjā leads off each of the pūjās as a preparatory rite for the longer pūjās; it is also performed monthly on the new moon day and other joyful occasions. The Pañcakalyāṇak Pūjā was performed to commemorate joyful events (weddings, anniversaries, birthdays, good fortune) and to mark the new year—it was not performed in Shivajinagar specifically on the anniversaries of the Pañcakalyāṇak (five auspicious moments) of Pārśvanāth to whom the pūjā is dedicated.[1] Vāstuk Pūjās were performed as a housewarming pūjā. Antarāyakarm Nivāraṇanī Pūjās were performed to remove obstacle-creating karma, in the name of a recently deceased relative, when one breaks the menses restrictions, or after a birth.

The various formal pūjās differ from daily pūjā in two central ways. First, the daily pūjā is a fluid and improvisational ritual in which the women draw from a collection of acceptable gestures and offerings to create a pūjā that reflects both their general understanding of worship and devotion and their personal—often varying from day-to-day—interpretations and practices. These are modified by time and energy, by whether the women are able to enter the inner sanctum, and by the particular balance of practices that each woman adopts according to her personal sentiment. Second, the formal pūjās are regulated by the evaluating eyes and words of other women and, in the case of the pūjā contest discussed later in chapter 7, men. The formal pūjās were usually shared public performances, which like other public performances are subject to the scrutiny of the audience and other participants. Insofar as the performance was advertised, anyone could attend, and it happened in the public location of the temple, I speak of these as public events. I speak of the formal pūjās which take place in homes as private, but the very presence of the maṇḍaḷ and the sponsoring family—especially when the sponsors are not connected with the maṇḍaḷ—provide a context for this kind of public scrutiny. Thus, the public formal pūjās (and the choices for stavan to perform in particular formal pūjās) are moderated by a negotiated understanding of orthopraxy and the shared goal of striving toward that orthopraxy.

During the time of my research there were numerous formal pūjās[2] and several other public events which both identified and celebrated the Jain community and which promoted an orthoprax/orthodox interpretation of Jain religious practice. By "orthodox" I refer to those texts or instructions written by mendicants or trained laity in vernacular languages—in Pune, they were almost exclusively in Gujarātī. These public pūjās and other programs (for Mahāvīr Nirvāṇ and Paryuṣaṇ) form a broader expression of the orthoprax assertions within the context of Jain lay praxis. In many households there were lay manuals which instruct the lay people on being Jains, and these were readily given to me to study. Few among the laity study or even hear recitations of most of the Agamic Sanskrit texts except the annual *Kalpa Sūtra* recitation during Paryuṣaṇ; women (except in few exceptional cases, such as the women in the Jainology doctoral program at Pune University) can only understand the textual bases of orthodoxy through the vernacular *śrāvakācāra* texts, interaction with mendicants, or other lay Jains. In addition, recall how Cort (1989) describes the two overlapping modes of being Jain: one based on liberation (religious acts aimed toward mokṣa) and the other on well-being (aimed at merit). These paths are not mutually exclusive but more a matter of prioritizing one's practice according to one's life—laymen should be good laymen and male mendicants should be good male mendicants—and an interpretation understood in conjunction with the belief that no one on earth can attain mokṣa in this era.

Formal pūjās derive their "liturgy" from texts written by male mendicants in the nineteenth century, which are collected into pūjā books. These vernacular narrative (rāso) style texts were written for a wide variety of occasions, probably to counter the popularity of Hindu magicoreligious ceremonies (yantra-mantra pūjā) among Jains.[3] The most common "complete" collection of these pūjās is the *Vividh Pūjā Saṅgrah* (edited by Paṁnyās Jinendra Vijay Gaṇī), of which the temple owned fifteen or so copies. Ranjana, Maluben, and several of the more involved women had this book in their families' collections. All the women in the maṇḍaḷ had books that gave the text of the formal pūjās. The most common pūjā manual in Shivajinagar and around Pune was the *Laghu Pūjā Saṅgrah* in Gujarātī, published by the Jain Prakāśan Mandir in Dośīvaḍa Poḷ, Amdāvād. It was readily available at the Jain Pustak Bhaṇḍār (bookstore) in Guruwar Peth near Goḍījī Temple.[4] Moreover, the temple itself owned ten or so copies of this text, as well as other pūjā text collections. The *Laghu Pūjā Saṅgrah* contains the texts of eight formal pūjās:

Śrī Snātra Pūjā
Śrī Pañcakalyāṇak Pūjā
Śrī Navāṇuṁ Prakārī Pūjā
Śrī Bār Vratanī Pūjā
Śrī Vedanīy Karmanī Pūjā
Śrī Antarāyakarm Nivāraṇanī Pūjā
Śrī Navpadjī Pūjā
Śrī Vāstuk Pūjā

It includes the version of the Snātra Pūjā written by Paṇḍitācārya Śrī Vīrvijayjī, the most commonly found Tapā Gacch version of this pūjā.[5] Although these manuals do not include all the possible formal pūjās, it was widely accepted that these were the pūjās that the maṇḍaḷ could perform without a more formally trained ritual specialist; some of the more complicated *mahāpūjās* (Siddhacakra Mahāpūjā, Bhaktāmar Mahāpūjan, Vīś Sthānak Mahāpūjan, Pārśvanāth 108 Abhiṣek Mahāpūjan, Śrī Śantī Snātra Mahāpūjan) included in the *Viviḍh Pūjā Saṅgrah* require either a layman ritual specialist (vidhikār) or a male mendicant, and are for most Jains—and virtually all women—prohibitively expensive. None of these pūjās had been performed in the Ajitnāth Temple during the year 1993–94. In 1999, Dadiji's family sponsored a Siddhacakra Mahāpūjā, which was the first of any of the large, complicated mahāpūjās to be performed at Ajitnāth Temple in Shivajinagar.[6]

Male mendicants are required (if only briefly) at the largest and most complex mahāpūjās: temple consecration (*pratiṣṭhā*), mendicant ordination (*dīkṣā*), and so on; the orthodoxy and orthopraxy of these pūjās are regulated in part by the male mendicant's recitations or his corrections of their actions and recitations. However, most of the formal pūjās are performed without a present and vocal mendicant guide; in other words, most of a pious Jain's praxis does not involve (or devolve from) direct instructions of mendicants. Lay experts are important for the performances of most pūjās. Whereas *vidhikār* are always referred to as knowledgeable laymen (*śrāvak*), in fact the knowledgeable experts of the most commonly performed Jain pūjās in Pune were—except at Goḍījī—women and women's maṇḍaḷs.

Each of the pūjās' texts begins with ritual instructions (*vidhi*), which explains the basic performance of the pūjā, but it does not dictate the bulk of the gestures and the exact activities surrounding that pūjā. Most of what happens during a pūjā is determined by a lay ritual specialist or women's maṇḍaḷ. The longer and more complex pūjā ritual instructions are considerably longer than that of the more common Snātra Pūjā; perhaps the editors felt the performers would already know the gestures of the Snātra Pūjā. Alternatively, the increase in direction may have been demanded by the relative complexity of the longer pūjās. I quote the first part of the ritual instructions of Vīrvijayjī's Pañcakalyāṇak Pūjā as given in the *Laghu Pūjā Saṅgrah* because it is the most explicit of all the ritual instructions in that collection—although much of what happens in the pūjā is not included:

> (1) First perform the Snātra Pūjā. Then put flowers in a dish and stand to make the offering. Once the first pūjā has been made, say the Mantra, then soon after place the flowers on the Jina. (2) In the second pūjā, put cloves, cardamom, betel, coconut, almond, grapes, seeds, pomegranate, orange, mango, banana or other juicy, fragrant, beautiful fruit in a dish. Holding the dish in your hands, recite the pūjā's reading, and toward the last Mantra, hold the fruit in front of God. (3) In the third pūjā, put brilliant unbroken grain (rice) in a dish. Holding the dish in your hands, recite the reading, and after the last Mantra, make a svastik in front of God and three sweepings (heaps) of rice. (*Laghu Pūjā Saṅgrah*, n.d., 12)

These instructions—except for the gloss over setup and the Snātra Pūjā—are quite specific; the pūjā could be performed by following these directions. In contrast, the ritual instructions of the Antarāyakarm Nivāraṇanī Pūjā reads in its entirety: "(1) pañcamṛt water, (2) saffron, (3) jasmine flowers, (4) eight-limbed incense, (5) lamp and likewise at this place hold a cotton rosary of 158 knots, (6) in a dish make a rice nandyāvart, (7) sweets, (8) fruit" (*Laghu Pūjā Saṅgrah*, n.d., 82). There are no further instructions anywhere in the text; to perform this pūjā, there must be either a knowledgeable participant or someone confident enough to improvise.

The differences between the text of a pūjā and the text in performance points to the kind of improvisational spirit—justified by one's having the proper devotional sentiments—that is shared by the individual's daily pūjā styles. The understanding of orthodoxy is fluid within what are commentary-like features of the pūjā—the stavan—as long as the text of the pūjā is sung accurately and the correct prayers and mantras are recited absolutely correctly. However, because the ritual instructions are far less explicit about what happens during a pūjā, the maṇḍaḷ women or the lay ritual specialist must draw on other sources for the exact details. It is useful to create a concordance between the ritual instructions (both written and internalized), pūjā text, and performance of a Snātra Pūjā; there is a lot of interpretation required to fit all the pieces together. Using the texts she referred to before (and during) a pūjā, and the actual performance of the pūjā to illustrate Maluben's strategy as a lay ritual specialist, I begin by describing the context and preparations which must come before the pūjā text (and its written ritual instructions) begin. But first I outline the kinds of Snātra Pūjās because the type of pūjā being sponsored alters the performance considerably.

The Snātra Pūjā in Context

At Ajitnāth, the Snātra Pūjā and its stavan in maṇḍaḷ performances varied very little. Vīrvijayjī (1773–1854) wrote the Snātra Pūjā text which the maṇḍaḷ used. It was primarily dedicated to the story of Mahāvīr's birth celebration. The Snātra Pūjā is performed at the start of all the longer pūjās, as well as on its own; notwithstanding prologue Snātra Pūjās, the Snātra Pūjā was still the pūjā most often performed both by the individual or the maṇḍaḷ. The Snātra Pūjā is a reenactment of the birth and subsequent bathing of the baby Mahāvīr. There are three basic types of performance of the Snātra Pūjā at Ajitnāth Temple: in the first, the individual "hires" Arun (the pujārī) to perform the pūjā on her behalf; in the second, the individual recites and performs the Snātra Pūjā herself with a small group (though with some assistance from the pujārī). In the third, the maṇḍaḷ performs the pūjā either on "hire" or as part of its group participation in Jain religious rites.

The first two kinds of Snātra Pūjā performances fall within the realm of personal daily worship—even when not daily—though they are indirectly regulated by the observation of public pūjā performance standards. The simplest of these is when the pujārī is "hired" to perform the Snātra Pūjā on someone's behalf. This was done as part of morning pūjā often to commemorate birthdays or anniversaries. Each sponsor brought a husked coconut to the temple as the fruit offering to leave on the rice table in front of the silver assembly hall stand holding the metal image of Mahāvīr that is worshipped during the Snātra Pūjā. Most women then gave Arun, the pujārī, five rupees directly (though occasionally, if he was not in the temple, it was left with the coconut).[7] Arun performed the Snātra Pūjā later in the day when he had finished the other work in the temple. This first type of Snātra Pūjā performance was—in a sense—not a performance (by the sponsor) at all. Arun performed the pūjā later, when virtually no one, not even the sponsor, was at the temple; the sponsor's participation is minimal.

Although individuals could perform a Snātra Pūjā alone[8]—as Arun does—they usually chose to form ad hoc performing groups. At Ajitnāth, a group of several women met to perform the Snātra Pūjā every morning.[9] There were usually about six women in the group—most of them older women who had a bit more available time—who met at the temple around eight o'clock. Because they recited—rather than sang—the text of the Snātra Pūjā, it rarely took them more than about twenty minutes. If there was a maṇḍaḷ pūjā in the morning, these women—some active members of the maṇḍaḷ, some not—instead participated in the maṇḍaḷ pūjā. This kind of participation centered around performing the circumambulations and recited prayer set (caityavandan) by performing the aspects of pūjā after the sponsor had done them herself or by the extension of pūjā efficacy by touching the person who is performing the act.[10]

On the day after the new moon—thus marking the new month—the maṇḍaḷ women performed a Snātra Pūjā in the temple at eight o'clock in the morning. Each month a different family sponsored the new moon Snātra Pūjā. The maṇḍaḷ did not charge for the performance of the new moon Snātra partly because, as the temple's maṇḍaḷ, they felt they had to perform the pūjā that morning, and partly because the maṇḍaḷ women performed the pūjā. Although each month a different sponsor performed the monthly pūjā, many of the maṇḍaḷ women came to the Snātra Pūjā in their pūjā clothes and thus were able to actively participate in the pūjā rituals. For the new moon Snātra Pūjā, each woman brought her own coconut to add the often quite substantial pile in front of the assembly hall stand. On particularly important new moon days (especially the Snātra during Paryuṣaṇ, which coincided with the day of the recitation of Mahāvīr's birth) other non-maṇḍaḷ people also brought coconuts to the Snātra Pūjā—including several men. Likewise, on the Marāṭhī New Year several men brought strings of pressed sugar cakes to hang on the assembly hall stand. Otherwise, the sponsor was responsible for the pūjā offerings. The Snātra Pūjā was, however, not an especially expensive pūjā and many observant families tried to sponsor one each year. The sponsor was responsible for the cost of the temple supplies (5 rupees), and for bringing the pūjā offerings (including, most important, flowers, fruit, sweets, rice, and coins[11]), the maṇḍaḷ gift—a token payment of 1, 5, or 11 rupees per performer or a gift (small steel dishes, pūjā bags, jewelry boxes)—and the prabhāvanā (a sweet or fruit for all Jains and others who come to observe and therefore participate as audience for the pūjā).

All other formal pūjās are preceded by a full Snātra Pūjā. Because of this, the maṇḍaḷ women (and their maṇḍaḷ scholar) were familiar with the Snātra Pūjā. (Most of the maṇḍaḷ women could—with prompting—sing the whole pūjā.) The prologue Snātras had a rushed and functional feel; they were sung very quickly (almost chanted) with few breaks and no stavan, in order to get to the real business of the day—the more complicated pūjā. The prabhāvanā is not distributed during this pūjā but saved until the last section of the longer pūjā. Likewise, the closing rites are saved until the end of the longer pūjā. The prologue pūjā serves simply to set the scene for the longer pūjā. Whereas the independent Snātra Pūjā ordinarily takes forty minutes to an hour, the prologue Snātra Pūjā took no longer than fifteen to twenty minutes.

The Snātra Pūjā Concordance: Monitoring Variations on a Theme

A close examination of the sponsor's actions and received instructions in a single Snātra Pūjā shows ways in which Maluben organized and interpreted the pūjā. During the Snātra Pūjā performance Maluben gave directions to the sponsor, within which she combined the elements of the written ritual instructions in the various pūjā manuals, the ways she had seen other maṇḍaḷs and individuals perform the pūjā, and her own particular understanding of Jain orthopraxy. The result is a complete set of actions intended to match both the text of the pūjā and the tone of the pūjā. Because most of my research activity focused on the singing during pūjās, I sponsored a pūjā to make sure I would be at least once on the receiving end of Maluben's instructions. It is from this particular pūjā that I construct this concordance.[12] This pūjā was unique in two ways: (1) its especially high attendance, which may have been due to its being my pūjā and/or to its being a new moon Snātra at the same time; and (2) the unprecedented participation of my husband Steve in performing the entire pūjā with me.[13]

Snātra Pūjā: Pre-pūjā Sponsors' Participation

On August 8, 1994 I arrived at the temple with Ranjana and Steve; I was to be sponsoring the new moon Snātra Pūjā myself. We had collected some white flowers (from a neighbor's jasmine bush) on the way to the temple. I was told to leave the sweets I had brought for prabhāvanā on the steps outside the temple. Were they to come into the temple they would no longer be acceptable for Jains to eat. Steve went with Arun, the pujārī, to be dressed in pūjā clothes[14]—borrowed from Satishbhai, Ranjana's husband. I handed my coconut, a handful of rice, and a 25 paise coin to Maluben. She made a svastik on the bottom level of the stand beneath the image and I put the coin on top of it. When Steve returned, red and yellow strings were tied around my wrist and Steve's and a third around the coconut, which was placed on the bottom shelf on top of the coin. Meanwhile, Maluben made five rice svastiks on the low table and set up the five pitchers, each of which also had a red thread tied around it, and each of which sat atop a svastik. I was told to put the rice in the small silver plate. The maṇḍaḷ began to set up in front of the image. We were handed sandalwood paste and told to perform sandalwood paste pūjā on the Snātra image. Then we washed our hands. When we returned Maluben drew a svastik of sandalwood paste on my right palm and told me to draw one on Steve's right palm. Meanwhile, new arrivals had been contributing coconuts for the pile in front of the image.

Śrī Snātra Pūjā, a small pamphlet with the text to this single pūjā, which, at an earlier Snātra Pūjā, was handed out as prabhāvanā (a gift given out at the end of a pūjā to all attendees) to all the members of the maṇḍaḷ (and me), contains ritual instructions for the Snātra Pūjā. The preparations listed in the small Snātra Pūjā (Vīrvijayjī's version) manual include arrangements made before our arrival—the reorganization of the assembly hall stand and the arrangement of the tables and pitchers—and the first acts required to set the stage for the performance of the Snātra Pūjā. Compare what has happened so far in the foregoing description to the ritual instructions given in the pūjā manual:

> (1) First, to represent the three-tiered fort, put the beautiful three-tiered stand together. (2) On the tier beneath the image (in the center), make a svastik design with sandalwood, and atop that another with rice, and put a coconut (with husks) on top of them. (3) Then, on tables in front of the sandalwood paste svastik, make four svastiks and put a pitcher tied with the ritual red and yellow thread on each. (4) In the middle of the lion throne in good fortune make a sandalwood svastik, then put rice and coins, and say three "Navkār Mantras"; then on this respectfully place the Jina image. (5) Further in front of the image make another svastik, and on this place the siddhacakra. (6) Put a standing lamp on the image's right side at the height of the image's nose. (7) Then tie the red and

> yellow thread to the hand of the Snātra performer, and put in that hand a pitcher filled with the five ambrosias (pañcamṛt).[15] While saying three "Navkār Mantras," the Snātra performer should bathe the image and the siddhacakra. (8) Brush the image and siddhacakra, bathe them with water and dry with a soft cloth three times, and then do sandalwood pūjā. (9) Then pass your hand through the incense smoke and make a mark with the sandalwood paste in the palm of the right hand. (*Śrī Snātra Pūjā*, n.d., 9–11)

These instructions are designed for a solo performer of the Snātra Pūjā. These instructions are identical to those given in the longest and most detailed pūjā manual, the *Vividh Pūjā Saṅgrah*, except that the *Vividh Pūjā Saṅgrah* starts the instructions with a bit more detail:

> In your own heart, you should have pure sentiments and after your own bath have contact with only pure things. This being done, mark your forehead with sandalwood paste. (1) Above you should hang the canopy [*candarvo*]. The area below should be clean and pure. In place of the three-tiered fort, set up a beautiful three-tiered stand and place on top of this the lion throne. (*Vividh Pūjā Saṅgrah*, n.d., 1)

The gestures include both the actions performed by the sponsor and those that the maṇḍaḷ—usually Maluben—did to set up the pūjā. Before we had even arrived, Maluben and Arun had set up the assembly hall stand in the center of the temple, in front of the central door to the inner sanctum. They also had set up the standing lamp, filled the pitchers with water and the five ambrosia, and generally gathered together all the necessary materials. Maluben collected from me a handful of rice and some coins and put the image and the siddhacakra in their respective places. The step of putting the coconuts on the silver chest (bhaṇḍār) in front of the assembly hall stand was begun with one of the two coconuts brought by the sponsor (in this case, me), but each person who came in with a coconut added to the pile. Though Maluben's procedure ended with the same setup, the order in which she prepared the pūjā was—in part—determined by the availability of materials and efficiency.

In the public performances of pūjās, other maṇḍaḷ members or participants rarely, if ever, saw, paid attention to, or participated in this setup process. In fact, few people aside from Maluben and the sponsor were even at the temple during most afternoon setups, and if they were, they were usually performing pūjā or busy with their own preparations for the pūjā. Most Snātra Pūjās coincided with the time of greatest temple activity. The morning Snātra Pūjās were often attended by large numbers of maṇḍaḷ members; even though the temple was often crowded, the "audience" was frequently busy doing their morning worship while listening to the pūjā.

The Snātra Pūjā Liturgy Performance

Between the sponsors' arrival and readiness, the maṇḍaḷ members usually did a certain amount of preparation. Each woman entered the temple and added her coconut to the pile in front of the image. Those in pūjā clothes performed eightfold pūjā to all of the Jina images in the temple. Meanwhile, the other women organized themselves into two facing lines and sorted out their bookstands, pūjā manuals, stavan notebooks, tambourines, dāṇḍiya sticks, hand cymbals, and (if they were in pūjā clothes) pūjā handkerchiefs. When the Snātra Pūjā was organized and the maṇḍaḷ was seated in their lines in front of the Jina image, it was time to begin. The sponsor stood to the image's left, and the maṇḍaḷ started by singing the "Navkār Mantra." After the Navkār was sung, the maṇḍaḷ began to sing and recite the text of the formal Snātra Pūjā, and Maluben instructed the sponsor on the correct gestures and offerings corresponding to the singing of the formal text, drawing from many sources, especially her attendance at hundreds of Snātra Pūjās. Continuing my concordance from my Snātra Pūjā on August 8, we see the extent of her decision making with regard to the details of the ritual:

> After everything was set up and the maṇḍaḷ had sat in their rows, I was told to stand to the image's left and Steve to my immediate right. Then Maluben told us to first hold the milk pitcher and then the water pitcher during the introductory prayers. When the maṇḍaḷ reached the Flower Offering (Kusumāñjali) section, we were instructed to sprinkle the image with sandalwood paste using a flower. Then Maluben tore up some flowers and mixed them in the rice and added sandalwood paste (or *barās*—a camphor-based mixture) to the mix. The maṇḍaḷ sang the Flower-Offering verses:
>
> > Bathe with the pure water pitcher. Clothe the precious limbs.
> > Keep this flower-water, O Ādināth, Bliss of the Jinas.
> > Washing the beautiful limbs of the Siddha, the soul is purified by tenderness.[16]
>
> At each of the seven Flower-Offering verses, we were told to take a pinch of the flower, sandalwood paste, and rice mixture and toss it at the image and the siddhacakra.
>
> When it was time for the circumambulations, Steve led the group (as the men are supposed to go first) with significant visual prodding from Maluben and finally a real prod from me. Behind Steve and me, there were several women from the maṇḍaḷ also doing the circumambulations. While making the three circumambulations of the assembly hall stand, the women all chanted the Siddhācal couplets that always accompanied the circumambulations[17]:
>
> > In this present era, one does not cross over the cycle of rebirth.
> > That cycle is broken by circumambulating three times.
> > In circling, one spirals far from the world's worries,
> > Right faith, right knowledge, and right action take the form of the three circumambulations.
> >
> > Fear of birth and death disappear, burnt away, when one sees God.
> > The three jewels bring gains. Take darśan of the Jina king.
> > Knowledge roots in this worldly life, from knowledge of the highest we are happy.
> > Without knowledge, the lives in this universe cannot hear the truth.
> >
> > That collection of karma, that restlessness which causes troubles,
> > Right action is simple, praise that storehouse of good qualities.
> > Right faith, right knowledge and right action, these are the three jewels of the steadfast.
> > These three circumambulations are for him, the destroyer of the sorrow of the world.
>
> We could not recite the words to the caityavandan, so it was recited by Ranjana, after which we did a speedy version of the agra pūjā: offering incense, the mirror and metal fan, the lamp, and the flywhisk, using Maluben's miniature silver set of pūjā tools, while the maṇḍaḷ sang the story of Mahāvīr's birth. This was followed by sandalwood pūjā and the offerings of fruit and money. Lastly, we poured milk and water exactly on the right foot of the image. The maṇḍaḷ began to sing "Bring, O Bring":

Bring, O Bring! The big merchant brings the bathing water each month.
Bathing Marudevī's son honors God.
The whole congregation cannot contain its happiness at bringing the bathing water.[18]
The Pārśva Maṇḍaḷ cannot contain its happiness at honoring God.[19]

During this song, I went down the middle of the maṇḍaḷ set handing out my gifts—a small steel plate and cup for each maṇḍaḷ member—and Steve went outside to hand out the sweets to everyone who had come to the pūjā. Then we were told to perform sandalwood pūjā again, and the image and siddhacakra were removed from the assembly hall stand to be cleaned and to have the decoration—here, made of silver foil—applied to the image. Ranjana continued to hand out sweets for us outside while most of the maṇḍaḷ women and others left the temple. I put a one-rupee and a twenty-five paise coin on the stand on top of the svastik and helped carry the image and the siddhacakra back to the assembly hall stand.

The ritual instructions of the Snātra Pūjā offer very little by way of explicit instruction (much less so than those of the Pañcakalyāṇak quoted earlier). The instructions for the actual pūjā performance are scant, but the performance is rich with detail. According to the ritual instructions in the Snātra Pūjā manual, at the pūjā's beginning, the first pitcher should be presented during the recitation of the first Mantra. Then the silver plate with "flower bath" offering is offered while the Flower-Offering verses are sung and the flowers are put on the image's right hand. After the Flower-Offering section is finished, the ritual instructions have the Snātra performer do the circumambulation and caityavandan. During our pūjā, the bulk of these prayers were recited by Ranjana as the prayers usually were in formal pūjās. Even though other women knew the caityavandan, only one woman was permitted (by Maluben) to recite at a time; the other women were told to be quiet.

There are no specific written instructions for the highly involved and very fast, expanded version of the eightfold pūjā performed while the maṇḍaḷ sang the section of the text that describes the eightfold offerings made to the newborn Jina. Maluben shouted commands at us (which I translated for Steve) as she did at all the sponsors, and we rapidly made each of the offerings. The maṇḍaḷ sang while we hurriedly completed the requisite acts. The rest of the pūjā was slower, but Maluben and Ranjana gave us our instructions about exactly when to do sandalwood pūjā, when to distribute the gifts and the prabhāvanā, and when to return to the front to complete the pūjā. The maṇḍaḷ began the Troṭak recitations with the shaking of tambourines and the ringing of the temple bells:

Then thought Indra in his mind: who is making this celebration?
It must be the birth of a Jina, that zenith of people, and everyone is blissfully happy.

The Snātra Pūjā text includes brief instructions at this point: "In this place ring the bell" (*Śrī Snātra Pūjā*, n.d., 20), marking the celebrations of the birth of Mahāvīr. Meanwhile the maṇḍaḷ has sung the sections that describe everything from the dreams of Mahāvīr's mother to the birth of Mahāvīr. The rest of the formal text of the Snātra tells the story of the celebration of Mahāvīr's birth, ending with the repetition of the line "In every house there was great joy." During this last section the prabhāvanā is distributed (though in a longer pūjā it is distributed in the final offering section), even though prabhāvanā is not described in any of the ritual manual texts I have read. Here, the women use their own social expectation about how to celebrate the birth of a son—a time when one gives sweets to all relatives and close friends—to choose the time for the prabhāvanā; to them it makes sense to hand out the gifts of appreciation at this point in the Snātra Pūjā. The last instructions for the Snātra Pūjā proper are as follows: "At this time, bathe the image with the water pitcher, and then with milk, yoghurt, ghee, water and sugar, bath with pañcamṛt. Finally do pūjā [which was understood to mean perform the sandalwood pūjā] and then place flowers" (*Śrī Snātra Pūjā*, n.d., 27). This is the final performance of sandalwood pūjā before the image is cleaned and the silver-foil decoration is applied.[20]

During this central section of the Snātra Pūjā, the actions we were told to perform were based on an interpretation of the pūjā liturgy. The sponsor acts out the gestures toward the Jina image which are being performed in the narrative of the liturgy; for example, when the liturgy states that the heavenly beings clean the area of Mahāvīr's birth, the sponsors made a sweeping gesture. A high-speed version of the eightfold pūjā plus the offerings of the flywhisk, fan, mirror, and dance were inserted into the middle of the Snātra Pūjā in the section that comes directly after the circumambulation of the image and the recitation of the caityavandan. After the eightfold pūjā was completed, the Jina image was bathed and a decoration of silver foil was put on. During these ministrations, there was no formal text to recite. Usually the maṇḍaḷ sang two stavan at this time: "My Golden Throne" and "Śankheśvar Svāmī" in that order. "My Golden Throne" lists the beautiful ornaments of the Jina, which are, as it was being sung, applied to the Jina in decoration, making a very neat fit between the context and stavan. It describes the image decoration with an opulence appropriate to the intensity of devotion:

> Your heavy gold crown sparkling looks so very beautiful.
> Your armbands and bracelets look so very beautiful.
> In your ears, the shining earrings look so very beautiful.
> The pearls in your nine stringed necklace look so very beautiful.
> The yellow campā, roses and jasmine flowers look so very beautiful.
> Like going to the jasmine bush, you look so beautiful.

The stavan represents more what the maṇḍaḷ members wish they were giving the Jina than what they can actually give, which amounts in this case to silver foil, flowers, and a small silver crown and earrings (purchased with money collected from several pūjās). In a devoted and somewhat lofty way, the maṇḍaḷ sang of dressing their images like real kings.

If the image decoration was not completed during the singing of "My Golden Throne," the maṇḍaḷ filled out the extra time by singing "Śankheśvar Svāmī" or "Mahāvīr Śrī Bhagavān." If there was a longer pūjā following the Snātra Pūjā, the image was decorated quickly. "Śankheśvar Svāmī" was shifted into the longer pūjā. As it was more a request for grace than a celebration of the glorification of the Jina, and about Pārśvanāth, not about Mahāvīr, it is not surprising that its place in the Snātra Pūjā was less fixed. However, by virtue of being addressed to their "patron" Jina, this particular stavan was considered always to "fit." It was included in most pūjās either in the Snātra Pūjā alone, during a Snātra Pūjā preceding a longer pūjā, or in the longer pūjā itself. Perhaps because it was a maṇḍaḷ favorite, because Pārśvanāth was ubiquitous to these Jains' imagery, and, perhaps most significantly, it was sung in the same key, tempo, and timing as "My Golden Throne." These two stavan were sung almost exclusively in the context of the formal pūjās. When "Mahāvīr Śrī Bhagavān" was performed as part of the Snātra Pūjā it differed from its solo performances by Nita or others primarily in its rhythm and tempo. Performed solo, this stavan was slow, with varied line lengths, but in the pūjā it was made rhythmically steady and up tempo by the pounding of the drum. Though it is, by virtue of its subject, appropriate to a pūjā about Mahāvīr, the stavan does not mention the birth or any of the auspicious times in Mahāvīr's life. Instead it is a reminder—it repeats his name over and over—of why Mahāvīr's birth is important to Jains, and it tells of the merit gained from having had devotion to Mahāvīr.

At the end of all the pūjās, the maṇḍaḷ always sang "Bring, O Bring," the stavan which listed all the members of the sponsoring family who had come to perform the pūjā and the attending members of the maṇḍaḷ. Even if other stavan describing the offerings devotees bring to temples were performed, this stavan was never replaced. Its use was clear—to name the participants. It was the only stavan that included the individual participants by name rather than by role, giving each of them recognition for their participation and expressing the maṇḍaḷ's approval of the sponsor's desire to perform the pūjā. In fact, it is the only recognition of individuals by name; though the pūjā announcements board recognizes the family and maṇḍaḷ, it does not do so individually.

Snātra Pūjā Closing Rites

Finally, after the distribution of prabhāvanā and the return of the decorated image to the assembly hall stand, formal pūjās were completed by two songs that accompany closing rites which were neither stavan nor a part of any specific pūjā text. The "Ādināth Āratī" is also performed at the close of the day when the Jinas are all offered an āratī lamp. Likewise, many families offered a lamp to their household shrines daily; this was the āratī song I heard in each house and the one the women told me they all sang:

> Victory to the lamp, O Ādināth, the Bliss of the Jinas, the son born of Marudevī.
> Let the first lamp be lit. Let man's devotion understand this flame.
> The second lamp gives compassion for the sick and the poor. In this city of dust, it is the Light of the World.
> The third lamp, O God of the Three Worlds, the Lord of Men, Indra, does your worship.
> The fourth lamp releases the soul from the fruits of desire giving complete liberation.
> The fifth lamp gives birth to merit. Sing the merits of Muḷcand Ṛṣabh.[21]

This Āratī song explains the meaning of the five wicks of the āratī lamp and moves, poetically, from devotion to Ādināth in general, through specific reasons for devotion, to the fruits of worship—liberation and merit—describing the path a devotee's mind must take to gain the merits of pūjā.

The Āratī is always followed by the Maṅgaḷ Dīvo, which is offered to counteract the possible ill effects of the Āratī. The Maṅgaḷ Dīvo is an offering of both a small single wick ghee lamp and a burning piece of camphor. Women explained this to me saying that the camphor, by virtue of leaving no mark when it burns, prevents any negative karma from attaching to the pūjā performer from the performance of the pūjā or Āratī. The Maṅgaḷ Dīvo, too, is always accompanied by a song:

Lamp, O Lamp, O holy lamp.
  Raise the lamp and live long.
In our decorated house on Dīvālī,
  In fancy clothes, our daughters dance.[22]
Saying the lamp prayer, the family of Ajuvāḷī
  Removes the obstacles with their devotion.
Saying the lamp prayer in this time of Kaḷī,
  King Kumārapāl raised the lamp.
Our house is blessed, your house is blessed,
  May the fourfold congregation be blessed.

Like the Vedic *prayaścitta*, these closing rites ensure that the pūjā's merit is gained and that any negative karma arising from mistakes within the pūjā are removed. It is not clear who is being petitioned. It does mention that the present is the time of *kalī* (during which no one will attain mokṣa) and thus the Jain devotee offers these lamps and their devotion to counteract the ill effects of their practice. This is an important rite, as it was widely held that to skip the Maṅgaḷ Dīvo resulted in bad luck as a result of one's bad karma.

If the Snātra Pūjā is the prologue for a longer pūjā, the Āratī and Maṅgaḷ Dīvo are performed at the end of the longer pūjā. If a longer pūjā was being performed, the maṇḍaḷ sang another Navkār Mantra between the Snātra Pūjā and the start of the longer pūjā. The Śantī Kalaś, a never-ending pitcher of the five ambrosia poured into a bowl with a sandalwood svastik, several coins, flowers and almonds at the bottom (see figures 5-2 and 6-1), which was almost always performed after the Maṅgaḷ Dīvo, is not required to complete the pūjā. The Śantī Kalaś and its accompanying text—the "Motī Śānti" (also called the "Bṛhatśānti")—were performed in order to bring peace (śānt) to the sponsor's home.[23] Often the sponsor's husband arrived at the end of the pūjā in time to perform the Śantī Kalaś with her. The instructions for these closing rites—the Āratī, Maṅgaḷ Dīvo, and the Śantī Kalaś—were scant in the pūjā manuals and not explained or described in the ritual instructions in the *Laghu Pūjā Sangrah*. The more complete pūjā manual, the *Vividh Pūjā Sangrah*, included the text of the "Motī Śānti" and brief instructions in its performance. The maṇḍaḷ women used the *Laghu Pūjā Sangrah* and thus relied on Maluben's knowledge of the details of their performance—especially for the relatively complex Śantī Kalaś—and on one of several women for the recitation of the "Motī Śānti." If the Śāntī Kalaś is performed, it marks the end of the pūjā; if it isn't performed, then the pūjā ends with the Āratī and Mangaḷ Dīvo. Thus the pūjā is concluded with the sense of the protection of the pūjā's efficacy through the Āratī and Mangaḷ Dīvo. In addition, pūjā efficacy is integrated into ordinary life by bringing the positive effects of the pūjā in the form of the Śāntī Kalaś into one's worldly life by carrying it (literally) out of the temple and into one's home. To illustrate the actual performance of these and the ways the sponsor and maṇḍaḷ tie up the loose ends of the pūjā, I will complete the description from our pūjā:

> Before offering the Āratī and Maṅgaḷ Dīvo, the lamps were both put on a large silver plate. We put salt and water in our joined hands and sprinkled it in a circle five times

FIGURE 6-1. Sānti Kalaś during the Nāvanu Prakāri Pūjā, Ajitnāth Temple, Shivajinagar, Pune, August 1994.

around the unlit lamps. Then the Āratī lamp was lit and waved in a clockwise circle while everyone, clapping and ringing the temple bells, sang the Āratī song. The Maṅgaḷ Dīvo was then put on the silver plate with some coins (Other women added coins to this plate as well as to the Śāntī Kalaś.) and a piece of camphor, and both were lit. This time the lamp was waved in a jagged pattern while the maṇḍaḷ sang the Maṅgaḷ Dīvo song and bells were rung again. During the Āratī and the Maṅgaḷ Dīvo, other women still at the temple briefly touched the silver plate on which the lamps were burning as a participation in the offering.

Finally, during the Śantī Kalaś, we sat cross-legged on the floor with Steve's hands on top of mine and poured milky-water from the main pitcher into the large bowl, which had a svastik, almonds and coins in the bottom. Sheelu was pouring the smaller pitcher into our pitcher to keep the stream unending for the duration of the prayers Maluben was saying. The remaining maṇḍaḷ women also briefly touched Sheelu's arm, participating in the act of pouring during the Śantī Kalaś. When the bowl was full and the prayers were done, the pitchers were sunk into the bowl, and the red and yellow threads were broken from our wrists and thrown into the milky water. After this, most women touched the water and then their eyelids and some women touched the milky water to the parts in their hair and left. We then gave a plate and cup set to Arun—who had done an image decoration of Ādināth, cleaned the image and applied the silver foil and generally helped set up and run the pūjā—and 5 rupees each to the man who cleans up the temple and to the woman who cooks the āyambil food. Steve changed out of the pūjā clothes in the mendicants' hostel and then we went back to the Alandikar's, where

I changed into regular clothes and we all had tea. I gave the remaining plate and cup to Lata since she had to stay home and keep the house in order while the others were at the pūjā. Her initial refusal of the gift—she said they should only go to pūjā performers—was perfunctory.

The closing rites of the pūjās ensure that the merit of the pūjā is not counteracted or compromised by possible mistakes made in the pūjās' performance. The text of the Snātra Pūjā supplies a model narrative and basic instructions which allow one to follow the ritual. However, when the maṇḍaḷ performed the Snātra Pūjā there were many more details in the actual performance than the text supplies.[24] The remaining actions are not passed through these written sources but through the attentive observation by these women of many (even hundreds) of Snātra Pūjās. Through maṇḍaḷ practice, attendance, and the observation of other pūjās, the women learn the specifics of Jain orthopraxy, and through public performances this orthopraxy is monitored. The Snātra Pūjā is an event during which, on a small scale, the women reiterate the proper performance of the pūjā and the correct recitation of the prayers.

Because the Snātra Pūjā preceded all other pūjās, the stavan in the Snātra Pūjā were present in all the pūjās. The placements and stavan choices were the same from performance to performance excepting the choice between "Śankheśvar Svāmī" and "Mahāvīr Śrī Bhagavān." The "fit" of the stavan in this pūjā—with the possible exception of "Śankheśvar Svāmī"—was clear: each addressing the very action at hand. The match of stavan to context is a central feature of the decision to perform a stavan in a pūjā context. In the previous chapter, the individual's personal devotion was the operative characteristic in stavan choices, but in the formal pūjās the maṇḍaḷ chose stavan whose meanings or styles reflected the intentions of the particular performances. The choices made in the actions performed during a pūjā are informed by the ritual instructions, by standard daily pūjā practices, and by a negotiated group understanding of what constitutes the features of proper worship. Although there is no single shared understanding of proper worship, there are limits to the range included within proper worship. In formal pūjās the combination of rehearsal by the maṇḍaḷ and the interactive environment of actual performance provides a place for the negotiation of various understandings to find a shared locus for that performance. It is in choosing stavan for inclusion in the pūjā performance that the women in the maṇḍaḷ were able to assert their own interpretations of the pūjā. Not only are there no instructions for choosing stavan for performance, there is no explicit or implicit reference to the performance of stavan at all. When Arun performs a Snātra Pūjā in someone's name, he does not include any stavan; however, the gestures he performs include all those described previously in the Snātra Pūjā except the prabhāvanā and the closing rites. Thus, stavan choice is a significant marker of the maṇḍaḷ's personal stamp on the meaning of the pūjā.

Stavan in Pūjā Performance

Pūjā performance knowledge inheres in places—stavan—that pair the ritual actions both with an orthopraxy and with the metaphoric/ symbolic event units in Jain mythology (e.g., the joining of the stavan "My Golden Throne," with its description of the decorated image, with the image decoration and the later coronation of Mahāvīr by

Indra during the pūjā performance). The text affects the timing of pūjā performance actions and the selection of accompanying stavan. Although a maṇḍaḷs' particularizations through the use and placement of stavan in formal pūjās may not be prescribed by the pūjā texts, these choices are consistent with that negotiated (in the context of the maṇḍaḷ and over time the non-maṇḍaḷ community) understanding of formal pūjā orthopraxy. The addition of stavan in between sections, new melodies for the opening verses or their replacement by stavan, and the dāṇḍiya-rās dancing are also dictated by a shared understanding of the meaning of a particular pūjā in its particular context. These choices are made in the context of various sources: the liturgical texts, the explanation of the pūjā, the context of the performance, and the musicality of the stavan. The variations between the text and performance show a place where the maṇḍaḷ can interpret the pūjā and use that interpretation to "spice up" their performance. The text, though central to the performance, is not fixed to the exclusion of individual interpretations; hence, the orthodoxy allows the performers to affix—in a sense—a commentary to the pūjā text. Even within the sphere of the ritual instructions, the written instructions for the pūjā performances are still limited; the maṇḍaḷ determined its performance primarily through negotiations at maṇḍaḷ practice.

The maṇḍaḷ practiced its performances of the pūjās, particularly those for which it had upcoming future performances. (They had, however, performed the Snātra Pūjā so many times by the time I came to do research that they no longer practiced it.) The source for correct performance of the pūjās was primarily the women's shared knowledge of the pūjās—though Maluben paid especial attention to make sure she knew exactly what happened when and that the pūjā sponsor was performing everything correctly. At a pūjā, the maṇḍaḷ, the sponsor, and any other participants are prepared to experience a particular set of actions based both on their previous participation in formal pūjā performances and on the number of pūjā manuals they have read. It was not unusual for a highly motivated laywoman like Maluben to take notes at another maṇḍaḷ's pūjā or to actively to seek out new books to read about pūjā performance. These books, as I showed earlier in this chapter, only outline the basic gestures and their timing. The actual pūjās are more complicated and involve a lot more activity than suggested in these books. This information is learned through participation and observation of pūjās over time. Clearly, the pūjā as a shared public ritual is a place for women to learn or refine correct praxis. It must inevitably also become a source of orthopraxy.

The relationships between the stavan texts and the contexts (starting with formal pūjās) in which they were performed illustrates some of the ways the laywomen understood the stavan's and pūjās' meanings. Particular performances of stavan are far from accidental; the women discussed the appropriateness of certain stavan in certain places, and repertoires evolved according to these discussions. If we can assume that the placement of certain songs is directly attached to their meaning and the singers' intentions (Ben-Amos 1982), then the actual repertoire of pūjās or daily pūjā is important for understanding what the stavan mean. There are essentially two kinds of stavan singing: stavan singing for the Jina alone (which I discussed in the previous chapter), and stavan singing in front of an audience that includes the Jina. The second category can be further divided into two types of performance: maṇḍaḷ performances at pūjās and hired singing sessions (*bhāvnā*s), and solo performances at singing sessions and programs. When the stavan are being performed in front of an audience, the notions of repertoire are different and the decisions about stavan choice are changed. The performance adopted an entertainment context where stavan can be easily expanded through repetition of lyrics, where stavan refrains are simple enough to allow the audience to participate in singing, and where stavan's melody and rhythm are lively—particularly when the audience is dancing. When there is a group of singers, even if led by a single singer, the repertoire must reflect a shared knowledge of stavan—even if only the melody is known and the lyrics are sung in a call-and-response manner. Singing-session performances will be talked about in the following chapter, but here my discussion focuses on the maṇḍaḷ performances of stavan in the context of pūjā performances.

The many formal pūjā performances all included stavan sung by the maṇḍaḷ. The repertoire of pūjā stavan was based in part on the text of the pūjās themselves. In the Vāstuk, Pañcakalyāṇak, and Navāṇuṅ Prakārī Pūjās, most stavan address the Jina being worshipped. Excepting the Snātra Pūjā, during which the same three stavan were sung in virtually all performances in the same places, the pūjās did not have a "set list." Choices were sometimes made spontaneously by one of the lead singers in the sense of a selection being chosen from the set of stavan that the maṇḍaḷ has practiced and decided are acceptable for performance. The maṇḍaḷ women were quite familiar with the pūjā texts and the meanings of the poetic sections and opening verses of the formal pūjā liturgy; the stavan were chosen to fit into the pūjā. In this regard, the pūjā text guided, but did not determine, stavan choices. However, the choices must be accepted by the group as appropriate (Abrahams 1976) or confusion or downright refusal by other singers to participate in singing caused the pūjā to be halted temporarily while a better choice was negotiated. When a stavan more subtly did not fit in the pūjā, the performance continued but it was dropped from the subsequent pūjā performances. The occasional mismatch of the stavan text with the exact wording of the opening verses—as I discuss later in the context of the Pañcakalyāṇak Pūjā—indicates that stavan were definitely selected for their meanings; stavan usually represented—in some global way—the sense of the text being replaced. For example, the text being replaced is often commentary rather than narrative (a stavan replaced narrative text only when the narrative episode was included elsewhere in the text). Stavan were often carefully selected so that they elaborated on the pūjā text. The focus seemed to be on the meaning of the liturgy as a whole or on the use-context of the pūjā more than on the particular words used in the text.

The major difference between a pūjā text as found in the pūjā manual and the same pūjā text as performed by a maṇḍaḷ were the stavan sung. The pūjā manuals do not list places for stavan to be performed. Stavan were used in three ways within the formal pūjās: (1) as filler between the sections of the pūjās—when the text finished before the ritual accompanying it was completed (as in the Snātra Pūjā); (2) tagged onto the formal text during the final pūjā of each of the longer pūjās in order to lengthen the music available for dancing—if people were having a good time dancing; and (3) in place of the opening verses that begin each section of the formal pūjā text as written. Certain stavan were used for each of these roles more often than others and not all the stavan were performed in each formal pūjā. However, some were used in the same place over and over again, suggesting a good match between the stavan and the maṇḍaḷ's understanding of the particular context. It is significant that the meaning of the opening couplet and the meaning of the stavan do not have to match, suggesting that the musicality of the stavan may take precedence over the meaning of the opening verse. All pūjā stavan shared two features: They worked well as group performances—either having easy melodies or lending themselves to a call-and-response form of performance—and had lively melody and steady rhythm. As the ensuing sections illustrate, the available contexts provide subtly different ranges of stavan choices, and the different types of pūjās further alter repertoire decisions.

Pañcakalyāṇak Pūjā

Vīrvijayjī's Pañcakalyāṇak Pūjā is a retelling of the five auspicious moments of Pārśva's life, through the Pārśvanāth image at Śankheśvar. In the Pañcakalyāṇak Pūjā, the maṇḍaḷ customarily divided up the stavan "Kesarīyā, O Kesarīyā,"[25] which opens this chapter, so that the appropriate verse was sung with each offering before the next opening verse. None of the pūjā text was replaced by this stavan. However, there are several places where the Pārśva Maṇḍaḷ inserted stavan in place of sections of the formal pūjā text. The second pūjā (the fruit offering) text has the opening verses:

> On Caitra's dark fourth, that god was conceived.
> That night, Vāmā, his mother, the incarnator, that virtuous store-house,
> Saw fourteen grand dreams, the mother saw them in the darkness.
> At night-time she went by herself to the temple, then returned to her happy bed to rest.

This opening verse is a shortened version of the story of Pārśvanāth's conception and his mother's subsequent dreams, which identify Pārśva as a Universal Ruler. The maṇḍaḷ replaced it with the stavan "Śankheśvar Svāmī," which does not tell the story of Pārśvanāth's birth but does address Śankheśvar Pārśvanāth, to whom the Pañcakalyāṇak Pūjā is dedicated:

> O Śankheśvar Svāmī, God of the Inner World,
> We praise you, Lord of Blissful Liberation.
>
> My resolve is only this, Lord,
> Let me be your servant.
> I breathe your name.
>
> You end all troubled times, Lord,
> And fulfill our desires, Lord.
> You destroy our sins and give us blissful liberation.
>
> Every day, I beg for you, Lord,
> I live at your feet.
> Meditating on your mind, I embrace your worship.
>
> Night and day, I am absorbed in you, Lord,
> I long to meet you.
> Rescue me from the sea of worldly sorrows.
>
> You are the ocean of compassion, Lord,
> The storehouse of grace.
> You are the ruler of the three worlds, the people's savior.

The stavan does not mention any of the auspicious moments in Pārśvanāth's life; it gives a list of praises and asks for the Jina's attentions. The first three (of the eight) sections in this pūjā are the story of Pārśvanāth's birth. The opening verse tells in a concise way what the longer narrative section (*dhaḷ*) expands on. While the opening verse is replaced with the stavan, Pārśvanāth's conception is still recounted (in more detail) in the narrative section; thus the maṇḍaḷ felt comfortable using a stavan here—on a permanent basis—which does not cover the same narrative events. It is perhaps most significant that the stavan sung here is not a birth stavan or one based in the celebration of Pārśvanāth's life; it is a reflection on Śankheśvar Pārśvanāth, the most popular Jina image for these—and many other—Gujarātī Jains (Cort 1988).

Every Pañcakalyāṇak Pūjā I heard also included the stavan "Sweetness in the Mind," which begins with a Pārśvanāth temple and goes on to name the Jina image at Śankheśvar. This stavan tells of Pārśvanāth's compassion and role as refuge for Jains, and the singer, by reflecting on these qualities is (at least according to the stavan text) filled with joy. It is a straightforward devotional song dedicated primarily to a single image;[26] whenever the temple bells ring—in any temple—the devotee is thinking of Śankheśvar Pārśvanāth:

> In Pārśvanāth's temple, bells are ringing.
> Bell, your tinkling puts sweetness in the mind.
> Sky and wind together are less beautiful than the abode of the Jinas.
> Bell, your tinkling puts sweetness in the mind.
> In your ears are earrings, and on you, the crown looks beautiful,
> Dādā, looking at your face, everyone's heart is charmed.
> See Śankheśvar's Lord and ring the bells,
> Bowing and clasping your feet, a devotee hopes for you.
> See the Lord of success' compassion rain from heaven.
> One who comes into your refuge swims from the ocean of existence.

It was a popular stavan to dance to, as it was sung to a Gujarātī folk dance (rās-garbā) melody. Unlike "Śankheśvar Svāmī," this stavan did not fall at a set time, nor did it usually replace the opening verse. In fact, the opening verse is often incorporated into the stavan, to extend the music for dancing. The rhythm of the opening verse is particularly well suited to this stavan's melody, which may well influence the choice of this stavan for this context. Being a particularly good dance tune, it often inspires enthusiastic and lengthy dancing during the dance part of the pūjā. It was sung over and over again, for as long as the women wanted to dance dāṇḍiya-rās. This pūjā was a celebratory one and was often sponsored to commemorate anniversaries or birthdays. Dance should therefore come as no surprise as it was a common part of other celebrations as well.

Because the Pañcakalyāṇak Pūjā was quite long, the maṇḍaḷ did not sing a stavan with each offering. Four or five stavan were usually sung, including "Śankheśvar Svāmī," "Sweetness in the Mind," and "Bring, O Bring." The other stavan in the Pañcakalyāṇak Pūjā varied from performance to performance and were rarely used more than once. They generally were not Pārśva stavan and therefore did not make as good a "fit," in the sense I have described. On January 1, 1994, the seventh offering's opening verse was substituted by "Knowledge Is Given" (a Mahāvīr stavan) written by a man in Pune's Ādarś Maṇḍaḷ for the previous Paryuṣaṇ, but this stavan was a mismatch (except for its good melody) and was not performed in another pūjā. A significant exception to content-based choices is the regular performance of the stavan "Kesariyā O Kesariyā," which, though dedicated to Ādināth, was performed regularly in the Pañcakalyāṇak Pūjā; however, this stavan's division into eight verses each about a different offering was a good match with the eight offerings sections in this pūjā, suggesting that its form was more important than which Jina was addressed. When the offering took longer than the text of the pūjā or there was a long empty space, the lead singers generally chose a stavan. These stavan were spontaneous performances, usually based more on the lead singer's perceived need for a stavan in the space than on a shared sense of a stavan's content and "fit" with the pūjā. On several occasions, two of the women started a stavan that was quickly preempted by a stavan with which the maṇḍaḷ felt more comfortable; the interrupted stavan was sometimes sung at the next opportunity or abandoned until another day. Some degree of permanence, then, seems to coincide with a stavan's fit either with the meaning of the pūjā text or with the flow of performance. As I show later, temporary changes can also have intentional implications.

With only two exceptions, the third opening verse of the Pañcakalyāṇak Pūjā was always replaced by "Come, Come, Everyone Come!," which listed the various items brought for the Jina: a crown, a garland of flowers, songs. This particular stavan—which focuses on the various roles devotees may adopt in doing pūjā—used the merit of singing as a refrain in the song, a popular sentiment among the maṇḍaḷ women, who centered their devotional activities around singing:

> Come, come, everyone come!
> Come and make your devoted pūjā!
> Bring, bring, everyone bring!
> Bring the flowers of devotion!
> Have cloth brought to the temple and dress our Lord.
> Sing powerful songs which remove the stain [of karma]
> O—With great devotion, everyone enters the temple to have darśan.
> Coming to the temple's beautiful image,
> People are enchanted like vines growing around the silent one.
> Singing songs of conscienceness come and bring your hearts.

On June 26, the maṇḍaḷ sang "Money or God"[27] instead of "Come, Come Everyone Come" as a critique of the woman performing the pūjā. It was a new stavan then and it was used one more time in place of the third opening verse when another Pañcakalyāṇak Pūjā was performed by someone who did not go to temple very often, suggesting a strong performative component in repertoire choice. Though the pūjā's sponsors may have been only marginally aware of the song's critique of their laxity, the maṇḍaḷ, having substituted it for a spirited celebration of singing, was collectively aware of (and, as it came out in many discussions with women from the maṇḍaḷ in the weeks after the pūjā, in agreement with) such a critique.[28] Were the women in the maṇḍaḷ uncomfortable with or in disagreement with the critique, not only would it have shown in their hesitance (or flat-out refusal) to sing the stavan, but it most certainly would have been a part of the post-pūjā discussions, as other issues arising from performance choices were. The Pañcakalyāṇak Pūjā stavan are based both on the particular dedication to Pārśvanāth and on the "fit" of the stavan with the actions—especially with stavan's articulations of the various roles of devotees and what they have to offer the Jina. The maṇḍaḷ varied their repertoire from performance to performance, sometimes introducing new stavan and using these changes to articulate their understandings of changes within the pūjā performance. Whereas stavan choices were made spontaneously during a pūjā performance, they were usually chosen from the set of stavan the maṇḍaḷ has practiced and decided are appropriate for this context.

The Vāstuk Pūjā and the Antarāyakarm Nivāraṇanī Pūjā

The Vāstuk Pūjā, written by Ācārya Śrī Buddhisāgarsūrijī (1874–1925) and usually performed when someone moves into a new home, is also dedicated to Śankheśvar Pārśvanāth. Every opening verse and narrative section praises Śankheśvar Pārśva as the bringer of well being. The first opening verse gives an extensive explanation of why this Jina is offered this pūjā and what the worshippers wish for:

Śrī Śankheśvar Pārśvanāth, the twenty-third Jina!
Dharaṇendra and Padmāvatī, the receivers of worship!
Pārśva's guardians are pleased by his worship. Doing it gets their attention,
And those who are full of Pārśvanāth meditating gain the joy of liberation.
This house's Vāstuk Pūjā gives great happiness.
Wealth, prosperity, happiness, and peace make an auspicious garland.
Five times, five things are placed in front of Śankheśvar Pās.
This pūjā is performed with affection. Let it be fruitful, that is my hope.
O Wish-fulfilling jewel, Pārśvanāth, your name is my touchstone,
One who meditates and sings for living creatures, does the work of the accomplished One.

These opening verses illustrate the efficacy of the Vāstuk Pūjā; the descriptions include the gains of the pūjā and how one gains these rather material benefits from Jina pūjā—in part through the intercession of the pleased Dharaṇendra and Padmāvatī. When the maṇḍaḷ performed Vāstuk Pūjās, all the opening verses were sung as well as additional stavan; the narrative texts did not cover the same material, and the meaning of the overall pūjā would be changed by removing these opening verses. The first section includes the birth of Pārśvanāth; the others extol the specific merits of worshipping Śankheśvar Pārśvanāth and performing the Vāstuk Pūjā. The text of the pūjā is all Pārśvanāth, yet the stavan used in this pūjā were not exclusively addressed to Pārśvanāth. The stavan repertoire for the Vāstuk Pūjā was fairly stable: "We Came," "Lord Pārśva," and "Bring, O Bring." "We Came" (the stavan which opens the book) was the only stavan written specifically for the Vāstuk Pūjā:

We came, we came, we came right here.
We are pleased to celebrate the Vāstuk Pūjā.
We went to the houses of our brothers in Shivajinagar.
We devoutly celebrated the pūjā in our sisters' homes,
O—We came to have God's darśan.

The Pārśva Maṇḍaḷ came right here
From devotion, we celebrated wildly.
  O—We devoutly celebrated with all our senses.
I say, we came to your door, God, because we have devotion.
The whole women's maṇḍaḷ is very happy.
  O—We came to Shivajinagar's God.
We decorated his image with all our gems.
O God, you are in the hearts of all my sisters.
  O—Because we are devoted, we performed your worship.

This stavan was usually used for dancing dāṇḍiya-rās. It focuses on the act of the image being installed, albeit temporarily, in the new home of a member of the congregation. The fact that the pūjā is performed in a person's home rather than in the temple makes it a more private event. The best attended Vāstuk Pūjā I went to still only had about fifteen or twenty people in attendance (besides the maṇḍaḷ women); generally, the only people usually at this pūjā would be the people who are going to live in the new house.

The other stavan performed at each Vāstuk Pūjā was "Just Once, Lord Pārśva," which was not specific to the Vāstuk Pūjā—though the stavan shares its addressee, Pārśva, with the pūjā—but was not sung at other pūjās either. It was set to a melody good for garbā dance, which may explain its presence in this pūjā, where more dancing was done than in any other pūjā:

Just once, Lord Pārśva, Come to my temple!
Come to my temple, that's my request.
My request is that you come, I beg you to do this.
That is my song's devoted wish.
Dark and daylight, my heart is large,
Thus, I came respectfully to you.
With the flowers of the soul, I spoke to you.
Take these flowers and bring back your precious ones.
In crushing illusion, one is your name,
One is your name, saying it is my work.

This stavan voices the conflict arising from the fact that the Jina images are not the Jinas themselves. By asking for true grace of the Jina rather than the worship of the Jina image, it expresses a strong sense of personal devotion and mildly challenges the notion of the efficacy of image worship. This reminds me of Ranjana's favorite stavan, "Inner Lord, Hear My Song," discussed in the previous chapter where the stavan demands some evidence of the compassion of the Jinas. The stavan asks the Jina to accept the flowers of pūjā and to give the devotee the Jina's more precious ones: his darśan. Despite this solemnly expressed desire to see the Jina, the stavan has a lively garbā melody.

During this pūjā, the maṇḍaḷ sang any two other stavan from a group of stavan that focus most commonly on devotees and their offerings: "Come, O Come," "Go to Pālītāṇā"—which praises Ādināth—and "Sweetness in the Mind," which, as we saw in the Pañcakalyāṇak Pūjā, primarily praises Śankheśvar Pārśvanāth. The order of the stavan was not the same from one performance to the next. Because these stavan were sung to augment the pūjā and add celebratory singing (it was always a fairly jolly pūjā with a fair amount of dāṇḍiya-rās), and because the repertoire was determined mostly by the joyous and somewhat worldly tone of the pūjā, musicality supplants meaning in decisions about "fit."

In contrast, the Antarāyakarm Nivāraṇanī Pūjā written by Virvijayjī (in 1817–18 C.E.) is sponsored by someone who needs to burn off a certain amount of antarāya karma—accrued through either a death in the family or some act of disrespect to Jain ideals. The pūjā itself is not dedicated to any one Jina and the stavan do not lean toward a particular Jina. The pūjā sponsor's intention was usually to offer a satisfactory sacrifice (in the form of expensive offerings and time) to counteract his or her bad actions. Though several stavan were sung during this pūjā's performance, all the opening verses, too, were sung. Because this pūjā has a direct effect—an actual decrease in antarāya karma (which, among other things, prevents one from performing worship meritoriously)—each verse was important. In general the stavan in this pūjā were slower and less celebratory than in the Snātra, Pañcakalyāṇak, and Vāstuk Pūjās. The repertoire varied from performance to performance, with the exception of "O Compassionate One." This stavan asks for mercy for sins and seems to express the emotional content of the performance of the Antarāyakarm Nivāraṇanī Pūjā:

> O compassionate Lord, your compassion has no end,
> O destroyer of troubles, is there no end to your mercy?
> My sin is doing this, I have forgotten to do your worship.
> O forgetter of my forgetfulness, is there no end to your mercy?
> I knew inside that I was playing sinful games.
> O lord who makes wrongs right, is there no end to your mercy?

The repetition of "O Compassionate One" reflects the need for the sponsor to ask for help to get back on track, to return to Jain ideals. The other stavan were generally somber and pointed to the need for the Jina's grace. The maṇḍaḷ's repertoire choices for both the Vāstuk Pūjās and the Antarāyakarm Nivāraṇanī Pūjās reflect the primacy of the tone of the stavan over the content or addressee, in part because neither of these pūjās tells a narrative. The pūjās' purposes—to bless a new home or to remove blocking karma—are the dominant themes in the performance. The Vāstuk Pūjā was always performed in the context of a housewarming, whereas the tone of the Antarāyakarm Nivāraṇanī Pūjā had a much more somber tone and no dance offering at all when it was performed as a post-funerary pūjā. In both, the specific purpose of that pūjā performance determined the tone of the stavan (and thus the set of appropriate stavan) used within them.

In sum, the women chose stavan in all these pūjās—Snātra, Pañcakalyāṇak, Vāstuk, and Antarāyakarm Nivāraṇa—bearing each pūjā's subject matter, tone, and purpose in mind. Some of the pūjās—the Pañcakalyāṇak and Vāstuk—were dedicated to the popular Śankheśvar Pārśvanāth, which assisted the maṇḍaḷ in their repertoire decisions. Others, like the Vāstuk and Antarāyakarm Nivāraṇanī Pūjās, required an examination of the stavan's tone to set the mood of the former's more joyful tone and the latter's somber one. By contrast, the Snātra Pūjā's frequent performance had, sometime before I began observing it, already negotiated a permanent—at least for now—repertoire. Stavan choices for pūjās are made balancing a variety of influences from liturgical narrative to tone, and from the need for dance music to a response to the ritual activities not accompanied by liturgical verse. Because there are scant instructions and virtually no male or mendicant regulation, these decisions are based on the laywomen's own interpretations of the pūjās. These interpretations arise out of broad knowledge about the context, tone, and meaning of both pūjās and stavan. The ways in which both formal pūjās and stavan intersect with lay religiosity have strong indications for the reconstruction of Jain theology focusing on devotion, particularly as these genres dominate Jain laywomen's praxis.

Pūjā Performance Evaluations

As a public event, the piety and practice of the sponsor is on display for the rest of the maṇḍaḷ and the others watching. The women customarily discussed the relative merits of each particular pūjā afterward during their tea and over the days which followed each pūjā performance or attendance. The primary criteria women used to evaluate each pūjā were divided between comments on their sense of the sentiment of the sponsor and the sponsor's family and the quality of the maṇḍaḷ contribution. For the most part the evaluations relied on positive statements about good pūjās rather than negative statements about bad ones; when there was a negative statement, it was a serious critique usually questioning the level of merit gained from the pūjā.

When the sponsor's sentiment is in question, the pūjā could be declared a disaster as it was at the Vāstuk Pūjā, which is discussed at length in chapter 8. However, the sponsor's sentiment was questioned on two other occasions without the pūjā being declared a "bad" pūjā, suggesting that the sponsors were not so out of line in their judgments to counteract the positive self-evaluation of the maṇḍaḷ's own contribution. However, if the sponsor and her family showed themselves to have strong devotional sentiments, it usually led to increased energy in the maṇḍaḷ's performance; likewise, if the family was enthusiastic about dancing, the maṇḍaḷ would sing stavan after stavan for dancing. The pūjās with long dance sections were all considered to be very good. The sponsors' sentiment was evaluated often in terms of the number of family members attending the pūjā, their behavior and perceived knowledge about Jain worship, and sometimes in terms of the quality of the gifts and offerings they brought.

Attendance by all the women in a sponsor's family at a temple pūjā was seen as a sign of a generally religious family, whereas the attendance of any adult man (besides the arrival of the sponsor's husband for the Śānti Kalaś) usually marked a particularly observant family about which the maṇḍaḷ women commented at some length. The maṇḍaḷ was less surprised by men's attendance at pūjās happening in their home, where it was assumed that the men in the family would try to be present. If a pūjā was held in the temple there was a sense that a good crowd (of an undetermined amount but generally suggesting crowdedness) was seen as congregational support for the maṇḍaḷ and part of what made a pūjā successful. There were a few kinds of knowledge that sponsors displayed which added to a positive assessment of the pūjā, especially knowledge of pūjā gestures and accompanying mantras. Knowledge—on the part of the sponsor—of how to perform the pūjā made the pūjā run more smoothly, and this knowledge often led to enthusiastic contributions from the sponsor and the sponsor's family; these were most often cited as reasons for a pūjā's being especially good. Large groups of attendees and evidence of the sponsor's knowledge about pūjā contributed to the maṇḍaḷ's sense that the sponsor was performing the pūjā with the correct sentiment of religious devotion.

The final locus for judgments about the sentiments of the sponsor was an evaluation of the economic contribution. The quality of the materials brought to the pūjā by the sponsor was always balanced against the women's perceptions about the economic status of the sponsor's family. Thus when a family perceived to have limited resources sponsored a pūjā there was an explicit adjustment of the expectations, a process I saw on several occasions. I never saw a pūjā where the women felt that the offerings were inadequate, perhaps because sponsors always prioritized the pūjā supplies, but the women did often comment on especially extravagant or beautiful offerings. This was often linked to praise of families that sponsored image decorations to go with their pūjā or that decorated their houses when a pūjā was to take place there. A second set of materials talked about was the gifts for the maṇḍaḷ and those that are distributed to all who attend a pūjā. These maṇḍaḷ gifts and the gifts distributed to all attendees were also marked mostly when they were seen as special relative to the giver. When a relatively wealthy woman gave a monthly Snātra Pūjā and gave silver lamps to everyone, it was seen as an especially good gift; likewise, when a relatively low-income family gave out small metal dishes for serving snacks it was spoken of as a good present as well.

As we know from other studies of paid specialists in South Asia, payment for ritual services often carries with it the stigma of being a receiver of the sin or inauspiciousness as part of a ritual. By paying the specialist (and thereby transferring the inauspiciousness to the specialist), the sponsor increases his or her auspiciousness (Parry 1994; Raheja 1988). Other times payment is used by the sponsor to justify seeing the paid specialist as a servant (at least temporarily) to the sponsor (Fuller 1984). The negotiation of status and control in those relationships often leads to accusations that one group or the other is overcharging or underpaying (Gold 1988; Parry 1994).

In the context of the Ajitnāth Temple the financial relationship between the Pārśva Maṇḍaḷ and the sponsors was controlled by the use of a fixed price system for performing pūjās; for example, the Snātra Pūjā cost 31 rupees and the Pañcakalyāṇak Pūjā cost 101 rupees. In addition, payment for the pūjā was made not to the maṇḍaḷ but to the temple trust directly—when the pūjā was performed in a house the sponsor (or usually her husband) came to the temple to pay the trustees for the pūjā in advance—and thus the maṇḍaḷ always saw its performances either as donation (dān) or as the maṇḍaḷ women's own participation in the pūjā. On the other hand, as part of the pūjā performance the sponsor is expected to provide prabhāvanā—presents to all who attend the ceremony—and gifts for the maṇḍaḷ performers. Thus, the sponsor's payment (as opposed to the gifts for the maṇḍaḷ women) was a question of giving to the temple. This meant that the maṇḍaḷ's complaints about a sponsor's payment for a pūjā were not a locus of financial negotiation between the maṇḍaḷ and the sponsor but a critique of the sponsor's sentiment behind his or her gifting to their temple. Although I never heard anyone complain outright about the practice of giving out coins or money as maṇḍaḷ gifts, I also never heard anyone compliment these gifts; I suspect the women were less enthusiastic about money gifts, partly because—being less personal—it seemed all too much like payment. It was clear that, in these discussions, the concern was not personal economics (the money gifts were small and the temple payment unrelated to the women's finances), but there was a sense of pride both in the quality of the pūjā and in the worthiness of their temple which contributed to the maṇḍaḷ women's critiques of the economic expression of the sponsor's sentiments.

There were criteria for the maṇḍaḷ's performance and participation which also led to judgments on the quality of the pūjā. The attendance of a good crowd (a figure that seemed to mean more than twenty at the temple and more than about twelve for a pūjā somewhere else) of the maṇḍaḷ women themselves showed both their general enthusiasm for pūjā performance and their appreciation of the sponsor herself. This usually meant a better performance (larger groups tended to meld together better), a better self-presentation to the sponsor, and usually a sense that it was more fun to perform the pūjā. Maṇḍaḷ performance, particularly the unity and enthusiasm of singing and dancing, was a major factor in the evaluation of a pūjā. If there was a dearth of strong lead singers, the maṇḍaḷ had difficulty staying unified in singing. Such pūjās were universally characterized as weak by those who were present. The maṇḍaḷ was at its worst if the members seemed distracted or disinterested in their own performance. I only saw this on two occasions—once when it was the third Snātra Pūjā on a single day and once when it appeared that the sponsoring family was disinterested (see chapter 8)—and both were considered disasters. As we saw earlier in chapter 3, the choices of stavan for maṇḍaḷ performance for particular pūjā contexts are negotiated and then practiced as a group. A shared, unified expression of the pūjā sentiments is central to their statements about the quality of the maṇḍaḷ's contribution, and thus practice becomes an important antecedent to every pūjā performance both on aesthetic and devotional grounds.

The pūjā instructions given in the liturgical texts are so scant as to demand the presence of a knowledgeable ritual specialist (vidhikār) who can guide the sponsor through the performance. For most of the commonly performed pūjās, the maṇḍaḷ women serve as the ritual specialists for sponsors who usually have little or no knowledge about the details of the pūjā. The maṇḍaḷ's choices for stavan, which arise out of the negotiations of maṇḍaḷ practice and decisions made during a pūjā performance, reflect the maṇḍaḷ's understanding of the content and tone of the formal pūjā liturgy. These choices were not necessarily made as full consensus—there were dissenting voices at practice and occasional nonparticipation (silence as dissent) at pūjā performances. If the maṇḍaḷ's stavan choices in a single performance were spontaneous, they were in some sense made by those women responsible for leading their particular stavan choice—though the long-term acceptance of a choice was a shared choice. In this chapter we looked at the decisions made by the maṇḍaḷ which attempt to unify the performance (stavan with liturgy, dance with music—recall the aesthetics discussion in chapter 4—maṇḍaḷ as a group, and sponsor's gestures with the liturgy); a unified performance was seen as a major contribution to the overall quality of a pūjā. The questions of pūjā quality that arise out of the maṇḍaḷ's evaluation of the sponsors' contribution become a locus for debates over prestige and authority, on which I focus in the next two chapters.

7

Jingle Jangle, Jingle Jangle,
Today in our temple there was a jingle jangle.
Glittering Sparkling, Glittering Sparkling,
Today in our temple there was glittering and sparkling.

That flower-seller came to the Jinas, praying and calling "Lord Pārśvanāth!"
He brought, he brought a garland of roses,
With this he did worship.

That jeweler came to the Jinas, praying and calling "Vīr O Vīr!"
He brought a crown, with him he brought the ornaments,
He decorated and dressed the Jina.

The Pārśva Maṇḍaḷ came, praying and calling "God! God! God!"
They sang auspicious songs for God and destroyed their karma;
They perform the devotion to God.

Transcription and translation of recording of ritual performance in Pune, Maharashtra, on 17 May 1994. Courtesy Śrī Pārśva Mahilā Maṇḍaḷ.

Expertise, Prestige, and Authority

The first time I heard this stavan it was performed by the Pārśva Maṇḍaḷ at the anniversary celebration of Ajitnāth Temple's image installation (May 17, 1994). Describing the possible offerings of various people who come to the temple, this stavan draws a picture of the temple decorated for a holiday celebration or pūjā; it posits the equality of offerings of wealth (jewelry) and offerings of praise (songs), undermining the jockeying for position between prestige (arising from large-scale donations of wealth) and expertise (donations of time, energy and knowledge) which was evident at several events I observed and discussed with Jain laywomen. The stavan itself suggests that what matters is that one is giving the best that one has. However, the equal status of material donation and donations of time and knowledge are not a given; the popularity of this stavan with the maṇḍaḷ women may point to tensions between these competing modes of authority which surrounded many of the public ceremonies Jain women performed. When the women sought more prestige for their devotion, they ran into a conflict between the ways the women's praxis usually was ordered and their urge to adopt the prestige practices usually associated with events dominated by laymen. In addition, high-prestige performances, such as bhāvnās (devotional singing sessions) in various temples during Paryuṣaṇ and at night after the Siddhacakra Mahāpūjā, are often marked by hiring outside professionals—usually male—to perform. This greater prestige was seen to augment the greater "glorification" of their devotion. Negotiations of authority took place at all levels of praxis: teaching pūjā, the annual Mahāvīr Nirvāṇ Program, the performance of the Navāṇuṉ Prakārī Pūjā, competitions in auctions (*boli*s), and the frequent struggle to be heard, literally, with the introduction of amplification into these ritual contexts.

The issue of religious authority hinges on the way that we understand authority and its relationships to both expertise and prestige. First, though, I must make it clear that I have observed two related but distinct components of authority: one that refers to a locus of control or influence and a second that identifies a locus of expertise. Although no one questioned the authority of the mendicants (particularly male mendicants in the Tapā Gacch) to speak authoritatively on issues of Jain orthodoxy and doctrine, there were certainly tensions surrounding the question of who is or has the authority to determine praxis (especially in relation to those practices intended to increase merit in ritual contexts of lay religiosity). Laidlaw (1995) writes of a pūjā context where the laymen asserted lay control and authority over a particular lay event by asking a male mendicant to hurry up and finish his talk. It must be remembered that Jain mendicants, though they sometimes lend a certain gravitas by making appearances at major events, remain largely peripheral in lay ritual life. Someone with prestige possesses influence, based on his or her success or rank in the public eye. One of the central ways of articulating prestige in the Jain social context is in substantial and public donations, especially in the context of Jain auctions or sponsorship of public events, acts that are primarily (though not exclusively) limited to men as they are most commonly the ones with access to sufficient capital. Expertise arises out of a combination of study and experience, and there is no question that women are the primary studiers and participants in most aspects of Jain ritual life.[1] The challenge of this chapter is to explore the ways in which prestige and expertise compete for the position of authority.

Authority within the Maṇḍaḷ

The women in the Pārśva Maṇḍaḷ of Shivajinagar did not express authority in economic terms; whenever a woman discussed a powerful woman, it was in terms of her knowledge. However, whereas knowledge was seen as a source of authority, knowledge without the time or forum to use it was no guarantee of power. Explicitly theological or philosophical knowledge, as such, was not usually included in the assessment; though it was highly valued, it was seen as the territory of the mendicants, not the layperson. "Knowledge" (in the abstract) to these women denoted religious knowledge,[2] which included primarily the knowledge of a large stavan repertoire and an understanding of the pūjās. Moreover, a woman's ability to read religious texts and the ability to write with facility were important factors when deciding which women should control maṇḍaḷ activities. Within the maṇḍaḷ the important negotiations were those that expressly determined who can lead the pūjās in the actions both of the sponsor and of the maṇḍaḷ and who can speak for the maṇḍaḷ in her negotiations with sponsors.

Maluben was in no financial position to make grand donations (as was Jyethiben—the donor whose gift paid for the construction of the Ajitnāth Temple), nor was her husband. Maluben's authority lay in her extensive knowledge of ritual texts and proper praxis and her assertion of this expertise over the years. She started the Pārśva Maṇḍaḷ in 1980 when the Shivajinagar Jains were worshipping in a household temple across the street from where Jyethiben later (in 1983) built Ajitnāth Temple. As Ajitnāth Temple's congregation had no male ritual specialist and, like most temples in Pune, had no men's maṇḍaḷ, this role was taken up by Maluben. When a pūjā was to be performed, the sponsor of the pūjā had to speak with Maluben, who instructed him or her in the proper items for the pūjā (i.e., how many coconuts, fruit, lamps, etc., were needed, the auspicious timing for the event, the cost, and other details necessary for its proper performance). She had most of this information and the exacting details of pūjā performance committed to memory. Though much of this was available in books and pamphlets, she was deferred to as the keeper and distributor of this information. Likewise, she knew the layout and gestures of each pūjā (information she learned from regular and committed attendance at literally hundreds of pūjās) and could recite with ease all the prayers necessary for all these pūjās.

Ranjana and Savita had the expertise and confidence to lead the maṇḍaḷ singing for the performances and jointly held the unspoken position of lead singer. Generally, these two alternately led during a pūjā, though other women (usually Pramila, Kamalben, or Sharmila) occasionally interjected a stavan. If Savita was not able to come, Ranjana led all the singing; she had an arrangement with her family that her presence at the pūjās took priority over her presence in the kitchen. Ranjana's access to virtually all the pūjās meant that she also had the ability to veto a stavan in performance if Savita did not come to the pūjā. This position required less administrative power but extensive musical memory and a knowledge of lyrics to many stavan. The lead singer introduced the melody to the pūjā section or chose and started an appropriate stavan when one was needed. It was the lead singer who chose when to sing which stavan in a pūjā—though some stavan were certainly geared toward a particular situation. Thus, when the maṇḍaḷ sang stavan that were critical of the sponsors—such as the one that begins the next chapter, it was to some extent a reflection of the lead singer's view. However, because the other singers occasionally interrupted a stavan or "sat out" if they did not think it was a good choice, their singing all the way through a stavan was a tacit approval of its inclusion. The primary positions of influence in the maṇḍaḷ, then, were those of the organizer and the lead singer; the former directed the sponsor how to properly conduct him- or herself, and the latter guided the maṇḍaḷ's creative choices that made each pūjā a new expression of devotion appropriate to the particular pūjā and situation.

There were two basic issues concerning the distribution of authority within the maṇḍaḷ—the first concerning ritual and musical knowledge and the second pertaining to those who had authority outside the maṇḍaḷ community. The latter group included women who had experience in negotiating with the community at large, those who had a certain amount of freedom to structure their time (either from their family's economic status or their valuing of the woman's religious activities), and those whose devotional sentiment and commitment was perceived to be very strong. Two maṇḍaḷ administrators ran their own businesses, which was another source of valuable knowledge, and had the confidence to assert themselves in interactions with other Jains, especially men (with whom pūjās were often coordinated). There was a certain lack of prestige associated with families in which the women have to work, but these are the same skills that make the women assertive and confident when dealing with sponsors. However, the sponsors themselves are hiring the maṇḍaḷ for its expertise so they are most interested in talking with someone perceived as an expert. Ultimately, expertise—linked with the time to increase and to use it—was the determining factor in maṇḍaḷ power relations because that kind of religious authority was needed to best conduct maṇḍaḷ activities.

Religious Education and Identification as Adults

Expertise (special knowledge, in this case, of Jain ritual literature and pūjā performance) is the primary qualification that Jains (both male and female, mendicants and laity) listed for the job of religious teacher both in the informal sense of who to learn "Jainism" from, and in the formal sense of who is authorized to teach one in both informal and formal Jain religious schools. Most Jains learn their primary worship (both the constitutive and regulative rules of Jain pūjā, basic prayers, primary theology) through temple going with their mother, paternal grandmother, and paternal aunts. However, there was informal religious education at many temples during the rainy season; at Ajitnāth, it was taught by a knowledgeable woman from the old city. I observed other informal Jain religious education groups in other temples in Pune, Mumbaī, Junnar, Karaḍ, and Sangamner during the rainy season. These were usually attended by girls and a few young boys. Their focus was on learning to recite daily prayers and the ritual confession and expiation of sins. In Pune's old city there was a religious education school that functioned more like the practice of American Hebrew School—it met only for an hour or so a day seven days a week and culminated in an extensive exam in which the students wrote from memory the text to various rituals: daily worship, the rite of confession and expiation (pratikraman̥), and so on.[3] Sheelu had received a certificate from this school two years earlier, which stated that she could lead Jain religious education for children in the more informal settings. She said that there were a large number of young women in this class. Almost all informal religious education was taught by women. It is interesting to note that the only context of formal religious education of Jain laywomen was not in Jain practice but in preparation for their roles in Jain instruction. Although it was assumed that Jain laywomen were qualified by virtue of their involvement in Jain praxis to give primary religious training, there were clearly certain women in each family who were best suited by their expertise (and temperament) to teach Jainism to the families' children.

Whereas some of the young men and boys I knew had gone to residential school for Jains (pāṭhśāḷā) during their vacations (in Pune this happened during Dīvālī vacation at the Gujarātī medium school campus), no women or girls had. These religious education camps are similar to the Vacation Bible schools to which young Protestant Christians are sent to learn the scriptures except that it is residential, so the boys live an "ideal" Jain life for a week. The boys are taught the prayers they need to do their pūjā, how to put on men's pūjā clothes, and how to perform worship, meditation, and the ritual confession and expiation of sins. The Jain vacation school was a relatively new phenomenon which seemed associated with urban middle-class life; no men over 40 or so with whom I spoke had gone to this type of school. In Junnar, there was a one-year Jain boarding school that accepted boys mostly from areas of India (especially Madras) where there was a smaller concentration of Jains. At the boarding school the boys lived according to the ideals of Jain lay life as dictated by the normative traditions—with emphasis on meditation, text study, and interaction with male mendicants. There were no boarding schools or camps for Jain girls, who learn their Jainisms from other lay women or through more informal religious education. In a sense, Jain laymen were being "created" in these contexts by differentiating their praxis (especially by standardizing their understandings of the rationale behind certain pūjā acts) from that of laywomen and children. However, I never heard a man speak of this as a corrective for a lack of women's expertise in religious matters; I found men to speak almost universally of women as the experts on Jain religion. It seemed more a way to encourage Jain boys and young men to understand Jain praxis as a part of Jain male adulthood rather than relegating Jain practice to something they did as a child.

The adult equivalents of the residential religious education are the Updhān Tap and the vow of *poṣadh* in which a layperson takes a vow to live a mendicant's life for multiples of twelve hours or, in the case of the Updhān Tap, forty-five days. Laidlaw (1995) speaks of residential camps called *updhān* where lay Jains live under the strict guidance of mendicants. At the end of these camps, the lay Jains are encouraged (and close to half of the participants in the group he observed did) to take the twelve lay vows. As part of the 2000 Updhān Tap in Katraj, the participants (who were almost all women) learned special prayers, observances, and new ways of performing certain rituals (especially the pratikramaṇ) associated with the praxis of mendicants which both expanded the numbers of practices they then performed and marked them in ritual contexts as those who had completed the Updhān Tap. Cort (1989) speaks of laywomen performing poṣadh in Gujarat. In addition, several women I knew had gone to Pālītāṇā for the whole rainy season, which can be seen as a Jain camp after a fashion. They live in pilgrims' hostels (*dharmśāḷās*) and eat in the Jain dining halls (*bhojanśāḷā*) for the whole time. These women are not involved in any of the harmful acts of household duties. They go to the sermons of the male mendicants every day and have long talks with both male and female mendicants who are in residence there for the rainy season. The central activities are to live as a Jain and to have the freedom from social and familial obligations that could distract the devotee from concentrating the mind on pūjā and Jain ideals under the watchful eye of mendicants and other observant Jains. While there were women in Pune who performed the Updhān Tap, spent the rainy season in Pālītāṇā with the mendicants, or, more modestly, took the vow of poṣadh, it was difficult after marriage to get the time off necessary for these kinds of vows.

When Jains signed up for (or more likely signed their children up for) religious education, as in the previous examples, those Jains have accepted the authority of the teacher to teach Jainism. This authority is granted in part by the certificates that professionalize religious education. When children are sent to the temple with someone to learn worship, prayers, or doctrine, the family has accepted the authority of that relative (virtually always female) to teach worship by acknowledging the expertise of that person in matters of religion. The extension of that teaching authority led to the discussion of monitoring performances. The monitoring and judging of religious practice is part of a number of rituals and events I observed in Pune.

Ajitnāth's Mahāvīr Nirvāṇ Program

The annual Ajitnāth congregation's Mahāvīr Nirvāṇ program (otherwise called the *snehasaṃmelaṃ*) on November 8, 1993, sponsored by the Pārśva Maṇḍaḷ, was a major social event. Approximately one hundred women and many children (boys and girls) and my husband—the only man—came to the mendicants' hostel.[4] The Mahāvīr Nirvāṇ program was a women's event sponsored by the Pārśva Maṇḍaḷ for all the women in the congregation to come to see the dances and drama the young unmarried daughters performed, and to have a congregation-wide party of women who were somehow tangentially connected to the maṇḍaḷ. The Mahāvīr Nirvāṇ program was the focus of social activity and thus presented an ideal opportunity to express the merits and values of maṇḍaḷ participation.[5] In the preparation leading up to the program, young women and girls are schooled by teachers (who were both active and nonactive maṇḍaḷ members—Kalpana, Savita, Sheelu—and another woman from downtown Pune who came for the rainy season to teach religious education in an informal school at Ajitnāth's mendicant hostel) in orthopraxy by incorporating aspects of the formal pūjās into the dance performances. The Mahāvīr Nirvāṇ program (and other all-congregation events such as the maṇḍaḷ picnic) encourages and educates the young women and girls in the socioreligious practices and expectations of Jain laywomen, an education separate from the general, shared, text-based education received in religious education classes.

A brief overall description of the program sets the moments I am discussing—the pūjā dance and speeches—in their context and illustrates the wide range of activities by women and girls that provide a greater number of opportunities (and models) for participation in Jain laywoman's identity. The program began with the Navkār Mantra and two stavan; I was introduced, and then a third stavan was sung. The unmarried young women performed a Gujarātī folk dance to recorded Gujarātī folk music (without lyrics). The younger girls performed a simplified version of the lamp dance accompanied by Ranjana's stavan singing. After several dance performances of folk dances were performed by the unmarried young women, to Jain stavan recorded with "disco-dāṇḍiya" (popular Gujarātī folk music and disco fusion) arrangements, the younger girls performed a pūjā dance to the stavan singing of Savita and Ranjana. After this dance there were a number of speeches and a gift was given to all the women in the maṇḍaḷ: a pūjā bag—a relatively common maṇḍaḷ-associated gift, which can be seen as yet another refocusing of social acts on religious practice. Once the speeches were completed, the young women presented a play about a young man (played by Soni) who is so devoted to the Navkār Mantra that he cannot be distracted even by his imminent wedding. The family is rewarded with new wealth for allowing the young man to be devout. The play was received with cheering, and then everyone was given a snack.

Savita and Ranjana had choreographed the pūjā dance for the young girls (ages 4 to 7). During the first verse of the stavan "Lord Mahāvīr," the first pair of the girls stood up with their pitchers and circumambulated a small table with a Jain image on it. When they finished their circumambulation, they poured milk and water over the brass image and then sat down. The second pair rose with the second verse, holding silver plates filled with flowers. They circumambulated the image, put flower garlands on it, and finally waved incense in front of it. The third pair was holding lamps and waved them in front of the image and then walked around the image afterward. The fourth pair each held a silver plate with a coconut on one and a papaya on the other, with which they circumambulated the image. There were rice tables with the beginnings of a svastik on them, and these two girls had to make rice designs from the rice piles and then put their fruit on them. Then they did three prostrations and returned to their places. Finally, the fifth pair danced with tambourines around and in front of the image. This pūjā dance was the only piece to which the audience paid much attention, probably in part because it was the worship of a Jina and in part because the little girls were so beautiful and pious. The whole dance can be seen as the instruction of how to perform pūjā, but, interestingly, it mimicked the structure and rigidity of a formal pūjā much more than the fluid style of the daily pūjā. Likewise, in daily pūjā, the inclusion of dance as an offering is unusual; it is only vaguely hinted at during the flywhisk offering in daily pūjā, but all formal pūjās included at the very least a short tambourine dance toward the end. The attentiveness of the audience, including one woman leaping up to correct one of the youngest girls when she started to circumambulate the wrong direction, suggests that the display was at least as much instruction (or monitoring instruction) as it was a performance.

There were several speeches given by various women from the maṇḍaḷ. These speeches were a recitation of the good and pious acts (fasts performed, donations given, pūjās sponsored, pilgrimages completed) of certain women in the congregation and words of thanks for those maṇḍaḷ women who had worked especially hard both on this program and on other events throughout the year. The speeches, which praised the women for their active and enthusiastic participation in those acts the maṇḍaḷ felt were important for Jain practice during the past year, constructed a sort of history of piety, raising the awareness both of individuals and of acts as pious. A similar history of the year's piety was recited at the annual all-Pune women's maṇḍaḷ program on Makar Sankranti where the program leaders listed the number of all the pūjās performed by maṇḍaḷs that year in Pune, who had performed fasts, how many women had taken special lifelong vows and congregation pilgrimages, and introduced the president of each of Pune's women's maṇḍaḷs. Attendance at this program clearly marked the female social membership in Pune's Jain community and the self-defined center of this community—the community of women's maṇḍaḷs. The Mahāvīr Nirvāṇ program served a similar role, marking female social membership in Ajitnāth's congregation and the maṇḍaḷ in a Jain public forum.[6] The maṇḍaḷ here was asserting authority over the sense of a female congregation and articulating what the religious practices and priorities of that community would be. The program also served as a place for women to encourage their daughters to participate in women's Jainism while reinforcing this representation of Jain orthopraxy.

Recitation Orthodoxy

A more explicit form of authority is the acceptance of a person's "right" to judge and correct the performance of others. In this context we see some of the more explicit negotiations of authority. Public recitation of prayers was a place where women corrected each other's inaccurate recitation and reinforced accurate recitation. In one's daily pūjā the prayers are recited so quietly that they can scarcely be heard, less so evaluated. However, it was the norm whenever several Jains were worshipping together that only one person would recite the prayers, even when all those present know the prayers; recall the discussion in chapter 5 of Soni and Sveta's interactive performance of daily pūjā in which they corrected each other at every turn, especially during the recitations. At the formal pūjā all recitations are clearly audible, and the other participants are actively quieted in order that everyone can both hear and benefit from the recitation. Because of the public listening, it was during the public recitations—especially those at pūjās—that I heard corrections in recitations. Through public recitation, the women's memories of the text were prompted and corrected and orthodoxy was reaffirmed.[7] The women never, in my experience, referred to a text to correct the words or to dispute anyone's correction; they accepted the corrections (or the multiple corrections) coming from other knowledgeable laywomen. Because of the importance of the correctness of the words in these prayers, the women did not hesitate to correct even Maluben.[8] On April 11, when Maluben was reciting the Motī Śāntī during the Śāntī Kalaś for a Snātra Pūjā, she was interrupted and corrected twice by the maṇḍaḷ. Although only one or two women actually spoke out the correct words, the incorrect recitation was followed by a general uproar. Generally, the women did not feel confident in correcting Maluben with regard to practice—an area in which she was far more trained than most Jains. However, many of the maṇḍaḷ women knew the text of "Motī Śāntī Stotra" and the importance of correct recitation outweighed the social tension arising from correcting an obviously knowledgeable woman. However, when the pūjā was over Maluben joked with a few women that she must be more confused than usual because her pregnant daughter had returned to her husband's house that day. It was clear that she wanted the tension dispersed and perhaps she was embarrassed that she had made a mistake.

The women recited a number of extended texts (including the caityavandan prayers, the "Motī Śānti" text, the various pieces of the different pratikramaṇs) in the course of my research; in all of these cases, it was especially important that all the words were absolutely correct and any mistakes would elicit corrections from even the most reserved members of the maṇḍaḷ. Not only the correctness of the words is important but the timing as well. It was very important that the "Motī Śānti" text be completed at the exact time that the Śānti Kalaś was finished. The women often slowed or sped up the pouring of the pitchers to accommodate the text. However, whenever a mistake was made in recitation, the reciter did not return to the beginning of the text—as he or she did if the ghee lamp went out or if someone sneezed. The misspoken section was repeated correctly and the recitation continued. There was no expiation (prayaścitta) to repair the recitation, as one finds in the Vedic ritual recitations; the words have to be correct but a mistake was corrected simply by saying the words right.[9] The mistake (here, like those discussed in chapter 5 and by Humphrey and Laidlaw 1994, which were not seen as disrespectful), if corrected, did not by itself decrease the amount of merit earned by the pūjā. Self-regulation (keeping the pūjā performance and text recitation within the frame of the regulative rules), by women in congregational groups and the maṇḍaḷ as a group, marked many of the maṇḍaḷ events and pūjā performances. However, it was rare to see maṇḍaḷ performances regulated by external authority as it was during the Snātra Pūjā contest.

The Snātra Pūjā Contest

During Paryuṣaṇ in September 1995, there was a Snātra Pūjā contest at Goḍījī Temple in Pune's old city.[10] Most of Pune's fifty-two Jain maṇḍaḷs joined in the competition. They were competing for prizes of 1,000, 500, and 300 rupees for first, second, and third places, respectively. The maṇḍaḷs were each given a date and time when they were supposed to perform their Snātra Pūjā. The Pārśva Maṇḍaḷ was given a slot on September 7, 1994, at 11 o'clock in the morning. The Snātra Pūjā contest was judged by three men from Goḍījī Temple who had run the mahāpūjās there as ritual specialists.[11] The maṇḍaḷs were to be judged primarily on the accuracy (read orthopraxy) of their Snātra Pūjā performances as determined by the judges. There were small numbers of points to be gained by the aesthetic qualities of the pūjā's presentation—how good the maṇḍaḷ singing was, how well the maṇḍaḷ decorated the area in which the Snātra Pūjā took place, and the flourishes added by each maṇḍaḷ—but the bulk of the earned points or demerits came from accuracy.

The maṇḍaḷ, through its practice sessions and performances, regulates its pūjā performances and creates a shared understanding of a correct pūjā. Because the ritual instructions of the pūjās do not explicitly direct the sponsor or the maṇḍaḷ in the exact details of the pūjā, and because getting these details right is considered to be of central importance, the judges of the annual Snātra Pūjā competition served as something like an ad hoc regulating committee for Pune's maṇḍaḷs. The contest rewards or penalizes the maṇḍaḷs' performances, and thereby attempts to standardize the performance to conform to the judges' understanding of orthopraxy. It was clear to me, however, that the particular standards of the contest did not completely match either the maṇḍaḷs' priorities in pūjā praxis or the maṇḍaḷs' customary practices.

For the whole 8 days of Paryuṣaṇ, Goḍījī Temple was the site of back-to-back Snātra Pūjās. Preparations for the Pārśva Maṇḍaḷ's performance began several days ahead of their slot as the maṇḍaḷ decided which decorations to bring or make for the pūjā, the schedule for the preparations and performance, and the details of how they would perform the actual Snātra Pūjā: who would take the role of sponsor, which stavan would be sung for the dance sequence, and when and how the young women's maṇḍaḷ would dance. Pramila, Manisha, and Maluben went during the week to Goḍījī Temple to see the other maṇḍaḷs perform their Snātra Pūjās. During the Saturday maṇḍaḷ meeting before their Snātra Pūjā time slot, the maṇḍaḷ decided that Ranjana should be the actual performer of the pūjā, because of her confidence and experience in performing the Snātra Pūjā. She also could sing the text of the entire Snātra Pūjā from memory and thus would be able to determine exactly where the maṇḍaḷ was in the text as she performed the pūjā. Significantly, the maṇḍaḷ women did not rehearse the Snātra Pūjā before the contest at all; they only made decisions about the performance and, in fact, put their efforts into practicing for an upcoming performance at another temple. The maṇḍaḷ women were clearly confident in the accuracy, and the efforts they gave to the Snātra Pūjā contest were directed toward the aspects of the pūjā that were understood to be extras: the dance and the decorations.

It seemed that every maṇḍaḷ woman's family contributed something to the decorations. For a Snātra Pūjā in the temple in Shivajinagar, the decorations amounted to the canopy and backdrop (*choḍ-caṇḍārvo*) for the assembly hall stand and occasionally a string of flowers to hang around the top of the assembly hall stand or an image decoration of the Mahāvīr image in the inner sanctum.[12] For the competition, the maṇḍaḷ brought a garland of leaves to string across the top of the porch area on which the assembly hall stand was located. The assembly hall stand itself was draped with garlands of colored tinsel, and Dīvālī-style, colored foil three-dimensional shapes were hung from the ceiling. In addition, young girls from the young women's maṇḍaḷ had made designs in flowers on long low tables for the area in front of the pūjā space, based on the image decoration backdrops they had seen so many times. Another girl made a fancy extended svastik with beads glued to a board. Two women had arranged flowers in baskets, and the fourteen silver images of the dreams of Triśalā—used in the reenactment of Mahāvīr's birthday during the reading of the Kalpa Sūtra during Paryuṣaṇ—were placed individually in decorated silver plates. There was a decorated silver plate with all the items necessary for performing morning eightfold offering pūjā. Perhaps most intricately, Savita built a miniature horsecart which carried a small Pārśvanāth image in it, in imitation of an image procession before temple installation. The whole area had a more than usually festive look to it. Aside from the string of leaves, the decorations were unregulated, though they were worth a few points in the contest and presented an opportunity to display the maṇḍaḷ's (and by extension the congregation's) level of devotion. Likewise, the extent and expense of the decoration indicated something of how the maṇḍaḷ is perceived by its own congregation, by showing how much time and money people were willing to contribute to the project of the Snātra Pūjā contest and ultimately displaying the maṇḍaḷ's prestige within its own congregation.

Pūjā decoration fits into the overall arts of decoration. The ability to create these decorations was an expression of another area of expertise. Hanchett (1988) writes of decorations made for household Hindu pūjā which are usually created by women and which often adopt familial or congregational styles; these decorations are seen as articulations of the proper offerings with the additional devotional sentiment expressed through the family's attention to detail. In the Jain context, the pujārī usually does the image and temple decoration and the women and girls of the family do the decoration for home rituals. However, most of the decorations for the Snātra Pūjā contest and part of those for the Siddhacakra Mahāpūjā were made by women involved with the pūjā, although Arun (Ajitnāth's pujārī) helped some of the young women and girls with their decorations. During Paryuṣaṇ, children and young unmarried women helped Arun prepare the daily image decorations by doing the smaller Jina images. This was understood to be pūjā and may be a place where Jains acquire decoration skills and aesthetic training.

In 1999, when Goḍījī Temple's congregation was hosting a large delegation of Jain mendicants who had walked from Mumbaī to bless the installation of a Padmāvatī image in the Katraj temple south of Pune, several groups of young women decorated a major intersection of the Mumbaī-Pune Road with complicated powder designs (*rangolī*). In each of these cases, women (and often men) spoke of the complexity and difficulty of the designs as examples of both the great skill on the part of the artists who created them and the commitment of a congregation to the religious event for which the decorations were made. Part of the expertise that inheres in Jain laywomen is the knowledge of decoration. Having a pujārī who is an expert at decoration adds to the relative prestige of a particular temple, suggesting here a place where the expertise of a particular person (or group of persons) hired or supported by the congregation leads to greater overall prestige for the congregation. This was also part of the rationale behind some of the congregational support in something like the Snātra Pūjā contest; to have an award winning maṇḍaḷ at the temple would add generally to the temple's prestige.

The maṇḍaḷ women arrived at Ajitnāth Temple at 9 o'clock in order to carry all the decorations and pūjā equipment to Goḍījī Temple. In a caravan of rickshas, all the items were piled on the laps of the women and brought to Guruwar Peth. The maṇḍaḷ women were all in their new matching lavender saris for the pūjā. The young women dancers were dressed in fancy saris, mostly borrowed from mothers and aunts. After leaving the pūjā things near the area in which the Snātra Pūjā was to be performed, everyone went into the main temple for darśan—putting the decoration of the pūjā space inside the frame of the pūjā itself. While the area around the assembly hall stand was being decorated, two women drew a large design made with colored powders (rangoḷī) on the floor. There was some discussion about how all the decor should be arranged so it would not interfere with the performance of the Snātra Pūjā or the special dance the young women had planned to perform during the pūjā. After the area was decorated, Ranjana asked me to come with her while she changed into her pūjā clothes. We went to her husband's aunt's house in the neighborhood. There, after a quick bath, Ranjana changed into her fanciest pūjā sari—one from her collection of wedding saris—and put on quite a lot of ornate jewelry, which she had borrowed from her co-sisters-in-laws for this pūjā. The borrowed jewelry served both as a statement of identification with Indrāṇī, the Queen of the Gods, and as a gesture to make sure that she looked properly dressed up; the latter connected to the prestige of both the maṇḍaḷ as a whole and of Ranjana's family.[13] I was sent to the nearby sweet shop to get the largest sweet they had, the largest being an example of giving the best one can give. When I returned to the temple, Ranjana had put on a cardboard crown covered with glass "gems" and flowers—in imitation of the crown of Indrāṇī—and prepared for the pūjā.

The Snātra Pūjā was performed smoothly. The maṇḍaḷ women had chosen ahead of time which melodies and stavan they would use for the pūjā competition and the usual flexibility about timing was replaced with a more formalized fluidity; there were no discussions or debates over whether to sing another stavan or who would dance. Because Ranjana (who knew the entire Snātra Pūjā by heart) was the sponsor, no instructions were necessary. She performed each part of the Snātra Pūjā corresponding to each part of the text, thus avoiding the dead space, awkward moments, and hectic frenzy usually brought on by a sponsor's lack of knowledge of the ritual details of the pūjā. Ranjana alone did the circumambulations and recited the temple prayers. Unlike a noncompetition pūjā, the women in the maṇḍaḷ stood aside and let the "sponsor" complete the pūjā while they watched without ever directly involving themselves in the offerings or the circumambulations. During the section when the maṇḍaḷ women were normally given their "gifts," the group of young unmarried women from Ajitnāth Temple's congregation performed their dance. This dance involved a modified version of a dance usually performed with the winnowing basket, but instead was more gently performed with silver plates decorated and carrying the fourteen dreams of Mahāvīr's mother. After each of the dreams was offered in front of the Jina, the young women returned to their places in parallel lines behind the maṇḍaḷ. During the Āratī and Maṅgaḷ Dīvo, Ranjana was joined by two other maṇḍaḷ women—Kanchanben and Ashaben. Shantaben performed the Śāntī Kalaś while Savita and Kanchanben poured the smaller pitcher and Ranjana did the recitation (see figure 5-2).

The maṇḍaḷ received third place (out of fifty) in Pune.[14] The judges had penalized them for four things. Within the performance of the pūjā, during the Śāntī Kalaś, they had forgotten to draw a svastik in sandalwood paste in the bottom of the bowl. There were two problems with the decorations: they had forgotten to hang the canopy over the assembly hall stand, and in the floor design some of the svastiks were backward (in mirror image to the others). The final problem was that some of the maṇḍaḷ women were late and some had to leave early. While the Snātra Pūjā contest pointed to four oversights in the Pārśva Maṇḍaḷ's Snātra performance, it also indirectly pointed to the complete orthodoxy of their performance; there were no criticisms to over twenty minutes of recitations and forty minutes of singing. The maṇḍaḷ was also reaffirmed in its orthopraxy, as the mistakes deemed significant were few. The maṇḍaḷ women had made only one of the two significant mistakes during the many pūjās performed during previous year; at a few pūjās they had not brought the over-hanging canopy with them.[15]

Maluben felt that the first two mistakes (forgetting the sandalwood paste svastik and the canopy) were more serious because they were constitutive of the proper performance of a pūjā, but she was still noticeably annoyed with the maṇḍaḷ for the second two mistakes. She felt they could have easily been avoided and the maṇḍaḷ might have won the contest. Ranjana was, on balance, pleased, because the maṇḍaḷ had performed the main features of the pūjā without a single misspoken or missung word, or a single gesture out of place. These two positions characterized the poles of the other maṇḍaḷ women's responses. Maluben had more control over her time than any other woman I met, and as she had only her husband and her unmarried adult son in the house, she had more free time as well. Thus she was less sympathetic about the women who were late or had to leave early. Ranjana, whose time was dominated by the work of a joint family and her husband and four children—though she herself was on time for this and most other pūjās—brushed aside this critique. When I asked whether it marked a lack of respect (which is how the men described it) or reflected the realities of women's lives, Ranjana said, "What would those men know about that [women's lives]?" The men who judged the pūjā were seen as authorities on the ritual structure of the pūjā, mitigated only by issues pertaining to the realities of the women's lives. Maluben, in spite of her exacting standards, was also quick to point out that the mistakes were all things they knew about but simply forgot in the nervousness before the contest; her perception was that the judges merely reminded (not taught) the maṇḍaḷ about these small (albeit important) details.

There were several differences in the pūjā performance here that arose out of the contest context. They can be divided into changes arising out of the desire for fluidity—a lone "sponsor" who knew the entire pūjā by heart, prearranged, choreographed dance—and a desire to exhibit the maṇḍaḷ's prestige—many decorations, Ranjana's especially fancy dress and jewelry, and the choice of the largest sweet. Although this pūjā was a real Snātra Pūjā, it was not a typical one, nor does it really typify an ideal pūjā. The ideal pūjā (as discussed in chapter 6) includes as primary characteristics the enthusiastic participation of all the sponsor's family members and the women in the maṇḍaḷ and a sponsor's very generous gifting (prabhāvana) to the temple and to the attendees, as well as a good maṇḍaḷ performance. The central difference between this and other pūjās was that the contest was more clearly a "performance" whereas in normal pūjās the "audience" does not usually remain aloof or critical: they participate. While these were pūjās in the senses both of complete and accurate performances and of conveying religious merit to the performers, the pūjā contest created also a pūjā artifact, in a way—less an idealized version of the women's own sense of correct praxis than a satisfaction of very context (contest)-specific aims. The maṇḍaḷ's changes (the fixed repertoire and dance) were less moves to correct pūjā performance mistakes than moves to polish up the performance in order to appear more organized, to make the pūjā run more smoothly, and to make the whole performance "fancier."

The changes here reflect some of the adjustments made in order to gain prestige for the maṇḍaḷ in the eyes of both the judges and the women of other maṇḍaḷs with whom they were competing. The contest served to monitor pūjā performance, but the maṇḍaḷ only changed aspects of their performance in an effort to win the contest in ways not directly related to ritual efficacy or orthodoxy—areas in which the women were confident in their expertise. The judges did indeed base most of their judgment on questions of expertise; decoration was a tiny fraction of the tally whereas recitation accuracy was central. The maṇḍaḷ's move to put a polish on the performance, then, indicated a sophisticated awareness of how to navigate prestige practices in an event putatively centered around displaying ritual expertise. The Snātra Pūjā contest hints at the adoption of prestige practices which marked the larger pūjās such as the Navāṇuṅ Prakārī Pūjā and the Siddhacakra Mahāpūjā, especially in the concerns over family, maṇḍaḷ, and congregational honor while performing under the watchful eye of these high-status Jain laymen judges and women from other maṇḍaḷs who came to watch the contest. This award could have a tangible effect on the maṇḍaḷ's future performance opportunities. The winners of the Snātra Pūjā contest gain the prestige in the form of local "fame," which could lead to additional performance opportunities as potential sponsors heard of good maṇḍaḷs to hire. The sponsors, likewise, gain prestige from hiring an "award-winning" maṇḍaḷ for their family's pūjā.

Performing Prestige and Prestigious Performance

Jain mahāpūjās, evening singing sessions (*bhāvnā*) at Paryuṣaṇ and other times, the various sites of Jain auctions, and the celebration at the Dādāvāḍī Temple for Kārtak Pūṇam are illustrative locations, because of their obvious expense in money and time, for examining the negotiation of religious authority and social prestige. These public events highlight issues of expertise versus prestige by the adoption of prestige practices such as hiring outside professionals, donation (discussed here in the form of voluntary donation or auctions as part of the Siddhacakra Mahāpūjā and Navāṇuṅ Prakārī Pūjā), and amplification. Prestige practices are more often encouraged and performed by Jain laymen and thus these practices are more commonly found at mixed events rather than women's events; however, the negotiations of prestige and expertise are more complex than a simple class-based or gender-based argument can explain.

Hiring Professionals and Prestige

The workings of expertise and prestige are linked here; one is more likely to hire a performer whose expertise is established. These performers become well-known and celebrated for their expertise, not for their cost. However, that being said, a greater prestige was accorded to performances with hired performers who came from far away, provided they demonstrated sufficient expertise. Quality matters: to hire an expensive specialist who had substandard expertise was to invite ridicule and critiques of being ostentatious and, worse still, foolish with one's money. These singing sessions often featured hired musicians from outside the congregation; likewise, men's maṇḍaḷs (and solo singers) are more often hired for prestigious "public" performances than are women's maṇḍaḷs. While men's maṇḍaḷs carry the prestige of being both expensive and unusual—there were only four in Pune—in Pune these men's maṇḍaḷs were not involved in pūjā performances and thus did not function as a locus of formal pūjā expertise. These maṇḍaḷs may not even have had the knowledge—which, as we saw in chapter 6, arises out of attendance as multiple pūjā performances—to do so. Thus for the celebration of Ajitnāth Temple's installation anniversary (*varṣgāṇṭh*), the congregation hired the Goḍījī Women's Maṇḍaḷ from Goḍījī Temple to perform a Pañcakalyāṇak Pūjā in the afternoon. This pūjā was ultimately performed by a mixed group of women from the hired maṇḍaḷ and from Ajitnāth's Pārśva Maṇḍaḷ. The Goḍījī Maṇḍaḷ had a young girl who performed the lamp-offering dance which was universally declared a major bonus from hiring this outside maṇḍaḷ. Here the Pārśva Maṇḍaḷ was intimately involved with the hiring of an outside maṇḍaḷ to perform a pūjā that they themselves performed with some regularity and with, arguably, more skill. This suggests that the hiring of specialists (here an outside maṇḍaḷ) adds prestige to the congregation's celebration. To do a "grand" program such as a mahāpūjā necessitates a certain gesture toward such prestige practices as hiring outside specialists. Likewise, we see here that the prestige of the performance was linked to both the performers' expertise and the difficulty (or sacrifice—especially in financial terms) required by the sponsor in hiring them.

Singing session performances illustrated a continuum of practices where the perceived publicness of the singing session was directly linked to the level of adoption of prestige practices. I attended singing session performances on several occasions: during the nights of the 1994 Paryuṣaṇ festival, in the evening of the 1999 Siddhacakra Mahāpūjā, as part of a pilgrimage in 1997, and as part of the 1993 Kārtak Pūṇam celebration at the Dādāvāḍī Temple. In 1994, the Ajitnāth Temple congregation sponsored singing sessions for three of the eight nights of Paryuṣaṇ. The first two nights of the festival, the temple hired men's maṇḍaḷs to perform these singing sessions, and the third night was sponsored and performed by the Pārśva Women's Maṇḍaḷ. The attendance at Ajitnāth's first singing session night (with the Gujarātī men's maṇḍaḷ) was light with a mix of men, women, and children; the second night (with the Ādarś Maṇḍaḷ) was packed with both men and women (at a ratio of about one man to two women), and the third night (with the Pārśva Maṇḍaḷ) was packed with women (and a few fathers of performing girls). The first night's program was a less well-known Gujarātī men's maṇḍaḷ, mostly of young men (and a few older boys) from the suburbs, who sang a variety of older lyrics and widely known new songs to existing melodies (from both film songs and Gujarātī folk music). They sat in a semicircle and had dhoḷak drums, hand cymbals and a harmonium; occasionally one man's daughter (age about 5) got up to dance with her tambourine. The second night's performance was by the well-known Ādarś Maṇḍaḷ, comprised mostly of late middle-age men whose published song collection (mostly written by members of their own maṇḍaḷ) was widely distributed in Pune, and whose performances were known to be lively and well executed. In their performance, these men, too, sat in a semicircle and performed with harmonium, drums, and hand cymbals for approximately two hours. Most of the songs' lyrics were written by members of their maṇḍaḷ to existing Hindi film or folk (here, Rājasthānī) melodies. Both men's maṇḍaḷs had melodic instrumentation, used microphones, and drew at least some men from Ajitnāth's congregation for the audience. Neither men's maṇḍaḷ used hand movements except for the ringing of hand cymbals, nor had a dance program been attached to their performance. The Pārśva Maṇḍaḷ's sponsored program on the third night of Paryuṣaṇ featured several dance performances by groups of girls and young women accompanied by stavan singing by the maṇḍaḷ (see figure 4-3). First the maṇḍaḷ performed a couple of stavan while arranged in facing lines in the middle of the temple—as they do for pūjās—and then Savita and Ranjana led the singing for the dancing and the maṇḍaḷ spread out to make room for dancing in the center. The Pārśva Maṇḍaḷ did not use any amplification. They sang with only the accompaniment of a single drum and hand percussion and dance performances.

During the 1994 Paryuṣaṇ festival, I also saw a women's maṇḍaḷ from the Camp area of Pune perform a singing session at the Timber Market Jain Temple; like the two men's maṇḍaḷs, this one also included the instrumentation of harmonium and tabla drums. They, however, embellished their performance with rās-garbā dancing—a long section of which was accompanied by dance performed by maṇḍaḷ members themselves. Both Pārśva Maṇḍaḷ performances of singing sessions that week (at Ajitnāth Temple and at the Karve Road Mahāvīr Temple) were likewise marked by the conspicuous presence of dance performances by young women and girls, and the seated dance performed by the singers themselves. The Pārśva Maṇḍaḷ was hired to perform a singing session at the Karve Road Mahāvīr temple on the sixth night of Paryuṣaṇ. The Pārśva Maṇḍaḷ again used only percussive instruments (a single drum and various hand percussion sounded by the women as part of their seated dance) and no sound system. Their performance that night was the same as that in their own temple except for the addition of the difficult lamp-offering dance performed by Manisha. Both the Pārśva Maṇḍaḷ's performance at the Karve Road Mahāvīr Temple and Pune Camp-based women's maṇḍaḷ performance at the Timber Market Temple had large audiences of men and women, suggesting that, at least for these two congregations, the hiring of a women's maṇḍaḷ was sufficiently prestigious to warrant a large turnout of the congregation's men.

I observed bhāvnā on four other occasions: two informal and private sessions (on pilgrimage and on the evening of a Siddhacakra Mahāpūjā at the sponsoring family's house) and two formal temple performances (at Ajitnāth Temple later in the evening after the Siddhacakra Mahāpūjā and at Dādāvāḍī Temple during the Kārtak Pūṇam celebration, discussed a bit later in the chapter). On Dadaji's memorial pilgrimage to several new Jain temples in Maharashtra in 1997, the members of Dadaji's family performed a devotional singing session one evening to celebrate the pilgrimage, to entertain the family with music, and to provide music for dancing. The singing was performed by women and children, and young men and women in the family danced. The singing that night was accompanied by a grandson's reasonably steady bongo playing and everyone's hand clapping. This informal singing session was an unstructured, interactive performance—people suggesting verses, singing along, clapping—with the enthusiastic participation of everyone in the room, especially in dancing. After the 1999 Siddhacakra Mahāpūjā and its reception were over, Dadiji's family returned to their apartment for dinner and after dinner for a short singing session before everyone headed to the temple for the evening's formal temple singing session performance. In the center room (where the Śānti Kalaś was placed after the pūjā) the professional singer sat facing the Śānti Kalaś and a photo image of Śankheśvar Pārśvanāth. The more enthusiastic singers (twenty to twenty-five) in the family—including Ranjana's brother who had come to visit for the pūjā—sat in the room as well. There were mostly women in the main room. Behind them in the living room sat the rest of the relatives (one hundred or so) who were there for the pūjā that day. The professional singer, who had been hired to sing at the pūjā earlier that day, started the singing with a stavan, followed by one led by Ranjana's brother. They were followed by four stavan led by women from the family with no percussion besides hand clapping. The session was rounded out with another stavan led by the professional singer. Both of these events memorialized Dadaji and shared a certain intimacy of familial ties. Here in the intimate setting of the family celebration the professional singer led others in singing—rather than singing solo—and was trading songs with the singers from the family. Both of these bhāvnā performances were less performances than participatory singing led by confident singers.

The singing sessions performed in temples by hired musicians exhibited a much more performative style and far less participation by the listeners. After the bhāvnā in Dadiji's family's main apartment, everyone headed to the temple for the evening's program. The Siddhacakra Mahāpūjā singing session in 1999 was the only temple-based singing session performance I saw which did not have a maṇḍaḷ;[16] the musicians on hand from that day's mahāpūjā were a hired singer, a harmonium player, and a *tabla* player, who led the congregation in singing stavan in the temple. They sang mostly commonly known stavan and women from the congregation sang along. During the temple program, Soni and Sveta each sang a stavan and Savita tried to get maṇḍaḷ women together to sing one too, but they were not sitting together. The singer rounded out the evening with a series of spirited stavan for dancing, during which most of the young women and some of the young men in the family danced dāṇḍiya. All singing session performances attempt to increase devotional enthusiasm through singing, but the workings of prestige change the ways in which that is done. Formal temple performances all share a sense of being a "performance" in a way that private singing does not. In private singing session performances the goal is to have everyone singing and participating. Formal temple singing session performances are more complicated; these performances balance the goal of getting everyone involved in the performance with the aim (which the sponsor, as well as the maṇḍaḷ, specifically seek) of displaying virtuoso singing, maṇḍaḷ precision, and—if it is a women's maṇḍaḷ—dancing.

The 1999 Siddhacakra Mahāpūjā is a fruitful event to consider in the discussion of hiring outsiders as a prestige practice. Because the sponsoring family (Dadiji's) is also closely linked with the Pārśva Maṇḍaḷ (all four daughters-in-law and one granddaughter are active members) we can see the hiring of paid outside professionals and other prestige practices for this mahāpūjā in the context of general respect and encouragement of women's maṇḍaḷs. This is not a case of class differences; here, the women's half of the sponsoring family are the same women who performed (in the Pārśva Maṇḍaḷ) many of the sponsored pūjā performances already discussed. Here we can see where both the presence of men in decision making and the importance of family honor and prestige come together. It is important to realize that whereas some sponsors of pūjās have no firsthand experience with maṇḍaḷ performance, all the maṇḍaḷ singers had from time to time been sponsors of pūjās themselves (both individually and as part of larger family celebrations).

When Dadaji was dying, he stated his wish that his family would one day sponsor a mahāpūjā at Ajitnāth temple. The second anniversary of his death seemed an appropriate time to do so, and his family planned a Siddhacakra Mahāpūjā for January 5, 1999. The Siddhacakra Mahāpūjā is the worship of the siddhacakra in direct imitation of the narrative heroine, Mayṇāsundarī, and her husband, Śrīpāl, whose worship of the siddhacakra healed his illness and brought them both health and prosperity.[17] Because this was the first mahāpūjā to be performed at Ajitnāth temple (the new courtyard was rapidly finished in order to be ready for the Siddhacakra Mahāpūjā) and because it was the first time their family had sponsored such an event, there was a lot of concern about how well they would perform the pūjā and also about the quality and generosity of the food served to all the guests. For this mahāpūjā, a male mendicant was required to recite several mantras. The family secured a male mendicant, Viśvamangaljī, to do the recitation of the mantras through consultation with Viśvakalyānji, a more charismatic mendicant whose presence the family would have preferred but whose predetermined wanderings were not anywhere near by to Pune. A recitation specialist and two ritual specialists (vidhikār)—one who specialized in creating pūjā designs and one who was familiar with the various details of the six-hour mahāpūjā—were hired from Mumbaī. The singer and his musicians were found through a family connection and came from Malegaon (about ten hours away). All these religious specialists were listed on both the invitation to the mahāpūjā and on the temple board where the pūjā was announced. A brahmin cook and two assistants were secured to produce both the snack offered to the 450 attendees after the mahāpūjā was completed and the lunch before and dinner after the mahāpūjā offered to about 150 relatives. Though the women in the family planned the menu and cleaned all the ingredients to Jain specifications and supervised much of the preparations, it was necessary to hire cooks to have all the food freshly prepared while the women of the family were busy performing the pūjā. These professionals were hired partly for the necessity of their expertise, which would ensure the proper performance of the ritual and its surrounding program, but also the choice of specialists from out of town increased the overall prestige of the event. As the first mahāpūjā at Ajitnāth, this event set a benchmark of prestige that the family simply had to live up to; upholding the prestige expectations of the event was unquestionably linked to the sense of family honor and the family's sense of the honor of their grandfather as an important member of the Ajitnāth congregation.

Auctioning, Donation, and Status

Enthusiastic showering of donations (dān) on the seven fields—Jina images, Jain temples, Jain texts, male mendicants, female mendicants, laymen and laywomen—is one of Hemacandra's markers of the difference between a Jain layman and a "great" layman (*mahāśrāvak*). In addition, Hemacandra's archetypal great layman also spends a great deal of time performing Jain pūjā and studying Jain texts (Cort 1991b). Prestige and wealth benefit the Jain layman primarily in conjunction with Jain religious values. In other words, Jain great laymen use their influence and wealth for the benefit of their family, their congregation, and the Jain community, though donations which come exclusively from self-centeredness are seen as less meritorious (Cort 1991b). The biographies found in the beginning of sponsored texts provide a location for examining both the ideal layman and the ideal laywoman. These texts reproduce much of the focus on donation and sponsorship for men whereas a woman's donations are included alongside the woman's fasts, pilgrimages, sponsorship of pūjās, and participation in maṇḍaḷs (Kelting 1996). For both the great layman and the great laywoman, a balance of high levels of expertise through practice, study and devotion often represented by enthusiastic participation in prestige practices identifies an individual as the ideal layperson.

At Mahāvīr Janam Dīvas the story of the birth of Mahāvīr is celebrated; it is at that point that the Kalpa Sūtra reading for Paryuṣaṇ reaches its zenith. The fourteen dreams of Triśalā presage the birth of a Jina and at this celebration each dream is specially garlanded. When the passage is read stating that Mahāvīr is born, his cradle is rocked. The privilege to perform these acts—and a few others that are part of the celebration—is auctioned off for considerable sums. The auctions at Mahāvīr Janam Dīvas are the primary fund-raising opportunities for the running budget of the temple for the coming year. Thus the event itself serves both as a celebration of Mahāvīr's birth and as a locus for prestige (Banks 1992; Cort 1989, 1991b, 1992; Laidlaw 1995; Reynell 1985b), which is doubly encouraged because it so clearly helps in the maintenance of the temple to have this prestige practice focus on giving to the temple in these auctions. Laidlaw (1995) provides an extensive discussion about Jain auctions during which he points to its role in competitive models of religiosity among Jains. In this model, lay Jains bid for the privilege to act as the paradigmatic patrons (often Indra and Indrāṇī, but also as Śreyāṃs in the role of first person to offer food to a new mendicant). Laidlaw argues that bidding distinguishes between "notables and citizens" (Laidlaw 1995), which clearly articulates the role of bidding in the claiming or restatement of familial and personal prestige (Banks 1992; Cottam Ellis 1991; Laidlaw 1995).

Paryuṣaṇ is marked by the annual rite of confession and expiation (Samvatsarī Pratikramaṇ) on the final day of the festival, but group confessions and expiations (pratikramaṇ) were performed daily throughout the festival. Each night a group of women—a mixture of those who were performing fasts that required a ritual confession every night, those who were doing this because it was Paryuṣaṇ and therefore a good time to be extra observant, and those who perform this ritual with regularity—gathered to perform this rite. At these nightly performances and at the annual rite—to which all Jains go as a matter of religious identification—the recitations of various prayers and the singing of the stavan are auctioned off before the recitation begins. These are women-only ritual groups. Most men, as a matter of course, only performed the annual rite of confession and expiation and they too auction the privilege to recite the text.[18] In 1994, the winning bids among the women were very low and the bidding moved along quite quickly. There were enough sections for each woman who showed an interest in participating to do so and women did not bid against each other during this auction. During Paryuṣaṇ auctions were held in the temple every morning for various acts. The bathing, first pūjā, dressing, or lamp offering for the Jinas, Bhairav, or Padmāvatī were all auctioned for small amounts most mornings to men, even though sometimes the winners passed the privilege of doing the act to the women in their families. In these daily auctions during the festival, there were often enough different actions and recitations for which one could bid that anyone who wanted to bid could find an affordable option; these auctions did not create a sense of competition for access to limited (and expensive) participation.

At the ordination of a new mendicant, there are several acts whose performances are understood to be especially efficacious: giving the soon-to-be mendicant a blessing mark on her forehead, carrying the mendicant's clothes to the ordination and presenting them to the mendicant, the first veneration (guruvandan), and the first feeding of the new mendicant. The first feeding receives the largest bids and can offset a fair piece of the cost (to the congregation) of the ordination ceremony. Laidlaw writes of the greatest prestige awarded to families that can pay for the entire ordination proceedings for their daughters (Laidlaw 1995). The 1999 Siddhacakra Mahāpūjā was entirely paid for by the family involved and was followed by a call for donations that highlighted the generosity of the sponsors by their giving yet more to the temple. In the context of mahāpūjās, the highest prestige goes to those families that can afford to sponsor such expensive events and therefore to those pūjās which are both expensive and not auctioned off.

As a family event there was no auctioning of the nine major pūjā sections and subsequent smaller offerings in the Siddhacakra Mahāpūjā; they were distributed by age to the Dadiji's five sons and their wives, two daughters and their husbands, eldest grandson and his wife, myself and my husband, and the smaller offerings and so forth distributed to the more distant cousins. Instead, after the pūjā was completed except for the Śānti Kalaś, the recitation specialist asked for donations toward animal welfare (*jīv dayā*) and as each married man in the family made a donation the name of the donor and the amount of money were recorded in the temple trust account book and broadcast over the sound system. Although a handful of people who did not perform the pūjā also donated money, the call for donations was more a public announcement of the extension of the sponsoring family's generosity. Beyond sharing some of the benefits of the pūjā with the crowd by distributing protective bracelets blessed by the mendicant, providing access to hearing the efficacious words and mantras of the pūjā, serving a snack to all the guests who chose to stay and eat, and giving a coconut to each guest as a post-pūjā gift in celebration of Jainism (*prabhāvanā*), their generosity was extended to include compassion for other life forms. Thus the call for donations during the Siddhacakra Mahāpūjā both highlights the family's unbounded generosity—in much the same way that the use of odd numbers (15, 21, 51, 101, etc.) is seen as evidence of the giver's unbounded generosity—and also asks for generosity from those Jains who came to the pūjā and thus likewise benefited, albeit indirectly, from the pūjā's efficacy. This extension of benefits counters the sense of the pūjā being performed exclusively for the family's benefit; the pūjā becomes a fund-raising opportunity for the temple.

Large-scale donation is associated with merit and prestige throughout Jain laymen's praxis (Banks 1992; Cort 1989, 1991b; Cottam Ellis 1991; Laidlaw 1995; Norman 1991; Reynell 1985b, 1987), and the predominantly male practice of donation held high prestige (as many male practices in India do) even for the women, for whom it is more difficult to attain. Most Jain women, in spite of their family's wealth or husband's willingness to donate, have relatively little direct control over the family's capital, yet what little the maṇḍaḷ women collected through their participation in the maṇḍaḷ events, they returned as donation (dān) through other pūjās or other religious sponsorship. Some women—either because their families had more money allotted for religious spending or because they had more control over the finances—were permitted to bid for pūjā performances or to sponsor pūjās more often. When sponsors gave money as the gift at a pūjā, the women almost always spent it on pūjā-related expenses—fancier fruit offerings, sponsorship of pūjās, the winning of auctions to perform sections of the annual confession and expiation of sins. This permitted the maṇḍaḷ participants a slightly (for they never received more than 21 rupees) greater level of participation. Virtually all women said that they wished they had more money to spend on religion, suggesting an internalized acceptance (though only partially so, as we will see later) of the privileging of the one part of Jain praxis in which they are less able to participate. Thus women were limited in their participation in public prestige practices—though they may be given the privilege of performing the act—by the same structures that limit their control over financial assets. For example, men placed less emphasis (both in their resources and in their interest in who won what) on the auctions at women's events—which would have no future positive effect on the family finances—than on their own more expensive auctions. Because of male priorities in spending, women (with the occasional exception of an elderly woman who is seen as the head of the household) were at a disadvantage when making requests for money to spend at auctions. Women were, likewise, at a disadvantage when amplification was introduced into the picture.

Amplification, Gender, and Authority

The Kārtak Pūṇam celebration included a singing session by the Ādarś Men's Maṇḍaḷ (the same group that performed on the second night at Ajitnāth Temple's Paryuṣaṇ program). The maṇḍaḷ was certainly not the focus of the event—making it distinct from all other singing sessions I witnessed—but rather one piece of the sonic action. While the maṇḍaḷ performed upstairs in the temple, the bulk of the activities at this celebration happened downstairs in the courtyard, where Jains from all over Pune circumambulated the model of Śatruñjay and then did sandalwood powder pūjā to a painting of Śatruñjay hung on the wall of the courtyard. While people did their pūjā, the sounds of the men's maṇḍaḷ unsuccessfully competed with amplified recitation cassettes and insistent and constant requests for financial donations to the temple and other Jain charities (not unlike the calls for donations at the end of mahāpūjās). Groups of women and individual women also sang their own stavan (unamplified) as part of their pūjā, both in front of the painting and in the room in which the men's maṇḍaḷ was performing. No one sound dominated the temple compound. Depending on where one stood, though, either the announcements or the maṇḍaḷ were the most audible (though barely understandable), followed by the cassettes. The women's singing was virtually inaudible in the amplified din unless one sat near the singers. The competition between men and women's singing and amplified sound illustrated the ways in which prestige practices can dominate the sonic (and also visual) environment.

At mixed events (with men and women), the microphones are literally in male hands; male voices dominated the sonic environment through volume. I saw this at events ranging from everything connected to the ordination of a new female mendicant to the small-scale auctions during Paryuṣaṇ at Ajitnāth during morning pūjā. Even in the case of the Ādarś Men's Maṇḍaḷ, which had to compete with recorded and other amplified voices at Kartak Pūṇam, these amplified voices were exclusively male. Recall that when women sang at the female mendicant's ordination, the men who controlled the microphone told them to be quiet so a particular man could repeat his song; when the women did not stop singing their songs, the men simply turned up the volume on the sound system. It was striking to me that the women sang throughout all of these events, sometimes ignoring and sometimes attempting to compete with the amplified sounds. Gold writes of a woman's joking about her assistant's microphone as an extension of his phallus (Raheja and Gold 1994). The women's jokes about the man who was singing into a microphone on stage at the February 1994 ordination followed the same line, suggesting that these women definitely saw control over amplification in explicitly gendered ways. Although the women did not often explicitly speak of these prestige practices (hiring performers, auctioning, and amplification) as male, they are, in fact, usually included in these events at the behest of men and are dominated by male voices.

The sponsor can, however, take control of the microphone and put it in a female hand in much the same way that the winners of auctions may choose—in the case of an ordination—to return the privilege to the family of the new mendicant, or, in the case of the Paryuṣaṇ auctions which are usually won by men, turn the privilege over to one's female relatives. At the Siddhacakra Mahāpūjā's formal singing session in the temple, the microphone was taken from the singer twice—both times so that young women from the sponsoring family (Soni and Sveta) could each sing a stavan. The authority to control the sound is the dominion of the sponsor (if the sponsors had not wanted these women to sing they would not have been heard) and is a mark of prestige at public events. The competition to be heard (and listened to) between men and women in Jain public performances suggests that the relationships between prestige, expertise, and authority are certainly a negotiated balance or perhaps a negotiated tension and one negotiated, in part, along the lines of gender.

Before the maṇḍaḷ performed the Navāṇuṁ Prakārī Pūjā, sound systems had not been used at any pūjā at Ajitnāth. Later, visiting male performers used amplification during the Paryuṣaṇ singing sessions and at the Siddhacakra Mahāpūjā for both professional reciter and the professional musicians. The role of amplification in the creation of prestige performances is widely observed by scholars of Hinduism (Henry 1988; Flueckiger 1996; Lutgendorf 1991; Manuel 1993; Marcus 1995). Here, in a Jain context this practice was adopted for the prestige that a sound system and the subsequent—if involuntary—local awareness of the Jain pūjā that the sound system brings. An anomaly in the Navāṇuṁ Prakārī Pūjā performance was that the Pārśva Maṇḍaḷ had hired a sound system to broadcast the pūjā and the maṇḍaḷ's singing into the street in front of the temple. There had already been some concern over whether the hiring of a sound system was a more meritorious use of the money raised than giving this money directly to the temple. In a sense, the issue was whether the public—Jain and non-Jain—knowledge of the pūjā performance was more valuable than the donation, which would be known and appreciated exclusively by the Jain community. After substantial debate, the sound system was ultimately determined to be central for the public glorification of the pūjā performance and therefore Jain devotion—especially as the maṇḍaḷ could hire the sound system and still make a donation of the silver garland. The maṇḍaḷ women seemed much more uncomfortable with the sound system (expressed by how they kept moving to sit further from the microphone, the quiet singing for the first part of the pūjā, and the continual readjusting of the microphone to point it away from any one person), which broadcast their singing into the neighborhood, than they seemed to be with my recordings, which were to go to a foreign country. (It is likely that my recordings did not make the pūjā seem as immediately unfamiliar as the sound system and its ambitious expectation did.)

The Navāṇuṅ Prakārī Pūjā

An examination of the Navāṇuṅ Prakārī Pūjā sponsored by the Pārśva Maṇḍaḷ demonstrates how these prestige practices work within a public and female context where there are not the obviously gendered articulations of relative status between men's and women's practices at a single event, and without the direct connection to negotiations of creditworthiness as seen in the prestige practices surrounding Mahāvīr Janam Dīvas. Here we can see women actively encouraging prestige practices among themselves. The Navāṇuṅ Prakārī Pūjā was chosen by the maṇḍaḷ when the members decided to perform a big pūjā because of its relative grandness, but the women did not agree on the ways to distribute and attribute access and merit. The same women within the maṇḍaḷ who welcomed the performances of the outside men's maṇḍaḷs for singing sessions and the outside women's maṇḍaḷ for the temple anniversary were uncomfortable with the adoption of other prestige practices in the case of the Navāṇuṅ Prakārī Pūjā. Grandness was in part equated with the public and ostentatious practices associated with Jain laymen. Here I am not arguing that a desire for prestige is necessarily the only reason behind pūjā sponsorship and donation, though that is an important part of these public performances. These attempts to "upgrade" the pūjā performance and to participate in male-dominated rhetoric about prestige were neither universally accepted nor without their practical challenges.

On August 8, 1994, the Pārśva Maṇḍaḷ performed the complicated and expensive Navāṇuṅ Prakārī Pūjā. It requires a huge number of offerings (ninety-nine) and is quite long (four and a half hours). This was the first time this pūjā had been performed at this temple. The maṇḍaḷ was concerned with doing an impressive job at the pūjā performance even though the members did not expect any nonparticipants to observe their performance: It was to be performed on a midweek afternoon and there were no invitations sent to other women. In the weeks prior to the pūjā, there was some learning and extra practice of new stavan deemed to be appropriate for the pūjā and a lot of discussion about how best to perform it. At crucial points during the planning and performance of this pūjā the women were not in consensus over whether to adopt practices usually associated with male-controlled events and men's maṇḍaḷs to make their pūjā more prestigious: Most significantly, there were questions about the use of amplification, and factions debating the auction of the constituent parts of the pūjā (a common, and usually a male-dominated, activity at mixed events) versus equal donation and equal participation which marked all (but the various pratikramaṇs) of the other Pārśva Maṇḍaḷ-sponsored events. On the Saturday before the pūjā at the maṇḍaḷ's weekly meeting, the different parts of the pūjā were auctioned off for the women to perform (table 7-1). Generally, pūjā auctions were won by women who were active in the maṇḍaḷ. In this case, all the women except one (Swagati Pungaliya) were women who regularly went to Ajitnāth temple. The auction and its songs took most of the time up from the maṇḍaḷ meeting. The total earned was 1,004 rupees. Ranjana and Maluben purchased all the necessary fruit, sweets, rice, and so on, and rented the sound system for the performance with the money collected from the auction. The remaining money was later used to buy a silver door garland to hang over the central door to the inner sanctum. This garland, notably, made its first appearance on the night of the Pārśva Maṇḍaḷ's singing session performance during Paryuṣaṇ.

The auction itself was interesting, especially as most scholars of Jainism are perhaps unaware—or see little of the extent—of women's participation in auctions (bolī) and donation (dān). Maluben led the Navāṇuṅ Prakārī Pūjā auction with what was clearly a practiced hand at auctioning. Whenever there was a lull in the bidding, some of the women started to sing bidding songs. Most of these songs had lyrics saying "say you'll give more," or "how good it is to give to one's temple."[19] Each song was followed by at least one more bid. Many times, Maluben directly asked someone who walked into the room to bid. For example, when Kavita walked in the room, Maluben said, "Kavita, how much will you give for the Āratī?" to which Kavita replied, "You have to ask Ranjana bhābhī. If she bids, then we will do it [the Āratī]." However, the women in Ranjana's family were both unprepared

TABLE 7-1. Navāṉu Prakari Pūjā Auction Results

Pūjā section	*Winning Bid*	*Winner of Bid*	*Maṇḍaḷ Status*
Dudh pūjā	21 rupees	Induben Osval	Inactive
Jaḷ pūjā	21 rupees	Sheelu Shah	Active (Maluben)
Kesar pūjā	21 rupees	Savita Shah	Officer
Phūl pūjā	41 rupees	Sadhana Shah	Inactive
Dhūp pūjā	61 rupees	Swagati Pungaliya	Non-member
Dīpak pūjā	181 rupees	Sriben Daga	Active
Akṣat pūjā	61 rupees	Lata Gandhi	Active
Naivedya pūjā	45 rupees	Pramila Shah	Officer
Phal pūjā	71 rupees	Taraben	Active
Āratī	101 rupees	Induben Osval	Inactive
Maṅgaḷ Dīvo	165 rupees	Vimla Khivansara	Active
Śāntī Kalaś	215 rupees	Kamla Solanki	Active

for bidding—they had not secured permission to spend money—and did not want this pūjā to be run by auction. The fact of their not bidding here presented the possibility of a loss of face, which visibly irritated them.

This is a mirror of the mechanism of bidding at Mahāvīr Janam Dīvas, where the congregation holds generalized expectations for high bids from particular key bidders who are addressed directly by the auctioneer (Cort 1989; Laidlaw 1995). Here in this bidding women were explicitly reproducing the kind of prestige practices that mark the larger scale auctions where men (usually) establish their family's status and credit-worthiness (Cottom Ellis 1991). This kind of pressured auction (to raise the bids generally and to get bids from individuals) was not part of the all-women's auctions (as part of the rite of confession and expiation) that I saw in 1993 and 1994. Likewise, in 2000 in the auction at the Samvatsarī Pratikramaṇ when Savita began a bidding song, she was shouted down by the women who wanted the auction to be as short as possible since the recitation itself is quite lengthy. Clearly, the Navāṇuṅ Prakārī Pūjā auction was mirroring the auctions at Mahāvīr Janam Dīvas or those held at pilgrimage sites for the privilege to be the first on a given day to worship a particularly powerful image.

There are, of course, economic limitations to men's participation in pūjās; only men with money can win auctions for pūjā participation, and this too necessitates familial discussion (with the other men in the family) when it involves large sums. This issue was mirrored at the auction for the Navāṇuṅ Prakārī Pūjā; only the few women with money of their own or permission to spend their husband's or the family's money could win the primary claim to perform pūjā, even though the amounts that won several of the auctions were quite modest. But the scale here is the difference; few men needed to get permission to make donations under 50 rupees, as the women did. Although for women not bidding involved a certain small loss of face, it was not likened to admitting a familial lack of creditworthiness or miserliness, a charge Laidlaw (1995) found in the rhetoric among men about bidding. In such auctions both the amounts of money and the level of financial control women had over general family resources were minimal. The other women who bid were doing so without the financial control to actively affect their family's overall prestige, except perhaps in the discussions surrounding weddings, but their bidding may have indirect effects on the familial prestige. The fact that these auctions do not really have the kind of affect on honor and prestige that the large-scale auctions at Mahāvīr Janam Dīvas do highlights the way these auctions are reframed as prestigious in and of themselves without reference to their social roles in other contexts. The auction itself becomes a marker of a prestigious event.

Later, over tea, Ranjana and Nita reported their dissatisfaction to Lata, their elder co-sister-in-law. Both of them were disappointed that the maṇḍaḷ meeting was all work, as the first Saturday of each month was usually devoted to social activities. They had prepared two contests based on pūjā performance skills (rice-svastik making and Navkār recitation races), but the time went instead toward the bidding—a competition based on money, not skill. Nita felt that the original idea was for the whole maṇḍaḷ to perform the pūjā equally; by auctioning off the parts of the pūjā, some women were doing more of the pūjā than others. The conflict seemed to be between the competitive model of access to pūjā performance through dān and the maṇḍaḷ's usual practices of equal sharing where no one woman gets "credit" for the pūjā, or of "first come, first served" (rota) models of access to pūjā performance. The women's auctions attached to the Navāṇuṅ Prakārī Pūjā re-created the limits set by the socioeconomic situations of the women (how much money they could bid or if they could bid at all), thereby limiting access to what had started out as a maṇḍaḷ-sponsored event. Several women had expected it to be a shared performance of the pūjā, like the distribution of different pūjā acts in the Siddhacakra Mahāpūjā, other family events, and other women's ritual performances such as the thrice-yearly devvandan. For example, the devvandan recitations were divided into sections and performed on a rota basis with no auction or focus on expertise—anyone who was capable of reading (or reciting from memory) and interested recited a section of the text. The auctions here worked against the sense of community within the maṇḍaḷ.

When the pūjā was actually performed, the idea of the pūjā as a shared maṇḍaḷ event was strong enough to exert pressure on each woman to pass on her piece of the pūjā (after the first round) to other women: first to women in her family and later to other women in the maṇḍaḷ. Most of the women in the maṇḍaḷ performed at least one of the offerings on one round. Recall though, again, that it is common practice for men who win auctions to pass them on to others. Although a woman had won the bid for the performance of the Āratī and another the Maṅgaḷ Dīvo, the whole maṇḍaḷ together joined in the performances of the 108-wick Āratī and the Maṅgaḷ Dīvo (see figure 7-1). There was some joining in during the Śānti Kalaś but

FIGURE 7-1. A 108-wick āratī during the Nāvaṇuṅ Prakārī Pūjā with Arun and the maṇḍaḷ participating, Ajitnāth Temple, Shivajinagar, Pune, August 1994.

not much, which may exhibit the relatively high status (and prestige) of the woman performing but also represents the usual practice of letting a single person or couple perform this rite (see figure 6-1). The women on the whole shared the performance of the pūjā as they did the monthly Snātra Pūjās. The maṇḍaḷ itself was responsible for the performance of the text and the donation of the money raised for the purchase of the door garland. As a group the maṇḍaḷ earned the merit of the donation of the garland and the subsequent donation of its award from the Snātra Pūjā contest, and no individual names were attached to the garland donation. The only name on the blackboard was that of the maṇḍaḷ as a whole. The importance of the donation reflected the women's participation in a prestige system usually considered the domain of laymen and—perhaps more important—the infiltration of auctions into the pūjā context where rotation had been the dominant model for access to performance.

The preparations, especially the bidding for the privilege to perform the pūjā sections, encouraged by Maluben, re-created some of the structures of the style of pūjās run by men. Although not all the women completely approved of this model, all of them felt that it was an "important" pūjā; they may have been reflecting on the prestige patterns usually associated with prestige-dominated mahāpūjās and the maṇḍaḷ's ability to re-create them in their own (female) public practice. To speak of prestige patterns in a gendered way is problematic as there are important exceptions to the association of prestige practices with men and expertise as authority with women's praxis: Women always bid for the privilege to recite various sections of the annual rite of confession and expiation, a woman gave the winning bid to take Mahāvīr's image home during Paryuṣaṇ 1994, and Ajitnāth Temple was built through a large donation by Jyethiben, a laywoman from the congregation. Likewise, men were the locus of expertise at the Snātra Pūjā contest, as ritual specialists for hire for mahāpūjās, and as hired musicians. Differing from the pūjā contest where the maṇḍaḷ was performing and being judged according to orthopraxic understandings of pūjā, the Navāṇuṅ Prakārī Pūjā performance was participating in the forum of economic prestige and women's intentional and unintentional acceptance of the norms that are usually acted out by men. Although the women were the arbiters of what the pūjā should be, they themselves accepted some of the models for prestige that actually diminished their own full access to the pūjā.

The prestige of a sponsor's program was in part connected to the expertise of those hired to perform the program. There was considerable prestige attached to hiring outside experts to perform the more complicated pūjās (such as the Siddhacakra Mahāpūjā) but also for the performances of evening devotional singing programs to celebrate events and holidays, even when there was a maṇḍaḷ associated with the temple that could perform the singing session. When the maṇḍaḷ was performing the auctions for the Navāṇuṅ Prakārī Pūjā, the members were in a sense using their pūjā as an opportunity to glorify Jainism through the prestigious practice of public (and broadcast) worship and through the auctions used as fund raising for the purchase of the silver garland for the temple door. For Ranjana and Nita, the movement from the high levels of involvement in skill- and knowledge-based events to the low level in economically based activities brought forth their criticisms. The maṇḍaḷ's usual practice of either taking turns (e.g., the rotating sponsorship of the monthly Snātra Pūjās) or awarding access to pūjā performance by virtue of expertise (e.g., Ranjana acting as the sponsor at the Snātra Pūjā at the contest) was replaced here with access by virtue of prestige where women gained access to the performance of sections of the pūjā by winning the auction for that action.

Judging pūjā like the Snātra Pūjā contest and the public recitations of texts at pūjās serves both to reward expertise by celebrating accurate performance and effective teaching and to monitor performances in a shared evaluation of women's expertise. The recitations that Ranjana performed at the Snātra Pūjā competition were evaluated for accuracy by the group of men. Although she was confident in her knowledge, she was visibly relieved when she had made no errors in front of them, demonstrating her concern for the opinions of others, an unusual exception to her usual unflappable demeanor. Pūjā performances are places where expertise is at the center of a shared goal. In the case of the Snātra Pūjā contest, the maṇḍaḷs from around Pune were competing for a prize; along with the prize money came prestige, which also had the potential for increasing the number of sponsors of a given maṇḍaḷ. Whereas the women, on the whole, retained their own sense of expertise with regard to Jain praxis—an expertise they (and usually the rest of their families) understood to be meritorious for themselves and their families—they also negotiated the social realities of the privileged position of prestige in the Jain context. In particular, several women spoke of their lack of (at least regular) access to a variety of "expensive" rituals: pilgrimages, mahāpūjās, Mahāvīr Janam Dīvas auctioned activities, or having sufficient hired help (or daughters-in-law) at home which would permit them to be more involved in temple and maṇḍaḷ activities.

The authority to teach or to critique comes from the community's acceptance of one as an expert. In a sense, whereas prestige allows significant influence over social events and considerable access to the more prestigious religious acts, it does not on its own afford the authority to critique Jain praxis. This social authority may also excuse prestigious Jains from the obligation of attaining high degrees of orthopraxy while still being important figures in the Jain community, but it does not make them experts of religious knowledge. Conversely, high levels of religious knowledge can carry with it a certain amount of prestige. I am talking about loci of authority—whether it arises out of prestige or expertise—as a place to see negotiations of ritual efficacy, honor, and the theologies arising out of both. Although there are certainly those who seek authority for its own ends (sheer power) or for nonreligious ends (business connections), this is not the whole picture, any more than a picture of Jains renouncing their wealth selflessly and without an eye to prestige would be. The articulations of competitive relationship between prestige and expertise over issues of authority point to more than simply gender- or class-based inequities within Jain practice. The balance between these two realms is precarious. It has established an important undercurrent in Jain theology that criticizes the nature of public Jainism by challenging the uneasy balance between the negotiations of material understandings of Jain karma with the workings of devotion within that karma theory and the social workings of prestige, expertise, and authority.

8

Money is dull stone and God is shining gold—
Tell me who you love, Money or God?

You love money and nothing else.
For two hours your heart is given pleasure, but for the third, darkness.
In happiness and sorrow, who is your true companion, Money or God?

You will gain, yes, but only worldly joy.
Every day you have new thirsts. Pay attention, what should you be doing for joy?
Who can give you liberation from even this great joy? Money or God?

Because of his true heart, God escapes the cycle of rebirth;
Your life is full of the worship of money, but you keep yearning for more.
Who is the giver of joy and ease, Money or God?

Soul and supreme soul,[1] follow the greater path,
There, find peace and contentment. Śaival explains the path:
Who arrives at the door of the liberated, Money or God?

Transcription and translation of recording of ritual performance in Pune, Maharashtra on 26 June 1994. Courtesy Śrī Pārśva Mahilā Maṇḍaḷ.

Laywomen's Authority and Jain Theology

Ranjana brought this stavan back to the Pārśva Maṇḍaḷ when she returned from a visit to her mother's house in Karaḍ. It was a relatively new stavan, sung to an older popular Hindi film melody ("Mere Mankī Gaṅgā"); I never found its lyrics in any publication. She had learned it from her sister-in-law, who was active in a maṇḍaḷ in Karaḍ. This stavan expresses a critique of those Jain laity for whom the pursuit of wealth interferes with being a good Jain. Being wealthy in and of itself presents no inherent conflict with piety (Laidlaw 1995), but the use of wealth and gifting (dān—charitable donation to religion) as substitutes for religious commitment—as demonstrated by praxis and having the proper intention or sentiment (bhāv)—was a concern for the maṇḍaḷ women, whose role as specialists for hire brought them in contact with Jains who are not regular temple goers. Questions about the relationships between the correct sentiment and merit (puṇya) arose for the women in the maṇḍaḷ with the presentation of every hired pūjā.

The foregoing stavan was first performed by the Pārśva Maṇḍaḷ during a Pañcakalyāṇak Pūjā (June 8, 1994) before the members really knew it well. When there was a pause after one section of the pūjā was complete, Savita encouraged Ranjana to sing the new stavan. The maṇḍaḷ sang the first two verses and then substituted the verses of the formal text of the pūjā. They retained, however, the stavan's chorus and the Hindi film melody. The sponsor was a wealthy woman from a fancy suburban development who rarely came to the temple. Unlike the other commonly performed formal pūjās, including the Snātra, Vāstuk, and Antarāyakarm Nivāraṇanī Pūjās, the Pañcakalyāṇak Pūjā is never a "required" pūjā;[2] she was performing this pūjā to mark her twenty-fifth wedding anniversary. The sponsor's husband had also sponsored a Pārśvanāth image decoration for that day (101 rupees). After the pūjā, the sponsoring family held a party at their home for two thousand people. It is the most expensive pūjā that I saw regularly performed. In addition to the relatively high cost of materials,[3] the temple trust would normally be paid 101 rupees for a Pañcakalyāṇak Pūjā. In this case, the sponsor donated only 31 rupees to the temple trust. At the next meeting of the maṇḍaḷ, Maluben commented that pūjā should not be used as "decoration," indicating that the sponsor—by shorting the temple 70 rupees (granted, this donation is supposedly voluntary) while spending literally thousands of rupees on a party—made the pūjā (and by extension the Jain religion) seem like a mere ornament for her party rather than a possible source of her future marital happiness. There was much murmuring consent. The assent among the maṇḍaḷ women and the presence of the hastily prepared and pointedly critical song, and many veiled (or not so veiled) comments I encountered after that, led me to suspect the presence of something more than simply resentment boiling over.

The stavan that starts this chapter and the maṇḍaḷ women's understanding and use of it to criticize the sponsor of the Pañcakalyāṇak Pūjā imply certain theological questions: Does merit (puṇya) come to those without the correct sentiment? When Jains pay for someone else to perform a pūjā are they actually doing pūjā? I never heard any of the women use language that suggested that they were participating directly in the textual tradition: One maṇḍaḷ woman expressed such criticism to me as follows: "They think they can just buy merit." Other maṇḍaḷ women often expressed this criticism less concisely. In a community whose public face involves competitive auctions, large-scale donations, and throwing handfuls of money in the streets, this concern becomes a substantial theological and social critique.[4] Sponsoring a pūjā is a form of meritorious giving, which fits into the broader category of gifting, which includes those more public acts. This concern picks up an old thread in Jain theology—whether action without intention or knowledge is meritorious—and places it at the center of this maṇḍaḷ's understanding of its own practice. This conflict resembles the Christian theological debates over the role of "good works" in one's salvation.[5] As opposed to the Christian conflict between, on the one hand, faith and works, and on the other, faith alone, Jain theology asks, Are works (*kriyā*) alone enough? Must action be accompanied by knowledge (praxis as opposed to practice), and what is the place of devotion?

The women in the maṇḍaḷ felt that their expertise in pūjā performance and their roles as ritual specialists for other Jains necessitated the maintenance of pūjā standards; it is for this reason that the question becomes one of great seriousness for the maṇḍaḷ women. The temple priests at the great Minakṣī Temple (Fuller 1984) and the funerary brahmins in Varanāsī (Parry 1994) both express contempt for the devotee clients, but the maṇḍaḷ women usually spoke of the sponsors in complimentary terms, for these sponsors were doing what was seen as an unquestionably good act: Jain pūjā. Perhaps the most significant difference between the brahmins and the maṇḍaḷ women is that the same women who perform in the maṇḍaḷ are at other times the sponsors who hire maṇḍaḷs. Once again, the tensions between prestige and expertise over the authority to control and construct the pūjā frame the competing desires of the sponsors (the sense of their privilege to control their own event justified by the fact of their buying a service) and the maṇḍaḷ (the sense that they can control and evaluate the sponsor by virtue of their expertise in matters connected to pūjā). Whereas the sponsors who hire maṇḍaḷs (and in fact, other ritual specialists) may see these women as mere functionaries in the production of their pūjās—as Babb neatly puts this: "In a sense the pūjā principals 'do,' while the others felicitate what is 'being done.'" (Babb 1996, 29)[6]—for the time that they are performing the pūjā, these same sponsors suspend their own authority as part of the project of doing the pūjā well. Conversely, the maṇḍaḷ women (and observant non-maṇḍaḷ women confronted with the less observant) themselves saw themselves as the experts in pūjā (for which they are hired) and showed no real concern over the opinions of the kinds of sponsors with whom they could have had conflicts, such as those in this chapter. The important thing to both sponsor and maṇḍaḷ was that the pūjā was performed correctly and then that it went smoothly, avoiding awkward and inappropriate breaks that could reflect badly on them.[7]

The laywomen's authority was expressed in the negotiations between the Pārśva Maṇḍaḷ and its patrons; this influence both affects and was affected by differing notions of merit. During a pūjā, Maluben was quite outspoken about the ways that a pūjā should be done. At most of the pūjās she was seated at the top of the maṇḍaḷ set on the "men's" side, where she could easily observe the actions of the sponsor, who stood on the women's side next to the pūjā image. From her key spot she shouted commands to the sponsor and halted the pūjā if things were not going correctly. Her proprietary claims on the performances of pūjās at Ajitnāth or with the Pārśva Maṇḍaḷ extended to performances at other houses and to other maṇḍaḷs performing in the temple. On October 30, 1993 during a Kacchi Maṇḍaḷ Snātra Pūjā at Ajitnāth, Maluben interrupted the other maṇḍaḷ's pūjā because the women were singing a section of the Snātra Pūjā before the sponsor had reached that point in the performance of the pūjā. Though Maluben was sometimes seen as "difficult," no one ever questioned the correctness of her ideas or the appropriateness of her expressing them. Generally, when Maluben was present and in charge of the pūjā performance, the sponsors' knowledge (or lack of it) was disguised under her flurry of instructions. When Ranjana led Vāstuk Pūjā on August 24, 1994, her initial hesitation showed, through the moments of awkward silence and inaction, her own lack of confidence in how to proceed and, more disturbingly, the sponsor's lack of knowledge. The maṇḍaḷ did not blame the faulty pūjā on Ranjana's leadership even in private discussions later; the maṇḍaḷ women only raised the possibility that the sponsors gained little merit because they knew next to nothing about how to proceed.

The layout of the performance also suggests the centrality of the maṇḍaḷ women in the performance; the maṇḍaḷ women literally had the best seats for seeing the Jina image (darśan) and the sponsors (except the person—or persons—who is prepared to perform the eightfold pūjā) sat to the side of and behind the maṇḍaḷ (see figures 1-4 and 4-1). In a sense the sponsors accepted the relatively lower religious status by admitting to their relative lack of knowledge. They were prepared to be told how to do the pūjā, what to put where and when, and what to say and when. In this sense they acknowledged their lack of expertise whenever they hired a maṇḍaḷ. Though the presence of auspicious singing is quite important for these pūjās, it is not necessary. One could theoretically perform the pūjās alone or with only a ritual specialist or pujārī; clearly, the maṇḍaḷ leaders serve as the ritual specialists within the congregation. For a Vāstuk Pūjā (or any other pūjā done in someone's home) the image must be brought to the house of the sponsor along with all the accoutrements for the pūjā, and the organization of this process is often a good part of the maṇḍaḷ's work at a pūjā performance. Hiring a maṇḍaḷ for these pūjās highlights the maṇḍaḷ's position as knowledgeable Jain practitioners. The presence of the maṇḍaḷ can also be seen as adding to the overall prestige of the event, but, as we saw in chapter 7, the specialists must have expertise or the impulse backfires. However, most of the pūjās were performed in the afternoon with no "audience" whose view of the family could be affected by the adoption of prestige practices. In such cases, maṇḍaḷs are understood more to provide auspicious singing for hire and to be ritual specialists who can guarantee the proper performance of the pūjā. The atmosphere of a pūjā is one in which the sponsors allow—even if they privately think that devout temple goers are superstitious—the maṇḍaḷ women to run the show.

The merit of a pūjā lay both in the hands of the maṇḍaḷ and in those of the sponsor. If the sponsor had devotional sentiments he or she would gain merit, but in a sense only through the expertise of the maṇḍaḷ. If the maṇḍaḷ did not instruct the performer correctly, the pūjā could be spoiled and hence fruitless. When the sponsor performed the pūjā, it was the maṇḍaḷ women who guaranteed the correct action and supplied the right knowledge through their knowledge of the prayers, the timing of the actions, and the appropriate stavan. The sponsors—especially when they were not regular temple goers—were not in a position to direct the pūjā and thus relied on the maṇḍaḷ women to correctly direct the pūjā.

Jain Theological Frames

To understand the discussions in which these women were participating, I must introduce a few frames within Jain theological discourse about how one accrues karma, the relationship between karmic materiality and the role of intentionality, and the ways that intention gets linked specifically to the question of merit and gifting. Most Jains (men and women) I questioned spoke of several ways in which one could gain merit:[8] (1) by doing the pūjā themselves (being the person who actually performs the acts of worship); (2) by having someone else do the pūjā, which could include the maṇḍaḷ's giving instructions to others in their pūjā performance and/or others hiring the maṇḍaḷ or pujārī to perform a pūjā; and (3) through the appreciation of others doing good acts (anumodan). As in Śānti Sūri's paradigm, this hierarchy privileged the more interactive approaches with higher merit. Generally, the women felt that as maṇḍaḷ participants they were participating on all three levels of meritorious behavior. Women often came to a Snātra Pūjā with a coconut to offer, and wearing pūjā clothes which allowed them to participate in the circumambulations, ritual bathing of the image (abhiṣek), and sandalwood pūjā following the sponsor's sandalwood pūjā. All members routinely performed the caityavandan prayer series and the singing and recitation of the formal text of the liturgy during a pūjā. Often, women not in the maṇḍaḷ came to watch a pūjā being performed and sing along in a clear case of appreciation (anumodan). However, the maṇḍaḷ women saw their role in the pūjā as central to its proper performance, not peripheral as implied by the term anumodan; they saw the maṇḍaḷ as a third group—in addition to the sponsor and the audience—serving as ritual specialists (vidhikār).[9]

Jain karma is understood to be a material substance capable of attaching itself to one's soul and one's intention matters primarily as another way of binding karma: through thinking about, saying something about, causing someone else to do, or appreciating someone else's doing an act. For example, if a Jain hits a bug to kill it, there are two sins: (1) killing the bug (*dravya*) and (2) wanting to kill the bug (bhāv). If one performs a harmful act, karma is accrued regardless of one's intention. For Jains, doing the wrong action is compounded by having the wrong sentiment; conversely, having the right sentiment increases the merit of good acts. The women also believed that if one has the correct sentiment, one's minor faults are lessened. This may arise from the way that Jains understand the experience of the fruit of one's karma. It is their understanding that the possible negative karma that accrues (from picking flowers for worship, digging dirt to build temples, etc.) during the performance of religious duties comes to fruition immediately and does not have a long-term effect (Cort 1995c; Dundas 1992). It is also their understanding that once one experiences the fruit of one's karma it shrivels up and drops away (Jaini 1979). However, this materialist model of karmic materiality is challenged by an equally powerful model of the centrality of intention in the workings of karma.

In Jain religious praxis, there is a widely held belief that a correct act cannot be done at all without the correct intention. For example, for a fast to be efficacious and to help rid one of karma, the fast must be preceded by a recitation of the statement of the intention to fast (paccakkhāṇ). If one forgets to eat or cannot find food one day, it is not automatically a karma-reducing fast; to decrease the amount of karma already bound to one's soul—the hoped for result of some fasts and expected result in the case of the pratikramaṇ—there must be a stated intention (Laidlaw 1995). Of course, the material workings of karma do mean that there is a decrease in the binding of karma because there is literally a decrease in action (in much the same way that unintentional acts still cause some binding of karma regardless of intention), but the fast cannot work to destroy existing karma. Here we can see how the women came to the understanding that without proper sentiment there would be no decrease in karma or increase in good karma and, if the sentiment was a bad one, the negative karma would outweigh the good.

In his study of Jain lay manuals, Williams reformulates a list of important factors for evaluating gifting from the Śrāvaka-Prajñapti: place, time, faith, respect, and due order of offerings (Williams 1963). The third, faith (*śrāddh*), is interpreted as purity of mind. In this formulation the sentiment of the giver must be "pure" if the gifting is to accrue merit. As early as the Tattvārtha-bhāṣya[10] one's sentiment directly affects the quality of one's gifting. If the right qualities, most significantly for this chapter and most commonly discussed as a "lack of desire for worldly result," are present, the gifting is meritorious (Williams 1963, 154). Though the Tattvārtha-bhāṣya Sūtra is speaking of gifting to mendicants, we can see the sponsor as participating in an acceptable form of gifting in that their payments go to the temple and to laywomen for the exaltation (prabhāvanā) of Jainism.

Gifting includes all money or goods donated ("strewn") by Jains upon the seven fields of merit: Jain images, Jain temples, Jain texts, Jain mendicants (male and female), and laypeople (men and women). For many of the families in the Ajitnāth congregation, large-scale donation was not economically possible; when there was an opportunity for donation, it was generally the province of the men in the family. Recall Ajitnāth Temple was built through the major donation of a laywoman, Jyethiben Sanghvi. As we saw in chapter 7, women's auctions were held for the chance to perform offerings in the maṇḍaḷ's Navāṇuṅ Prakārī Pūjā and to recite or sing sections of the rites of confession and expiation. But most of the women in the maṇḍaḷ had few opportunities for donation in their own names. In 2000 the relative prosperity of the congregation was evident as virtually all the auctions at Mahāvīr Janam Dīvas were won by members of the congregation. However, in 1994 during the auction (*bolī*) on Mahāvīr Janam Dīvas (the birth of Mahāvīr as celebrated during Paryuṣaṇ), only one of the expensive auctions was won by a regular templegoer. The largest bid—for the privilege of taking the Mahāvīr image home for the next four days—went to a family that had come from Goḍījī Temple's congregation where, I was somewhat cynically informed by one young Jain layman, taking Mahāvīr home was more expensive. However, as the same person said, the money from the bids would support the temple for the coming year. This demonstrates the gifting conflict: there is not much devotional sentiment in bargain hunting, but, then, the results of the gifting are undeniably good; this is the merit. This issue of ostentatiousness and gifting has been discussed in several works but with an eye to the social workings of Jain donation.[11] The laywomen—both maṇḍaḷ singers and non-maṇḍaḷ performers—considered one's sentiment to be of central importance for determining the merit of acts; virtually all descriptions of good acts included an account of the doer's devotional sentiment. The relatively few negative critiques that I heard asked with which sentiment a gift—or donation—was given: one lacking in desire for worldly result, or one filled with self-aggrandizing? When the women were forced to question why (if not for merit of any kind) a sponsor had sponsored the pūjā at all, the critique went beyond an evaluation of the sponsor's sentiment to questions about the sponsor's Jain identity.

The Vāstuk Pūjā

To illustrate the way that the maṇḍaḷ women formulated and expressed their theological critiques, I will describe the Vāstuk Pūjā on August 24, 1994, in which the hesitant progress and the sponsors' clear lack of knowledge led to explicit and implicit critical commentary.[12] When we arrived at the sponsor's house at 3:30, someone had already retrieved the stand and the image from the temple and set them up in the living room. Because Maluben was absent (Sheelu, her daughter, had just had her baby), Ranjana, Asha, and Savita were setting up all the pieces of the pūjā. When it came time for the placement of the coconut under the Pārśvanāth image, Ranjana asked the family who would be performing the pūjā. There was a long silence. Ranjana asked, "who is in pūjā clothes?" No one was dressed to do pūjā. It seemed that the family had expected the maṇḍaḷ to perform the entire pūjā for them. The family either would have required a transfer of merit from the maṇḍaḷ to the family (theoretically not possible in a Jain karmic context) or would have been relegated to receiving only the benefits of appreciating a good act (anumodan).

The father sent the youngest daughter-in-law to the living room to clear this up. Ranjana, showing some irritation, asked whether the daughter-in-law could change to pūjā clothes, and she seemed not to have any. The maṇḍaḷ women gathered around and finally Ranjana said, "Do you have any new saris you haven't worn?" The daughter-in-law said "yes" and was sent to the back room to change into one of her wedding saris. While she was gone, Pramila wondered aloud whether she had a new blouse and all that,[13] but either no one heard it or everyone chose to ignore her comment. The daughter-in-law came back and joined Ranjana and Asha in the front of the room near the pūjā stand. Pramila called out for the daughter-in-law to cover her mouth with a handkerchief and she looked bewildered. The father came in and handed a handkerchief to Ranjana who folded it (with the nine prescribed folds) and told the daughter-in-law to tie it so it covered her mouth and nose. Then one of the old women in the family told the daughter-in-law to cover her head with her sari.

The maṇḍaḷ began the pūjā with Ranjana instructing the daughter-in-law at every step and the daughter-in-law following directions the best she could. The only person in the family who seemed to be paying attention to the pūjā (except for the daughter-in-law) was the father; he said the prayer to begin each section of the pūjā.[14] Others were sitting around catching up on family gossip and wandering in and out of the room. When it came to the circumambulations, Savita had to show the daughter-in-law how to do a prostration (praṇām),[15] and Savita also recited the

"Khamāsamaṇo Sūtra" that always accompanies prostrations before a Jina image. When it was time for the caityavandan prayers, no one in the family was willing (or, as many of the maṇḍaḷ women speculated later, able) to recite one. Ranjana recited the prayers in their place. There was little of the usual enthusiasm that marks a Vāstuk Pūjā—the maṇḍaḷ seemed to be rushing through the pūjā performance, and when it was time for the dancing the maṇḍaḷ women perfunctorily danced for only one short stavan. Not surprisingly no one in the family was interested in dancing.

After the bulk of the pūjā was done, the maṇḍaḷ women (except for Ranjana, who was finishing up the pūjā) went to a side room, where they were given snacks. Kamla put hers down without touching it. When Savita looked at her, she said, "In the rainy season, one has to be extra careful." During the rainy season, Jains are enjoined to be meticulous about their food restrictions and other observances. Kamla was not known for taking on extra food restrictions; none of the women finished their snack, though most ate the sweets. As we gathered to leave, Nita said to me, "I don't know how much merit one gets from a pūjā like this." Nita's explicit criticism questioned the efficacy of a pūjā done with incorrect sentiment, and what appeared to her to be a lack of respect ties in directly to the debate about what is meritorious. The lack of interest in the pūjā, the idle conversation, and the general carelessness of the family's participation in the pūjā seemed clearly to be disrespect for Jainism. The maṇḍaḷ women interpolated this view from the spirit of the list of the disrespectful faults (āśātnās) which Jains should avoid, and these acts were, as we saw in chapter 5, commonly understood instances of disrespect. Thus Nita saw disrespect in the variety of actions performed (and, perhaps more important, not performed) by the sponsoring family which she considered inappropriate during a pūjā. Even I was surprised by their behavior, and I optimistically speculated to Ranjana that maybe the daughter-in-law was Sthānakavāsī (a non-image-worshipping sect of Śvetāmbar Jains) by upbringing and had married into an image-worshipping family. Ranjana just shook her head—"no." The maṇḍaḷ women were quite upset at the time by the obvious lack of Jain practice (and praxis) in the family. Likewise, they were upset by their connection to such a pūjā. Kamla's rejection of the family's snack (a clear insult, as commensality among Jains is a central value of the community) asks an even more crucial question: Are they Jains?

Maṇḍaḷ Critiques and Jain Theology

Though no woman showed real familiarity with textual details from the Sanskrit or Prakrit traditions—including precise terminology—the ideas come to the women through the filtering conduits of discussion with other laywomen, lay manual texts, mendicant interaction, and the shared understandings of Jain practice. In the Jain textual tradition, Śānti Sūri's Dharma-Ratna-Prakaraṇa provides a discussion of four levels (*nikṣepa*) of Jain-ness that resembles the spirit of some of the critiques I heard among the women:[16]

(i) *nāma-śrāvaka*—one who is a Jaina in name only, just as a slave may bear the appellation of a god

(ii) *sthāpanā-śrāvaka*—the statue of a layman

(iii) *dravya-śrāvaka*—one who carries out the rites obligatory for a Jaina but who is empty of spirituality

(iv) *bhāva-śrāvaka*—a believing Jaina (Williams 1963, 36)

To the maṇḍaḷ women, the non-temple-going Jains who suddenly hire a maṇḍaḷ when they need a Vāstuk Pūjā could seem, were they familiar with the text, more like ones just performing their obligations (dravya-śrāvaka) than "believing" Jains. It is not that it is a problem to have a specialist perform a ritual function for another individual—recall how single individuals recite prayers for whole groups, how women asked Dadiji to recite difficult prayers for them, and how maṇḍaḷ women themselves hired specialists for their events. It is more a question of the context of that request; in sum, they were concerned about the sentiment with which the individual was asking someone else to perform the ritual.

The maṇḍaḷ women voiced their criticisms of the quality of a sponsor's pūjā in two ways. First, as we saw previously, they would question the sponsor's sentiment or intention in performing the pūjā. Second, they could draw attention to the sponsor's lack of knowledge of Jain prayers and rituals. The maṇḍaḷ women, based on their own experiences, had certain expectations of other laypeople's knowledge; a basic assumption was that any Jain knew the "Navkār Mantra" as a matter of Jain identification, even going so far as to say, "Even Digambar Jains say this Mantra. All Jains do." The next level of expertise, which was learned by most of the children I knew at around 8 or 9 years of age, was how to perform proper prostrations, including the "Khamāsamāṇo Sūtra." Then they learned how to perform the veneration of Jain mendicants, and soon after they learned the basics of the morning prayer series. Once a child knew this, he or she could function as an independent Jain layperson, though as a matter of practice children did not go to temple alone for several more years. Knowledge of the entire Snātra Pūjā was less common; its length and complexity distinguished more pious Jains from the ordinary (and in the view of the maṇḍaḷ women, adequate) Jains. Several maṇḍaḷ women knew the text by rote; this kind of familiarity with the Snātra Pūjā marked a person as having an active temple-going life and maṇḍaḷ participation. In the case of the Pañcakalyāṇak Pūjā, even the women in the maṇḍaḷ who rehearsed it from time to time rarely remembered how all the sections went without the help of a lead singer or a pūjā manual. This kind of knowledge was clearly beyond most expectations; it often marked those who are or will become maṇḍaḷ leaders.

During a pūjā as performed by a maṇḍaḷ there are spaces at the beginning of each section when a prayer ("Namo'rhat Sūtra"—a shortened form of the "Navkār Mantra") is recited. Usually, a woman from the maṇḍaḷ asked one of the men (if there were any present) to recite this prayer. If there were no men, the oldest woman in the sponsor's group was asked first and then other women were asked to recite the prayer. The sponsors usually responded with some shyness but would recite their prayer—usually the "Navkār Mantra" as an acceptable substitute for the other prayers, and one most people felt comfortable reciting. In the pūjās that were considered good ones, the women sponsors usually got involved in the singing and by the end were eager to recite their passages. Sometimes even two or three began simultaneously; Maluben chided them to speak in turn, but it was clear that the maṇḍaḷ appreciated this kind of enthusiasm.

There were some pūjās at which the mantra did not come so spontaneously. Then the pūjā stopped and Maluben or whoever was leading the recitation asked if anyone wanted to say the mantra. On more than one occasion, after some silence someone would ask: "Does anyone know the 'Navkār Mantra?' " In most cases at this point some woman would pipe up with the Mantra. If no one did, which happened only two times, Maluben prompted with the first line of the mantra: "*Namo Arihantānaṃ*?" and then "No one knows the Navkār?" On the two occasions I witnessed when no one was willing or able to say the mantra, the maṇḍaḷ said it for the group. However, whenever this happened the sponsor was tacitly admitting to having less knowledge than the children of the maṇḍaḷ women, who could all recite the "Navkār Mantra" by the age of 4 or 5.

With this paradigm of expectations for religious behavior (somewhat more exacting than Śānti Sūri's), knowledge of correct praxis is the basic criteria by which a person's "Jain-ness" is judged. However, faced with a failure to meet these expectations, the maṇḍaḷ also sometimes questioned the intention or sentiment of the sponsor. In the earlier case of the Pañcakalyāṇak Pūjā, the Vāstuk Pūjā, and also clearly in the stavan that begins this chapter, it is the sentiment of the sponsor that is under scrutiny. The sponsors' lack of knowledge and ability to perform rites correctly makes them, at best, Śānti Sūri's "sthāpanā-śrāvaka," but the maṇḍaḷ was clearly more upset by the total lack of devotional sentiment that their lack of knowledge implied than by the lack of knowledge itself.

Through their questions about the role of the sponsors in a pūjā and their skepticism about the merit earned by the sponsors, the maṇḍaḷ women touch on an important debate within Jainism: What is the relationship between knowledge, intention, and merit? In general the women did not actively engage in explicitly theological discussions with me; if a question of mine was explicitly theological, I was told to ask a mendicant. This reticence, however, does not preclude the women's having theological questions (and answers) and complex understandings of Jain philosophy. For the women, the incredibly complex textual and philosophical traditions were an issue of everyday life that ranged from what to cook during the hot season when the only vegetables available (potatoes, eggplant) were not acceptable to questions about which of the observances should take precedence when several conflicted. Although a women was, of course, in dialogue about Jain practice and belief with others—other laywomen and also mendicants and laymen—these discussions had more practical aims than systematically theological ones. In the absence of explicit theological debate, each woman had to come to her own understanding within the Jain tradition. The maṇḍaḷ women have a theology that favors their praxis-oriented religion and offers real positions of power and authority for them in the congregation. It is straightforward and practical (in both the praxis sense and the realistic sense): The greater the degree of practice (which leads to knowledge and therefore a further greater degree of praxis) and the purer the sentiments of devotion, the more merit one acquires. This stress of the praxis side of Jain religiosity and the importance of performing pūjā in order for anyone to understand Jain religiosity focused my research and determined my fieldwork method. The women insisted that in order to write a thesis about Jain laywomen's religious understandings, I had to understand pūjā; the only way to understand pūjā was to learn from them how to perform pūjā. The sense was that knowledge would arise from action—like the female mendicant's use of the magnet image to describe pūjā efficacy in chapter 5—and that correct sentiment led to correct action which was necessary for the acquisition of knowledge.[17] This conflicts with a common catch phrase that right action arises naturally and exclusively from right knowledge—like the stavan in chapter 3 where Sarasvatī grants knowledge as a necessary antecedent to correct action. Hence, when women were faced with what seemed to be wrong sentiments or wrong knowledge, they often expressed concern over whether right action was even possible. This conflict remains, like many tensions within Jain theological negotiations, unresolved.

If the maṇḍaḷ women felt that the sponsors displayed a lack of knowledge and practice, the sponsor's sentiment was called into question. If one is not committed enough to Jainism to go to the temple and to learn how to do worship, is it possible to have the correct intentions? The maṇḍaḷ women were skeptical of the sentiments of someone who did not perform worship at the temple, but this alone did not draw criticism. It is the distinction between being "bad" Jains and not being a Jain at all. When the maṇḍaḷ's question is whether the sponsor is or is not a Jain, it is more than a question of a generalized lack of enthusiasm—which itself could be a sign of insufficient devotional sentiment or being a "bad" Jain. The sponsors here seemed to be performing pūjā to fulfill some sense of social expectation without an interest even in the merit it might bring. Of course, if the sponsor were really uninterested in the whole event—not even interested in the social prestige or sense of duty—the event would not have taken place at all.

The stavan texts and the women's commentaries on the texts and rituals and the way the laywomen used their knowledge to explore theological questions (within their own idiom) make it clear that women have a "voice" in the development of contemporary and future Jainism. The wording of the song was clear: money or God. The conflict is a given (as we saw in chapter 7 and here in this chapter) that their position as ritual performers brings to the fore. Their theology privileges Jain practice and ritual expertise—all with the correct sentiment—over other approaches; because of these women's high level of praxis and knowledge of praxis, they see themselves as having the authority to express their theology publicly. They do so through their choices of stavan and the ways that they use the authority they gain through expertise.

Understanding Jain women and their beliefs illustrates a major source of much of contemporary Jainism. However, because authority is often understood in terms of men's priorities, social structures, and patterns of awarding prestige, much of the women's participation in the creation and functioning of Jain communities is overlooked. My examination here of contemporary Jainism, to understand present articulations and tensions of the religion, shifts attention from the Sanskrit and Prakrit to the vernacular, from economic to religious power among laypeople, and from individual sponsors to other ritual participants. Ritual expertise and authority were negotiated among the women and transmitted (often by singing) into the Jain community as a praxis-centered theology that reformulates the relationship between knowledge, practice, donation, and devotion in Jainism. This reformulation opens up new questions for the scholar of Jainism about the place of devotion and grace; the sources of alternative role models; the relationship between gender, class, and status; and a multitude of new opportunities for seeing Jainism as the changing, negotiated tradition that it so clearly is.

I heard the following stavan (the "Śrī Śāntināth Stavan," from the *Śrī Sudhāras Stavan Saṅgrah*) again and again at the conclusion of many Jain events where Jains came together as a congregation. In the face of the kinds of theological debates in which Jain laity participate and negotiate their practice, it was striking that the closing statement of community at these public events was articulated in devotional (rather than theological or philosophical) language. The hope of a congregation is articulated in a request for the Jina to give them darśan and thereby to restore peace to the community. Thus it seems right to end this book about the representations, debates, negotiations, and reconstructions of Jain devotion with the words so many Jains themselves sang when faced with seemingly inexplicable or unresolvable challenges:

Accept my praise, King! Excellent Lord Śānti!
O Acīrājī's son, we came lovingly to you for darśan.
O Lord whose faith delights us, our devotion brought us to you.

Your promise is to reduce sorrow, our hope is the same.
You are passionless and free, what is the state of our consciousness?

People say: "Don't go before God with demands."
But this child does not know how else to approach the beloved.

You are so kind and powerful, Lord, how can I do less than obey?
O Jewel of the mind, I am bound in a knot with you, whose work is whose?

O Sun of Spiritual Knowledge, you lifted my heart defeating the darkness of ignorance in a moment.
O Victory of the lotus, the servant of your words sings with auspicious devotion.

Transcription and translation of a ritual performance in Pune, Maharashtra, on March 21, 1994. Courtesy Malathi Raman Shah.

Notes

CHAPTER 1

1. I translate the word *Prabhu* as God for two primary reasons: first, and most important, God was the word used by Jains to translate Prabhu and also when they used English to speak of the Jinas; second, the other possibilities—Lord (which seems to carry the scent of the King James version of the Christian Bible) and husband (which would really be incorrectly translating the meaning and use of the term in this context)—both seem to misrepresent the relationships with the Jinas that these women described to me. I used the term Lord when translating words for the Jinas which carry with them the sense or the meanings of dominion over the Jains (i.e., *Sahib*)—in the sense of kingship or lordship which is often attributed to the Jinas. To speak of Jains as atheists conflates the term God with the notion of creator (Cort 1989). Jain doctrine does not accord creator status to the Jinas or to anyone else; the world is uncreated and eternal. Jains speak of the Jinas in language suggestive of the idea of God (Bhagavān); however they do distinguish—in their vocabulary—the Jinas from guardian gods and goddess (śasan devatā), lineage goddesses (kul devī), and Hindu gods and goddess (dev and devī or mātā).

2. I use the name Mumbaī—rather than Bombay—in line with recent legislation about the name of the city and, more important, because it was the way everyone I knew pronounced it. The same holds true for Amdāvād (Ahmedabad). I make an exception when I refer to these cities during the periods in which they were more commonly known by the latter names in the West.

3. Śatruñjay is a temple-covered hill in the town of Pālītāṇā and the most popular Śvetāmbar pilgrimage site.

4. However, virtually every Jain temple I saw—outside of Pālītāṇā and Rāṇakpur—was under some kind of construction. Michael Meister, in personal communication, said to me that a "loved" Jain temple is one under construction, pointing to the role of donation in religiosity. Renovation is a Jain religious project. For more, see Meister 1998.

5. I use the word *image* here in part because I do not distinguish generically between mūrtis (which are formally installed sculptural images of Jinas), and other images, including pictural images in the temple and in houses and household sculptural images, which have not been formally installed. When this distinction is relevant, I include more specific information. Humphrey and Laidlaw 1994 have an interesting argument for the use of "idol" to translate *mūrti* where they posit that the use of "image" tacitly accepts the negative associations that are found in Protestant Christianity. I do feel that Humphrey and Laidlaw's critique is based on three features that do not really apply in my study: (1) that the Jains involved themselves see the worship of Jina images as problematic (something I never heard once); (2) that these Jains are aware of the kinds of associations connected with the use of "idol" in the Judeo-Christian audience of their study (a discourse I never encountered in any of my research discussions); and (3) that the Jains used the English word *idol* themselves, but the women with whom I did my research did not use English with me or with anyone else with whom I saw them speak.

6. The images (mūrtis)—except for that of Gautam Svāmī—named here are of Jinas (sometimes called *tīrthankar*s) who are the twenty-four teachers/sages who revitalized and taught Jainism in this era. Temple worship of Gautam Svāmī was not noticeably different from that of the Jinas.

7. For basic surveys and introductions to Jainism, see Dundas 1992 (for Jain history and Jain doctrine); Cort 1989 (for Jain laymen's practice and Jain normative theology); Folkert 1993 (for Jain canon); and Jaini 1979 (for Jain doctrine and normative models).

8. If we project the 1991 Pune City percentage figure to the present based on the 1996 figure of the United Nations, we might expect to find approximately 68,200 Jains in Pune Municipal Corporation (pop. 3,100,000). The 1971 census gives Maharashtra a population of 703,664 Jains (27 percent of Jains in India and 1.4 percent of the population of Maharashtra) and Pune District Jains make up between 0.5 and 2 percent of the total district population (Sangave 1980). The population of Jains in Greater Bombay grew at the highest rate of any Jain community in India: from 1951 to 1961 at 43.86 percent and from 1961 to 1971 at 44.88 percent (Sangave 1980). This suggests the centrality of Maharashtra for Jainism now and in the future.

9. United Nations figures come from web site www.undp.org/popin/wotrends/urb/furb.htm as of April 20, 1999, where they define the urban agglomeration as "the population contained within the contours of continuous territory inhabited at urban levels of residential density without regard to administrative boundaries." This area more closely resembles the region referred to as "Pune" by the Jains I knew.

10. Dating the life of Mahāvīr is still inextricably linked to dating the life of the Buddha (Dundas 1992). However, this debate is not one that in any way impinges on the Jains I knew who believed Mahāvīr to have lived from 599 to 527 B.C.E. and that Jainism itself is eternal and without beginning.

11. I found that Jains I knew also participated in other Hindu (or pan-Indian) festivals and pūjās without giving them a "Jain" gloss: Ganapati Pūjā, Satyanarāyaṇ Pūjā, Hanuman Jayanti, Navrātrī, Makar Sankranti, Rakṣabandhan, and having darśan in various (vegetarian) Hindu temples wherever they happened to be when out on a picnic, traveling, or on pilgrimage. I plan to look into the ways Jains understand their participation in Hindu festivals in the future.

12. Jains conceive of time as a wheel with an ascending (*utsarpiṇī*) and descending (*avasarpiṇī*) side. During the period at the bottom of the spiritual decline, mokṣa is not possible on this continent (Jain geography posits concentric continents around a central island) but is possible on the continent of Mahāvideha where the Jina Simandhar Swāmī is alive and where Jains can attain mokṣa.

13. Whereas Amdāvād (Ahmedabad) and Mumbaī (Bombay) have greater concentrations of Jains, the highest (Mumbaī has slightly fewer Jains) number of Jains in a single region is in this region, which includes Kolhapur and Belgaum districts (Carrithers 1991).

14. Though the more important celebration of Mahāvīr's birth was celebrated during Paryuṣaṇ.

15. There are strong similarities between Gujarātī and Mārvāḍī languages, though they are written in different, but related, scripts.

16. Gujarātī language retention in Pune is especially high for a migrant group (Chandhari and Kunte 1971; Dhonge et al. 1989).

17. The oldest temple, in Kālevāvur, was not then in the city proper (Deo 1950). The original shrine of the Dādāvāḍī Mandir was built in 1586 (Samvat 1642). The temple was built in 1938 (Deo 1950). A large separate Jina temple was consecrated there in 1990. S. B. Deo (1950) also writes that in 1891, when the Jains built the Sacapir Street Mahāvīr temple in the Pune Cantonment, the British required that the exterior of the temple look like a house—the temple dome was enclosed within a building—so that British Christians would not have to see the temple. This narrative must be understood in the context of Deo's research time—just after Indian Independence. Whether the Sacapir street temple was legislatively hidden or whether it is a reflection of the havelī temple style (Asher, forthcoming; Laidlaw 1995)—popular in Rajasthan from where the earliest Jains in Pune came—ultimately matters less than the idea that Jains express their position as a "hidden" community.

18. The term śrāvak denotes Jain laymen, exclusively, but I suspect the British use of the term included Jain laywomen too. If not, the Jain community was considerably larger than this figure.

19. Although Jains certainly would have come from neighboring towns for such a large event, some of the Pune Jains would have probably been manning their stores and homes.

20. The two visual markers I encountered were subtle: a very small sandalwood mark put on the forehead at the temple and the particular kind of protective bracelets distributed at Jain pūjās. Both of these were identified as Jain; when people (especially Jains) saw them on me, I was immediately asked whether I was Jain.

21. I am in debt to John Cort's 1989 dissertation for most of the Pāṭaṇ history.

22. If there had been Digambar Jains in Pune, their history has effectively disappeared.

23. If a developer wants to get Jains to move into a new development it must have a Jain temple. Likewise, as soon as a Jain community is settled in a new area—in India, East Africa, Europe, Japan, or North America—they build temples (Banks 1992, 1994; Cort 1989; Laidlaw 1995).

24. The annual rite of confession and expiation of sins, the Saṃvatsarī Pratikramaṇ, is performed with one's congregation unless one cannot be in the city. People came home—from service jobs, school, and so on—over some distance to perform the rite together with their congregation.

25. A start can be found in the work of scholars such as Orr 1998, who is reconstructing some Jain and Hindu women's social history from donative inscriptions.

26. No one with whom I spoke discussed castes, except when they spoke in the global sense of refering to all Jains as Vāṇiyā—the more generic term that subsumes the castes of most Jains—and references to two downtown temples as the Osvāl and Poḍvāl temples. When I asked what caste (*jnati*) people were, I almost always got the answer: Śvetāmbar. However, there were two caste-based organizations in Pune which a few men I knew had joined. These were the Viśā Śrīmalī Trust (in which I knew several men), which owned a building in downtown Pune that people could rent for functions, and the Viśā Śrīmalī Marriage Service (in which I knew two men), which published a list of eligible young men in their caste to help prospective families find potential grooms. No women I knew—including women from the families of the men who joined these organizations—were members of any caste-based groups, nor did they ever speak of caste. For discussions of Jain castes, see Babb 1996; Banks 1992; Cort 1989; Cottom-Ellis 1991; Laidlaw 1995. I suspect that in Pune District religious and ethnic identities were ultimately more significant because of the role these identities have in the sense of difference from the dominant culture: Maraṭhī-speaking Hindu.

27. Mendicants are consulted on mundane and secular issues, as well as on theological ones (Shanta 1985)—true also of Hindu laity and holy personages (Narayan 1989)—and even after ordination the families and the mendicants acknowledge the familial relationships through conversations and photographs. (See Cort n.d. a; Laidlaw 1995; Reynell 1991 for discussions about the relationships between Jain mendicants and laity.) This issue was less important in central Maharashtra where there are still few mendicants compared to the number in Gujarat and Rajasthan.

28. There have been several good studies of Jain mendicant movements spanning diverse issues (Caillat 1975; Carrithers 1989; Cort 1991a; Holmstrom 1988; Jaini 1991; Shanta 1985; Tatia 1981). Caillat's and Tatia's studies are textual compilations and analyses of normative models of the Jain mendicant traditions; Carrithers', Holmstrom's and Shanta's studies are ethnographies of Digambar Jain male mendicants, Terapanthī Jain female mendicants and Jain female mendicants, respectively. A 1999 University of Toronto doctoral thesis, "Women and the Ascetic Ideal in Jainism," by Anne Vallely, discusses Terapanthī Jain female mendicants in Ladnun.

29. For extensive discussions about the role of Jain temple worship in lay religiosity, see Babb 1996; Cort 1989, 1991b, 1994, forthcoming; Humphrey 1985; and Humphrey and Laidlaw 1994.

30. Personal interview with and lecture by Tapā Gacch female mendicant, Śirur, July 31, 1994.

31. There are three photos of men and women together: one of a newly married couple performing an āratī, one of women assisting men in performing a Śāntī Kalaś, and one of three Jains (two men and a woman) entering the temple together. Compare this with the sixty-seven photos of men alone or in groups performing all the various acts associated with worship.

32. Tapā Gacch women are permitted to touch any Jina image, provided they observe the same level of cleanliness required of men. However, Tapā Gacch Jains observe the menses restriction against entering the temple. After a birth (even the attendants on a birth are restricted) or death, there are varied periods of restriction against temple entrance and entering the inner sanctum. However, a woman who does not menstruate or is not menstruating is permitted to perform all acts of worship. Khartar Gacch women (at least in Jaipur) do enter the inner sanctum despite a past historical prohibition, although I expect that they follow a menses restriction as well.

33. I see the women's agency as one that considers the social (as well as logical) limitations of their acts. However, following Whitehead (1929), I see that the fact of limitation—which men also face—is not a negation of their agency.

34. There was one ad hoc children's maṇḍaḷ which I have not discussed here.

35. See Blackburn 1988; Dhere 1988; Flueckiger 1996; Fuller 1984; Gold 1988; Henry 1988; Lutgendorf 1991; Lopez 1995; Mallison 1989; Parry 1994; Slawek 1986; Thompson 1987; and Wadley 1991.

36. For starters, see Archer 1985; Dhruvarajan 1989; Flueckiger 1996; Harlan 1992; Henry 1988; Narayan 1986; Raheja and Gold 1994; Tewari 1977; Trawick 1988; and Wadley 1975. For a place to begin looking at further studies on women and music outside of South Asia, see Koskoff 1987.

37. My questions about the use of the terms *orthodox*, *bhakti*, and *devotionalism* for Jain and Buddhist practices and materials was greatly influenced by a pair of lectures given at Harvard in the spring of 1995 (and the unpublished papers that accompanied them) by John Cort and Charles Hallisey.

38. See the following studies for an overview of bhakti poetry scholarship: Barz 1976; Barz and Thiel-Horstmann 1989; Hawley 1981; Hawley and Juergensmeyer 1988; Hess 1983; Lutgendorf 1991; and Werner 1993.

39. In addition, Neelima Shukla-Bhatt, a graduate student at Harvard Divinity School, is working on Gujarātī bhakti literature, especially Narsi Mehta. This study will be of great importance for understanding the ways in which devotionalism is understood in Gujarat and among Gujarātīs.

40. The importance of the *Śrī Sudhāras Stavan Saṅgrah*—the most popular stavan collection—as a normative hymnal for communal singing may point to a future role of hymnals as women's literacy rates rise and publication costs shrink. However, Jain women have had a relatively high literacy rate for several generations and the diaries—kept individually by women or by families—serve as hymnals without the homogenizing effect of a single published hymnal edited by a single group. The *Śrī Sudhāras Stavan Saṅgrah* collection itself is not fixed. In 1985, the collection was 125 pages long, in 1993, it had 144 pages, and in 1995 the collection had ex-

panded yet again, to over 200 pages. My most recent edition from 1999 had expanded to 384 pages. The women's repertoires and diaries included favorite stavan from the *Śrī Sudhāras Stavan Saṅgrah* collection.

41. For information about Jain laymen's manuals, see Cort 1989, 1991b; for Hindu manuals for women, see Leslie 1989 and Pearson 1996.

42. Until fairly recently, the available scholarship on Jains has focused primarily on the textual traditions of Jainism through translation (most notably, H. Jacobi) and on normative (doctrinally prescribed) models of Jainism according to the textual ideals. For critiques of these models, see Cort 1990 (for an illustration of the ways in which previous scholarship imposes limiting constrictions about what constitutes Jainism), Dundas 1992 (for a model for the use of a wider range of materials for studying Jainism), Folkert 1993 (for a discussion of the effect of Protestant scholarship on the study of Jains), and Jaini 1976; (for an analysis of the relationship between western and Indian scholars of Jainism).

43. For studies of contemporary Jains, see these field research–based studies: Babb 1996; Banks 1992; Carrithers and Humphrey 1991; Cort 1989, 1991a; Humphrey and Laidlaw 1994; Laidlaw 1995; Mahias 1985; and Reynell 1985a, 1991.

44. Śvetāmbar Jain Tapā Gacch female mendicant, personal communication. January 16, 1993, Ajitnāth's mendicant hostel in Pune.

45. This mantra is recited at the start of almost all Jain rituals, as well as at the start of secular activities—setting out on a trip, opening a store, and, for many, first thing in the morning and last thing before sleeping:

Namo Arihantāṇaṃ	Praises to the Liberated (Arhats)!
Namo Siddhāṇaṃ	Praises to the Perfected Ones (Siddhas)!
Namo Āyariyāṇaṃ	Praises to the Mendicant Leaders (Ācāryas)!
Namo Uvajjhāyānaṃ	Praises to the Mendicant Teachers (Upadhyanas)!
Namo Loe Savva Sāhunaṃ	Praises to all mendicants!
Eso Pañcanamukkāro	This five-fold salutation,
Savva Pāvappaṇāsano	Which destroys all sin,
Maṇgalāṇaṃ Ca Savvesiṃ	Is the most holy,
Padamaṃ Havai Maṇgalam.	Of all holy things!

46. I use the term *knowers* here after Gadamer 1975. My thinking on this point has been greatly enhanced by feminist epistemology, especially Code 1991; Gergen 1988; Hekman 1990; Mariniello 1998; and Stanley and Wise 1993.

47. One cannot be aware of all social dynamics in any situation; the reader can only take it on faith, but I was not aware at the time (nor have I been made aware in the intervening years, during which I have kept up a steady correspondence with several women in Shivajinagar and made three further visits) of any relationships damaged at the hands of my research. But perhaps most important, I have made this concern central to the way I think about doing research. For scholarly discussions on the effects of field research and writing, see Behar and Gordon 1995; Feld 1987; Kumar 1992; Lavie 1990; Limón 1994; Rosaldo 1984; and Stacey 1991.

48. I am aware of the Derridian critique of Heidegger's notion of responsibility (Spivak 1998). However, I still feel that the concept of forestructure—if not taken to limit one's ability to change and have empathy—is a valuable tool for thinking

about how to do less authoritarian research particularly when the forestructure itself is also seen a locus for deconstruction.

CHAPTER 2

1. The words in this translation were given to me by Ranjana but could be found in the stavan collection of many maṇḍaḷ women. Although the women said that the melody was then only 3 years old, no one could remember who had brought the stavan to the maṇḍaḷ. In *Cassette Culture*, Manuel (1993) suggests that the melody for the Hindi film song, "Ek, do, tin," was based on a Marāṭhī folk song of the same name. As no one suggested this source—all were clear about the melody source—I must assume they were not aware of the possible connection, which reflects their general lack of interaction with Maraṭhi-speaking culture.

2. For more about Paryuṣaṇ, see Cort 1992; Folkert 1993; and Laidlaw 1995.

3. This term carries with it a history of the discourses surrounding its use and the understandings of the ideological complex surrounding the idea of a sati in contemporary Hindu religious and political identity, its connection to the British discourse about "suttee," and feminist (both Indian and Western) discourses. My next project will focus on the ways in which the term *sati* and its ideology are used by Jain sources and by contemporary Jains. Śvetambar Jains honor a group of satis who are honored as the pinnacle of female (and in some ways human) virtue. None of these women performed the Hindu rite of following one's dead husband onto the funeral pyre nor are they especially devoted to their husbands, whom they often leave to become Jain mendicants (excepting Rājīmatī). Balbir (1994) suggests that this name comes from the women's devotion to their husbands; however, in the vernacular literature, this is not the case. In addition, the Sthānakavāsī Jains call their female mendicants *mahāsatīs*. I assume the term in the Jain context is used in its more generic form—"a chaste and virtuous woman" or "one knowing the truth"—rather than the more specifically Hindu understanding where it is an extension of a woman's dedication to her husband. It would not be virtuous for a Jain woman to become a satī by dying with her husband, as this would be seen as suicide and suicide is considered an irredeemable act of violence. Again, the relationship between suicide and satī is as tricky for Hindus as the suicide and fasting to death (*sallekhana*) issue is for Jains. For more about this, see the works of Hawley 1994 and Mani 1989 for Hinduism; or Tukol 1976 for Jain materials. Of course, this term may have arisen in an effort to encourage Jains to worship virtuous Jain women rather than the women considered virtuous by Hindus. It would not be the first—or last—time religious groups co-opted another group's rhetoric.

4. Yaśodhara is Mahāvīr's wife (Ācārāṅga Sūtra) and Nandivardhan is Mahāvīr's elder brother. Śvetāmbars believe that Mahāvīr was married and had children before he renounced the world, but the Digambar Jains do not accept this view. This couplet is probably borrowing its tableau from the Rāmāyaṇ here because there are few mentions of Mahāvīr's brother in the Jina's narratives.

5. The Candanbālā story as retold here is based on both the version in a tract about virtuous women (*Sulasā Candanabālā*) and retellings I heard. They match with the versions told to Reynell and Shanta, which they both record in their works (Reynell 1985a; Shanta 1985).

6. Hemacandra's argument for celibacy can be found in his Yogaśāstra Book 2, verses 76–105.

7. In the Khartar Gacch (Laidlaw 1995) there are some female mendicants who themselves write religious tracts and give sermons based on some of the materials prohibited to women in the Tapā Gacch.

8. For further information on the ways Hindu women derive their theologies from vernacular or oral texts, see Erndl 1993, Gold 1988, Henry 1988, Pearson 1996, and Wadley 1975.

9. Research which has begun to use these materials, though still scanty, can be found in Balbir 1993, 1994, Dundas 1992, and Granoff 1990, 1998.

10. Jain laity more often look to the lives of illustrious laity for role models. See discussions in Babb 1996, Cort 1998, and Dundas 1992. This area of Jain religiosity will be greatly enhanced by Steve Heim's future University of Chicago dissertation which looks at those most illustrious of Jain laymen: Vastupāl and Tejpāl. Shanta 1985 suggests that the female mendicants drew most of their role models from the vernacular narrative tradition as well.

11. See Christ 1987 and 1989; Olsen 1989. There are newer, more nuanced studies of goddess worship and gender. See Brown 1998, Caldwell 1999, Coburn 1991, Erndl 1993, Feldhaus 1995, McDermott 2000, Pintchman 2001, and Sax 1991.

12. This, of course, is totally unacceptable to Digambar sources, for she is not only a woman but a householder, neither of whom are believed by Digambars to be capable of attaining mokṣa.

13. Contemporary research shows demographically that most Jain female mendicants take their ordination vows before marriage—opposing the previously held view that Jain female mendicants are widows (Jaini 1979, 1991; Sangave 1980). My research with female mendicants, though limited, and the women's descriptions of ordinations confirm these patterns. Cort 1991b also shows that the Śvetāmbar male mendicants take their ordination vows early in their lives (before age 30) and thus choose a lifelong vocation rather than, as he puts it, "a retirement option."

14. Although this paccakkhāṇ serves a purpose—an announcement of intention—similar to the *sankalp* in Hinduism, it has a relationship with the whole family and the mendicants.

15. During my 1993–94 research period I knew one man who was performing a varsītap; in addition, in 1994 several other men and boys performed fasts: Mukesh's two days upvās during Paryuṣaṇ, Nilesh's ekāsan and Āyambil, and Satish's and Ashok's Āyambils during Oḷī. Moreover, all the men performed the Saṃvatsarī fast. During Paryuṣaṇ in 2000, all but three of the men in Ranjana's extended family did fasts beyond the Saṃvatsarī fast. Since then I have known of several men who took on Jain fasts, but it is true that the most strenuous fasting is usually performed by women. Laidlaw 1995 points to the life of Śriman Amarcandjī Nahar as a male example of extreme fasting while opening fruitful possibilities for understanding how it is the choice of performing austerities on the male body that becomes the icon of fasting there.

16. This use of the term vrat should not be confused with the vows called *mahāvrat* or *anuvrat*; the women were clear that these fasts were not a part of "Jain" religious practice but were efficacious for the attainment of certain desired results. For more about Hindu vrats, see McGee 1987 and Pearson 1996.

17. Laidlaw (1995) has an extensive discussion of fasting variation and narratives and gives a list of six basic kinds of fasts as *naukārsī, porisi, upvās, ekāsan, āyambil*, and *nivi*. Cort 1989 lists them as *naukārsī, porisi, upvās, ekāsan, beāsan, caūtth* (not eating until the fourth meal), *chaṭṭh* (not eating until the sixth meal), and *aṭṭham* and separates the dietary restrictions of *āyambil* and *nivi*.

18. I found the same kind of knowledge of ritual performance without knowing the narrative explanation common in Jain performance of pūjā or darśan in Hindu temples (except Lakṣmī and, sometimes, Ganapati).

19. Reynell 1991 also writes of the connection between wedding photos and fasting photos.

20. This fast lasts for fifteen days and ends on Samvatsarī Day (in conjunction with the Samvatsarī Pratikramaṇ and fast); once started it must be performed for four years in a row. The women eat only one meal at midday and can drink water from midday until sunset.

21. This stavan, "Fast-breaking Day," was brought to the maṇḍaḷ by Pramila who had found the words in a stavan collection called *Śrī Pārśva Parāg* which she no longer owned so I cannot give a full citation here

22. Reynell 1991 suggests that it is used to prove the continued chastity and virtue of a woman after marriage, but I never saw any definite evidence of this or evidence directly against this interpretation. In Hema's case, an extremely charismatic male mendicant, Viśvakalyāṇjī was staying in her town and with him a charismatic female mendicant, too. I suspect they encouraged her to perform the fast. It may have been connected to her eldest daughter's reaching marriageable age while she was still in school getting her doctorate.

23. These fasts are so strenuous that women sometimes die from a heart attack while undergoing them. I rarely heard of this in Pune, but I suspect it was not a topic the women talked about unsolicited, especially when someone they knew was at risk, and I was unaware of any cases until after I left in 1994. When I was in Pune for Paryuṣaṇ in 2000 there were no deaths, but there were serious concerns when an elderly woman with a heart condition decided to undertake an eleven-day fast.

24. As in all sections taken from my field notes, editing has instilled a certain cogency.

25. In addition, mendicants, especially, would repeatedly encourage women to fast.

26. Reynell 1985a discusses—along with fasting—women's performance of regular daily meditation (samāyik) and temple worship.

27. The only ordinations in Pune during my stay were three of women (two young unmarried women and one middle-age woman). There were no male ordinations in Pune that year. There have been historically more female mendicants than male. The young unmarried woman whose ordination I describe later was Mārvāḍī, and the other two ordinations were of Gujarātī women.

28. It would be interesting to see if widows also wear the wedding attire when they take ordination, but I did not see the ordination of a widow and did not think to ask about this. I am indebted to Kirin Narayan for pointing out this fruitful possibility.

29. For a fascinating study of the role of pictures and picture taking in India, see Pinney 1997.

30. For studies of Hindu renunciation (dīkṣā), see Dumont 1970, K. Narayan 1989, and Patrick Olivelle 1986–87.

31. These are understood by both lay and mendicant Jains to be legitimate reasons for taking ordination, but they were colored with a sense that both the family (or community) was not able to support itself economically—or was too greedy to give what it would take to marry the daughter—and the ordination was somehow unreligious because it did not conform to the renunciation rhetoric.

32. For example, the Tapā Gacch female mendicants cannot study the Cheda Sūtras or give formal sermons—though they do in the Kalāpūrṇsūri Samuday in Kacch. John Cort, personal communication.

33. Holmstrom 1988 writes however that this time was often used as free time to nap or chat.

34. See also Reynell 1991. I saw Jain men being observant in ways often dismissed as socioeconomic, such as buying only from Jain stores, which I interpret in part as an extension of their "support of moral and virtuous people."

CHAPTER 3

1. The forty-five Āgam texts include the central theological treatises and mendicant manuals. Folkert 1993 provides the best overall discussion of theories and categories of Jain canon.

2. The only place I found this Jñān Pancamī stavan was the section of the *Śrī Pañca Pratikramaṇ Sūtra* where stavan were given for each holiday.

3. There was a decidedly Sthānakavāsī tone to the study group (four Sthānakavāsī women and two Mūrtipūjak) and one of two the Mūrtipūjak women told me she went to the temple (but not until we were alone).

4. Digambar Jains also worship their texts in a festival called Śruta Pañcamī (Jyestha sud 5, May/June) with manuscript donation. See Jaini 1979.

5. I use the term Kalpa Sūtra to mean both the Prakrit root text and the Gujarātī commentary, as the women considered them to both be constitutive parts of one text. The Prakrit root text is sometimes called the Bārasā Sūtra, but the women did not speak of either of these texts very often—only during the recitation at Paryuṣaṇ. See Cort 1992 and Folkert 1993 for extensive discussions about these two texts and their performances.

6. This celebration bears a striking resemblance to the Puṣṭimarg Vaiṣṇav celebration of Kṛṣṇa's birth on Janmāstamī, highlighting the long-standing interaction between these two communities in western India. I do not have the evidence to speculate on the origins or the history of this ritual now, but for my purposes here the origin is immaterial. However, for a further discussion of the relationships between these two communities, see Babb 1996.

7. The *Laghu Pūjā Sangrah* is an abbreviated version of the *Vividh Pūjā Sangrah*, which serves as the central pūjā text for Tapā Gacch Jains. Although some women owned the longer version and the temple had a pile of copies, many women used the shorter edition because it was lighter and contained all the pūjās they actually performed.

8. Historically, there is a relationship between Gautam Svāmī and knowledge (Dundas 1998), but at Ajitnāth Gautam Svāmī was treated exactly the same as the Jinas. He was only noted individually on Mahāvīr Nirvāṇ when people worship his pictures with sandalwood powder (Cort 1995a; Laidlaw 1995), where his worship seemed more about wealth than knowledge.

9. Śrutadevī is addressed in the "Kallāṇa-kandam" (verse 4) in the Samsāra-dāvā; in addition, while women recite the "Kamala-dala" to Śrutadevatā, the men recite the "Jīse Khitte" verse to Khetarpāl in that spot. Thanks to John Cort for pointing this out.

10. This merit was sometimes transferred to a deceased ancestor (Cort 1995b). The concept of merit transfer in Jainism is discussed in Cort (forthcoming).

11. I'm not sure if they have or would have touched non-Jain religious books during their menses. I suspect they would not, because when a group of women asked me to sing a Christmas carol, they made one woman who was menstruating leave the room. Several women who had completed the Updhān Tap in 2000 had also taken a vow not to read any books, magazines, or newspapers during their menstrual cycle because they had been made to understand it would decrease their overall existing knowledge to read anything at that time.

12. The active repertoire itself was not fixed, as stavan were learned sometimes only one week in advance of their performance and others were dropped without comment from the performance repertoire.

13. The second group may have begun as one of the locally produced versions for festivals and programs, but time and also editing have removed those parts that would mark them as such. An in-depth study of stavan books such as the *Śrī Sudhāras Stavan Sangrah* is necessary to look at the development of this semicanonical text. I hope to pursue this topic in future writings.

14. In my personal collection I have a copy of each of these stavan books as well as others produced in Pune by Pune groups and several I acquired while in Amdāvād (there are also Pālītāṇā editions). None of the Amdāvād collections (that I count as the locally produced ones) were present in any of the Pune temples or personal collections I encountered.

15. All Śvetāmbar/ Pune (twenty-one temple collections catalogued, some temples have more than one building with separate central images—mūl nāyak), Alandi (one), Dombivli (two), Karaḍ (three), Junnar (two), Mumbaī (five), Sangamner (two), and Śirur (one) in Maharashtra; Amdāvād (seven) and Pālītāṇā (nine) in Gujarat; Jaipur (two), Jaiselmer (three), Lodruva (one), Udaipur (four), Ranakpur (one) in Rajasthan, and the personal collections of the all the Jain families with which I worked. Likewise Cort (1989) and Zwicker (1984–5) refers to its ubiquitous presence in Gujarat.

16. Many Jains carry a box or bag (often quite ornately decorated) to and from the temple when they go to morning worship—though some families left their boxes at the temple. These boxes usually contained rice, whole almonds, rock sugar chunks, a rosary or two, a copy of the Sudhāras collection, some coins, and sometimes photos of Jina āngīs—in short, the items needed to perform their morning pūjā offering.

17. The 1993 (Amdāvād) *Sudhāras* collection includes thirteen bolavānu stutis,

the prayers to accompany pūjā, nineteen caityavandans, forty-eight stavan, three chands, instructions for the Navānu "99" pilgrimage, three sets of dohas, kalaś, Āratī, Maṅgal Dīvo, instructions for pilgrimage to Śatruñjay, the "Ratnākar Paccīśī" prayer, and the Bhaktāmara Stotra in Gujarātī.

18. Padmavijay (eight), Udayratna (two), Jñānvimalsuri (two), Śubhavir (two), Manemuni (two), Jinaharṣ (two), and Jas (two).

19. The ubiquity of this collection has made certain caityavandans and other prayers the norm through widespread usage.

20. Nemichand Solanki (twenty-seven), Kevalchand Jain (sixteen), Hansaraj M. Ranka—the deceased (fifteen), Megharaj K. Jain (thirteen), Jalamchand J. Dalavat (ten), M. Manmohan C. Osvāl (six) and Dr. Pravin B. Osvāl, Ganeshmal Kavediya, Nemichand Osvāl, Ganeshmal C. Osvāl (two each) and Dinesh D. Jain, Kundanmal Phulakagar, Pratapachand J. Dalavat, Vimalchand Sanghvi, Valachand M. Jain, Kumchand N. Solanki, Jetalal L. Osvāl, Jetamal N. Surana, Kantilal Surana, Champalal N. Solanki, Shantilal K. Ranka, Amarchand M. Jain, and Madankumar Solanki (one each), plus three attributed to the Ādarś Men's Maṇḍaḷ as a whole.

21. At Ajitnāth there was a collection box marked simply "jñān" in which people put money to support the production and worship of knowledge.

22. It also makes "good business sense" to use standards on cassettes, a practice that ensures popularity and sales.

23. These cassettes do not list the possible sources for the stavan or the authors of the lyrics. It is possible that the singer or producers have written some of the stavan, but I was unable to find out that information. However, many of the stavan melodies could be found on other devotional tapes or Gujaratī folk song and dandiya rās-garbā tapes.

24. The effect this has on Gujarātī folk music is still unstudied, but Qureshi's work on qavalī suggests that these cassettes might narrow the performance repertoires of rās-garbā music (Qureshi 1995). Many of the changes in Hindu devotional music, including the sex of the singer, the narrowing of genres to those with sexual lyrics—in rasiya songs (Manuel 1993), or the replacement of live music by recorded music (Marcus 1995) have not happened to Jain devotional music. The only change represented within the cassettes is in the reliance on differing instrumentations; however, most stavan singers do not draw their musicality from stavan cassettes as much as from the rās-garbā tradition (both live and recorded). Some stavan cassettes participate in the bhajan tape phenomenon through the use of light classical musical style, the use of complex instrumentation, and the standardization of recorded performances. One cassette of the Bhaktāmara Stotra is performed by Anuradha Pauḍvāl, who started her career as a playback singer (a singer who provides the voice of the actress for Hindī film songs) and now records primarily bhajan cassettes in a light classical style (Marcus 1995). It remains to be seen what effect, if any, these cassettes may have on stavan singing as a part of Jain worship.

25. Though I did not hear anyone articulate a restriction against marrying someone within the same city, I also only knew one woman over thirty who had married someone whose family lived in Pune and the man she married already lived in Mumbaī. However, women who have gotten married in the last five to ten years are increasingly likely to be married in Pune. In Pune, it was not understood as ex-

ogamy but a necessity arising out of other factors. The reason given was usually finding a groom sufficiently distant in relation (more than seven generations) and of comparable socioeconomic background and family (which may have included caste). According to Cort 1989, in Gujarat Jains do not practice village exogamy. The research by Cottam Ellis 1991, Reynell 1985a, 1991, and Singhi 1991 suggests that the Jains in Rajasthan also do not practice village or city exogamy.

26. In the active repertoire there were stavan that had previously been brought in by Sheelu and Maluben, but I was unable to see the process of their integration. None of Sharmila's had been adopted yet but her enthusiasm will likely bring her to the fore of this practice. By 1999, her choices were part of the repertoire and now Soni, Ranjana's daughter, is the youngest member bringing stavan to practice.

27. Not really an unusual phenomenon: Recall that even the art musicians of Europe wrote pieces intended for a single performance (e.g., Bach's "St. Matthew Passion" or Handel's "Fireworks Music"), some of which have been incorporated into contemporary symphonic performance repertoires.

28. When she sang the stavan for me she did so, as she told me, because I had not heard a memorial stavan and she felt my collections and therefore my "book" might be incomplete. She was also pleased with the poetic results of her labor in writing the stavan.

29. Likewise, an adaptation of Hema's niece's fasting song could easily work its way into the Śirur maṇḍaḷ's repertoire.

30. There were two men's maṇḍaḷs associated with Goḍījī Temple in Guruwar Peṭh, one associated with Dādāvāḍī Jain Mandir near Saras Bagh and one in Yerawada. There are also twelve known "house temples" and fifty-seven additional Mūrtipūjak temples in the surrounding area.

CHAPTER 4

1. One may find a historical source for stavan and the formal pūjā texts by looking at the history of Sanskrit/Prakrit, Apabhraṁśa, Old Gujarātī and Medieval Gujarātī Literature, and the Jain, Vaiṣṇav, and Śakta literatures of western India (Jhaveri 1978; Krause 1952; Munshi 1954; Sandesara 1953, 1990; Schubring 1959; Shah 1981; Vaudeville 1986).

2. *Rāṇai Bhejyā jahar piyālā, imirat kari pī jāṇā*. My translation.

3. B. D. Jain (1950) speaks of Jain poetry in Persian, suggesting a source for this and other unusual (for Jains) images in their poetry. The use of Persian script by Mārvāḍī Mahājans in Rajasthan (Cottam Ellis 1991), likewise, suggests real possibilities for familiarity with Persian literature. See also Dundas 1996.

4. The chanting and recitations are usually melodic and rhythmic—which makes them sound at first like singing—but the use of the same stock "melody" for most performances of any stotra, stuti, and sūtra was more similar to Sanskrit recitation than to singing. Likewise, the women used the verb *gāvu* (to sing) for stavan, but the verbs *vācavu* (to recite) and *bolvu* (to speak) for stotra and stuti. In other areas these stotras may be sung, as John Cort heard the Bhaktāmara Stotra sung (Cort, personal communication), but even the cassettes I heard were more like recitation or chanting.

5. The use of one term to denote both the whole of something and also the de-

finitive part of the whole is common in India taxonomy: See pūjā and formal pūjās, *ālāp* and *ālāp*, tabla and tabla in classical music and a multitude of other multivalent terms. I must thank Warren Senders for an informative discussion about this use of language. In general, I use the term caityavandan in its second sense (the whole series of prayers) because the women rarely spoke of the individual caityavandan prayers. However, the prayer and stavan collections often have many caityavandan texts (in the shorter more specific sense) for a Jain to choose from for use within the caityavandan (in the larger serial sense). The caityavandan texts were short poetic praises addressed to specific Jinas (like the stavan) but were recited without refrains or repeated lines, musical devices shared by all the stavan. The praises in the caityavandan are more similar to a litany of epithets than to a lyric or narrative poem.

6. Jaini uses *stava* to mean contemporary singing as well, though this form, rather than stavan, denoted old verse in my experience in Pune and was not commonly used to mean the Gujarātī and Hindī texts, nor was it used in common speech.

7. I cannot emphasize enough that far more research needs to be done in this area. Thousands of volumes of Jain poetry and songs from the medieval period to the present have yet to be as much as commented on.

8. The roots of stavan texts also include the sajjhāy texts.

9. Because my focus is the role of singing and song texts in Jain practice, I examine here only the stavan and the formal pūjās and do not explore the variety and theology of other texts: caityavandans, stutis, and stotras. However, a study of these genres would add much to our still embryonic understanding of Jain bhakti, praxis and literary history.

10. There is scholarship on Jain poetry in Hindī and Gujarātī, but these poets have not been included in the burgeoning bhakti poetry scholarship in the Western academy. Even Narsi Mehta, who is widely studied in Hindī and Gujarātī language examinations of bhakti poetry, is mostly excluded from Western scholarship, though Neelima Shukla-Bhatt's translations and dissertation (presently in process at Harvard Divinity School) will eventually fill some of the lacunae.

11. See Barz and Thiel-Horstmann 1989, Harlan 1995, Hawley 1983, Kishwar and Vanita 1989, Lynch 1990, Mukta 1994, and Thiel-Horstmann 1983a, 1983b as a sampling of some of the new studies of bhakti saint poets and their influence on Hinduism.

12. Though in the *Śrī Sudhāras Stavan Saṅgrah* the stavan include the poets' names in the final line, the bulk of the stavan I heard did not include them. Perhaps the singers have at some point dropped the last verse in their performances, but I think more likely the names are not being included in more contemporary compositions.

13. The many other poetic works in the Jain tradition include works based in all the rasas. The didactic nature of such works—showing how all these emotions are to bad effect—did not stop the writers from using the *rasas* well in evoking the mood they wished to reject. See especially the Tamil Cīvakacintāmaṇi, whose overbearing erotics are intended to disgust (Ryan 1985, 1998).

14. This general misunderstanding of Jain aesthetics is perhaps even more pronounced in the scholarly work on art history where Jain art is summarily dismissed

for being not Hindu and not Buddhist (Leoshko forthcoming). For example, see the works of Hutchinson and Vincent Smith; for more evenhanded Jain art treatments, see U. P. Shah 1955 and P. Pal 1994. Though there are several works on Jain literature they are mostly not available in the United States (or outside Gujarat) and are written in Gujarātī (which few of the Western scholars read). In these works, Muslim writers in Gujarātī are given an even worse treatment than the Jain writers, suggesting the need for a better basic work on Gujarātī Literature, one less tied, perhaps, to Hindu nationalist and romantic constructions of history.

15. As it is in Hindu traditions as well (see Slawek 1986; Thiel-Horstmann 1983b). The world as an ocean is an analogy shared by Hindus, Buddhists, and Jains.

16. The *ṛ* is pronounced *ru* in Gujarātī (and Marāṭhī) and not *ri* as in Hindī and Sanskrit. Thus *Kṛpālū* would be said *Krupālū* rather than *Kripālū*, and likewise *Amṛt* is pronounced *Amarut* rather than *Amrit.*

17. In a literal word order translation, the line reads: "My forgetfulness's forgetter," but I have rendered the line in a way much easier to pronounce, reflecting, I hope, the tumbling quality of the Gujarātī without creating a tongue twister.

18. Another name for the siddhacakra.

19. I did occasionally hear "rejected" stavan in the personal repertoires of the women.

20. By *phrasing*, I mean the relationship between melody and rhythm. Because the stavan came to the maṇḍaḷ orally, there was no music to refer to as an authority; the maṇḍaḷ determined the phrasing often quite differently from the way the stavan was introduced.

21. In dānḍiya rās the dancers form a circle with half the dancers facing clockwise and the other half counterclockwise. It is performed with an undulating stepping pattern which ultimately brings the dancers from one partner to the next in a circle, while the stick-clashing patterns involve a repeated—though changing—series of clashes with one's own sticks or one's partner's. Garbā is also danced in a circle, but one in which all face the same direction. The gestures are hand sweeps and sometimes fine gestures combined with clapping and snapping. The stepping moves the group again in an undulating pattern forward and back, either as a circle or in movements toward the circle center and back out. For example, the stavan "Jingle, Jangle" was sung to the same melody as the garbā, "Mar Diyā Jāy, Choḍ Diyā Jāy" and "Lord Mahāvīr" was sung to melody of the garbā, "Ghor Andhārī Re." Both of these (as well as others mentioned) are on a popular cassette "41 Nān-Stop Dhamāl Gujarātī Lokgīt." Other stavan melodies are shared with songs I found on "Taraṇe, Tarane Meḷe: Gujarātī Garba," "Ratī Cundalaḍī: Non-stop Garba," "Ambājīnā Meḷe" "Lumbe, Jhumbe: Rās-Garba," "Bamboo Beats: Garbā No Rang, Sājan ne Sang," and so forth.

22. Stevenson ([1915] 1970) gives an example of a man performing a Snātra Pūjā singing while accompanying himself on the harmonium, but I never saw or heard anyone speak of this kind of performance in a temple.

23. See Gordon Thompson's 1987 dissertation for the most thorough discussion of Gujarātī folk music available. This extremely popular music is still relatively unstudied.

24. There were five stavan sung to Hindi film song melodies, three to absolutely

ubiquitous film melodies: "Phulonsa Chehra"; "Ek, Do, Tin"; and "Mere Mankī Ganga." In one collection of men's maṇḍaḷ stavan, there were three stavan written to "Phulonsa Chehra." Likewise, Manuel (1993) writes of the wide variety of songs written to the tune of "Ek, Do, Tin."

25. However, the recitation cassettes—like those of the Bhaktāmara Stotra—were presented in a high-pitched light classical style with a strong drone played behind the singer, Anurādhā Pauḍvāl. On the whole, however, the classical aesthetic one finds in Puṣṭimarg havelī singing is not transmitted into the Jain context (Gaston 1997). Havelī sangīt relies on classical music knowledge and norms and trained professionals to the exclusion of the other devotees; the heavy instrumentation and use of specific classical rāgs require classical training, whereas the Jain singing is based on the Gujarātī folk music with which most Gujarātī Jains are familiar. The daily practice of devotional singing, during which many women spend hours perfecting their vocal techniques, is training, but I intend to say, rather, that one woman's training does not mean that the "untrained" are excluded from the performances. Though some Jain maṇḍaḷs have achieved semiprofessional status, Jain musicians at the temples need not be—as they must be in the Vallabhan temples (Gaston 1997)—professionals.

26. This kind of seated dance was universally identified as Jain by the Jains and Hindus I asked. It is performed at Jain pūjās in North America and the United Kingdom as well.

27. John Cort (personal communication) said that he saw men perform extended flywhisk (cāmar) dances (several minutes long) at the larger pūjās.

28. There are a few accounts of possession among Jains (Babb 1996; Humphrey and Laidlaw 1994), but these speak of possession in the context of worship of the Jina's guardian deities. The only first- or second-hand accounts of Jains in Pune getting possessed that I heard was of a woman who had, in 1998, begun to be possessed by the goddess Āmbajī during the Hindu Navrātrī festival. I intend to look further at this issue in future research.

CHAPTER 5

1. For example, this is seen in the Vaiṣṇav repetition of "Hare Kṛṣṇa, Hare Ram" and in the Śaivite "Śiv Śakti" (Alper 1989; Henry 1988). There are similarities to the nām smaraṇ when one enters or leaves a house, starts a letter, or begins a journey. Shivajinagar Jains use the Jinas' names (often Śankheśvar Pārśvanāth) and, occasionally, three repetitions of the Navkār Mantra. Although these are not specifically mantra recitation, they do express the efficacy of saying the name of God. Saying the name of a Jina (i.e., "Śrī Mahāvīray Namo") was a common mantra for recitation on a rosary as well.

2. In Khartar Gacch Jain practice, the worship of the Dādāgurus—magically charged male mendicant reformers—can be a source of prosperity, because they are not fully liberated beings. See Babb 1996, Humphrey and Laidlaw 1994, and Laidlaw 1995 for discussions of Dādāguru pūjā.

3. At one time I was told by a group of five Jain laywomen that pūjā was not very important. However, after some discussion I discovered that three of these women were raised as Sthānakavāsī Jains and one as a nonobservant Mūrtipūjak

Jain who had decided as an adult to study Jain philosophy at Poona University. The fifth woman told me privately that she went to the temple every day. Among some of the wealthier Pune Jains there was a move away from daily temple worship, which may result in a more abstract understanding of Jain religiosity, but even among the Sthānakavāsīs, rituals of recitation, confession, and stavan singing were still important.

4. Household pūjā does not include sandalwood pūjā, which is only offered to consecrated images—unless the house has a consecrated temple (ghar derāsar). If an image has had the eye opening (*anjan śalākā*) performed, it should be bathed daily (*nitya snān*).

5. Other household shrines more or less reflected this setup: usually a small metal Jina image at the center and a combination of silver coins with images and photos of images. Likewise, most Jain house shrines included guardian deity images connected with their lineage or important pilgrimage temples. Most also had images of deities who are understood to be not exclusively Jain such as Lakṣmī. Ranjana's shrine was obviously heavily worshipped—everything had a thick layer of sandalwood powder on it; the disorder reflected the number of people who used the tools of pūjā.

6. This was linked to the lamp offered in front of photos of recently deceased relatives (within a year usually) and the lamp some families left burning near their water pot at sundown.

7. This is quite different from the guru shrines at Khartar Gacch temples where they are worshipped for help in worldly affairs (Babb 1996; Laidlaw 1995). Also, Goḍījī Temple in Guruwar Peth has a small shrine to several Jain mendicants who were considered especially powerful, but the worship in that shrine is not intermingled with the worship of the Jinas in the way that Gautam Svāmī's worship is. One woman told me that the siddhacakra should not be worshipped until after all the Jinas are worshipped because the siddhacakra contains images of unliberated beings. To offer worship to unliberated beings before the Jinas who are liberated would be an act of disrespect. This same woman did not articulate any hierarchy between the Jinas and Gautam Svāmī, who is an enlightened and liberated being (siddha) but not a Jina.

8. Padmāvatī is a Jain goddess associated as the protectoress of Pārśvanāth. She is usually paired with Dharaṇendra, but as the canonical pairings of guardian deities are often broken in Pune District, she is paired at Ajitnāth Temple with Nākoḍā Bhairav, as she seems to be in the Dadabari Temple described by Humphrey and Laidlaw (1994). Likewise, Ajitnāth is theoretically paired with Mahayakda and Ajitabala. However, only in the neo-orthodox śāstrik temples is there a real attention to these pairings. Padmāvatī and Nākoḍā Bhairav are a popular pairing in contemporary worship and it is not surprising to see these two in a new temple together.

9. J. E. Cort (n.d. b) I owe the bulk of the information in this paragraph to his very important article.

10. The Rāyapaseṇī (Sanskrit Rājapraśnīya) and Nāyadhammakahāo (Sanskrit Jñātṛdharmkathāḥ) Suttas are two canonical sources with descriptions of image worship (mūrtipūjā) from at least the fifth century C.E.

11. Barz 1976 and Natavar (n.d.). For further discussion of Puṣṭimarg Vaiṣṇav

practices and beliefs, see also P. Bennett 1983, 1990; Gaston 1997; Redington 1983; and Toomey 1990.

12. Of course, this itself presents the problem of whether one can (or should) try to cool the image if the Jina is not present in the image. The question whether the image is inhabited is complicated by the "eye-opening" ceremony in the image installation ritual.

13. Bengali Vaiṣṇavism focuses on *Mādhurya bhāv* as the highest one while Puṣṭimārg tends toward *vātsalya-bhāv*.

14. For a specific discussion about this in the context of Śankheśvar Pārśvanāth, see Cort 1988.

15. Aside from the Kalpa Sūtra, which is recited and discussed every year during Paryuṣaṇ, I asked about the Yogaśāstra by Hemacandracarya. The response was recognition of the name of the famous Ācārya and usually the rejoinder that I really should talk to Jain mendicants about those books. Several women intimated that only through doing pūjā would I ever understand these texts—in effect saying that knowledge would come directly from practice. This view has been casually recorded by other scholars of Jainism. In fact, only one Jain mendicant spoke to me of these texts—Muni Harishbhadra Vijayji—and he suggested I look at more "useful" texts that were available at the Jain Pustak Bhaṇḍār.

16. In 1999, I was twice shown the new volume, *Daīnīṅg Tebal* (Dining Table) by Hemaratnavijay (the same mendicant who wrote the relatively common *Cālo Jinālaye Jaiye*) which outlines Jain dietary restrictions. However, it didn't seem that anyone yet knew what was in this volume.

17. Most of these teaching sessions came at the very beginning of my research time when I still was unfamiliar with the temple routine. The example given here occurred toward the end of my research time; thus my description and understanding of the rhetoric of pūjā were much more complex. Therefore, I use this as my example here. Because I could not recite the caityavandan by myself, I was not considered able to go to the temple by myself and was always sent with someone who knew the whole series, which facilitated my observation of different women performing their morning worship. In 1993–94, I went to morning worship more than two hundred times with seventeen different women: Ranjana, Lata, Kavita, Nita, Padma, Soni, Sveta, Maluben, Dadiji, Hema, Moni, Vimal, Aparna, Savita, Vanita, Sangita, and Varsha. In addition, I observed many women performing pūjā in the morning other than those with whom I had come to the temple. The caityavandan is printed in several stavan books and lay manuals and on a hard laminated board at the temple, but reading was slow and seen as somewhat inferior to having someone else recite the text for you. Before children can be sure to know the whole caityavandan prayers, they only perform darśan pūjā alone if there is no woman present to assist them.

18. Unfortunately I didn't think at the time to ask her about barās pūjā—when a sandal and camphor mixture is wiped all over the Jina with the right hand.

19. I could not hear her quick and indistinct recitation clearly over the temple din, but I suspect it was a prayer stating the "proper" meaning of the pūjā.

20. Jain temples share with Hindu temples this gender division regarding each image; the women should stand on the central image's left, the men on the right. In

the outer temple, men and women divide with the men in the front and the women behind them—incidentally, the same way a mosque is divided. I do not think this derives from any other tradition but simply develops in the environment of a culture where women are socially subordinate to men. Interestingly, in North America the "sides" of the temple are reversed, with women on the deities' right hand (though the left side of the room from the women's point of view) and men on the left in Jain temples, and in the few Hindu temples I have seen.

21. The snakes in Pārśvanāth's snake-hood are also worshipped with sandalwood paste but with the ring finger as the Jina is. Even though they are technically the heads of a guardian deity, they are treated as a limb of Pārśvanāth.

22. She brought the vial back home to her pregnant daughter.

23. The nandyāvart is a form of extended svastik considered one of the eight auspicious signs (aṣṭamaṅgalam) and is also the identifying marker of the eighteenth Jina, Aranāth. I suspect the knowledge of this symbol derives from the ubiquitous aṣṭamaṅgalam. I only once saw a separate image of Aranāth and it was in the Katraj temple, which has an image of each of the twenty-four Jinas of this era.

24. It is this understanding which makes hiring a maṇḍaḷ or having the pujārī perform a pūjā for you acceptable. However, as you will see in chapter 8, sponsorship is not without its internal challenges to its efficacy.

25. The further education of the boys—after they turn 12—is also not taken on by the men in the family. The boys would have to learn this from informal or formal pāṭhśāḷā. Only once did I see a man overtly instructing his children in the temple. A man brought his two grandchildren (by his daughter who was visiting him) into the temple and told them to get incense and come to the center image to make the offering. It was more like a reminder than real instruction but was, I suspect, part of his generally teaching about the temple when they came to visit him.

26. There were a few women in the Ajitnāth congregation—indicated by their presence at the annual rite of confession and expiation (Saṃvatsarī Pratikramaṇ) and the all-congregation dinner—who did not come to the Shivajinagar temple very often. I was not really able to observe their worship, which may have been performed at other temples or at home. Some of these women (like Pramila) reported to me that they performed pūjā every day in the temple near their homes, but I was not able to either join them or observe them at their morning worship. Reynell's survey in her 1985 thesis has the following statistics: of the sixty-three married women, fifty-eight went to the temple daily, and of the thirty-three unmarried women surveyed, twenty-three went to the temple daily. Reynell does not separate temple going into its various acts within the temple. I did find that young, unmarried women were much more likely to skip daily temple attendance or to abbreviate it. The observance by the married women may reflect the need for married women to have private time of their own as much as their identification of pūjā performance with being an adult woman.

27. I asked whether all the women followed this rule and they said, "yes." Although this is certainly not hard-and-fast truth—coming as it does from a third party—the women do know when the other women have stayed home with menses and when to expect to see them at the temple again. Although there seemed to be some embarrassment for young women who were new to experiencing their menses

and to the public nature of the menses restrictions, there was not the sense of shame associated with menses that I had expected. In an environment in which this is public knowledge, there was an earthy matter-of-factness that one does not find in the presumably uninhibited United States.

28. Humphrey and Laidlaw 1994 found a similar model, which they call the nesting model of pūjā. I found that while darśan includes aspects of agra and bhāv pūjā, it was not spoken of as the same as those; darśan was a separate category with shared actions in it.

29. The mendicants are not permitted to perform dravya pūjā (the material offerings to the Jina) and thus they offer only bhāv pūjā to the Jinas. Sthānakavāsī pūjā is exclusively bhāv pūjā and without even the Jina images to focus on visually. For a translation and description of the caityavandan in English, see Cort 1995d.

30. Reynell 1985a found this to be true among Jain laywomen in Jaipur as well.

31. The variation among the women's pūjās may stem partly from the fact that they learned to do pūjā in a wide range of towns, villages, and cities and have come to Pune through their marriages or the movements of their husband's families. Similarities may owe to the fact that the granddaughters learned much of their worship from the two older women.

32. The prayers Dadiji spoke were so quiet that standing next to her I could not hear them. There are many versions of what should be said at this time, but on the whole they are a set of prayers designed to focus the worshippers' minds on acceptable Jain understandings of their actions. This does not mean that there is a single acceptable understanding which the women should share, and I suspect that any number of Jain interpretations would be acceptable to even the most orthodox male mendicants. See Cort 1989 for an example of these prayers or Humphrey 1985 for an analysis of Jain pūjā according to these prayers. See also Humphrey and Laidlaw 1994 for a critique of the text-based model for understanding Jain pūjā.

33. Dadiji was renowned in Shivajinagar for knowing all the prayers; this was literally a daily event.

34. These are rosaries that most often have 108 beads. They are usually made of cloth or sandalwood, though I have seen silver māḷās in some of the more prosperous temples.

35. However, all the women I knew who were of that group still did work in the house when the work load was especially heavy; at the same time husbands who had retreated from worldly obligation were much more apt to have taken a formal and therefore lifelong vow.

36. The equivalent of writing down the entire order of the mass, which observant Catholics or those at Catholic schools sometimes do.

37. John Cort said that he was told that touching the goddess beneath her waist is an act unacceptable because of its associations with sexuality and fertility; it may be especially unacceptable for Soni as an unmarried young woman who should not be participating in sexuality and its rhetoric yet. He saw this as the reason for the skirt on the goddesses. This fits with the general practices I saw as well. I noticed that the woman's intervention did not stop Soni from doing this during pūjā to Padmāvatī on future days.

38. In the earlier example of teaching pūjā, Maluben obliquely critiqued others'

pūjā practices but did so only in the context of explaining to me how to perform pūjā—correcting someone else's "mistake" for my education. However, even Maluben would not have directly criticized someone's daily pūjā. This is quite different from formal pūjās where Maluben saw herself as responsible for the propriety of the maṇḍaḷ pūjās.

39. "Middle-aged women" includes women who in the United States are not yet considered middle aged. It starts at about 30 and seems to continue until the first son is married or the first daughter has a child (based on my casual observations).

40. Sometimes the visit would be quite short—especially for school-age kids and young men—but its "dailiness" never faltered.

41. Although there were women who did gossip (spoke negatively about others for no apparent reason), most speech about others was tied to information that either made women's lives easier—planning involves others—or strengthened ties between the women and the person discussed.

42. In a concerted effort to minimize the sense of obligation, I rarely asked anyone to take me to or show me anything in particular. Instead, I allowed myself to be taken, educated, and generally controlled by the intentions and suggestions of the women themselves.

43. For other descriptions of Jain temple worship, see Babb 1996; Cort 1989, 1994; Humphrey and Laidlaw 1994; and Laidlaw 1995.

44. I hope to examine this question about the interpretation of brahmacarya vows in the context of pūjā in future work. I include this here—despite its incomplete discussion—because it is evidence of the link between devotion and vow taking and of the rationale behind differences in some women's daily worship.

45. There is also a division in the worship of Bhairav and Padmāvatī based on ethnicity. Mārvāḍīs performed most of the daily worship of Bhairav and won most of the bids in auctions associated with Bhairav, while Padmāvatī's worship was dominated by Gujarātīs. This is still anecdotal, but I will be pursuing this line of research in the future.

46. Here I am specifically playing off Humphrey and Laidlaw's use of the phrase "getting it right" (Humphrey and Laidlaw 1994).

47. One exception I noticed was that whereas many people left their shoes at the base of Śatruñjay hill—suggesting that the whole hill is a temple—most did not change to pūjā clothes until they were at the top of the hill, where they took their bath and changed.

48. I question the caption under a photo—showing men in kūrta-pajāmā eating—in Carrithers and Humphrey (1991, 90), which states, "Śvetāmbar Jain businessmen wear ritually pure clothing to eat restricted food during a fast, Jaipur 1983." In Pune, both in normative sources and actual practice, eating is in a direct conflict with notions of ritual purity. It could be different in Jaipur where I did only the briefest survey, but the restriction is so prevalent everywhere I went that I doubt it. It is possible that the men had never eaten in these clothes before and had just done pūjā in them—though again, it is not common for men to do pūjā in clothing other than dhotī-khes—and then sat down to eat; however, the moment they sipped their water, the clothing would have no longer been acceptable for pūjā.

49. All of them were quite careful not to bring the vegetable bag into the tem-

ple. Partly, I believe, as a sign of the abandonment of worldly thoughts and partly from the belief that any food that comes into the Jina's line of sight is considered dev-dravya and is not acceptable for Jains to eat.

50. Mekhala Natavar (personal communication).

51. Caṇiyā-colī is a Gujarātī outfit that consists of skirt (sometimes called by the Rājasthānī term *ghāgharo* when separate from its blouse and *oḍhaṇī*) and blouse with an oḍhaṇī (a half sari worn on the upper body). When Mārvāḍī women adopted dress that marked them as ethnically distinct—for example, at weddings and religious functions—they wore ghāgharo-oḍhanī. In addition to the taxonomical differences, there were differences in the materials used: the caṇiyā-colī usually features intricate dye-work and mirror-work embroidery, while the ghāgharo-oḍhanī features intricate embroidery on very light fabric. Wearing a sari "Gujarātī" style—which, incidentally, even Mārvāḍī women I knew called it—indicated that the *pallav* (the designed end) was displayed in the front. This is as opposed to "Bombay" style, where the pallav hangs down the back over the left shoulder, and "Mahārāṣṭri" style with the nine-yard sari worn in part like a dhotī (which I never saw any Jain woman wear). Both wearing the caṇiyā-colī and wearing the sari Gujarātī style were identified as expressions of Gujarātī (sometimes equated with Jain) ethnic identity, but the divisions of who wore which were usually based on the age and marital status of the wearer. For example, though several of the young married women usually wore their saris Bombay style, they would switch to Gujarātī style for maṇḍaḷ performances, family events, and when I wanted to take a formal family picture. Likewise, the caṇiyā-colī was the preferred "dress-up" clothing for girls who were often seen in *salwār-kamīz* (in Pune commonly called *Pañjābī sūṭ* / Panjābī suit) on regular days.

52. Although a few women seemed concerned about the use of silk for pūjā clothes because of the violence inherent in its production, most women seemed more concerned with its ostentatiousness. Of course, silk is understood in a pan-Indic way to be resistant to pollution making it a preferred fiber for pūjā clothing generally. This is similar to the Hindu understanding of dedicating one's goods to god, and it is also in line with the Jain understanding that a certain amount of one's property should be used for religious purposes. Though it is a subtle distinction between goods offered in the temple—which Jains cannot use—and the use of pūjā clothes first for pūjā, the practice is not inherently contradictory: Pūjā clothes are not intended to be used for the benefit of the temple, nor are they themselves given up—only the attachment to them is given up. A notable exception was a sari purchased for a wedding when the sari was worn first to the wedding; however, the bride usually would be doing pūjā before the wedding, so in her case it may still be seen as first offered for pūjā.

53. In 1994 Nita won second place, I was proudly told on the phone after I returned to the United States.

54. Because most of the women saw performing stavan for me (to put on my tapes or in my book) as the glorification of the Jinas and their teachings, and because they had a genuine interest in helping me with my project, stavan singing often happened in contexts in which it might not otherwise have been performed—while having tea, while ironing (though they would stop the actual ironing for

singing), and with everyone sitting around watching the "interview." However, in these cases the women would do, as Savita did, as much as they could to make it "religious" (dharmik).

55. While many Jains have certain images for which they have special devotion—such as Śankheśvar Pārśvanāth—I was surprised at the number of women who had favorite Jinas. Jinas themselves are theoretically interchangeable, but in stavan choice women show definite preferences for stavan addressing a particular Jina. For example, Nita's repertoire was dominated by Mahāvīr stavan. This question of Jina-specific devotion needs further attention.

56. This stavan is called "Sri Śankheśvar Pārśvanāth Stavan" in the *Śrī Sudhāras Stavan Sangrah*. Because of the large numbers of stavan that address Śankheśvar Pārśvanāth, women sometimes called it by its first line, "Antarjāmī suṇ alavesar." All Śvetāmbar Mūrtipūjak Jains share a regard for the Ādināth image at Pālītāṇā, but Śankheśvar Pārśvanāth is seen as a sort of patron Jina for Gujarātī Jains, especially for those whose families originated, as Ranjana's did, in the same region (Mahesāṇā) within Gujarat as Śankheśvar.

CHAPTER 6

1. Babb 1996 writes that the Pañcakalyāṇak Pūjā was performed in Jaipur to celebrate the birthdate of Pārśvanāth. He gives an excellent description and analysis of the pūjā there.

2. During my twelve months of fieldwork in 1993–94, I attended twenty-two formal pūjās performed by the Śrī Pārśva Mahilā Maṇḍaḷ of Shivajinagar. I saw the maṇḍaḷ perform eight independent Snātra, six Pañcakalyāṇak, one Navāṇuṅ Prakārī, four Antarāyakarm Nivāraṇanī, and three Vāstuk Pūjās. In addition, I saw the Kacchī Mahilā Maṇḍaḷ perform two Snātra and one Pañcakalyāṇak Pūjā. I regularly (two to three times weekly) watched groups of women perform the Snātra Pūjā as part of their morning worship at Ajitnāth Temple. I also observed the Navpadjī Pūjā being performed by a group of older women at the conclusion of the Āyambil Oḷi fast. In the summer of 1997, I attended an additional two Snātra Pūjās and one Pañcakalyāṇak Pūjā performed by the Śrī Pārśvanāth Mahila Maṇḍaḷ, and in January 1999, I attended two Snātra Pūjās performed by the Śrī Pārśvanāth Mahila Maṇḍaḷ and a Siddhacakra Mahāpūjā. In the summer of 2000, I attended three Snātra Pūjās performed by the Śrī Pārśvanāth Mahila Maṇḍaḷ and two Snātra Pūjās performed by groups with the help of Maluben and Ranjana.

3. John Cort (personal communication) suspects that these texts were written specifically to prevent the hiring of Hindu specialists, especially for pūjās such as the Vāstuk Pūjā. These texts followed much of the aesthetics and format of Gujarātī rāso literature. For more, see Kelting 1996.

4. The Jain bookstore in Pune was just outside the main Śvetāmbar temple complex, and although there was a Digambar temple in the neighborhood, the books in this store were decidedly Śvetāmbar. The presence of a large Tapā Gacch mendicants' hostel and the predominance of this gacch in this neighborhood and in Pune in general was reflected in the bookstore's collection. In 1998, a new Jain bookstore opened in the same neighborhood.

5. Babb 1996 refers to the Khartar Gacch version written by Śrī Devcandjī in a

text called, *Śrī Devcandjī Kī Vidhi Sahit Snātra Pūjā* (Ajmer: Cāndmal Sipāṇī, 1979), and Cort refers to the *Vividh Pūjā Saṅgrah* as the one used in his studies with primarily Tapā Gacch Jains in Gujarat with whom he did his research.

6. I only heard once about any of these pūjās happening in Pune (though I'm sure there were others): one Śanti Snātra at Goḍijī in 1994. These pūjās were not generally performed by the members of the congregation or by others in Pune, or I suspect that it would have been more common for them to be pointed out to me. The one Śanti Snātra was performed by a men's maṇḍaḷ and only a few women attended.

7. The maṇḍaḷ women often used the money they received from maṇḍaḷ performances to buy the coconut and to pay Arun for solo Snātra Pūjās on another day.

8. Stevenson describes the Snātra Pūjā being performed in the early part of the 20th century at Śatruñjay by a layman without a maṇḍaḷ: "The present writer saw a man at Satrunjaya perform the cheapest service—the Sanatana pūjā—for which privilege he had paid only two annas, though at Abu he would have paid at least five-and-a-quarter. After bathing and donning the two cloths, he marked the idol in fourteen places and filled up time by playing on a harmonium. He then took in one hand a tray containing roses, almonds, rice, saffron, and sugar, and in the other a jug containing water and milk, and round the jug and round his wrist he tied a red thread. After performing Dipa pūjā and Aksata pūjā, he did what is called Camari pūjā (i.e., he gently waved a brush of cow's hair in front of the shrine, while the paid officiente was decking the big idol in its jewelry.) He then placed a little image of a Tirthankara in front of the larger image in the inner shrine and bathed it and marked it with the auspicious marks. It was interesting to notice that while doing this, he kept showing the little idol its own reflection in a pocket looking glass, as a thoughtful ladies' maid might have done to her mistress as she assisted at her toilette; he completed his service by offering the articles on the tray to the Tirthankara" (Stevenson [1915] 1970, 252–53).

9. John Cort (personal communication) encountered these Snātra Pūjā Maṇḍaḷs in Ahmedabad in the fall of 1995 as well as singing maṇḍaḷs and Bhaktāmar Stotra recitation maṇḍaḷs. There were groups of women who performed the Navpadjī pūjā at the conclusion of the Āyambil Oḷi fast, and during other fasts there were groups of fasters who performed the requisite pūjās together. However, the Snātra was the only pūjā they performed daily. They were not formal or organized maṇḍaḷs like the Pārśva Maṇḍaḷ. At Ajitnāth Temple, the only group that called itself a maṇḍaḷ was the Śrī Pārśva Mahilā Maṇḍaḷ, which focused on singing stavan and performing formal pūjās.

10. Tambiah 1970 speaks of the extension of ritual efficacy in Thai Buddhist rituals as well, and Jamison 1996 describes the role of "taking hold of from behind," a kind of touch efficacy, in her analysis of Vedic ritual suggesting a possible shared origin for these variations of the extension of ritual efficacy through touch.

11. Maluben based her setup instructions on a pamphlet, *Vividh Mahāpūjan Tathā Pūjā Upayogī Sāmagrīnuṅ Līsṭ*, her brother had given her.

12. In the summer of 1997, I sponsored a second Snātra Pūjā to double-check my description and to see whether there had been any change in performance over the intervening three years. There had been no significant change in the performance:

The same pūjā gestures, melodies, stavan, and dance gestures were performed in the same order. During the preparation time of most pūjās, I was setting up my equipment for recording and also observing the maṇḍaḷ women's activities. My attempts to observe closely the setup and close-down of other pūjās was somewhat discouraged by Maluben—I believe because my endless questions and photos inevitably slowed down the process—although I was able to record them on several occasions.

13. However, John Cort (personal communication) tells me that it was common in Pātaṇ for men to bid for the monthly Snātra Pūjā and then perform it with their wives. These new moon Snātra Pūjās were not performed with a maṇḍaḷ as they were in Pune. I sponsored this pūjā toward the end of my research period when I had already observed twenty Snātra pūjās performed by the Pārśva Maṇḍaḷ and three by the Kacchi Maṇḍaḷ. At this time I was fairly confident about what happened when and I knew the sections of the text and stavan. During the pūjā I had to translate Maluben's instruction to my husband, who did not understand her blend of Gujarātī, Marāṭhī, and Hindī; Sheelu took pictures of the pūjā for us. It was interesting to see how she chose to photograph what were for her the salient features needing to be recorded. Because of my studies and the fact that the pūjā was toward the end of the year, I was relatively well versed in both the ritual and liturgy of pūjā—perhaps even more so than some of the pūjā sponsors during the year.

14. Steve did not own his own Jain pūjā clothes (dhotī-khes) and had never put one on before. Most men did not perform the entire pūjā and thus did not change into pūjā clothes just to perform the Āratī, Maṅgaḷ Dīvo, and Śantī Kalaś. However, if they were performing the whole pūjā they would have their own pūjā clothes and most likely would not need help putting them on.

15. In the Jain context, this includes ghee, yoghurt, milk, sugar, and either boiled and filtered water or clove.

16. Each verse of this section is different and the chorus line changes from "Keep this flower, O Ādināth, Bliss of the Jinas" to address Śantināth, Nemināth, Pārśvanāth, Mahāvīr, all twenty-four Jinas of this era as a group, and all Jinas of all eras as a group.

17. The couplets I heard women recite were the same as those printed in the *Laghu Pūjā Saṅgrah.*

18. In each subsequent verse, the names of each of the sponsors are substituted where "the whole congregation" appears in this line.

19. In this line, the names of all maṇḍaḷ women present are substituted where "the Pārśva Maṇḍaḷ" appears. The last verse often substitutes "My sisters" for "Pārśva Maṇḍaḷ."

20. After the silver foil is applied, like any other decoration, sandalwood pūjā is not performed; only vāskep or agra pūjā can be performed atop the decoration.

21. My translation was made from recordings of women singing. Their version seems to ultimately come from the *Śrī Sudhāras Stavan Saṅgrah.* The version quoted in the pūjā instruction manual was slightly different and was not the one sung. The same holds true for the Maṅgaḷ Dīvo song. The versions here are the ones I have heard at all the temples and homes I've seen in India and the United States. Although I have heard variations in the melodies, the words have been the same.

22. The verb *khelvuṅ* (to play) was often used to mean "to dance rās-garbā."

23. John Cort (personal communication) observed that women often brought the kalaś home on their heads and placed it in the family shrine—especially if they wanted children. Though I only saw this once—after the close of the 1999 Siddhacakra Mahāpūjā—it may be that on previous occasions when a pūjā was performed in someone's house, they left the kalaś in their shrine for a time before returning it to the temple.

24. This Snātra Pūjā as an actual performance is not very different from the actions performed in a Khartar Gacch Snātra Pūjā as described by Babb 1996, even though the text is different.

25. Kesarīyā is the name of the Ādināth image at the temple and the religious name of that temple's town, formerly called Rishabhdeo. I was told the following story as an origin for this temple. It derives from a story in which a man who wanted a child offered to give the child's weight in saffron to the temple.

26. Dādā usually refers to the Ādināth image at Śatruñjay and sometimes to the Dādāgurus and thus seems slightly out of place in this stavan, which frames the whole stavan in a Pārśvanāth temple. However, Dādā can refer to other Jinas generically as it does in this song, but that is somewhat unusual.

27. This stavan was sung in other pūjās as well—as a critique—but was not generally set in the more permanent repertoire for those pūjās.

28. Daily pūjā performance and other markers of regular practice were valued highly by the rather religious maṇḍaḷ women; temple going seems to be less central in Jain religious identity among men, especially those of the highest economic class (Babb 1996; Cort 1989; Laidlaw 1995). Reynell 1985a found that regular temple going was a part of laywomen's practice in Jaipur as well. However, irregular pūjā performance as a locus for criticism only came up in conjunction with other critiques, such as the seeming priority of social prestige over religious devotion here.

CHAPTER 7

1. The dominance of women in Jain ritual life is widely reported. See Babb 1996, Cort 1989, Humphrey and Laidlaw 1994, Laidlaw 1995, Reynell 1985a, 1991, and so forth.

2. They used here the word *jñān*. Though my presence as a scholar of religion clearly may have influenced how they selected their vocabulary, these same women were influential and powerful in the maṇḍaḷ.

3. In 1994 this school was directed by Harishbhadra Vijay, who showed me a weekly exam that involved writing, from memory, ten to twelve pages of prayers in Prakrit and Sanskrit.

4. The presence of Steve for the first half of the program did not seem to affect the performance or speeches that were all chosen, practiced, and/or written in advance. He was not introduced, sat in the back and, after a few minutes of giggling by the young women sitting near him in the back, seemingly ignored; moreover, I was not made aware when he left after an hour or so.

5. At Paryuṣaṇ, the unmarried young women prepared Gujarātī folk dances for themselves and the younger girls to perform at the Paryuṣaṇ program in the temple

and the fast-breaking ceremonies, but it is for the Mahāvīr Nirvāṇ Program that more explicit rhetoric of Jain orthopraxy was integrated into the dance and drama performances.

6. Religious membership in the congregation is marked primarily by participation in the congregational confession on Samvatsarī and secondarily by attendance at the temple installation anniversary and its subsequent feast.

7. This is reminiscent of the importance of recitations for the preservation of the Jain texts. See Dundas 1992.

8. She was unusually meticulous in all religious activities. Maluben's expertise in ritual activities was highlighted by her confident ability to instruct others in how to perform a pūjā.

9. Thanks to David Knipe for pointing out this difference. The only exception to this is the *cīnk vidhi* (the sneeze ritual), which is performed if someone sneezes during the performance of a ritual confession and expiation of sins.

10. The annual contest was already several years old by 1994 and was increasing in popularity, although it has not been held since Paryuṣaṇ 1997.

11. I was unable to get more details about the judges at the time because I left the country that week, and when I asked in letters no one seemed to be able to remember who the men were. This suggests to me that they were in fact an ad hoc rather than a standing "standards" committee.

12. On the Mahārāṣṭrian New Year, there was a Snātra Pūjā and many people festooned the assembly hall stand with strings of shell and star-shaped pressed sugar cakes.

13. It was similar to the way a young woman of marriageable age was dressed up when a family was coming to meet her during the search for suitable marriage partners for her or frankly whenever those potential families might be present. She would never be expected (by either family) to wear merely her own clothing and jewelry.

14. They received third place again in 1995.

15. Because of the economic class and households of many of the women in the maṇḍaḷ and the fact that several maṇḍaḷ members had to come to the maṇḍaḷ events by rickshas, lateness and leaving early were common issues and ones I doubt they can resolve.

16. There was a performance of stavan by a solo singer with harmonium and dhoḷak as part of the All Pune Jain Maṇḍaḷs Makar Sankranti Program discussed in chapter 3.

17. There is a shorter, less expensive, and simpler worship of the siddhacakra attached to the Āyambil Oḷī fast called the Navpad Oḷī Pūjā, which does not require a mendicant's presence. Both of these arise out of the narratives of Mayṇāsundarī and Śripāl discussed in chapter 2.

18. I was not present at the men's confession but I was made to understand that it was similarly performed. Accounts by other scholars of the annual rite of confession do mention the auctions for the recitations—much like the women's auctions—and do not suggest that these are highly contested auctions either. For excellent descriptions of this ritual, see Banks 1992, Cort 1989, Folkert 1993, and Laidlaw 1995.

19. I regret that I was not able to record any of these bidding songs because I too was unprepared for the auction.

CHAPTER 8

1. Here I am translating "*Ātmā Paramātmā*," which clearly harkens to Hindu imagery of the relations of souls returning to a single soul. This is not really in line with Jain thinking about the nature of souls—where each soul (jīv) is individual and upon liberation they rise to (but do not dissolve into) the region of liberated souls (siddhalok) (Dundas 1992). In the description of the kinds of souls—outer, inner, and supreme (*parama*)—given to Humphrey and Laidlaw by a Khartar Gacch female mendicant, the supreme soul is—rather than a combination of all souls—the purified and perfect essence of one's soul having removed all its karma (Humphrey and Laidlaw 1994).

2. I also observed Pañcakalyāṇak Pūjās performed for an important birthday, when a new bride entered a family, and as an upscale observance of the monthly celebration (parv), which was usually marked by a Snātra Pūjā, especially if the Snātra Pūjā was being performed by someone else in the morning. There are other pūjās which are "required" in certain contexts: Snātra Pūjā on new moon days, New Year's days (four were observed while I was in Pune), and other auspicious days, especially those associated with Mahāvīr; Vāstuk Pūjā when one moves into a new house; and the Antarāyakarm Nivāraṇanī Pūjā when one has acquired *antarāya karm* (e.g., after a death in family, or a birth, or if a women has accidentally broken a menses restriction) in order to cleanse oneself karmically. Relatively few of these non-temple-going Jains would tend to sponsor a Snātra Pūjā, yet virtually all families sponsored a Vāstuk Pūjā when they moved to a new home. It blesses the house with peace (śānt) and allows the family to throw a party after the maṇḍaḷ performs the pūjā. There was often Gujarātī folk dancing and the pūjā was followed by tea with fancy snacks and sweets for the maṇḍaḷ, the family, and any friends who may have been invited to the pūjā. However it is a semiprivate ritual, unlike a Pañcakalyāṇak Pūjā in the temple which is posted on the blackboard and open to the public. At the Vāstuk Pūjā the gifts after the pūjā were usually a bit fancier than the 1 rupee and a *mosambī* or *potāsa* usually given at the temple pūjās; at various Vāstuk Pūjās, I received small, shaped plates, a bag to bring to the temple, and sets of 11 and 21 rupees.

3. A Pañcakalyāṇak Pūjā is a relatively expensive affair (especially as a large temple pūjā).

4. Laidlaw 1995 provides an excellent and extensive study of the tensions between Jain religious values (especially renunciation) and the lifestyle of the wealthy Jains with whom he worked.

5. I am indebted to John Cort for pointing out this parallel.

6. Babb 1996 discusses Khartar Gacch pūjā in Jaipur and Amdāvād in light of these similar questions of pūjā hierarchy, though Babb's research points to a clearer distinction between "doers" and "audience," a universal distinction not reflected in my research in Pune.

7. There were acceptable breaks within a pūjā (between the major sections) while the lead singer would suggest the next stavan as Maluben would prepare the next

offering and brief the sponsor on the next section. But it must be understood that these breaks were only minor punctuation in an event that more often than not proceeded with a sort of breakneck inevitability. Long or frequent pauses in the process were unusual.

8. These categories existed as early as the Ācārāṅga Sūtra 1.1.1.5 where they are used to point out three ways of accruing sin (pāp) rather than as levels of merit. The sense of hierarchy between them comes from my observation. Cort (1989) also notes the use of these categories for types of meritorious acts.

9. For this role as ritual specialist, they used the verb "to speak" (*bolvuṇ*) rather than "to have done" (*karāvuṅ*). The latter was used when the women had the pujārī perform a Snātra Pūjā (without a maṇḍaḷ) for them on special personal occasions or to describe the request that someone do pūjā for them in a pilgrimage spot. (In this case the Gujarātī post-position *vatī* was added to their names to indicate something being done for their sake.)

10. There is debate over when this text was written and who wrote it, but, according to Paul Dundas (personal communication), it cannot postdate the 5th century which certainly qualifies this as an early text.

11. For examples of this approach, see Banks 1992; Cort 1989; Humphrey and Laidlaw 1994; and Reynell 1985, 1991.

12. Chapter 1 briefly addresses the question of Mārvāḍī and Gujarātī antagonism and regional identities in group formation, and in the case of this Vāstuk Pūjā, this conflict may well inform the level of vocality and the strength of the criticisms. However, there were Mārvāḍī women maṇḍaḷ members present at this pūjā who also expressed their concerns about the pūjā.

13. The dedicated clothing should include not just sari and blouse but also the petticoat and underwear to which Pramila was euphemistically referring.

14. Namo'rhat Sūtra: "Namo'rhat Siddhācāryopādhyāyasarvasādhubhyaḥ" a condensed version of the Navkār Mantra.

15. pañcaṇg pranīpat: the posture of five limbs (two palms, two knees, and forehead) on the ground, a gesture of great respect reserved for Jina images and Jain mendicants.

16. nāma, sthāpanā, dravya, and bhāva are themselves the four nikṣepas and as such are categories available for application to various discussions. See Dundas 1992. Williams dates this text in the eleventh century.

17. For this reason, it was difficult for many of the women to believe that I would be able to perform Jain pūjā and not consider myself Jain. Most said that I was somehow Jain without knowing it.

Glossary

abhiṣek bathing of an image, usually with water or pañcamṛt

ācārya religious leader

Ādināth the first Jina of this era

agra pūjā literally, "in front of" worship, performed in front of an image or outside the inner sanctum, as compared to ang pūjā, which is performed on the image directly

Ajitnāth the second Jina of this era and the central Jina honored in the Ajitnāth Temple

akṣat "unbroken," rice offering in the context of Jain pūjā

ang pūjā "limb worship" referring to the part of the eightfold pūjā that is done directly on the image: bathing, barās, sandalwood, flowers

angī a decoration of the Jina or other image in temple

Antarāyakarm Nivāraṇanī Pūjā "obstacle karma removal pūjā" and its liturgy; performed to remove the specific karma that prevents one from worshiping correctly; often performed in the name of a deceased relative

anumodan appreciation of the good acts of others, which is a source of merit

aparigrah "nonattachment," referring to the vow of nonpossession and the ideal of nonattachment

āratī the offering of a ghee lamp in a clockwise direction, often marking the end of a ritual; sometimes, the lamp or the song accompanying the ritual

arhat Jina

aśātnā a fault, an act disrespectful to the Jain religion

aṣṭaprakārī eightfold worship; more specifically the eight offerings of water, sandalwood, flowers, incense, lamp, rice, fruit, and sweets

āvaśyaka originally, the six daily obligations of a Jain mendicant; later lay versions have also been also created

āyambil bland food associated with the Oḷī fast

barās mixture of watery sandalwood paste and camphor used in ang pūjā

Bhagavān God

Bhairav a guardian deity said to protect Jain temples and Jains

bhakti devotion

bhaṇḍār treasury; storehouse; bookstore

bhāv sentiment; mental intention

bhāv pūjā worship done through meditation on and recitation of praises to the Jinas; includes the daily caityavandan, sāmāyik, and stavan singing

bhojanśāḷā eating hall, often serving special foods during fasts

bolī the practice of auctioning off the privilege to perform certain parts of a Jain ritual; the auction itself

brahmacarya a complex celibacy vow including the restrictions against any interaction with the opposite sex and the use of cosmetics

caityavandan a series of prayers recited as part of the full daily pūjā; also, short prayer always included within the daily prayer series

cakravartin universal emperor

cāmar flywhisk made of cow tail hair or of silk and/or wool

caṇiyā-colī a skirt and blouse combination considered traditional to Gujarat and always worn with the oḍhaṇī—a half-sari worn over the skirt and blouse—in a style similar to the Gujarātī-style sari

cāturmās/comāsu the four-month long rainy season during which the mendicants remain in one area and the laity observe more food restrictions

caturvidh saṇgh the fourfold community of male mendicants, female mendicants, laymen, and laywomen

caturviṃśati-stava a prayer listing the names of the twenty-four Jinas; its recitation is one of the daily obligations

Dādāguru any of the four venerated (and miraculous) male mendicants from the Khartar Gacch lineage

Dādāvāḍī "house of Dādā," a shrine to the Dādāgurus, also Dādābāḍī, "garden of the dādā"

dān donation or charity to acceptable recipients (e.g., temples, Jain books, Jain mendicants, and, least meritoriously, Jain laity)

dānḍiya rās a Gujarātī folk dance with short sticks, which may have had its origins in the goddess festival of Navrātrī; now danced at weddings and holidays; very popular also among Maharashtrians during Navrātrī

darśan seeing a Jina, god or goddess, but in a mutual way that blesses the human seer

derāsar "Jain temple" in Gujarātī and Mārvāḍī (mandir in Hindī or Marāṭhī)

dev god

devī goddess

devvandan a prayer and song series based on the caityavandan; recited three times yearly

dharm religion or duty

dharmśāḷā a hostel for pilgrims

dhotī-khes a pair of white cloths worn by Jain men for pūjā

dhūp incense; one of the eightfold offerings

Digambar "skyclad"; one of the sects of Jainism, popular primarily in the South and parts of Rajasthan; though very important in many parts of Maharashtra, these Jains are the smallest group in Pune

dīkṣā the rite of initiation that changes a Jain layperson into a mendicant

dīkṣārthī one who has the intention of taking dīkṣā; a mendicant-to-be

dīpak ghee-lamp offering

Divālī festival of lights celebrated by both Jains and Hindus, which focuses on the worship of Lakṣmī, the goddess of prosperity; also the New Year in much of western India; for Jains the time of Mahāvīr's attainment of mokṣa

dravya material; pertaining to material offerings made to the Jinas

dravya pūjā worship using material objects, as opposed to bhāv pūjā or mental worship

gacch a school of Jain mendicants; a further subdivision within Jainism of mendicants and their followers; in Pune, as in Jainism as a whole, the largest was the Tapā Gacch, though there were also Khartar Gacch Jains in Pune's Śvetāmbar Mūrtipūjāk community

garbā a Gujarātī women's folk dance, probably with its origins in the goddess festival of Navrātrī; the name refers to the lamp-pot with which the women dance

Gautam Svāmī the most important disciple of Mahāvīr, venerated in Jain temples alongside the Jinas

gīt "song," especially welcome songs (svāgatam gīt) or fasting songs (tapasya gīt)

guṇasthān one of the fourteen stages of spiritual development

guru teacher or specific mendicant to whom one may have a special attachment; generically, any mendicant leader

guruvandan a short prayer spoken to a Jain mendicant, which includes questions about the mendicant's needs, praise, and a request for forgiveness of sins

Indra/Indrāṇi the king and queen of the gods, paradigmatic Jain devotees

jal "water," usually referring to water used to bathe an image

jap repetition of prayers, mantras, or the name of god usually counted on a rosary or hands

Jina "victor"; one of the omniscient teachers of who revitalizes the Jain religion; there have been twenty-four Jinas in the present era, and there will be a future cycle of twenty-four when the next era of time begins

jñān "knowledge"; usually religious knowledge

kalaś water pot used in the bathing of images

karma "action"; in the Jain context, the material substance that adheres to one's soul and prevents it from rising to the abode of the liberated; specific forms of karma determine the future destiny of a soul

Kārtak Pūṇam the last day of comāsu and the day Jain mendicants resume their wandering after the rainy season retreat; also the day on which Jain pilgrimage resumes after the ban during the rainy season

kesar "saffron"; sometimes refers to mixture of saffron, sandalwood, camphor, and water used to anoint the mūrtis in a Jain temple

Khartar Gacch a lineage of Jain mendicants popular in Rajasthan, marked by female mendicants giving sermons and by the worship of the Dādāgurus

Laghu Pūjā Saṅgrah a popular book with the text of several pūjās

mahāpūjā great worship ceremonies; formal pūjās understood to require a sādhu's presence

mahārāj honorific title added to the name of the lead mendicant in a group traveling together; the feminine form mahārāṇī is not used; female leaders are called sādhvī mahārāj

Mahāvideh a different continent on which there is presently a Jina (Simandhar Svāmī) preaching, and therefore a place from which mokṣa is possible in this era

Mahāvīr the twenty-fourth and last Jina of this era and continent

Mahilā woman

mālā garland or rosary

Mallināth the nineteenth Jina; for Śvetāmbars, a woman

maṇḍaḷ "circle"—a group which meets for a religious practice; in Pune, usually a singing group

mandir "temple"; sometimes used in Hindi or Marāṭhī for Jain temple

maṅgaḷ dīvo a type of lamp; an offering at the close of a pūjā which removes any possible negative karma from religious rituals

mantra formulaic short prayer for recitation

mārg path

Mārvāḍī people or things from the region Mārvāḍ (Marwar) in southern Rajasthan; a major ethnic group within the Jain community

mokṣa "liberation"; release from the cycle of rebirth

Mumbaī Bombay

mūrti "image"; particularly installed sculptural images in temples

Mūrtipūjāk those who do worship to images, a major sect within Śvetāmbar Jainism; the two others are Sthānakavāsī and Terapanthī, neither of which accept image worship

naivedya sweetmeats in the context of Jain pūjā

nandyāvart a complex Jain svastik with nine corners in each arm

Navāṇuṅ Prakārī Pūjā the "ninety-nine offering" pūjā liturgy associated with the first Jina, Adināth, and particularly with his image at the pilgrimage site, Śatruñjay

Navkār Mantra the basic Jain mantra recited as part of all rituals; it honors the five worshipful beings: the Jinas, liberated ones, mendicant teachers, mendicant leaders, and all mendicants

Navrātrī the "nine nights" of the goddess, a Hindu festival honoring nine manifestations of the goddess

Nemināth the twenty-second Jina of this era

ṇisīhi "it is abandoned"; a formula recited upon entering a Jain temple or the inner sanctum before performing pūjā

Oḷī "line"; a nine-day Jain festival (probably created to match Navrātrī) during which there is emphasis on fasting for saubhāgya and worship of the nine worshipful things represented on a siddhacakra

paccakkhān "intention"; public statement of the intention to fast

Pañcakalyāṇak Pūjā the "five auspicious moments" pūjā and its liturgy dedicated to Pārśvanāth; the five auspicious moments present in the life of every Jina are conception, birth, dīkṣā, omniscience, and liberation

pañcamṛt "five nectars," usually consisting of raw milk, ghee, yoghurt, sugar, and water that has been purified by boiling or other means usually adding a clove, and that is used for bathing the Jina images

pāp "sin"; actions that lead to the accumulation of bad karma

Pārśvanāth the twenty-third (second to last) Jina of this era

Paryuṣaṇ an eight-day festival near the end of the rainy season during which there is increased lay-mendicant interaction, fasting, and religious activity generally

pāṭhśāḷā school or academy; Jain religious schooling

phal fruit

phūl flower

poṣadh a formal but temporary vow made by laity to live as a mendicant for a fixed period

potāsā a flat cake of sugar often distributed as prabhāvanā at a Jain pūjā

prabhāvanā "illumination"; any act that draws positive attention to the Jain religion; small presents given to all participants at a ritual

pradakṣinā "circumambulations" of the inner sanctum of a Jain temple; sometimes pilgrimage—either is usually accompanied by prayers

praṇām "prostrations"; accompanied by the recitation of the Khamasamāṇo Sūtra (a prayer asking for forgiveness) if before a Jina

pratikramaṇ the rite of confession and expiation of sins

pratiṣṭhā image installation or temple inauguration

pūjā "worship"; generally, the performance of worship liturgies or daily worship

pujārī a temple functionary—usually Hindu—who keeps the temple cleaned and supplied and ensures that each image is worshipped every day

puṇya "merit"; the karmic result of meritorious acts as opposed to pāp or sin

pustak book

Puṣṭimārg a sect of Vaiṣṇav Hinduism started by Vallabhacarya in the fifteenth century

rangolī a design drawn with colored powder in front of the door of a house or temple, or in front of an image during holidays or pūjās, or drawn around thālis at an important meal

ras/rasa one of the eight or nine emotional sensibilities associated with Sanskrit aesthetic theories

rās/raso a medieval poetry form widely adopted by Jains for devotional poetry

rāth yātra chariot procession of a temple image

sādhu male mendicant

sādhvī female mendicant

Śakra another name for Indra

sāmāyik formalized meditation usually for forty-eight minutes

samavasaraṇ the assembly hall built instantly by the gods whenever the Jinas preach; also the thronelike stand that holds the mūrti used for formal pūjās

saṃvatsarī the final day of Paryuṣaṇ on which virtually all Śvetāmbar Jains perform both the annual rite of confession and expiation and a total fast overnight

saṅgh "community" or "congregation"; either the Jains who worship at a particular temple—articulated through their presence at the annual congregation feast or the Saṃvatsarī Pratikramaṇ—or the sum of all Jains

śānt peace or equanimity

Śāntī Kalaś "peace water pot," into which blessed water is poured as part of a ritual to bring peace to an individual; often done to close formal pūjās

Śāntināth the sixteenth Jina and giver of peace to devotees

śāsan-devatā the protector deities who, as Jain devotees, protect the Jinas and assist human Jains

satī a "true woman"; for Hindus usually a self-immolated wife of a recently deceased man; for Jains, a virtuous woman who is true to her religion, sometimes in conflict with her obligations to her family

saubhāgya "state of well-being"; usually a woman's state of being while she is married to a living man

siddha a liberated soul

siddhacakra a symbolic representation of the nine elements of Jainism worthy of worship: the Jinas, the liberated souls, the mendicant teachers, the mendicant leaders, all mendicants, right faith, right knowledge, right action, and right austerities

siddhalok the abode of all liberated souls from which souls cannot return to the world

Snātra Pūjā "bathing pūjā" reenacting the birth of Mahāvīr and its celebration; it is the most common pūjā liturgy

śrāvak "he who listens"; Jain layman, also Sanskrit śrāvaka

śrāvakācāra lay manuals usually written by mendicants

śrāvikā "she who listens"; Jain laywoman

Śrutadevī one of the Jain names for the pan-Indic goddess of learning, also called Sarasvatī or Śāradā

stavan Jain devotional hymns

stavanāvalī collection of Jain hymns

Sthānakavāsī sect of Śvetāmbar Jainism which rejects image worship, founded by Lonka Shah in the twelfth century

sthāpnā the invocation of the deity or guru for a ritual

Śrī Sudhāras Stavan Saṅgrah a particularly ubiquitous stavan collection

svastik swastika

Śvetāmbar "white-clad"; the larger of the two major sects of Jainism, popular primarily in western India from Rajasthan to Maharashtra; this community is increasing in size in Maharashtra and is the larger group in Pune; marked by a belief in the ability of women to attain mokṣa

svarūp the embodied image of Kṛṣṇa worshipped in Puṣṭimārg Vaiṣṇav rituals

tap "austerities"; almost exclusively fasting; includes various kinds of restrictions: one sitting (ekāsan), two sitting (beāsan), or eating bland foods (āyambil), among others

Tapā Gacch the largest ascetic lineage in Śvetāmbar Jainism

tarj melody, as opposed to a classical rāg or scale

thāli a metal plate: steel for eating, brass for a musical instrument, and silver for performing Jain worship

tilak a blessing mark on the forehead, usually of either vermilion or sandalwood paste

tīrthankar "fordmaker"; another name for a Jina

upaśray mendicants' hostel

Updhān Tap a complex vow where a lay Jain lives the life of a mendicant for an extended period of time (usually forty-five days), during which the lay Jain performs extensive fasting and learns those parts of mendicant praxis the laity can perform

upvās a full fast with no food at all; if it includes water, it is a tivihar upvās such as the eight-day (aṭhṭhaī) fast or monthlong (māskhamaṇ) fast, and if water is omitted, it is a cauvihar upvās such as the samvatsarī fast or two and a half-day (aṭṭham) fast

Vaiṣṇav pertaining to worship of Viṣṇu or his incarnations, usually Kṛṣṇa or Rām *vāskep* a powder of sandalwood and saffron which (after a sādhu has blessed it) is used in a variety of Jain worship acts

Vāstuk Pūjā a pūjā which blesses a new home

vidhi ritual instructions

vidhikār a ritual specialist

vītarāg passionless, detached

vrat "vow"; for Jains, both Jain vows and Hindu vows undertaken by Jains

yantra a mystical diagram used in worship

Bibliography

In section I, which lists source materials, the titles are arranged alphabetically. In section II, books and articles are entered according to the name of the author.

I. Jain Texts

Ācārānga Sūtra. In *Jaina Sutras, Part I* (*Ācārānga Sūtra*). Edited and translated by Hermann Jacobi (pp. 1–216). New York: Dover Publications, 1968.

Ādarś Stavanāvalī. By Śrī Ādarś Maṇḍaḷ. Puṇe: Manmohan Saṅgīt Vidyālay, n.d.

Bhakti Gīt Mālā. By Śrī Jain Bhakti Sevā Maṇḍaḷ. Puṇe: Śrī Jain Bhakti Sevā Maṇḍaḷ, 1979.

Bhakti Preṛṇā. By Jain Praray Mahilā Maṇḍaḷ. Amadāvād: Bhurābhāī Phūlcand Śāh, S. 2025 (1968).

Cālo Jinālaye Jaiye. By Pannyāsapravarśrī Hemaratnavijay Gaṇī. Ahmedabad: Aarhad Dharm Prabhavak Trust, 1993.

Gīt Mālā. Puṇe: Abhinav Jain Yuvak Maṇḍaḷ, 1993.

Jain Stavans: Hindi-Gujarati-English. Edited by Ila D. Punater. Dayton, Ohio: Jain Center of Cincinnati-Dayton, 1993.

Jain Tithi Darpaṇ Vīr Samvat 2520 (A.D. 1993–94). Edited by Ācārya Manoharakīrtisāgarsūrī Mahārājā. N. p., n. d.

Jinadarśan. By Bhadrabāhu Vijay. Mahesāṇā: Śrī Viśvakalyāṇ Prakāśan Trasṭ, 1991.

Kalpa Sūtra. In *Jaina Sutras, Part I.* Edited and translated by Hermann Jacobi (pp. 217–312). New York: Dover Publications, 1968.

Laghu Pūjā Saṅgrah. Amadāvād: Jain Prakāśan Mandir, n.d.

Pratimā Pūjan. By Śrī Bhadrankaravijayjī Gaṇivar. Ajmer: Caṅdamal Sopaṇī, 1990.

Prayer Book. Edited and translated by Jain Society of Rochester. Rochester: Jain Society of Rochester, n.d.

Ragīle Phūl. By Śrī Vardhamān Śramaṇ Sanghīy Śrī Keval Munijī. Byāvar: Śrī Jain Divākar Divya Jyoti Kāryālay, V. S. 2470 (1943).
Sāmāyik. By Muni Harishbhadra Vijayji. Bombay: Navjivan Granthmala Trust, n.d.
Śraddhanuṁ Sangīt Yane Samskar Śibir. Sāglī: Vardhamān Sanskṛtidhām, n.d.
Śrāvak Ko Kya Karnā Cāhiye? By Mukticandra Vijāyjī. Vaḍhavāṇśhar: Kalyāṇ Sāhity Prakāśan, n.d.
Śrī Ārādhanā Tathā Tapavidhi. By Munirājśrī Vivekcandravijayjī. Pālītāṇā: Somcand D. Śāh, 1984.
Śrī Devvandanamālā (Vidhi Sahit). By Ācārya Śrī Jitendrasūrijī. Sirohī: Śrī Piṇḍavāḍā Jain Sangh Jñān Khātā, V. S. 2048 (1991).
Śrī Snātra Pūjā (Caityavandananī Vidhi, Śānti Kaḷaś Sahit). Pālītāṇā: Piyūś Prakāśan, n.d.
Śrī Śrīpāl Rājā no Rās. Amdāvād: Jain Prakāśan Mandir, 1997.
Śrī Sudhāras Stavan Saṅgrah. [Śankheśvar edition] Pālītāṇā: Somacand D. Śāh. n.d.
Śrī Sudhāras Stavan Saṅgrah. Pālītāṇā: Somacand D. Śāh. n.d.
Śrī Sudhāras Stavan Saṅgrah. Amadāvād: Śrī Jain Prakāśan Mandir. n.d.
Śrī Taporatna Mahovidhi. Śāntipurī (Saurāṣṭra): Śrī Harṣapuṣpāmṛt Jain Granthamālā, 1989.
Stotrasār Samuccay. Belgāum: B. D. Caugule Press, 1978.
Sulasā Candanabālā. By Phatahcand Srilalji Mahatma. Udaypur: Phatahcand Śrīlāljī Mahātmā, 1987.
Sūtrakṛtaṅga. In *Jaina Sutras, Part II.* Edited and translated by Hermann Jacobi. New York: Dover Publications, 1968.
Triṣaṣṭīśalākapuruṣacaritra. By Hemacandra. Translated by Helen M. Johnson. Baroda: Oriental Institute, 1931–62.
Vividh Mahāpūjan Tathā Pūjā Upayogī Sāmagrīnuṁ Līsṭ. Muṃbaī: Śrī Vardhamān Jain Bhakti Maṇḍaḷ, n.d.
Vividh Pūjā Saṅgrah. Edited by Paṉnyās Jinendra Vijay Gaṇī. Sivana: Tapāgacch Jain Saṅgh, 1986.
Vividh Pūjā Saṅgrah. Amadāvād: Śrī Jain Prakāśan Mandir, n.d.
Yogaśāstra. By Hemacandra. Translated as *The Yoga Shastra of Hemchandracharya (A 12th-Century Guide to Jain Yoga)*, by A. S. Gopani. Jaipur: Prakrit Bharti Academy, 1989.

II. Secondary Sources

Abrahams, Roger. "The Complex Relations of Simple Forms." In *Folklore Genres*, edited by Dan Ben-Amos (pp. 193–214). Austin: University of Texas Press, 1976.
Abu-Lughod, Lila. *Veiled Sentiments.* Berkeley: University of California Press, 1986.
———. "Can There Be a Feminist Ethnography?" *Woman and Performance* 5 (1990a): 7–27.
———. "The Romance of Resistance: Trading Transformations of Power Through Bedouin Women." In *Beyond the Second Sex*, edited by Peggy Sanday and Ruth Goodenough (pp. 311–337). Philadelphia: University of Pennsylvania Press, 1990b.
———. *Writing Women's Worlds.* Berkeley: University of California Press, 1993.
Adey, L. *Class and Idol in the English Hymn.* Vancouver: University of British Columbia, 1988.
Alper, Harvey P., ed. *Mantra.* Albany: State University of New York Press, 1989.
Archer, William. *Songs for the Bride.* New York: Columbia University Press, 1985.
Asher, Catherine. "Hidden Gold: Jain Temples of Delhi and Jaipur and their Urban Context." In *Festschrift for Professor Padmanabh S. Jaini*, edited by Olle Qvarnström. Lund Studies of African and Asian Religions. Lund: Almqvist and Wiskell, forthcoming.

Aslet, Christopher. "Some Reflections on Hindu *Bhakti* Iconography." In *Love Divine*, edited by Karel Werner (pp. 207–212). Richmond Surrey, U. K.: Curzon Press, 1993.

Babb, Lawrence A. *Absent Lord: Ascetic and Worldly Values in a Jain Ritual Culture*. Berkeley: University of California, 1996.

Babiracki, Carol M. "What's the Difference?: Reflections on Gender and Research in Village India." In *Shadows in the Field*, edited by by Gregory F. Barz and Timothy J. Cooley (pp. 121–136). Oxford: Oxford University Press, 1997.

Bajpai, Gita. *Agrarian Urban Economy and Social Change*. Delhi: Daya Publishing, 1989.

Balbir, Nalini. *Āvāsyaka-Studien: Introduction Générale et Traductions*. Stuttgart: Franz Steiner Verlag, 1993.

———. "Women in Jainism." In *Religion and Women*, edited by Arvind Sharma (pp. 121–138). Albany: State University of New York, 1994.

Ballard, Roger, ed. *Desh Pardesh: The South Asian Presence in Britain*. London: Hurst, 1994.

Banks, Marcus. *Organizing Jainism in India and England*. Oxford: Clarendon Press, 1992.

———. "Why Move?: Regional and Long Distance Migrations of Gujarati Jains." In *Migration: The Asian Experience*, edited by Judith Brown and Rosemary Foot (pp. 131–148). Oxford: St. Martin's Press, 1994.

Barz, Richard. *The Bhakti Sect of Vallabhācārya*. Faridabad: Thomson Press, 1976.

Barz, Richard, and Monika Thiel-Horstmann, eds. *Living Texts From India*. Wiesbadan: Harrassowitz, 1989.

Bauman, Richard. *Story, Performance, and Event*. Cambridge: Cambridge University Press, 1986.

Behar, Ruth. *Translated Woman*. Boston: Beacon Press, 1993.

Behar, Ruth, and Deborah A. Gordon, eds. *Women Writing Culture*. Berkeley: University of California Press, 1995.

Belsare, M. B. *An Etymological Gujarati-English Dictionary*. New Delhi: Asian Educational Services, 1993.

Ben-Amos, Dan, ed. *Folklore Genres*. Austin: University of Texas Press, 1976.

———. *Folklore in Context: Essays*. New Delhi: South Asian Publishers, 1982.

Bennett, Lynn. *Dangerous Wives and Sacred Sisters: Social and Symbolic Roles of High-Caste Women in Nepal*. New York: Columbia University Press, 1983.

Bennett, Peter. Temple Organization and Worship among Puṣṭimargīya-Vaiṣṇavs of Ujjain. Ph.D. dissertation, School of Oriental and African Studies, University of London, 1983.

———. "In Nanda Baba's House: The Devotional Experience in Pushtimarg Temples." In *Divine Passions: The Social Construction of Emotion in India*, edited by Owen Lynch (pp. 182–211). Berkeley: University of California Press, 1991.

Blackburn, Stuart H. *Singing of Birth and Death: Texts in Performance*. Philadelphia: University of Pennsylvania Press, 1988.

Brown, C. Mackenzie. *Devi Gita: The Song of the Goddess*. Albany: State University of New York Press, 1998.

Bynum, Caroline W. *Holy Feast, Holy Fast*. Berkeley: University of California Press, 1987.

Bynum, Caroline, S. Harrell, and Paula Richman, eds. *Gender and Religion: On the Complexity of Symbols*. Boston: Beacon Press, 1986.

Caillat, Collete. *Atonements in the Ancient Ritual of the Jaina Monks*. Ahmedabad: L. D. Institute of Indology Series, 1975.

Caldwell, Sarah. *O Terrifying Mother: Sexuality, Violence, and Worship of the Goddess Kali*. New York: Oxford University Press, 1999.

Campbell, James M., ed. *Gazetteer of the Bombay Presidency: Poona*. Vol. 18, Parts I, II, and III. Bombay: Government Central Press, 1885.

Carrithers, Michael. "Passions of Nation and Community in the Bahubali Affair." *Modern Asian Studies* 22 (1988): 815–44.

———. "Naked Ascetics in Southern Digambar Jainism." *Man* 24 (1989): 219–35.

———. "The Foundations of Community among Southern Digambar Jains." In *The Assembly of Listeners*, edited by Michael Carrithers and Caroline Humphrey (pp. 261–86). Cambridge: Cambridge University Press, 1991.

Carrithers, Michael, and Caroline Humphrey, eds. *The Assembly of Listeners*. Cambridge: Cambridge University Press, 1991.

Chaudhari, K. K. and B. G. Kunte, eds. *Maharashtra State Gazetteers: Language and Literature*. Bombay: Directorate of Government Printing, 1971.

Chitre, Dilip. *Says Tuka* (*Tukaram*). New Delhi: Penguin Classics, 1991.

Christ, Carol. "Toward a Paradigm Shift in the Academy and in Religious Studies." In *The Impact of Feminist Research in the Academy*, edited by C. Farnham (pp. 53–76). Bloomington: University of Indiana Press, 1987.

———. "Symbols of Goddess and God in Feminist Theology." In *The Book of the Goddess: Past and Present*, edited by Carl Olsen (pp. 231–251). New York: Crossroad Press, 1989.

Clifford, James, and George Marcus, eds. *Writing Culture: The Poetics and Politics of Ethnography*. Berkeley: University of California Press, 1986.

Coburn, Thomas B. *Encountering the Goddess*. Albany: State University of New York Press, 1991.

Code, Lorraine. *What Can She Know? Feminist Theory and the Construction of Knowledge*. Ithaca: Cornell University Press, 1991.

Cort, John E. "Medieval Jaina Goddess Traditions." *Numen* 34 (1987): 235–54.

———. "Pilgrimage to Shankheshvar Pārshvanāth." *Center for the Study of World Religions Bulletin* 14 (1988): 63–72.

———. Liberation and Well Being: A Study of Svetambar Murtipujak Jains of North Gujarat. Ph.D. dissertation, Harvard University, 1989.

———. "Models of and for the Study of Jains." *Method and Theory in the Study of Religion* 2 (1990): 42–71.

———. "The Śvetāmbar Mūrtipūjak Mendicant." *Man* 26 (1991a): 651–71.

———. "Two Ideals of the Svetambar Murtipujak Jain Layman." *Journal of Indian Philosophy* 19 (Dec. 1991b): 1–30.

———. "Svetambar Murtipujak Jain Scripture in a Performative Context." In *Texts in Context*, edited by J. Timm (pp. 171–194). Albany: State University of New York Press, 1992.

———. "Following the Jina, Worshiping the Jina: An Essay on Jain Rituals." In *The Peaceful Liberators: Jain Art From India*, edited by Pratapaditya Pal (pp. 39–56). Los Angeles: Los Angeles County Museum of Art, 1994.

———. "Absences and Transformations: Ganesh in the Shvetambar Jain Tradition." In *Ganesh the Benevolent*, edited by Pratapaditya Pal (pp. 81–94). Bombay: Marg Publishers, 1995a.

———. "The Jain Knowledge Warehouses: Libraries in Traditional India." *Journal of the American Oriental Society* 115 (1995b): 77–87.

———. "Jain Questions and Answers: Who Is God and How Is He Worshiped?" In *Religions of India in Practice*, edited by Donald Lopez (pp. 598–608). Princeton: Princeton University Press, 1995c.

———. "The Rite of Veneration of Jina Images." In *Religions of India in Practice*, edited by Donald Lopez (pp. 326–32). Princeton: Princeton University Press, 1995d.

———. "Tantra in Jainism: The Cult of Ghaṇṭākarṇ Mahāvīr, the Great Hero Bell-Ears." *Bulletin d'Études Indiennes* 15 (1997): 115–33.

———. "Who Is a King?: Jain Narratives of Kingship in Medieval India." In *Open Boundaries*, edited by John E. Cort (pp. 85–110). Albany: State University of New York Press, 1998.

———. "Communities, Temples, Identities: Art Histories and Social Histories in Western India." In *Ethnography and Personhood*, edited by Michael W. Meister (pp. 101–28). Jaipur: Rawat, 2000.

———. "Doing for Others: Merit Transfer and Merit Motility in Jainism." In *Festschrift for Professor Padmanabh S. Jaini*, edited by Olle Qvarnström. Lund Studies of African and Asian Religions. Lund: Almqvist and Wiskell, forthcoming.

———. "Devotion of Asceticism among Svetambar Murtipujak Jains." Unpublished article, n.d.a.

———. "Bhakti in the Early Jain Tradition." Unpublished article. Harvard University, Photocopy, n.d.b.

Cottam Ellis, Christine. "The Jain Merchant Castes of Rajasthan: Some Aspects of the Management of a Social Identity in a Market Town." In *The Assembly of Listeners*, edited by Michael Carrithers and Caroline Humphrey (pp. 75–108). Cambridge: Cambridge University Press, 1991.

De Jong, M. " 'I Want to Be Like Jesus': The Self-Defining Power of Evangelical Hymnody." *Journal of the American Academy of Religion* 54 (1986): 461–93.

Deo, Shantaram B. "Jain Temples, Monks and Nuns in Poona (City)." *Jaina Antiquary* 16 (1950): 17–33.

Dhere, Ramchandra Chintaman. "The Gondhali: Singers for the Devi" (translated by Anne Feldhaus). In *The Experience of Hinduism: Essays on Religion in Maharashtra*, edited by Eleanor Zelliot and Maxine Berntsen (pp. 174–189). Albany: State University of New York Press, 1988.

Dhongde, R. V., and S. R. Sharma, Krupa Kulkarni. *Minority Language Communities: Islands or Icebergs*? Pune: Deccan College, 1989.

Dhruvarajan, Vanaja. *Hindu Women and the Power of Ideology*. Granby, Mass.: Bergin and Garvey, 1989.

Dimock, Edward C., et al., eds. *The Literatures of India*. Chicago: University of Chicago Press, 1974.

Doniger, Wendy. "Fluid and Fixed Texts in India." In *Boundaries of the Text*, edited by Joyce B. Flueckiger and Laurie Sears (pp. 31–41). Ann Arbor: University of Michigan South and Southeast Asian Studies Center, 1991.

Dumont, Louis. "World Renunciation in Indian Religions." In *Religion, Politics and History in India* (pp. 33–60). The Hague: Mouton, 1970.

Dundas, Paul. "Food and Freedom: The Jaina Sectarian Debate on the Nature of the Kevalin." *Religion* 15 (1985): 161–98.

———. *The Jains*. London: Routledge, 1992.

———. "Somnolent Sūtras: Scriptural Commentary in Śvetāmbara Jainism." *Journal of Indian Philosophy* 24 (1996): 73–101.

———. "Becoming Gautama." In *Open Boundaries*, edited by John E. Cort (pp. 31–52). Albany: State University of New York Press, 1998.

Elwin, E. F. *Indian Jottings*. London: John Murray, 1907.

Enthoven, R. E. *Tribes and Castes of Bombay*. Vols. I, II, and III. Bombay: Government Central Press, 1920–22.

Erndl, Kathleen. *Victory to the Mother*. New York: Oxford University Press, 1993.

Feld, Steven. "Dialogic Editing: Interpreting How the Kaluli Read Sound and Sentiment." *Cultural Anthropology* 2 (1987): 190–210.

Feldhaus, Anne. *Water and Womanhood*. New York: Oxford University Press, 1995.

Flueckiger, Joyce Burkhalter. "Genre and Community in the Folklore System of Chhattisgarh." In *Gender, Genre, and Power in South Asian Expressive Traditions*, edited by Arjun Appadurai, Frank Korom, and Margaret Mills (pp. 181–200). Philadelphia: University of Pennsylvania Press, 1991a.

———. "Literacy and the Changing Concept of Text: Women's Ramayana Mandali in Central India." In *Boundaries of the Text*, edited by Joyce B. Flueckiger and Laurie Sears (pp. 43–60). Ann Arbor: University of Michigan South and Southeast Asian Studies Center, 1991b.

———. *Gender and Genre in the Folklore of Middle India*. Delhi: Oxford University Press, 1996.

Folkert, Kendall W. "The 'Canons' of 'Scripture.' " In *Rethinking Scripture*, edited by M. Levering (pp. 170–79). Albany: State University of New York Press, 1989.

———. *Scripture and Community: Collected Essays on the Jains*, edited by John E. Cort. Atlanta: Scholars Press, 1993.

Foucault, Michel. *Power/Knowledge*. New York: Pantheon Books, 1980.

Fuller, C. J. *Servants of the Goddess*. Cambridge: Cambridge University Press, 1984.

Gadamer, Hans-George. "Hermeneutics and Social Science." *Cultural Hermeneutics* 2 (1975).

Gaston, Anne-Marie. *Krishna's Musicians*. Delhi: Manohar, 1997.

Gergen, Mary M. ed. *Feminist Thought and the Structure of Knowledge*. New York: New York University Press, 1988.

Gilligan, Carol. *In a Different Voice*. Cambridge: Harvard University Press, 1982.

Glushkova, Irina, and Anne Feldhaus, eds. *House and Home in Maharashtra*. Delhi: Oxford University Press, 1998.

Gold, Ann Grodzins. *Fruitful Journeys: The Ways of Rajasthani Pilgrims*. Berkeley: University of California Press, 1988.

Graham, William. *Beyond the Written Word: Oral Aspects of Scripture in the History of Religion*. Cambridge: Cambridge University Press, 1987.

———. "Scripture as Spoken Word." In *Rethinking Scripture*, edited by M. Levering (pp. 129–69). Albany: State University of New York Press, 1989.

Granoff, Phyllis, ed. *The Clever Adulteress and Other Stories: A Treasury of Jain Literature*. New York: Mosaic Press, 1990.

———. *The Forest of Thieves and the Magic Garden*. New Delhi: Penguin, 1998.

Hanchett, Suzanne. *Coloured Rice: Symbolic Structure in Hindu Family Festivals*. Delhi: Hindustan Publishing, 1988.

Harinārāyaṇjī. *Mīrā Bṛhatpadāvalī*. Jaipur: Rājasthān Prācyavidyā Pratiṣṭhān, 1968.

Harlan, Lindsey. *Religion and Rajput Women: The Ethic of Protection in Contemporary Narratives*. Berkeley: University of California Press, 1992.

———. "Abandoning Shame: Mīrā and the Margins of Marriage." In *From the Margins of Hindu Marriage: Essays on Gender, Religion, and Culture*, edited by Lindsey Harlan and Paul B. Courtright (pp. 204–27). New York: Oxford University Press, 1995.

Hawley, John S. *At Play with Krishna: Pilgrimage Dramas From Brindavan*. Princeton: Princeton University Press, 1981.

———. "The Sectarian Logic of the Sūr Dās Kī Vārtā." In *Bhakti in Current Research, 1979–1982*, edited by Monika Thiel-Horstmann (pp. 157–70). Berlin: Dietrich Reimer Verlag, 1983.

———, ed. *Sati, the Blessing and the Curse*. New York: Oxford University Press, 1994.

Hawley, John S., and Mark Juergensmeyer. *Songs of the Saints of India*. New York: Oxford University Press, 1988.

Hekman, Susan J. *Gender and Knowledge: Elements of a Postmodern Feminism*. Cambridge (U. K.): Polity Press, 1990.

Heidegger, Martin. *Being and Time*. London: SCM Press, 1962.
Henry, Edward O. *Chant the Names of God*. San Diego: San Diego State University Press, 1988.
Hess, Linda. "Rām Līlā: The Audience Experience." In *Bhakti in Current Research, 1979–1982*, edited by Monika Thiel-Horstmann (pp. 171–94). Berlin: Dietrich Reimer Verlag, 1983.
Holmstrom, Savitri. Towards a Politics of Renunciation: Jain Women and Asceticism in Rajasthan. M.A. dissertation, University of Edinburgh, 1988.
Humphrey, Caroline. "Some Aspects of the Jain Puja: The Idea of 'God' and the Symbolism of Offerings." *Cambridge Anthropology* 9 (1985): 1–19.
Humphrey, Caroline, and James Laidlaw. *The Archetypal Actions of Ritual*. Oxford: Clarendon Press, 1994.
Jain, Banarsi Das. "The Persian of Jain Hymns." In *Siddhabhāratī, Part One*, edited by Bandhu Vishva Bandhu (pp. 47–49). Hoshiarpur: V. V. R. Insititute, 1950.
Jain, Satish Kumar, ed. *Perspectives in Jaina Philosophy and Culture*. New Delhi: Ahimsa International, 1985.
Jaini, Padmanabh S. "The Jainas and the Western Scholar." *Sambodhi* 5 (1976): 148–56.
———. *The Jaina Path of Purification*. Berkeley: University of California Press, 1979.
———. *Gender and Salvation*. Berkeley: University of California Press, 1991.
Jamison, Stephanie W. *Sacrificed Wife, Sacrificer's Wife: Women, Ritual, and Hospitality in Ancient India*. New York: Oxford University Press, 1996.
Jhaveri, Mansukhlal. *History of Gujarati Literature*. New Delhi: Sahitya Akademi, 1978.
Kaiwar, Vasant. "The Colonial State, Capital and the Peasantry in Bombay Presidency." *Modern Asian Studies* 28 (1994): 793–832.
Karve, Irawati, and Jayant Sadashiv Ranadive. *The Social Dynamics of a Growing Town and Its Surrounding Area*. Poona: Deccan College, 1965.
Kelting, M. Whitney. Hearing the Voices of the Śrāvikā: Ritual and Song in Jain Laywomen's Belief and Practice. Ph. D. dissertation, Department of South Asian Languages and Literatures, University of Wisconsin, 1996.
———. "Who's Running the *Pūjā*: Jain Women's *Maṇḍaḷs* and the Authority to Recreate Jain Theology." In *Approaches to Jain Studies: Philosophy, Logic, Rituals and Symbols*, edited by Olle Qvarnström and N. K. Wagle (pp. 275–90). Toronto: University of Toronto Centre for South Asian Studies, 1999.
———. "Constructions of Femaleness in Jain Vernacular Devotional Literature." In *Festschrift for Professor Padmanabh S. Jaini*, edited by Olle Qvarnström. Lund Studies of African and Asian Religions. Lund: Almqvist and Wiskell, forthcoming.
Kendall, Laurel. *The Life and Hard Times of a Korean Shaman*. Honolulu: University of Hawaii Press, 1988.
Kishwar, Madhu, and Ruth Vanita. "From Poison to Nectar." *Manushi* 50–51–52 (Jan.–June 1989): 74–93.
Koskoff, Ellen, ed. *Women and Music in Cross-Cultural Perspective*. New York: Greenwood Press, 1987.
Krause, Charlotte. *Ancient Jaina Hymns*. Ujjain: Scindia Oriental Institute, 1952.
Krishnaraj, Maithreyi, and Karuna Chanana, eds. *Gender and the Household Domain*. New Delhi: Sage Publications, 1989.
Kumar, Nita. *Brothers, Friends, and Informants*. Berkeley: University of California Press, 1992.
———, ed. *Women as Subjects: South Asian Histories*. Charlottesville: University of Virginia Press, 1994.
Laidlaw, James. *Riches and Renunciation: Religion and Economy among the Jains*. Oxford: Oxford University Press, 1995.

Lavie, Smadar. *The Poetics of Military Occupation*. Berkeley: University of California Press, 1990.

Leoshko, Janice. "Inside Out: 19th-Century Views of Jains and Jain Art." In *Festschrift for Professor Padmanabh S. Jaini*, edited by Olle Qvarnström. Lund Studies of African and Asian Religions. Lund: Almqvist & Wiskell, forthcoming.

Leslie, I. Julia. *The Perfect Wife: The Orthodox Hindu Woman According to the Stridharmanpaddhati of Tryambakayajvan*. Oxford: Oxford University Press, 1989.

Limón, José. *Dancing with the Devil*. Madison: University of Wisconsin Press, 1994.

Lopez, Donald, ed. *Religions of India in Practice*. Princeton: Princeton University Press, 1995.

Lutgendorf, Philip. *The Life of a Text*. Berkeley: University of California Press, 1991.

Lynch, Owen, ed. *Divine Passions: The Social Construction of Emotion in India*. Berkeley: University of California Press, 1990.

Mahias, Marie-Claude. *Délivrance et Convivialité*. Paris: E. M. S. H., 1985.

Mallison, Françoise. "Development of Early Krisnaism in Gujarāt: Viṣṇu-Raṇchoḍ-Kṛṣṇa." In *Bhakti in Current Research, 1979–1982*, edited by Monika Thiel-Horstmann (pp. 245–56). Berlin: Dietrich Reimer Verlag, 1983.

———. "From Folklore to Devotion: Dhoḷ Songs in Gujarat." In *Living Texts From India*, edited by Richard K. Barz and Monika Theil-Horstmann (pp. 87–102). Wiesbaden: Otto Harrassowitz, 1989.

Mani, Lata. "Multiple Mediations: Feminist Scholarship in the Age of Multinational Reception." *Inscriptions* 5 (1989): 1–23.

Manuel, Peter. *Cassette Culture: Popular Music and Technology in North India*. Chicago: University of Chicago Press, 1993.

Marcus, Scott. "On Cassette Rather Than Live: Religious Music in India Today." In *Media and the Transformation of Religion in South Asia*, edited by Lawrence Babb and Susan S. Wadley. Philadelphia: University of Pennsylvania Press, 1995.

Mariniello, Silvestra. "Introduction." In *Gendered Agents: Women and Institutional Knowledge*, edited by Silvestra Mariniello and Paul A. Bové (pp. 1–16). Durham: Duke University Press, 1998.

McDaniel, June. *The Madness of the Saints*. Chicago: University of Chicago Press, 1989.

McDermott, Rachel Fell. *Singing to the Goddess*. New York: Oxford University Press, 2000.

McGee, Mary. Fasting and Feasting: The Vrata Tradition and Its Significance. Unpublished Th.D. dissertation, Harvard Divinity School, 1987.

Meister, Michael. "Sweetmeats or Corpses? Community, Conversions, Sacred Places." In *Open Boundaries*, edited by John E. Cort (pp. 111–38). Albany: State University of New York Press, 1998.

Mohanty, Chandra Talpade. "Under Western Eyes: Feminist Scholarship and Colonial Discourses." *Boundary* 2 (1984): 333–58.

Mukta, Parita. *Upholding the Common Life: The Community of Mirabai*. Oxford: Oxford University Press, 1994.

Munshi, Kanaiyalal M. *Gujarat and Its Literature*. Bombay: Bharatiya Vidya Bhavan, 1954.

Nāhṭa, Agarcand, ed. *Jain Maru-Gurjar Kavi Aur Unkī Racanaeṅ*. Vol. 1: *11th to 16th Century*. Bikāner: Sumatilāl J. Śāh, 1975.

Narayan, Kirin. "Birds on a Branch: Girlfriends and Wedding Songs in Kangra." *Ethos* (1986): 47–75.

———. *Storytellers, Saints and Scoundrels*. Philadelphia: University of Pennsylvania Press, 1989.

Narayan, Kirin, with Urmila Devi Sood. *Mondays on the Dark Night of the Moon*. Oxford: Oxford University Press, 1997.

Narayanan, Leila. *Ethnicity in Urban Context: Gujaratis in Madras City*. Jaipur: Rawat Publications, 1989.

Natavar, Mekhala. The Lord's Pleasure. Unpublished article. Department of South Asian Studies, University of Wisconsin, Photocopy, n.d.

Norman, K. R. "The Role of the Layman According to the Jain Canon." In *The Assembly of Listeners*, edited by Michael Carrithers and Caroline Humphrey (pp. 31–40). Cambridge: Cambridge University Press, 1991.

O'Flaherty, Wendy Doniger. *Other People's Myths*. New York: Macmillan, 1988.

Ojha, Catherine. "Feminine Asceticism in Hinduism: Its Tradition and Present Condition." *Man in India* 61 (Sept. 1981): 254–85.

Olivelle, Patrick. *Renunciation in Hinduism: A Medieval Debate*. Vienna: Institut für Indologie der Universität Wien, 1986–87.

Olsen, Carl, ed. *The Book of the Goddess Past and Present*. New York: Crossroads, 1989.

Ong, Aihwa. "Colonialism and Modernity: Feminist Re-Presentations of Women in Non-Western Societies." *Inscriptions* 3 (1988): 79–93.

Orr, Leslie. "Jain and Hindu 'Religious Women' in Early Medieval Tamilnadu." In *Open Boundaries*, edited by John E. Cort (pp. 187–212). Albany: State University of New York Press, 1998.

Oza, Shantilal S., and Ramanbhai G. Bhatt. *The Modern Combined Dictionary: English into Gujarati and Gujarati into English*. Bombay: R. R. Sheth, 1991.

Pal, Pratapaditya, ed. *The Peaceful Liberators: Jain Art From India*. Los Angeles: Los Angeles County Museum of Art, 1994.

Parry, Jonathan. *Death in Banaras*. Cambridge: Cambridge University Press, 1994.

Patai, Daphne. "U. S. Academics and Third World Women: Is Ethical Research Possible?" In *Women's Words: The Feminist Practice of Oral History*, edited by Sherna Berger Gluck and Daphne Patai (pp. 137–53). New York: Routledge, 1991.

Pearson, Anne Mackenzie. "*Because It Gives Me Peace of Mind*": *Ritual Fasts in the Lives of Hindu Women*. Albany: State University of New York Press, 1996.

Pinney, Christopher. *Camera Indica: The Social Life of Indian Photographs*. Chicago: University of Chicago Press, 1997.

Pintchman, Tracy. *Seeking Mahadevi*. Albany: State University of New York Press, 2001.

Qureshi, Regula. "Recorded Sound and Religious Music: The Case of Qawwālī." In *Media and the Transformation of Religion in South Asia*, edited by Lawrence Babb and Susan Wadley (pp. 139–66). Philadelphia: University of Pennsylvania Press, 1995.

Raheja, Gloria Goodwin. *The Poison in the Gift*. Chicago: University of Chicago Press, 1988.

Raheja, Gloria Goodwin, and Ann Grodzins Gold. *Listen to the Heron's Words*. Berkeley: University of California Press, 1994.

Ramanujan, A. K. *Speaking of Śiva*. Harmondsville: Penguin, 1973.

———. *Who Needs Folklore? The Relevance of Oral Traditions to South Asian Studies*. South Asia Occasional Paper Series, No. 1. Honolulu: University of Hawaii, 1990.

———. "Towards a Counter System: Women's Tales." In *Gender, Genre, and Power in South Asian Expressive Traditions*, edited by Arjun Appadurai, Frank Korom, and Margaret Mills (pp. 33–55). Philadelphia: University of Pennsylvania, 1991.

Redington, James. *Vallabhacarya on the Love Games of Krishna*. Delhi: Motilal Banarsidas, 1983.

Reynell, Josephine. Honour, Nurture and Festivity: Aspects of Female Religiosity amongst Jain Women in Jaipur. Unpublished Ph.D. dissertation, Cambridge University, 1985a.

———. "Renunciation and Ostentation: A Jain Paradox." *Cambridge Anthropology* 9 (1985b): 20–33.

———. "Prestige, Honour and the Family: Laywomen's Religiosity amongst Svetambar Murtipujak Jains in Jaipur." *Bulletin D'etudes Indienne* 5 (1987): 313–59.

———. "Women and the Reproduction of the Jain Community." In *The Assembly of Listeners*, edited by Michael Carrithers and Christine Humphrey (pp. 41–65). Cambridge: Cambridge University Press, 1991.

Rosaldo, Renato. *Culture and Truth*. Boston: Beacon Press, 1989.

Rosenberg, Neil V. " 'It Was a Kind of Hobby': A Manuscript Song Book and Its Place in Tradition." In *Folklore Studies in Honour of Herbert Halpert*, edited by K. Goldstein and N. Rosenberg (pp. 334–51). St. John's, Newfoundland: Memorial University of Newfoundland, 1980.

Ryan, James. The *Cīvakacintāmaṇi* in Historical Perspective. Unpublished Ph.D. dissertation, University of California-Berkeley, 1985.

———. "Erotic Excess and Sexual Danger in the *Cīvakacintāmaṇi*." In *Open Boundaries*, edited by John E. Cort (pp. 67–84). Albany: State University of New York Press, 1998.

Said, Edward. *Orientalism*. New York: Pantheon, 1978.

Sandesara, Bhogilal J. *Literary Circle of Mahāmātya Vastupāla and Its Contribution to Sanskrit Literature*. Singhi Jain Series, No. 33. Bombay: Bharatiya Vidya Bhavan, 1953.

———. "Gujarati Literature of the Jainas." *Journal of the Oriental Institute* (Baroda) 39 (1990): 255–62.

Sangave, Vilas A. *Jaina Community*. Bombay: Popular Prakashan, 1980.

Sawant, Shashikant. B. *The City of Poona: A Study in Urban Geography*. Poona: University of Poona, 1978.

Sax, William. *Mountain Goddess: Gender and Politics in a Himalayan Pilgrimage*. Oxford: Oxford University Press, 1991.

Schubring, Walther. "Aus der Jainistischen Stotra-literatur." In *Jñānamukhtāvalī*, edited by K. Vogel (pp. 194–220). New Delhi: International Academy of Indian Culture, 1959.

———. *The Doctrine of the Jainas*. New Delhi: Motilal Banarsidass, 1962.

Scott, Joan Wallach. *Gender and the Politics of History*. New York: Columbia University Press, 1988.

Shah, Jagdish. *Madhyakalin Gujarati Bhakti Kavita*. Amadavad: Gurjar Granthratan Karyalay, 1981.

Shah, Umakant P. *Studies in Jaina Art*. Banaras: Jaina Cultural Research Society, 1955.

Shāntā, N. *La Voie Jaina*. Paris: O. E. I. L., 1985.

Singer, Milton. "The Radha-Krishna Bhajanas of Madras City." In *Krishna: Myths, Rites, and Attitudes*, edited by Milton Singer (pp. 90–138). Chicago: University of Chicago Press, 1966.

Singhi, N. K. "A Study of Jains in a Rajasthan Town." In *The Assembly of Listeners*, edited by Michael Carrithers and Caroline Humphrey (pp. 139–61). Cambridge: Cambridge University Press, 1991.

Slawek, Stephen Matthew. Kīrtan: A Study of the Sonic Manifestations of the Divine in the Popular Hindu Culture of Banāras. Ph.D. dissertation, University of Illinois at Urbana-Champaign, 1986.

Smith, William Cantwell. "The Study of Religion and the Study of the Bible." In *Rethinking Scripture*, edited by M. Levering (pp. 18–28). Albany: State University of New York Press, 1989.

Spivak, Gayatri Chakravorty. *In Other Worlds*. New York: Methuen Press, 1987.

———. "Can the Subaltern Speak?" In *Marxism and the Interpretation of Culture*, edited by C. Nelson and L. Grossberg (pp. 271–313). Urbana: University of Illinois Press, 1988.

———. "Responsibility." In *Gendered Agents: Women and Institutional Knowledge*, edited by Silvestra Mariniello and Paul A. Bové (pp. 19–66). Durham: Duke University Press, 1998.

Stacey, Judith. "Can There Be a Feminist Ethnography?" In *Women's Words: The Feminist Practice of Oral History*, edited by Sherna Berger Gluck and Daphne Patai (pp. 111–19). New York: Routledge, 1991.

Stanley, Liz, and Sue Wise. *Breaking Out Again: Feminist Ontology and Epistomology*. London: Routledge, 1993.

Stevenson, Mrs. Sinclair. *The Heart of Jainism*. New Delhi: Munshiram Manoharlal, [1915] 1970.

Stokes, Martin, ed. *Ethnicity, Identity and Music: The Musical Construction of Place*. Oxford: BERG, 1994.

Stoller-Miller, Barbara. *Love Song of the Dark Lord: Jayadeva's Gītagovinda*. New York: Columbia University Press, 1977.

Tambiah, Stanley J. *Buddhism and the Spirit Cults in North-East Thailand*. Cambridge: Cambridge University Press, 1970.

Tamke, S. *Make Joyful Noise unto the Lord*. Athens, Ohio: Ohio University Press, 1978.

Tatia, Nathmal, and Muni Mahendra Kumar. *Aspects of Jaina Monasticism*. New Delhi: Today and Tomorrow's, 1981.

Tewari, L. B. "Ceremonial Songs of the Kanyakubja Brahmans." *Essays in Arts and Sciences* 6 (1977): 30–52.

Thiel-Horstmann, Monika, ed. *Bhakti in Current Research, 1979–1982*. Berlin: Dietrich Reimer Verlag, 1983a.

———. *Crossing the Ocean of Existence: Braj Bhāṣā Religious Poetry from Rajasthan*. Wiesbaden: Otto Harrossowitz, 1983b.

Thompson, Gordon Ross. Music and Values in Gujarati-Speaking Western India. Unpublished Ph.D. dissertation, University of California at Los Angeles, 1987.

Tiwari, Maruti Nandan Prasad. "Saraswati in Jaina Art." In *Perspectives in Jaina Philosophy and Culture*, edited by Satish Kumar Jain. New Delhi: Ahimsa International, 1985.

Todorov, Tzvetan. *Mikhail Bakhtin: The Dialogical Principle*. Minneapolis: University of Minnesota Press, 1984.

Toomey, Paul M. "Krishna's Consuming Passions: Food as Metaphor and Metonym for Emotion at Mount Govardhan." In *Divine Passions*, edited by Owen Lynch (pp. 157–81). Berkeley: University of California Press, 1990.

Trawick, Margaret. "Spirits and Voices in Tamil Songs." *American Ethnologist* 15 (1988): 193–215.

Tubb, Gary A. "Hemacandra and Sanskrit Poetics." In *Open Boundaries*, edited by John E. Cort (pp. 53–66). Albany: State University of New York Press, 1998.

Tukol, T. K. *Sallekhana Is Not Suicide*. Ahmedabad: L. D. Institute of Indology, 1976.

Valley, Anne. Women and the Ascetic Ideal in Jainism. Ph.D. dissertation, University of Toronto, 1999.

Vaudeville, Charlotte. *Bārahmāsā in Indian Literatures*. Delhi: Motilal Banarsidass, 1986.

Vergati, Anne. "Les Rois et Les Deesses: La Fête de Navaratri et Dasahra au Rajasthan." *Journal Asiatique* 282 (1994): 125–46.

Visweswaran, Kamala. *Fictions of Feminist Ethnography*. Minneapolis: University of Minnesota Press, 1994.

Wadley, Susan S. *Shakti: Power in the Conceptual Structure of Karimpur Religion*. Chicago: University of Chicago Studies in Anthropology Series, 1975.

———. "Why Does Ram Swarup Sing? Song and Speech in the North Indian Epic Dholā." In *Gender, Genre, and Power in South Asian Expressive Traditions*, edited by Arjun Appadurai, Frank Korom, and Margaret Mills (pp. 201–23). Philadelphia: University of Pennsylvania Press, 1991.

Werner, Karel, ed. *Love Divine: Studies in Bhakti and Devotional Mysticism*. Richmond Surrey, England: Curzon Press, 1993.

Whitehead, Alfred North. *Process and Reality*. New York: Macmillan, 1929.

Williams, R. *Jaina Yoga*. London: Oxford University Press, 1963.

Wolf, Diane L. "Situating Feminist Dilemmas in Fieldwork." In *Feminist Dilemmas in Fieldwork*, edited by Diane L. Wolf (pp. 1–55). Oxford: Westview Press, 1996.

Wolpert, Stanley. *A New History of India*. Oxford: Oxford University Press, 1982.

Zwicker, Thomas. Unpublished fieldwork notes, in archives of University of Pennsylvania Museum, 1984–85.

Index